DAVID BEN-GURION
Politics and Leadership in Israel

DAVID BEN-GURION

DAVID BEN-GURION

Politics and Leadership in Israel

Edited by

Ronald W. Zweig

Tel Aviv University

 FRANK CASS • LONDON

YAD IZHAK BEN-ZVI • JERUSALEM

First published in 1991 in Great Britain by
FRANK CASS AND COMPANY LIMITED
Gainsborough House, 11 Gainsborough Road,
London E11 1RS

and in the United States of America by
FRANK CASS
c/o International Specialized Book Services, Inc.
5602 N.E. Hassalo Street, Portland,
Oregon 927213

British Library Cataloguing in Publication Data

David Ben-Gurion : politics and leadership in Israel.
1. Israel. Statesmen
I. Zweig, Ronald W.
956.94092
ISBN 0-7146-3423-9

Library of Congress Cataloging-in-Publication Data

David Ben-Gurion : politics and leadership in Israel / edited by
Ronald W. Zweig.
p.   cm.
1. Ben-Gurion, David, 1886–1973. 2. Zionists—Palestine–
–Biography. 3. Prime ministers—Israel—Biography. 4. Zionism–
–History. 5. Israel—Politics and government. I. Zweig, Ronald W.
DS 125.3.B37D39 1991
[B]   91-3206
                                                             CIP

Typeset by Yad Izhak Ben-Zvi Press, Jerusalem

Printed in Great Britain by BPCC Wheatons Ltd, Exeter

CONTENTS

313   Contributors

PREFACE

When the centenary celebrations to mark David Ben-Gurion's birth were being planned, it was proposed to publish an English-language collection of the major scholarly essays available on his career. The intention was to bring to a wider audience the fruits of Israeli research on the historical role and personality of the leader of the Jewish community in Mandatory Palestine and later Israel's first prime minister. It quickly became apparent, however, that the necessary pool of articles in Hebrew simply did not exist. Much had been written about Ben-Gurion, but little of it had come from the pens of historians. The events had been too recent, official records had not yet been opened to research, and the public controversies concerning Ben-Gurion's remarkable career had been too current for most historians to feel the distance and the detachment necessary to write dispassionately. As a result, articles for this collection were invited from a wide range of historians, each of whom has researched one or another aspect of Ben-Gurion's life.

Only one article was immediately available for inclusion in this volume, Israel Kolatt's "Image and Reality." Kolatt wrote as an engaged historian, and he directly addressed the question of Ben-Gurion's leadership at a time when it was being challenged increasingly. This focus on the quality and nature of political leadership expressed in the career of one of the foremost figures in contemporary Jewish history is the theme that binds all the essays in this book.

The subjects discussed in the seventeen articles presented here cover many aspects of Ben-Gurion's long political career, both in the pre-state years and after 1948. Many of the articles draw on material that has only recently been opened for research. Ben-Gurion's own papers and diaries have not been made available all at once, but progressively, roughly paralleling the availability of governmental records in Israel. In selecting the essays for this volume, an attempt has been made to include both established scholars in the periods under discussion and younger Israeli historians whose work has only recently become known.

While some articles present fresh insights into issues that have been discussed elsewhere, other contributions break new ground in the very questions they address. Ben-Gurion's response to the realities of the mass immigration in the early years of the state; his role in determining Israel's foreign policy between the two power blocs of international diplomacy; his advocacy of reparations negotiations with Germany; the factors behind his decision to withdraw from Sinai in 1957; his view of the legal and moral issues involved in Israel's trial and execution of Adolf Eichmann; his role in creating a public education system in Israel—these are issues which are discussed here for the first time.

Most collections of scholarly essays are based on the proceedings of a conference or symposium. This book is the direct result of the initiative of Yad Ben-Zvi in Jerusalem to present the fruits of Israeli research to a wider audience. Editing such a work has its own rewards and tribulations. A large number of people have been involved in this project at one stage or another, and I am grateful to the following for their assistance: Robert Amoils, Channa Biderman, Yossi Gevir, Yohai Goell, Hanna Levij, Zvi Volk, Orit Wertheim, and Zvi Zameret. I would particularly like to acknowledge the encouragement of Professor Amnon Cohen, without whose intervention this project would not have been completed.

Tel Aviv University   RONALD W. ZWEIG

The Praxis of Leadership

BEN-GURION AS I KNEW HIM

Shimon Peres

On David Ben-Gurion's 80th birthday, we went, as was our custom each year, to visit him at his home in Kibbutz Sedeh Boker in the Negev.

We flew there by helicopter. I had invited the great Israeli writer and Nobel laureate S. Y. Agnon to join us. Agnon loved Jerusalem and was a virtual recluse in the city. He was disinclined to wander afield and did not take part in social gatherings. Thus, this was the first time in his life that Agnon had seen the desert landscape south of Beersheba, a panorama which both amazed and disturbed him. Although he was a religious man, he voiced strong words of rebuke against God, assuming that from the helicopter they would reach their destination more quickly. He looked down on the bare hills, on the barren stones, on the strange shapes which the canyons carved in the terrain, on the reddish peaks — and argued with his Maker that it was not right to be so cruel to nature, to run rampant with the land, making it intractable and forbidding, without according man, who is also the handiwork of the Creator, a foothold in this broad territory.

When we approached Sedeh Boker, Agnon turned to me with growing emotion and said: "I have always believed that, in the final analysis, every Jew is just a little frightened of the Gentiles — of the Gentile as a man, and of the Gentile landscape. It would appear that Mr. Ben-Gurion is not afraid of the Gentiles." And, with a mischievous sparkle in his eyes, he added: "It seems that Mr. Ben-Gurion is not afraid of the Jews either." Were he afraid, he would not have brought them to such a place.

Indeed, it may well be that genius begins where fear ends: not to be afraid to question what is known, not to be afraid to be original. David Ben-Gurion did not try to imitate anyone.

He was not an easy person, or a congenial one, or a person who strove to be liked by others. He did not indulge others and did not expect or want to be pampered by them.

His personality was very complex, distinguished as it was by an exceptionally strong character, tremendous willpower, and stubbornness. He was also endowed with a mind that sought out what was new and was capable of penetrating the deepest recesses.

David Ben-Gurion was a decisive man who formulated an opinion on any subject with which he came into contact. He questioned the accepted interpretation of the Exodus from Egypt. He wrote to President Kennedy that he must establish relations with the People's Republic of China, ten years before the United States did so. He debated Buddhism with U Nu, and he argued that Spinoza was the greatest Jewish philosopher. He was convinced that energy would be derived from the atom, that seawater would be desalinated, and that an artificial brain would be developed.

But, first and foremost, he challenged every Jew who believed it was the fate of the Jews to live in the Diaspora, and he believed that the Jews could be a nation of farmers, industrialists, soldiers, pioneers, and not only scientists and intellectuals. He decided that the time had come to establish a Jewish state, yet once it had been founded, he was not satisfied—it must be an exemplary state, a chosen state.

Ben-Gurion could not for a moment remain noncommittal in his views. He did not know a moment of neutrality. He was always prepared to acquire knowledge, but he refused to abandon his views. Ben-Gurion once said to me, "All experts are experts on what was. There are no experts on what will be."

He enjoyed arranging his 20,000 books (in seven different languages) on the shelves of his library, books that accompanied him in every period of his life: philosophy and sociology, geography and history, biology and physics. He died an inquisitive man. He certainly never knew a day of boredom, even when he lived alone.

When Ben-Gurion decided to settle in Israel, he studied the geography of the land and traversed the country on foot. Finally, together with his friend Izhak Ben-Zvi, he published a geography, *The Land of Israel, Past and Future*, in which he wrote:

> If we wish to fix the borders of the Land of Israel today, especially if we view it not only as the legacy of the Jewish past, but also as the land of the Jewish future, of Jewish settlement, and of the Jewish National Home—we can take into consideration only the ideal borders promised to us by tradition, which are too broad in the conditions prevailing today. We cannot simply adhere to the historical borders, which have so often changed and are the product of chance, which are generally too narrow and do not conform to the natural lay of the land.

In 1931, Ben-Gurion published the book *Our Neighbors and Ourselves,* calling for coexistence between Jews and Arabs, which he believed to be vital for the return of the Jewish people to their land. While serving as secretary-general of the Histadrut from 1921-1933, he read widely on socialism and revolution, and on the psychology of the masses. He once told me that he used to spend entire days in the New York City Public Library immersed in the study of psychology books. He read the works of Marx, and all those of Lenin. He preferred Marx for his intellectual ability but was not won over by his teachings. Marx, he claimed, was not a Marxist. Lenin he preferred as a leader, although he totally rejected the Communist regime.

In fact, my first conversation with Ben-Gurion was about Lenin. While still a very young man, I was invited to accompany him from Tel Aviv to Haifa. He was already then a legend in the eyes of the people, and I was very excited at the chance to speak with this great man. To my disappointment, I found that Ben-Gurion was not a man of idle talk, and during most of the journey he remained immersed in his own thoughts and said almost nothing. Only on the outskirts of Haifa did he turn to me and say, "You know, Trotsky was not a true leader." To this day, I do not know what brought Trotsky's spirit into the car on the road to Haifa. But since I wanted to pursue the conversation , I asked, "Why?" At which Ben-Gurion exploded and said,

"What is 'no war and no peace'? This isn't policy; this is a Jewish invention. Either go to war and take the risk, or make peace and pay the price. Lenin, who was intellectually inferior to Trotsky, became the leader of the Russians because he took decisions."

However, his admiration for Lenin did not prevent him from attacking Leninist Communism in a long series of strongly worded polemic essays, and he was even more strongly opposed to Stalinism.

Ultimately, he published his own view of socialism: *From Class to Nation*. He did not seek a class war. He aspired to a time when the entire nation would become a nation of workers, a productive nation of citizens who would live by the work of their hands and their minds. He saw the role of the working class as constructive, not revolutionary: to rebuild the people, to cause the land that had been laid waste to bloom again. He believed that only the people—and not necessarily the wealthy and distinguished members—were capable of rebuilding themselves, of bettering themselves, of becoming the true architects of their new homeland. He was opposed to the self-isolation of the workers. He called for the dissolution of the labor trend in the schools, a trend which he himself worked to establish as secretary-general of the Histadrut, in favor of state education. He sought education to labor values for all children, not particularistic education for one segment of the people. He also advocated the transformation of the Histadrut labor exchange into a state labor exchange.

Ben-Gurion visited the Soviet Union, at the head of a Histadrut delegation attending an agricultural exhibition, in the early 1920s. He came to view Communism as the antithesis of Judaism. The Bible, and not *Das Kapital*; Hebrew, not Russian; the Land of Israel, and not the Soviet Union—these would save the Jewish people from their fate. The debate over the position to be adopted toward the Soviet Union continued even after the establishment of the State of Israel. It also caused a split within the Israeli workers' movement for many years. Until the "Doctors' Trial," portraits of Stalin were displayed in more than a few homes of leaders of the Israel labor movement. If not for Ben-Gurion, together with his friend and companion Berl Katznelson, it is doubtful whether the labor movement would have freed itself from the effects of this great revolution.

Ben-Gurion also contended with the religious public, which in part identified with the Zionist movement and in part rejected it, as well as with the Revisionists. He argued that Judaism is not a religion, but a faith. To Ben-Gurion, the classical religions are, in effect, vast administrative systems, which serve as intermediaries between God and the congregation of the faithful. According to the Jewish view, man was created in the image of God, and between God and man, every man, no intermediaries are needed. Judaism, in his view, is universal, inclusive, all-embracing. It is a compound that grew out of the history of the Jewish people as a nation. He therefore criticized the institution of the rabbinate, which tried to assume powers not founded in Jewish tradition.

As for the Revisionist movement, Ben-Gurion felt that it had introduced into Zionism a large dose of rhetoric and gesticulation, as an apparent shortcut. He believed that this movement disregarded two fundamental precepts of authentic policy: that one must build gradually and methodically, and that the time for joyful declarations was after the completion of the work, not before. Grandiosity, Ben-Gurion believed, was the illegitimate child of false messianism, and had turned the heads of the leaders of the Revisionist movement.

The disagreement with the Revisionists continued even after the establishment of the state. The I.Z.L., the military arm of the Revisionist movement, brought an arms ship, the *Altalena*, to the shores of Israel, and Ben-Gurion suspected that they intended to use these arms for combat in areas not included within the partition map. He did not hesitate to order the Israel Defense Forces to fire on the ship, believing that the I.Z.L. had not accepted the authority of the new national government. Thus he put an end not only to debate, but also to secession.

In his later years, Ben-Gurion fought still another battle: the "Lavon Affair." Pinhas Lavon, then minister of defense, had accused the head of army intelligence, Binyamin Jibli, of having ordered acts of sabotage in Egypt without explicit approval. Jibli claimed that Lavon had issued such an order. The cabinet wanted to act as judge, but Ben-Gurion argued that "ministers are not judges." Very few joined him in this battle, which he waged with unbelievable intensity, despite his advanced age.

Ben-Gurion's relationship with the intelligentsia was ambivalent. He respected them, because he knew that without a deep-seated partnership between the workers and the intelligentsia, it would be difficult to create a focus of unity within the people. He was also wary of them, because he saw in them much intellectual weakness, hesitancy, and a tendency toward criticism for its own sake.

There were many intellectuals whom Ben-Gurion admired in the fields of philosophy, history, literature, and poetry, and he himself had launched several literary enterprises. He initiated the translation into Hebrew of great works of world literature. He encouraged archaeology and the writing of history. He transformed the Israeli army into a school for the teaching of Hebrew. He encouraged instruction in the Hebrew language for all ages, and through his efforts the Bible became a more widely read book. He corresponded with the greatest thinkers and writers, studied their views, and continually engaged them in dialogue.

Although his relations with the intelligentsia embodied conflict, they were also ones of kinship. The context of all his intellectual disputes was mutuality and respect. As a result, no unbridgeable rift arose between his adversaries and himself. That, too, may have been a manifestation of his greatness.

BEN-GURION: IMAGE AND REALITY

Israel Kolatt

I

Historians are in the habit of shattering monuments. Heedless of the masses' devotion to a leader, they reveal the element of chance in situations, the hesitations affecting decisions, the multiplicity of factors involved, and the extent of that which is unavoidable. It is said that no measure of greatness can withstand the evidence of a servant or that of a private secretary, who have seen the great man, with all his petty human frailties. Similarly, documentary research detracts from a hero's monumental stature, setting him in the context of complex relationships and circumstances, and shedding light on his moments of weakness and doubt. The image of a leader, foreseeing the future and decisively calculating his moves in the light of a clear objective, is liable to collapse under the weight of facts thus revealed. Historians also know that even the greatest of human achievements is far from final and unequivocal. They are aware of the dialectic process whereby problems grow out of solutions and seeds of failure are sometimes hidden within the laurels of success. A relatively long time span is required to evaluate an achievement's ratio of lasting versus ephemeral effect.

In the case of David Ben-Gurion, the historian has been spared much of this iconoclastic labor. It would appear that Ben-Gurion himself sought at one time to shatter the monumental image which forced the great man to retire, wreathed in clouds of glory, from public life. He still felt strong enough to fight, and spurned the idea of preserving an image at the expense of what he regarded as just and essential. In this particular case, therefore, it would seem that it is of greater importance to rehabilitate and re-interpret greatness than to shatter it.

An evaluation of Ben-Gurion might distinguish between the creator of a historic enterprise on the one hand, and a human figure, on the other. This would be in apparant contradiction to Ben-Gurion's own evaluation, according to which one tends to equate a man with his endeavor—a tendency which on occasion leads to the absolute identification of that endeavor with the man. The ordinary Israeli might well wonder whether his fate was determined by a man of virtue and whether historical action and achievement are possible while observing moral rules and

This is an abridged version of an article which was originally published in 1972 and which appeared in the author's book, *Fathers and Founders* (Hebrew), Tel Aviv, 1975.

principles, or whether the great creator has his own code of ethics and makes his own laws. Does history elect persons of virtue, or are power and virtue mutually exclusive?

Ben-Gurion's actions, at least since his return from Sde Boker in 1955 (to become Minister of Defence and later Prime Minister), were controversial—as is well known—with the controversy sharper in matters involving personal evaluation than in those relating to political affairs. The "Lavon Affair" agitated the public more than the Sinai Campaign's justification, for example. The spotlight was focused more on the personal drama than on its historical significance—despite the fact that leaders' personalities are also an integral part of public life. The personal struggle was explained with the aid of symbols from folk literature and fable—the giant in the land of dwarfs or King Solomon losing his magic ring; King Lear ensnared by lies or the aged ruler seeking to lay a trap for his successors; a knight fighting for justice even at the price of his glory; or a retiring leader denouncing his successors' impotence.

Many of his contemporaries' complexes were directed toward the figure of Ben-Gurion. They were overcome in 1948 when, in the words of poet Nathan Alterman, "marching, and making headway with blind obstinacy, without retreat or return," he found the saving, and as it were irrational, solution to a seemingly insoluble situation, thus devastating the self-confidence of many of his opponents. For the lifespan of an entire generation, they dared not disobey his word. They became accustomed never to take anything he said or did not only at face value but rather as having a discrete meaning. It was this habit that would eventually help cause many of the failings which they were later to bemoan.

II

Ben-Gurion is one of those twentieth-century leaders who, after Machiavelli and Deutscher (in his book on Trotsky), may be described as "an armed prophet."[1]

> It must be considered that there is nothing more difficult to carry out, nor more doubtful of success, nor more dangerous to handle, than to initiate a new order of things. For the reformer has enemies in all those who profit by the old order, and only lukewarm defence in all those who would profit by the new order, this lukewarmness arising partly from fear of their adversaries, who have the laws in their favor; and partly from the incredulity of mankind, who do not truly believe in anything new until they have had actual experience of it. Thus it arises that on every opportunity for attacking the reformer, his opponents do so with the zeal of partisans, the others only defend him half-heartedly, so that between them he runs great danger. It is necessary, however, in order to investigate thoroughly this question, to examine whether these innovators are independent, or whether they depend upon others, that is to say, whether in order to carry out their designs they have to entreat or are able to compel. In the first case they invariably succeed ill, and accomplish nothing; but when they can depend on their own strength and are able to use force, they rarely fail. Thus it comes about that all armed prophets have conquered and unarmed ones failed.[2]

It was through this combination of prophet and arms bearer that Machiavelli tried to relocate the creator of norms and laws, the bearer of the word of God, within the concrete context of political reality, within the realm of human affairs. Here, force is not part of the given reality of struggle and violence, where one tries to achieve limited objectives, with weapons being an unavoidable evil. Here, force serves the loftiest of possible aims. The changing of beliefs and customs, the "prophet's" interjection of a virtue into reality cannot be the fruit of preaching alone—for the strength of that which is extant and entrenched is greater than the might of an aspiration which is but a dream and a word. Carrying weapons is intended to fulfill the prophecy, but once arms are taken up they become holy, since their function, after all, is not only to check the spread of evil but also to inaugurate a world of total goodness.

Ben-Gurion's leadership aimed at changing a historical reality, the entire fate of a people, and a social regime. The revolution at whose head he had wished to stand almost since his youth, was deeper and more comprehensive than those revolutions which Machiavelli had described. He sought to remold a traditional society in a place which, while being an ancient homeland, was actually new. Obstacles from within Jewish society preceded those from without. The anti-Zionist and anti-socialist antagonism among the Jews preceded that of non-Jews. Internal opposition could be overcome only by verbal influence and persuasion—at least until the establishment of the state. There was a time when Ben-Gurion thought that the external obstacles as well could be overcome by goodwill and mutual persuasion, and that the Great Powers, including the British, and the Arabs would extend aid to the Jewish endeavor.

We shall see how this hope did not materialize. Ben-Gurion was forced to join the "prophets" of his generation who resolved to realize their principles by force. Force, when in the service of truth, may be more justified; it is also more dangerous and extreme. The greater the validity of the truth and the more overpowering its power to uproot, the more ruthless are the weapons at its disposal. Against the backdrop of the revolutionary movements of his youth, Ben-Gurion had been influenced by the bold idea of replacing an old idea for a new one, and by the principle which posits that this end justifies violence. Like Lenin and Trotsky, Pilsudski and Ataturk, he did not restrict prophecy to the logic of the spoken word.

Movements and peoples striving toward revolution are not motivated solely by great misery and by a destructive urge born of protest and of a sense of humiliation. They are guided as well by a comprehensive vision of a new and better society—not only as a personal dream, which might be arbitrary, but as something revealed by the iron-clad logic of history. In their eyes, history is not only a sum of existing factors but also a substantive process leading beyond society as it now exists.

This view of the inevitable process was interpreted, of course, by socialist theory in two different ways, one of which might be referred to Kautskyist and the other—Leninist. The former relies upon the unavoidable process, assiduously interpreting reality while taking care to draw conclusions from the doctrines in question. It views the world of its aspirations as growing and developing from the existing world. The latter approach seeks to change the world, using the theory of history as a warranty, thereby deflecting accusations of arbitrariness. Yet it defines that theory freely, drawing concepts from it for support and changing them to meet requirements. It does not serve concepts; rather, it masters them. It is the god which creates and destroys worlds at will. The "historical process" is interpreted differently in different periods. And when history becomes obstreperous, ceasing to seem a rational process which leads toward the desired solution, it does not hesitate to employ force in order to fulfill its purpose.

In Ben-Gurion's own movement, as well, there were currents favorable to both concepts of the historical process. But though Ben-Gurion did not relinquish the perception of his movement as being embedded within an overall context of change and world revolution, he always adhered more to the idea of voluntary struggle than to a process described in any specific doctrine of historical development. For he preferred the act of revolution to diagnostic and prognostic deliberation.

Ben-Gurion's attitude towards Lenin is attested to by a brilliant passage from his diary published in his memoirs:

> When I read Lenin's words at the Seventh Conference, when the Party was faced with the question of war or peace, at the time of Brest-Litovsk, the secret of his influence became clear to me. This is indeed a great man. His penetrating gaze perceives reality as through a clear prism, impeded by no formula, proverb, phrase or dogma. For this man has been blessed with the ingenious ability to look life in the eye, to articulate matters neither in concepts nor in words, but rather in the basic terms of reality. And the man's courageous, bold thinking, unhampered by conventional, routine concepts, and his far-reaching vision, peering penetratingly deeply into life's complexities and hidden depths, drawing forth the future's prevailing forces from the sources of contemporary reality. Yet a definite objective, a route, stands before the master tactician, who refuses to veer off-course, either to the left or to the right, despite his ability to reach his goal by a variety of means, each in accordance with the situation. For he actually has only one path — that which leads to the objective. "If you are unable to adapt yourself, if you are unwilling to crawl on your stomach through the mire, then you are not a revolutionary but a prattler, and it is not because I like the idea that I propose this course, but rather because there is no other way." These words, uttered in the above speech, express Lenin's conceptual and spiritual essence.[3]

And later on:

> Is not the destiny of Lenin — the prophet of the Russian Revolution, its leader and teacher, its ruler and spokesman, its legislator and guide — the destiny of Communist Russia? Here is a man who is the quintessence of revolution, single-minded, disdaining all obstacles, faithful to his purpose, knowing neither surrender nor concession, a radical of radicals who knows how to crawl on his stomach through deepest mire to gain his end; an iron-willed man who spares neither the lives of grown men nor the blood of innocent children in order to further the revolutionary cause; the tactical genius who knows how to retreat from battle in order to gather forces for a new assault; who is not afraid to deny today what he supported yesterday, and to support tomorrow what he denied today; who does not permit webs of phrases to entrap his thought and refuses to be entangled either by formula or docrine. For this sharp and clear vision sees only naked reality, the brutal truth, and the actual balance of forces. But throughout all the struggles and retreats, the complexities of battles and upsets, one single, unchanging objective burns searingly

before him:... the great, fundamental revolution, uprooting the existing reality,
shaking a rotten perverted society to its very foundations.[4]

Ben-Gurion found in Lenin the prototype of power capable of transforming an
aspiration — nourished by an overwhelming sense of right and justice, but sheathed
in theory — into a decisive fact. It may be from Lenin that Ben-Gurion learned to
transform a voluntary, idea-oriented, social movement into a tool capable of forging
reality. Like Lenin, Ben-Gurion learned not to be "virtuous but defeated." He
became aware of the price to be paid for tactical retreat or for pretense designed to
ensure historic realization.

He was also Lenin's contemporary in the sense that he continued to believe that
"the boat struggling against the worldwide forces of nature" sought in the end to
reach that "mysterious wonderland, still unseen by the eyes;" that there is a final,
wondrous solution for social movements, and that after all the difficult turns in the
road, they would eventually reach their chosen land. He eventually merged the State
of Israel with the image of his dream, and a re-interpretation of Jewish history was
conceived in order to acquire this new meaning.

The emphasis upon the State of Israel, not as the result of circumstantial desires
and exigencies, but rather as an expression of "the vision of generations" and as "the
word of Jewish history," came mainly after the state's establishment. As the event
itself was transpiring, however, the great creator stood before infinite bits of data
and mountains of obstacles; the solution inherent in "the vison" was neither explicit
nor assured.

III

The British historian Charles Webster's assessment of Chaim Weizmann was based
upon the ratio between Weizmann's power and the problems he faced, on the one
hand, and his political achievements, on the other. Similarly, one may assess Ben-
Gurion's achievements on the basis of the ratio between the obstacles which stood in
his way and his moments of despair, on the one hand, and his undertakings, on the
other. More than once, Ben-Gurion witnessed the dissipation of his achievements,
with his movement facing an impasse. During the 1920s, the Histadrut, which he
served as secretary-general, was continually threatened with Communist secession, a
threat which was indeed realized when a part of Poalei-Zion (Left) and later a section
of the Labor Brigade (a communal force within the Histadrut which undertook to
fulfill pioneering functions in the years 1920-1927) seceded and allied themselves with
the Communist camp. The economic crisis of 1927, accompanied by hunger and dire
need for welfare assistance, positioned Ben-Gurion as a leader piloting an entire
camp, starving for bread and a new society, to its demise.

Zalman Aranne's memoirs contain two impressions of Ben-Gurion at that time. In
one, Ben-Gurion is the leader of a Jewish youth camp in the Russian diaspora,
entrapped by troubles and dreams, for which he viewed himself as responsible. "A
young face and white head, a penetrating glance, a voice of iron, and vital hands...."[5]

The second is of Ben-Gurion in another extreme of distress, in Palestine of 1927. Addressing a crowd of unemployed, who shout at him: "Leader, give us bread," Ben-Gurion can respond only: "I have no bread. I have a vision." He succeeded in turning this crisis into a springboard for strengthening the Histadrut, in a way very different from what he had attempted during the 1920s. It was no longer destined to take the place of the private sector, but rather to be built alongside that sector, even, to a great extent, to be built by it.

During the early 1930s, the Zionist movement faced: pressure from hosts of youth overseas wishing to immigrate to Palestine; a political crisis vis-a-vis the British government; the restriction of immigration; fears that cooperation with Britain might come to an end. The Zionist movement's budget shrank due to the economic depression in America; Revisionism aimed blatantly and threateningly to wrest control over the Zionist movement. Ben-Gurion feverishly formulated out political programs and procedures, at the same time initiating practical political activity vis-a-vis Ramsey MacDonald's Labour Government. Zionism survived this crisis, only to plunge into an even worse one at the end of the 1930s, by which time the strength of the Jewish community in Palestine (the Yishuv) had already grown immeasurably.

Ben-Gurion was a leader at the time that the Jewish people found itself caught between pressure for emigration from Europe and closed gates around the world and in Palestine as well. An era of distress and duress, characterized by the necessity of cooperating with Great Britain in its fight against the Nazis, while fighting Great Britain's attempts to implement the policy of its 1939 White Paper. A time when a mass of Holocaust survivors and a community of 600,000 Jews in Palestine challenged the then-victorious British Empire; a period when this small community stood up against the Arab invasion of 1948.

A leader on the verge of a great decision, the unfathomable future before him, seeks to rely upon a force beyond that of human fallibility. The leader, who set out to change national destiny and dispelled the charm of socialist utopia, found confirmation for his approach in a "vision of generations." In retrospect, history can be made into a normative entity, a commanding force. But as it transpires, history is but a plethora of evaluations, positions, decisions and actions made both by leaders and by the public at large.

History contains various aspects for its makers. On the one hand, it is the multifaceted composite of those circumstances in which the public finds itself, and is thereby an open-ended process. On the other hand, history is the choice which transforms a potential-laden future into an immutable past. Ben-Gurion knew that during the 1940s the choice was not clear-cut. "History" stood by mute, offering no guidance, providing no solutions. A large part of the Yishuv clung to British patronage, afraid to break away from it. The left, which opposed that patronage, sought to submit itself to yet another patronage, i.e. that of the so-called "socialist revolutionary" camp, in an arrangement that would be less practical and more binding than the British one. The intellectual heritage of many of the members of the Yishuv was incompatible with the conclusion that there was no peacable solution nor consensual formula for dealing with the Jewish-Arab conflict. Many opposed the use of force for achievement of political goals; many more feared a military confrontation. The Mapai Party split up, in 1944, and precisely that activist section with which Ben-Gurion felt affinity—left. There was fear of an activist movement of despair within the Yishuv, which would sweep aside existing frameworks and loyalties. On the other hand, there was also fear of Palestine-centered "yishuvism," which might well opt for calm under a British aegis. The underground movements stressed violent action and rebelled against organized authority, which was based upon the status quo, and which would not readily accept the risk of a war for political aims.

At that time, Ben-Gurion succeeded in welding together the conflicting elements, in harnessing them to his objective, and in besting them while they were at their weakest. The Biltmore Program, whose formulation allowed for a variety of options, became a means for rallying the Yishuv and the Zionist movement around the demand for a state. Ben-Gurion credited himself with the fact that he perceived the danger in its entirety, undeluded, and yet did not back away from it. At an almost impossible moment, Ben-Gurion steered Israel toward a state at the heavy price of partition and war.

It would seem that the figure of Lenin previously held up as Ben-Gurion's model was joined at this point by that of Churchill in World War II: the leader guiding his people from the edge of disaster, to victory. Facing personal and public challenges, utilizing a variety of ways and means—whose necessity will remain a subject for debate among historians—he achieved his aim. Like Churchill not so long before, and like Lenin whom he attempted to emulate in 1923, Ben-Gurion paid no small price for achieving his goal.

IV

Ben-Gurion's political methods gradually changed in scope, orientation, and procedure. During the Second Aliya and at the beginning of World War I, Ben-Gurion had faith in the Ottoman Empire and in its potential for reform. He believed that it would be forced to grant increased autonomy to national entities, and accordingly attempted to integrate the Yishuv in Palestine with the Jewish proletariat which was expected to immigrate to Palestine, in one politically-conscious national unit within the framework of the Empire.

At the end of World War I, Ben-Gurion believed that an international authority would arise, along the lines of the League of Nations or a revolutionary Socialist International. Within this framework, a worldwide Jewish polity would be established, gaining the right to build up the Land of Israel as a Jewish "labor center." He expected recognition of the Zionist labor movement by the victorious Socialist International, much as the Entente Powers and the League of Nations recognized the Zionist Organization.

Ben-Gurion's efforts during the 1920s, and to a certain extent during the 1930s as well, to conduct a dialogue with the Soviet Union, indicate the remnants of his internationalist ideology. These efforts represent a kind of search for the fragments of a shattered world.

After his hopes for the International and the world Jewish polity were dashed, Ben-Gurion began to view the Histadrut and its partners in the Yishuv and the Diaspora as the standardbearers of Zionist creativity and achievement during the 1920s. Their task was to jointly build a labor-oriented Palestine.

While concentrating during this decade upon the development of the Histadrut, Ben-Gurion did not ignore matters of national policy. He believed that areas of dense Jewish settlement and units of territorial autonomy, would lead eventually to a Jewish state. Territorial autonomy would at the same time facilitate self-government for the Arabs in their areas of the country.

The idea of developing a Jewish state in the Land of Israel based upon autonomous national territorial units was an alternative to the proposal to develop self-rule in Palestine through a Legislative Council. At that time, the members of the World Federation of Poalei Zion, headed by Shelomo Kaplansky, supported the principle of self-government for the citizens of the country, with guarantees for the Jews. This would have left the Jews, at least temporarily, as a minority within the Council. Ben-Gurion rejected this acquiescence to formal democratic principles. He believed that Jewish-Arab cooperation would result not only from the previously mentioned territorial autonomy, but also from the ability of parallel Jewish and Arab social classes to communicate with each other, regardless of national differences. *Brit Poalei Eretz Israel* (a federative organization which included the Jewish Histadrut and some Arab trade unions) was the expression of this principle within the working class. Ben-Gurion assumed that Jewish and Arab merchants, orchard owners and others would cooperate on similar lines.

During the early 1930s, Ben-Gurion still believed in the possibility of Arab-Jewish dialogue under British patronage. In his estimation, through the advancement of Arab independence, both local and regional, and by assisting in the creation of an Arab Federation, the Jews could gain the the Arabs' goodwill. He assumed that if executive governing power were shared with the Arabs, it would be considered sufficient compensation for their acquiescence to Jewish immigration. He proposed equal representation for Jews and Arabs in the national government, with the British participating as a third party. During the early 1930s, Ben-Gurion still believed that the region, and the entire British Empire, might develop along the lines of socialist internationalism. This movement would also recognize the rights of the Jewish people. But as early as then, Ben-Gurion made a point of emphasizing that his acceptance of "parity" rule between Jews and Arabs in Palestine was in contradistinction to "binationalism," which equated the rights of the existing local Arab community with those of the entire Jewish people over the Land.

Ben-Gurion's faith in the possibility of an Arab-Jewish political agreement and socialist harmony between the various national demands notwithstanding, he already started, in the early 1930s, to consider the possibility of a resolution reached by force. During a crisis in relations with Britain in 1930, he spoke of "blowing up the British Empire."

V

Far-reaching changes occurred not only in Ben-Gurion's political methods, but in his attitude towards the subject for the realization of his ideas, as well. His creative and formative life was ruled by a guiding idea, a historical view, and commitment to his public. The idea was that of a Jewish renaissance in the Land of Israel, a renaissance which he never limited to the political sphere, but rather included the social concept of a "liberated working community" also. Subsequently, he included in it the entire gamut of Jewish and human experience, as expressed in religion and philosophy. "Our class consciousness is illuminated by the light of the vision of redemption": such was a typical Ben-Gurion expression during the 1920s and 1930s, when the pathos of total change and creation was part and parcel of intellectual analysis and social action.

Rather than follow in the footsteps of his movement's rank-and-file, Ben-Gurion utilized his leadership in order to set the movement's goals. Nevertheless, at least until the creation of the state, he recognized "all the workers" as the ultimate authority, one which was not only an aggregation of interests but also the embodiment of "historic destiny," the illuminating idea.

It would be wrong to say that Ben-Gurion entertained a romantic concept of the public, ignoring the limits of ordinary human capabilities. Letters written in his youth reveal that he was always aware of the limits of disinterested action and recognized that only a select few are at all capable of such action.

During the 1920s, Ben-Gurion tried to incorporate within Ahdut Ha'avoda ("The Union of Labor," a party to which Ben-Gurion belonged and which dominated the Histadrut until it merged with "Hapo'el Hatzair" in 1930, thereby creating Mapai) and the Histadrut the idea of total linkage between individual and community. He wanted to establish the Histadrut and the Hevrat Ha'ovdim (which represented the economic aspect of the Histadrut) as centralized bodies, within which there would no longer be a distinction between private and collective property, on the one hand, and the rule of the working class, on the other. He opposed any tendency to set up autonomous intermediate bodies within the Histadrut economy and society.

Through his untiring demand for integration and his opposition to viewing the Histadrut as "a federation of parties," he hoped to strengthen the authority of the community and of its leadership. His opponents saw this as an attempt to stifle any semblance of distinct, independent identity. According to Ben-Gurion, "the class" was meant to be the bold builder of the new Jewish society, by making use of all personal and public resources.

During the early 1930s, the other facet of Ben-Gurion's attitude towards the community began to stand out. In his work as secretary-general of the Histadrut, he often took into consideration the need to safeguard veteran workers and to assure their employment as well as their professional rights.

During the 1940s, Ben-Gurion continued to view and present his party as dominated by his mission and its members as "mobilized". He demanded from them "complete subservience to the liberation and redemption of our people." However, he was well aware that this type of subservience is limited to times of crisis and to fateful issues. The state alone provided him with a tool through which one might tear down the barrier between the individual and the community. On the other hand, once the State had been established, he continued to be fully aware of the necessity of compensating his supporters.

For most of his life, Ben-Gurion sought to exert far-reaching influence and refrained from maintaining doctrines which did not enjoy a favorable public response. However, Ben-Gurion's definition of the "public" involved the individual's complete identification with the mission which history had destined for him, an elevation beyond a personal level of existence to one of destiny and achievement.

VI

The political system which Ben-Gurion tried to establish in the early 1930s, based upon a Jewish-Arab-British constitutional arrangement, was unsuccessful. The Yishuv's growth, in size and in strength, during the first half of the 1930s was not due to any newly formed constitutional framework, favorable from a Zionist standpoint. It came about due to the Zionists' success in preventing constitutional changes that might have proved unfavorable to their cause. The Zionist achievement of that period grew out of successful exploitation of the Mandatory framework, astute policy vis-a-vis British rule, and from economic and settlement initiatives. Ben-Gurion played a role in all of these.

It was, however, in the sphere of internal Zionist policy that Ben-Gurion's formula "From Class to Nation" bore fruit splendidly. During 1932-1933, he succeeded in turning the vacuum that had been created within the Zionist movement by the end of Weizmann's presidency, and the attacks by Revisionists and General Zionists on Labor positions, into a springboard from which he attained hegemony in the Zionist movement. Within his own party, he faced opposition to his methods from those who claimed that the attempt to attain a majority for the labor parties at the Zionist Congress would fail and only cause harm, since it would unite the labor movement's adversaries and sabotage fund-raising activities. Ben-Gurion could only answer that, dangerous though this daring move might be, the alternative — inactivity — was far more dangerous: specifically, a drop in pioneer immigration and budget cuts for labor settlement liable to be implemented by a hostile majority within the World Zionist Organization.

Ben-Gurion formulated a new ideological position — which one might refer to by a phrase that he coined, "From Class to Nation" — and developed tactics in anticipation of the 1933 Congress. Both the position and the tactics have withstood the test of history. The new ideological formulation no longer adhered to some of the basic tenets of the 1920s, according to which Palestine's development by private capital was neither possible nor desirable, and that such capital had, at best, a marginal role to play. He no longer even restricted the labor movement primarily to the field of developing the national economy. Henceforth, private capital was permissible as long as it utilized Jewish labor and increased the prospects for both Jewish immigration and a Jewish economy. The labor movement was being called to assume the nation's political leadership.

During the early 1930s, Ben-Gurion claimed that Palestine's increasing practical importance in Zionist life was exacerbating class differences within the Zionist movement. The General Zionists in the Diaspora were ceasing to be "general" and were joining forces with farmers and various bourgeois groups in the Yishuv. In actual fact, there were great differences, especially in political orientation, between the farmers and the bourgeoisie, and among the various bourgeois groups themselves.

Ben-Gurion's attacks upon the bourgeois sectors of the Yishuv were not directed at their consolidating themselves through private capital. Rather, he took them to task for their lack of national solidarity in demographic and national organizational affairs. At a time of fateful conflict over the country's future, the employment of Arab workers, and the reduction in the number of Jewish workers which ensued, wreaked havoc with the prospects for immigration and the growth of the Jewish population. The farmers' disassociation from the organized Yishuv and their resignation from the Va'ad Leumi ("National Council," the representative body of the organized Jewish community of Palestine during the Mandate period) were evidence of the overall national interest being undermined by the interest of private property owners. Ben-Gurion claimed that the national organization (Va'ad Leumi) was being sabotaged by farmers, fearful for their property and apprehensive about the taxes which the Council might levy.

In opposing the stand of the property-owning circles in the Yishuv and the Zionist movement, Ben-Gurion demanded that his own party should work out a Zionist program of action which would also be capable of accommodating "popular circles" and those possessing private capital, both in the Diaspora and in Palestine. He attacked the circumscribed, class-based orientation of the Jewish workers' movement. This position derived, in his view, from the Jewish Bund which had not sought to attain a majority within the people and to lead them. Ben-Gurion made up his mind that within the World Zionist Organization the various working class parties would speak in the name of the entire people. His 18th Zionist Congress election campaign in Poland in 1933 was intended, in effect, to demonstrate that on such vital topics as "general education, responsible politics, Yishuv organization, general franchise, popular settlement, and nationally-owned land"[6], the workers represented the entire nation.

VII

The election results for the 18th Zionist Congress in 1933 transformed the labor faction into the largest party in the World Zionist Organization. This fact, coupled with Chaim Arlosoroff's murder, made it incumbent that Ben-Gurion join the Executive. During the period between 1933 and 1935, Ben-Gurion was formally just another member of the Executive; he continued to serve as secretary-general of the Histadrut. It was only at the end of this period, in 1935, that the position of Executive Chairman was revived, and Ben-Gurion was elected to the post.

In fact, however, even before this Ben-Gurion was no ordinary member of the Executive. His great power and extensive authority during this period derived from his leadership of Labor, the largest and strongest movement in the country and in the World Zionist Organization. His status was also a consequence of the vacuum that had been created in the Zionist Executive and in Zionist leadership in general.

Ben-Gurion began his work in the Executive after having gained experience as an ideological and party leader. However, he used ideology differently from other members of his party. For him it was the key to understanding the impersonal forces which comprise the historical situation. He rejected analogies, determinism, and doctrines. For example, he opposed importing to the Palestinian context the European labor movement's attempts to struggle against fascism. He felt that such an analogy would lead to paralysis. He rejected the simplistic sociology which posited a necessary link between the decline of the Jewish middle class in Eastern Europe and a resultant attraction to the fascist movement of the Jewish people, which was, according to many, Revisionism. Ben-Gurion claimed, instead, that human situations and behavior are unique, induplicable phenomena. He set about his position as Executive member without accepting existing situations as foregone conclusions and without being bound by conventions. He tried in a variety of ways to re-include in Zionist activity elements that had withdrawn from it, to revive shelved options, and to create new ones. He was not to be bound by his predecessors' methods or style nor by the personal relationships which they had formed.

Ben-Gurion's identification of the national advantage—a concept which in and of itself constituted a kind of deviation from the principles of the labor movement—with the interests of that movement, also guided him in the development of his attitude towards private capital and industrial development. In a speech made during the 19th Congress, he ascribed new meaning to the term "national capital." Its scope was broadened to include private capital which employed Jewish labor. This was contrary to the position adopted by his colleague, Yitzhak Tabenkin, with the argument between them taking place within the Labor faction at the Congress.

Industrial development, which had been low in the labor movement's traditional order of priorities, was accorded a new status within the Ben-Gurion conception. To a certain extent, this was a return to the movement's early Poalei-Zion and Borochov origins. His visit to the USSR during the 1920s also taught Ben-Gurion the importance of industry. Recognition of the importance of both industrial and urban growth for population growth and economic development were associated with the know-how of German Jews in this field and the capital that they possessed.

VIII

During his first years in the Zionist Executive, Ben-Gurion tried to implement his party's programmatic formulas in the field of Jewish-Arab relations, as well. At that time he believed that a solution to the problem of Jewish-Arab-British relations in Palestine was possible through an approach of general harmony. He continued to favor mass Jewish immigration and the aggregation of a Jewish majority in Palestine, but believed that this could be achieved in concert with the Arabs. Ben-Gurion strongly criticized the methods of his predecessors in the Zionist leadership, who had tried to obtain Jewish-Arab agreement by dispensing bribes and special privileges to the Arabs. He accepted the Arab national movement and sought to fulfill its aspirations by offering assistance toward all-Arab independence within a federative framework. Such help was intended to compensate the Arabs for Jewish settlement. Indeed, during 1934-1935, Mapai's "parity" formula, originally put forward in 1931, was still mentioned, sometimes to counter the attempt to set up a Legislative Council. But the main focus of possible Jewish concessions to the Arabs moved from national equality within Palestine to dialogue with Arab nationalism on a regional scale. The combination of maximalist Zionism and a federation with the Arabs might have facilitated a Ben-Gurion-Jabotinsky foreign policy rapprochement. Ben-Gurion told Jabotinsky that during the 1920s, he (the latter) had himself, expressed support for the Arab independence movement outside Palestine.

Thus, armed with this outlook, Ben-Gurion commenced his contacts with Arab leaders. His book — *My Talks with Arab Leaders*[7] — indicates the extent of his disappointment. He had not only become disillusioned regarding the possibility of an agreement with the Arabs, but also learned to see things from their point of view. This perspective produced no shift in his Zionist outlook. Rather, he learned that the road to its realization would be paved with harsh struggles, and that the idyllic socialist prognosis would be of no avail. It was his unfulfilled hopes of agreement with the Arabs, coupled with his disillusionment about the chance of convincing the British through moral argumentation, that made Ben-Gurion into an "arms-bearing prophet."

In light of Ben-Gurion's position during the statehood period, when he refrained demonstratively from visiting almost any Arabs and supported the retention of military government over them, his openness to Arab claims and Arab-Jewish dialogue during the 1930s may seem surprising. However, once he became convinced that armed struggle would precede any agreement, he viewed the fate of relations between the two peoples as sealed. For Ben-Gurion neither toyed with matters nor dealt with them amateurishly. His 1952 Knesset appeal to Naguib and the revolutionary officers in Egypt was probably a vestige of his old belief that a change of regimes in the Arab countries might lead to peace with Israel, and that Arab progressiveness also meant the possibility of dialogue between peoples.

IX

When the Arab Revolt began in 1936, Ben-Gurion felt that it was the duty of the Zionist movement to check violence as much as possible, in order to prevent the breakdown of the Mandatory framework. For at that time he still regarded Britain as the Zionist movement's major negotiating partner. Ben-Gurion sought to take advantage of the riots in order to achieve greater economic independence for the Yishuv and military cooperation with the Mandatory authorities. The fruits of this policy were the construction of the port of Tel Aviv and the Supernumerary Police.

During the first stage of the disturbances, no change occurred in Ben-Gurion's fundamental political outlook. He continued to maintain his previous conception of a Jewish-Arab settlement through equal Arab and Jewish participation in the national government and the option of joining an Arab federation. One precondition seemed to him absolutely essential: unrestricted Jewish immigration. Regarding this issue, he disagreed with Weizmann on the diplomatic level and opposed initiatives on the part of various groups in the Yishuv for negotiating with the Arabs on this basis.

The change in Ben-Gurion's political outlook began with the Peel Commission; the shift in the methods he employed in the struggle occurred during the years 1938-1939. The Royal Commission's conclusions made it clear to him that the impetus for Zionist advances was no longer maximum immigration within the Mandatory framework, nor a settlement with the Arabs—but rather the establishment of a Jewish state, even in part of Palestine.

The need to justify a Jewish state in a partitioned Palestine created many ideological difficulties for the labor movement in the Yishuv. It was not only the relinquishing of part of the country which made the Peel Commission's recommendations difficult to accept. The very idea of establishing a state before the "Ingathering of the Exiles," before the transition from "class society" to "laboring people," before a Jewish-Arab agreement—all this contradicted deep-rooted beliefs of the labor movement. A Jewish state at that stage implied agreeing to a partition of government between Jews and Arabs, and acknowledging the inability of a socialist solution to deal with the country's nationalities problems. In this great argument, Ben-Gurion decided in favor of the political consideration at the expense of ideological principles. 1937 and 1938 were formative years for Ben-Gurion as a political leader. During this period, his disillusionment with the influence of public opinion in England and in the world upon the policies of the government came to a head, and the limited effect of moral argumentation was revealed. The limits of relations with Britain came to be seen clearly, as well. It is true that Ben-Gurion began his political career during a period of mistrust vis-a-vis imperialist Western powers, and that during 1918-1921 he labored hard to find an international base for Zionist policy in the form of an international body or an international Jewish Congress. Yet his reservations regarding Britain, which began in the late 1930s, did not stem from some abstract, ideological, ideal formulation, but rather from a search for a realistic arrangement.

The use of one's own force to obstruct undesirable policies or to effect desirable ones was now found to be justified. Allies were now to be selected, not according to theoretical derivatives but rather according to tangible interests. In the place of a harmonic understanding of international relations, one which aspired to the appeasement and conciliation of all parties, came the concept of national struggle. The Yishuv was intended at first to block the implementation of an anti-Zionist solution, and later on to open the door to an unabashedly Zionist one.

World War II presented Ben-Gurion with a revolutionary situation fated to assist in the implementation of a revolutionary solution of the Zionist problem. Ever since 1929, the leaders of Mapai, among them Ben-Gurion and Arlosoroff, had realized that a revolutionary solution to the Jewish question was required, and that the leap from a Jewish minority to a Jewish majority in Palestine should transpire with the greatest possible speed. The large-scale immigration of 1933-1935 accelerated the pace of Zionist achievement, though not to a revolutionary extent. The proposed partition of Palestine in 1937 augured well for the Yishuv's rapid growth, by way of a Jewish state in part of Palestine. Ben-Gurion hoped that Great Britain's withdrawal of support for Zionism in 1938-1939 was a temporary setback, deriving from the situation in Europe at that time and from the orientation of Chamberlain's government.

With the onset of world war, Ben-Gurion hoped that Britain's need for Jewish involvement would help bring about a positive change in its attitude towards Zionism. Churchill's rise to power seemed at first to provide this chance, but hopes for an imminent shift were quickly dashed.

Nevertheless, Ben-Gurion was aware of the radically changed situation which the war had created in the sphere of international relations. From 1941 onwards, the growing influence of the United States and the Soviet Union began to function as a new and promising factor for Zionist policy.

The Holocaust and the creation of mass pressure for immigration to Palestine provided the Zionist movement with potential that it had lacked in the fluid situation which followed World War I. Ben-Gurion sought to take advantage of this combination of factors in order to effect the rapid transfer of between one and one and one-half million Jews to Palestine within a short period of time. In this way, he intended to solve the problem of European Jewry and to settle the issue of Palestine's political future. The post-World War I Greek and Turkish population exchanges served, in his view, as a model for possible rapid transfers. The demand for independence opened up possibilities of acquiring allies other than Great Britain. Ben-Gurion was of the opinion that independent capabilities were more likely to gain potential partners than a pro-Soviet ideological stance. His dream of a large-scale, rapid solution was realized only through struggle and concessions. The muddle in which Zionist policy found itself at the end of the war made a revolutionary solution possible only through compromise and strife. The compromise was in agreeing to the partition of Palestine in 1946; the strife was with the British, and subsequently with the Arabs.

X

Ben-Gurion, who gradually shifted from the dogmatic, frozen conception of historical process to an active conception which does not deny a supra-personal process, but continually re-defines it, changed considerably in his attitude towards his party, its members, and its direction. He forged loyalties but did not hesitate to question them. His failure in the referendum regarding the agreement with the Revisionists in 1935 taught him that one cannot drag the party from one policy to another without adequate preparation. Once the state was established, he did not hesitate to enrage his loyalists by declaring that scientific activity was a form of pioneering and that air force service was a public mission, or by demanding hired labor in the kibbutzim or by attacking the World Zionist Organization. As one of the molders of the sanctified truths, he regarded himself as entitled to question them. Thus the leader was revealed not only as a guardian of the movement's "assets" but as their master as well, protecting them from dereliction but altering them at will.

Ben-Gurion came from a movement which was supremely devoted to values and ideologies, which was reared on inexhaustible talkativeness and which treated heartfelt whims as if they were immutable truths. He knew how to maintain a continual link with the public and to take its moods into consideration. But he did not consider the essence of the leadership to be public-oriented attentiveness which determines policy decisions. He learned to search, amidst the mass of details and aspirations, for the essential Archimedian point. He ignored the endless yearnings for human and social renewal expressed in "heart-to-heart" discussions and instead directed party loyalty into patterns of political action. He was assisted in this by the emergency which cast its shadow upon the Yishuv. Indeed, his thinking at this stage became more pragmatic and schematic, losing a good deal of the felicity of expression and feeling which had characterized his early writings. He came to exemplify what Lenin (following Goethe) had said: "Theories are gray, only the eternal tree of life is green."

More than once, Ben-Gurion risked adopting positions which cast him as an eccentric in the public's eyes, only later to demonstrate vigorously that what had appeared bizarre and unrealistic was in fact both just and justified. This was the case when in 1932 he demanded that the labor movement "conquer" the Zionist movement and later, during the days that he anticipated the Arab invasion of 1948.

Ben-Gurion's way of thinking was influenced by his upbringing within an ideological movement and by his law studies. Nevertheless, the man of action within him strove to face reality and deal with it head-on. Ben-Gurion was not an empiricist in his outlook, mode of thinking, or manner of expression. He made no distinction between facts and attitudes; he ignored human and social nuances; he did not read "belles lettres". He refused to circumscribe his thinking or his desire for action and repeatedly said that experience teaches only about the past and not about the future. When he indulged in scientific pursuits or made statements on the subject, the undisciplined, unbridled aspect of his thinking was obvious. He always sought the all-encompassing impetus of science, man's rational link with the world, but he never accepted the limitations imposed on this impetus. Despite his urge to encompass the world of emotion and history, to conduct an analysis more logical than empirical, and to subordinate thoughts to deeds, Ben-Gurion was controlled and careful in his decisions. Comprehensive, ideological thinking did not cut him off from reality but rather enabled him to break through the restricted boundaries of experience and to raise himself above endless detail. The rhetoric of his expression did not cloud his situational judgment.

As the years passed, a shift occurred from a concept of reality, which included a grasp of those roots of a situation which lay beyond tangible phenomena, to a personal historical outlook whose touch with reality might be considered doubtful.

Impatience with persuasion and negotiation was not typical of Ben-Gurion when he first started out. This developed during the 1950s. While he was leading the movement, he was willing to sit and argue with groups, even with individuals, for hours on end. During his visit to Poland in 1933, he warned local party workers not to make light of anyone, since either victory or defeat might depend upon that person. He never enjoyed argument for its own sake, despite his disputatious nature. All his argumentative and persuasive efforts were aimed at creating popular forces and achieving defined objectives. These efforts lost his personal stamp only after the establishment of the state, when he became used to appealing directly to the masses over the heads of party political organizations, which he sometimes tried to neutralize or exploit.

Ben-Gurion always emphasized action, scoffing and raging at those who possess ideas but do not bring them to fruition. But it would be a mistake to regard this call for realization as only a personal, moral demand. His main interest was not the personal tests faced by the individual but rather the need for the realization of historical necessity. Of course he made demands of the individual, but the moment he required other tools to achieve his aim, even faulty tools, he did not hesitate to make use of them. It was not the individual's intention which guided him but rather the actual result.

His attitude to Zionists and the World Zionist Organization serves as an example of this. During his early days in Palestine, before World War I, Ben-Gurion ridiculed Zionists who did not immigrate. This was also his attitude after independence. Yet under the circumstances which evolved during the period after Word War I, Ben-Gurion was very far from regarding immigrants alone as the basis for establishing a National Home. For that purpose, he strove to organize the Jewish communities of the world, which represented the present, functionary activity, and day-to-day reality. Between the two wars, particularly since the end of the 1920s, he found the Zionist Organization to be an appropriate base for his activities. At that time, he did not insist upon equating ideological support with a requirement for personal immigration to Palestine. He formed coalitions with various allies, never hesitating to endorse those whom he had previously invalidated, or to invalidate those whom he had recently endorsed. In 1935, he succeeded in forming a broad coalition in the Zionist Executive, regarding this as one of his major achievements.

Ben-Gurion's use of social devices as circumstances required meshed with his tendency to assess human characteristics in terms of temporal exigencies. In one of his letters to his wife, Paula, Ben-Gurion assessed Moshe Sharett. He claimed that Sharett was incapable of making decisions "in matters demanding great intellectual and moral courage." In order to decide "in difficult and complicated questions," "vision" and "profound thought" are required.[8] He learned from experience that historical activity, does not permit man to remain "blameless and upright," fearing God and shunning evil (Job 1:8). Cruel struggles require means which go beyond the conventional boundaries of personal morality. Nonetheless, he knew that the movement must not be corrupted from within, and that internal trust and unity must be preserved if the goal is to be reached.

Starting in the 1920s, it seems that Ben-Gurion acquired the art of those political tactics which strike one's opponent mercilessly at his moment of weakness and in his most vulnerable spot. He exploited internal differences and extreme expressions of opinion within his opponents' camp in order to publicly expose his adversaries. He enjoyed a good fight and, at the peak of his career, was astute enough to cast the die at the appropriate moment. He was always conscious of the threat of malice against the ruler[9] and did not hesitate to anticipate his opponents and to make use of force before they were properly organized. For him, the challenge took precedence over the quest for peace, and achieving the objective preceded public consent.

As time went on, his self-confidence grew, reinforcing his impatience with his partners and friends. He admired persons of intellect but did not like people who pursued intellectual truths as an end in itself. A blend of sharpness and character, sense and strength: this, in his view, was what the historic circumstances mandated. He saw before him a stratum of young people who would bear the standard of "biblical man".

XI

In every period, Ben-Gurion oriented himself towards the pursuit which seemed to him to be the focal point of that time. Sometimes he erred and had changes of heart, but generally his judgment was sound. He came to Palestine because he understood that personal immigration was the best argument against Zionism's detractors, one which makes the vision of Eretz-Israel tangible. He rotted away in solitude in Salonika in a bold attempt to master the Turkish language so that he could devote himself to political activity within the Ottoman Empire. He deluded himself into thinking that military cooperation with the Turks at the beginning of World War I was feasible. He did not hesitate to abandon his young wife in America shortly after their marriage, when he volunteered for the Jewish Legion.

After the formation of Ahdut Ha'avoda and the split within the World Poalei-Zion movement (1920), he went to the London office of Poalei-Zion, apparently believing in the value of world socialist and Jewish political action. After a short time, he returned to Palestine and built up the Histadrut, during the 1920s, with drive and self-discipline. Although his strong political interest continued to grow at the end of the 1920s, and with it his concern over the rift between Weizmann and his Revisionist opponents, which had developed within the Zionist movement, it is doubtful whether he intended to undertake any direct political activity in the Zionist arena. It would seem that his election to the Zionist Executive after Arlosoroff's murder was not at his initiative. He was neither shy and retiring nor was he repelled by political power, but under the then-existing circumstances, he continued to regard the Histadrut as the vital tool for action in Palestine. Even without his executive post, his position in the Histadrut and in Mapai provided him with sufficient influence upon Zionist policy. It was only the political crisis following the 1936 disturbances which convinced him that the focus was in the Zionist Executive; at the 1937 World Labor Zionist Council, he announced that for the first time he was putting forward his candidacy for the Zionist Executive, his objective being the creation of a Jewish state: "This will be my life's objective in the near future."

He continued to function within the Zionist Executive until the establishment of the state, but did not hesitate to resign in 1943 when it appeared to him that Weizmann's policy was contradictory to his own views. Until his retirement to Sde Boker, in 1953, he regarded his leading political stature as his main means for action. In 1947, he added security affairs to this.

Even his first retirement to Sde Boker can be explained, not only as a personal need, but as recognition that the character and destiny of the State of Israel would be decided not by its conventional rulers but by the personal example set by its leading individuals and by its spiritual profile. Ben-Gurion's retirement revealed the sin lurking upon the threshold of man's loftiest longings. It proved a hindrance to his successors; in the end, the combination of spiritual authority and political control threatened to undermine both.

XII

Ben-Gurion, the implementer of theory, did not subject action to theory, but rather theory to action. He even refrained from regarding that action and social and historical reality as a partial reality, incapable of encompassing all that is hidden within human and ideological potential. Despite his intellectual forays towards ahistorical doctrines, he always granted an edge to reality, and to the fulfillment of the historical process and the intellectual structures related to it.

Ben-Gurion was interested in Plato and in Buddha. But whereas Platonic ideas are always beyond sensual reality, and Buddhism even dismisses the world of desire and illusions, Ben-Gurion took an antithetical stance. To the extent that he sensed intellectual or emotional needs of his own or of his contemporaries, he always sought to account for them in reality. All the rest was "talk." And indeed, in the case of the Jews and their state, reality was not only a context for realizing values of justice, morality, and beauty, but also an arena for a life and death struggle, wherein defeat means the end of all values and their bearers.

One must not underestimate Ben-Gurion's personal urge to journey into the world of the intellect. A leader who stands alone, facing lengthy struggles and weighty decisions, seeks relief in the form of a vision rising above ordinary details. He attempts to break out of the limitations of his personality and to feel part of an all-encompassing comprehensive entity, to question the relationship between his limited personality, the extensive sphere with which he has been entrusted and the weight of his decisions in the lives of individuals and the community. This urge brought Ben-Gurion to Spinoza and to Buddha—to the desire for inclusion in a suprahuman destiny. It led him toward the link between fate and freedom, to a vision beyond the eye of man, to wish for the unity of matter and spirit, to the superiority of spirit over matter. Eventually, he began to take an interest in biology and to search for "the secret of life" beyond the existence of the individual personality. However, he never sought to reach, nor did he, "a brow of peaceful god, all-seeing eye" (Tchernichovsky), which would mean ignoring the individual. His attitude toward Israel's war dead expresses his approach to the individual who sacrifices everything in the service of History, and nevertheless remains an individual, the son of a father and a mother, a victim whose individuality has not been erased by his sacrifice.

During the early period of the state, Ben-Gurion still stood primarily upon socio-political ground and did not soar up into the realm of philosophical and historical speculations. At one of Ben-Gurion's first meetings with intellectuals and philosophers as prime minister, Martin Buber sought to grasp the final aim of the state and its society. Ben-Gurion replied that the aim was for the multitude to ask "For what purpose?" since man's superiority over other creatures was inherent in this question. The ingathering of many Jews from Europe and the Islamic countries to a life of security and comfort allowing for such spiritual questions to be asked—this seemed to him to be a sufficient aim. In actual fact, as early as the mid-1940s, Ben-Gurion began searching for the spiritual meanings of Jewish existence. He was impelled toward this not so much by the Holocaust and political hardship as by the challenge posed by Communism following Russia's entry into the war, in 1941. Ever since 1917, Ben-Gurion and his generation had been faced with the need to justify themselves in the light of the promised universal redemption of the Revolution. This prospect created a comprehensive worldwide loyalty which overrode Jewish loyalties, rendering them pointless. It also promised a change in the world order, which would set the Jewish destiny right, not a partial, localized solution like Zionism. During the early days of the Revolution, Ben-Gurion sought to protect Zionism by declaring that the redemption of the Jewish people was a goal in its own right. The Palestine labor movement's slide toward "the revolutionary world," during the 1940s, uncovered the threat embedded in Communism. This, more than any topical political question, was the major cause of rifts and alliances within the labor movement during 1944-1948.

Ben-Gurion sought to view the struggle against Communism in the broader context of the battle to guard Judaism's historic uniqueness in the face of Hellenism and Christianity. The era following the establishment of the state taught him that changing social circumstances are insufficient to fill the world of the young Israeli. The Israeli's stance vis-a-vis himself and the world, the Jewish past and present, necessitated a vision.

Ben-Gurion's own shift beyond the political and social context apparently began during the early 1950s, subsequent to his first retirement to Sde Boker. He saw that the new generation which was growing up in the State of Israel lacked that sense of ties with the Jewish people which was felt by his own contemporaries; this new generation no longer knew the distress of dispersion, deprivation, and the fear of atrocities. "Career" now preceded "mission." Ben-Gurion felt the need to supplement the military, political, scientific, and economic activity, then being pursued by the new Israeli generation, with a sense of destiny. In such activity, Jew and non-Jew are undistinguishable, whereas the State of Israel was intended to express the Jewish people's unique destiny. Ben-Gurion applied his view of the future to the past as well, a past which was now subordinated to the existence and progress of the State of Israel. On the one hand, he considered his own generation to be at the pinnacle of his people's history, the predecessors possessing, in his view, no advantage over their successors. For each generation must be seen as sovereign in its own right, even though it builds upon foundations laid by its predecessors. On the other hand, he sought to steep his generation in the Bible, which appeared to him to be an expression of that "Jewish genius" whose "unity of matter and spirit" or "supremacy of spirit" would be expressed, in modern times, in science.

The Bible possessed several qualities from Ben-Gurion's vantage-point. For him, it was not merely an expression of the spontaneous feeling of belonging of the native-born to one's land and to one's ancient forefathers, but also an expression of a clearly Jewish life, which is a life of human endeavor. This was the life of a delimited nation, land and monarchy, with an eventually universal fate, a life which earned the Jewish people its place in world history. It is this life which makes state history superior to non-state history and to the existing Diaspora. In our times, it is the "scientific genius" which earns the Jewish people's universal status. The State of Israel, blending "matter and spirit" and stressing the "supremacy of spirit," is, as it were, the expression both of the Jewish genius of the past, as described in the Bible, and the genius of the present, which finds its form in science. Just as Marxism discerned in the realization of socialism a vision of the meeting of "subject" and "object" and of the removal of the divisions between consciousness and reality, so Ben-Gurion sought to see in the creation of the State of Israel the removal of still another cognitive and historical separation between "matter" and "spirit."

One finds it difficult to follow the lines of this conception and to see the connection between the universal meaning of the Bible and the scientific endeavors of Jews. And one need not add that Einstein, Freud, and others had no deep ties with the Bible. It can be said that the Bible in and of itself, and universal science in and of itself, have even led Jews away from Judaism. The average Israeli is far from a biblical hero, and the problems of his worldview cannot be solved by the deeds of a hero like Joshua, nor apparently by an Isaiah. The Bible exerts a tremendous spiritual presence in Israeli life, but it is doubtful whether it is rooted enough to be an organic and creative element.

Ben-Gurion's envisaged the establishment of the state as a leap forward, designed, as it were, to shake its contemporary generation out of the historical and spiritual continuity of the previous generation, into a new world, which would be closer to the ancient biblical world. Ignoring this generation's web of direct, close links, only ensnares it in miracle and myth, until it ceases to have the ability to assess its own reality, having lost its bearings, no longer knowing where it comes from and where it is going. And by any autonomous account of this generation, the policies of Weizmann and of Ben-Gurion himself are no less relevant than the biblical figure of King David.

Furthermore, shifting the discussion away from actual policy issues to a retrospective consideration of the founders of the Petah Tikvah colony, for example, made contemporary elected institutions seem, in effect, empty vessels in comparison with the grand scope of the historical vision. It distracted, as it were, the public from a rational political consideration of its problems, leading instead to the intuition of the leader, who has been privy to the mysteries of the "kingdom's" birth and who now scrutinizes its proceedings. This shift toward the ideal of "a chosen people" possessing moral and intellectual superiority, "a light unto the nations," screened the tangible, crude, social reality of Israel. Ben-Gurion sensed the inability of the traditional Zionist and socialist concepts to come to grips with the demands of this reality, or to satisfy the aspirations of Israel's young people. One would be hard-pressed to say that this intellectual incompatibility disturbed him in and of itself. Words and symbols mattered to him only when related to forces and means. Criticism of traditional Zionism and socialism enabled him to break away from dogmas which seemed outdated to him, and from social organizations which had become guardians of vested interests. He severed loyalties in order to be free to affect both the nation's political direction and its social and spiritual image. Indeed, Ben-Gurion was one of the few members of his generation who found a common language with those young people whom he drew closer. It is doubtful whether they accepted his biblical vision, but they did accept his broad, sober view of reality and the vigor in the historical sphere to which he guided them. They left to him the reckoning with "Israel's eternal destiny" and threw themselves into frenzied, enthusiastic, and sometimes unrestrained action in the service of that destiny.

Ben-Gurion's mastery of the reality which is visible and perceptible to ordinary mortals allowed him not only to advocate a leap towards danger and its concomitant potential but also to perceive the fallacies of that very achievement. Since the State of Israel was established, he never ceased to warn of the danger of its destruction. The near-catastrophe of 1948 made an indelible impression upon him, and no one knew better than he how narrow the distance had been from defeat and annihilation. He also knew well that the State of Israel's historical and geopolitical status were far from stable. His appeal to the Western Powers in 1963, on the eve of his final resignation, to guarantee Israel's security in the face of one of the short-lived proposals for an Arab Federation constitution, is incisive proof that he sensed his achievement's limitations and even the limitations of Israel's self-reliance (exemplified in his dictum "It is not important what the Gentiles say, it is important what the Jews do "). His way of using force, both in policies that he initiated and in ones to which he reacted defensively, was always to react with utmost caution. His fear of entanglement with a European power is well-known.

One of the means of evaluating a great historic act is to try to "isolate" the personality of the leader and to inquire how matters would appear without his personal seal. In Ben-Gurion's case, it is apparent that this was not merely the addition of a personal "touch" to various processes, but rather the shaping of these processes in a comprehensive historical context. He did not allow his movement to become addicted to the "assets" which it had acquired or created with great difficulty, or to think that these assets would automatically yield the future that the movement hoped for. As times and methods changed, he forced it to face up to danger. He did not regard leadership as an honorary reward or laurel wreath, but as a kind of imperative and challenge. He was obliged to secure his movement's consent to his leadership, but once he had acquired it, the quality of his leadership derived not from his formal election but from its own right, a quality which altered his movement and its norms. He believed in historical destiny, but knew that it had to be willfully forged. He believed in the public, but knew that one must lead it to the goal and not follow in its footsteps. It is doubtful whether his decisive role in the establishment of the State of Israel will be understood in the future in the historical and philosophical terms which he himself attempted to coin. It may well be that different interpretations will only enhance Ben-Gurion's greatness as a leader.

Notes

1 Deutscher, *The Prophet Armed: Trotsky, 1829—1921,* New York and London: 1954.
2 Machiavelli, *The Prince and The Discourses,* New York (Modern Library): 1950, p.22
3 David Ben-Gurion, *Diaries I,* Tel Aviv: 1971 (Hebrew), pp. 254-255 (1923).
4 Ibid., pp. 267-268 (1923).
5 Zalman Arranne, *Autobiography,* Tel Aviv: 1971 (Hebrew), p.201.
6 David Ben-Gurion, *Diaries I,* p.541.
7 *My Talks with Arab Leaders,* New York: 1972.
8 From a letter to Paula; October 7, 1937.
9 *Ben Sira* 7, 5.

BEN-GURION'S THEORY OF SOVEREIGNTY: THE TRIAL OF ADOLF EICHMANN

Michael Keren

Adolf Eichmann was brought to Israel in 1960. He was placed on trial and sentenced to death for his role in the planning and organizing of the murder of European Jewry. In 1962 he was executed. The trial aroused great interest throughout the world. There had been no precedent for Eichmann's crimes, nor was there a precedent for Israel's actions.[1]

During the trial and afterwards, there was considerable debate regarding the legal and political questions pertaining to it. Who should judge Eichmann? Was Israel entitled to represent the Jewish people? Could Israel extend its jurisdiction over acts that were committed before the state was even established? What was the practical and educational significance of the trial? What should be done with Eichmann after his conviction?

Two opposing viewpoints were expressed in these debates—the "tribal" position, and the "universal" position. The former conceived of the trial as an expression of a social, categorical imperative: an eye for an eye. According to this stand, there exist self-evident principles of behavior which stem from every society's need to preserve itself. One of these principles, which has been valid since man's beginning as a social animal, is the automatic punishment of the person whose guilt toward the community is clear and discernible. Even a complex legal system must, according to this view, take account of the primeval instincts upon which it is based. This is all the more certain in the case at hand, in which the criminal has transgressed all bounds of human and cultural comprehension. Accordingly, vengeance remained the principal foundation for judgment.

In comparison, the universal position postulated that the beginning of every human action requires a rational understanding that by its very nature transcends tribal and national boundaries. According to this view, a trial is perceived as a basis for the discussion of fundamental issues, such as the nature of the crime, the motives of the criminal, the relationship between the criminal and his environment, the role of punishment, and so on. The legal system is expected to act in accordance with the norms that emanated from such discussions which took place "within the family of nations" and not out of parochial passions. It is hardly necessary to point out that while the tribal position is widely held, the universal position is the domain of only a limited number of intellectuals.[2]

David Ben-Gurion adopted a position between these two approaches. He saw the Eichmann trial first and foremost as a legal act of a sovereign state. Ben-Gurion's concept of political sovereignty and its relationship toward social imperatives on the one hand, and to universal values on the other, found its most outstanding expression in the debate associated with the Eichmann trial.

Political sovereignty is the right of the state to enact laws and behave according to concepts of justice which it has defined. However, the sovereign state since its inception at the close of the Middle Ages, is engaged in a confrontation with concepts of justice, both tribal and universal, which prevail within and without. These concepts are frequently contradictory. The ability of a state to realize its sovereignty is dependent to a large degree on the ability of its leaders to find a balance between these forces and place the state in a condition of equilibrium. The state cannot behave as a tribe or as a solitary intellectual, nor can it operate in a world which is normatively neutral.[3] Ben-Gurion's stance on the Eichmann trial affords us a better understanding of his conception of the sovereign state as well as of the norms associated with sovereignty.

The State and Historical Justice

The announcement of the capture of Adolf Eichmann on May 23, 1960, was very dramatic. After Ben-Gurion had convened the cabinet for a special meeting, he decided to announce the capture formally to the Knesset.[4] The following day, he wrote a letter to a young girl who had approached him regarding the issue of arms deals with Germany. He availed himself of the opportunity to draw a distinction which he zealously maintained throughout the trial:

> I am writing to you by coincidence, one day after I announced in the Knesset, the capture by our security services of the despicable Nazi criminal, Adolf Eichmann. My attitude toward him is similar to yours, but there are other Germans.

Ben-Gurion drew a distinction between Hitler and his "shattered" regime, on the one hand, and the government of West Germany on the other. He stressed that the world had changed since 1945, and the ruling forces in the world were different. Not for a minute would the Eichmann trial constitute for him a symbol of the struggle between nations or between historical forces. On the contrary, in his letter, one day after his announcement to the Knesset, he stressed the need for friendship with Germany for one could not,

> bring back to life the six million who were slaughtered and burnt in Europe.... In Egypt and Syria, the disciples of the Nazis want to exterminate *Israel* and this is the grave and principal danger which we face....[5]

On the same day, the President of the World Zionist Organization, Nahum Goldmann, expressed the opposite opinion: "I am satisfied that they found Eichmann.... I hope that the case against him will serve as a classic judgment by the Jewish people in Israel."[6] For Goldmann, as for a number of politicians and intellectuals, the trial was indeed to be "classic" throughout its entire course; the Jewish people against its oppressors; humanity against evil. Goldmann emphasized that the success of the "Jewish people" in apprehending Eichmann was a matter of great historical importance. Similarly, in a question to the Minister of Justice, Peretz Bernstein contended that "turning the Eichmann case into a normal criminal proceeding would not only injure the feelings of every Jew, but the very significance of the trial itself."[7]

However, for Ben-Gurion, it was precisely the ability of the sovereign State of Israel to conduct a normal criminal trial that endowed it with uncommon significance. This was the reason for his irate reply to a suggestion broached by Goldmann in a newspaper interview, that an international tribunal should be assembled to decide the Eichmann case.[8] The suggestion stated that a court composed of justices from all the countries which had been conquered by the Nazis, and which had suffered under the Nazi regime, should convene in Jerusalem, with an Israeli justice presiding. Goldmann noted that he was not doubting Israel's right to try Eichmann. He expressed his confidence in Israeli justice, but he stated that this would be a meaningful gesture.

Ben-Gurion's response cannot be comprehended solely on the basis of his problematic relationship with Goldmann, who was then visiting Israel at the initiative of the government. Goldmann had been summoned to give an account of his controversial political contacts overseas. In the discussion that took place on the subject at the Mapai Party Center on January 2, Ben-Gurion rebuked Goldmann publicly: "You are a wandering Jew."[9] Beyond these other points of conflict, however, Goldmann's proposal for setting up an international tribunal struck at the heart of Ben-Gurion's concept of Israeli sovereignty.

In a letter to Goldmann, Ben-Gurion contended that placing Eichmann on trial was the decision of the government and of all the people in Israel. This point was emphasized when Ben-Gurion alluded to Goldmann's non-resident status: "In Israel there is full freedom of speech, not only for Israeli citizens, but also for tourists who sojourn here for a long or short time." The prime minister stressed the singularity of the Holocaust, as opposed to the other atrocities committed by the Nazis during World War II. He wrote that the obligation to exact retribution for this unique crime rested on the sole sovereign authority of its victims—the state of Israel:

> This is perhaps the first case in human history of historical justice, where a small people, whose enemies and persecutors are so numerous, was afforded the opportunity to place on trial, in its sovereign country, one of the chiefs of its oppressors for atrocities committed against hundreds and thousands of its children.[10]

In Ben-Gurion's words, historical justice and the honor of the Jewish people demanded that this "should be done only by an Israeli court and in a sovereign Jewish state."

Goldmann responded that he did not understand why his suggestions should be construed as a serious blow to the feelings of the people in Israel and to the honor of the state. In his opinion, "it should be a great honor for the state, if the other countries would send their justices and would participate in a tribunal over which an Israeli justice would preside." If his proposal was unacceptable, he added, "it would be worthwhile to at least invite observers from the states whose many citizens were also exterminated."[11]

Ben-Gurion's position was not easy to understand. The poet Nathan Alterman attempted to clarify it:

> The feeling of greatness inherent in this event stems from the fact that this criminal is going to answer for his crimes not before strangers, but before the public seat of judgment belonging to the people against whom he committed his crimes. This judgment combines, for the first time in the history of the Jewish people, a public judicial legality with the chapter of law and retribution, something hitherto unknown in the saga of the Jewish nation.

Therefore, Alterman asserted, Israel would not relinquish this trial and would not transfer it to others. The reality of its rebirth and existence were never more apparent than in the scales of justice which it presently wielded.[12]

The trappings of justice at the disposal of the state, including the judicial bench, robe, and gavel, were, in Ben-Gurion's eyes, not only symbols, but the very basis of Israeli independence. Believing that the physical and the spiritual are intertwined, Ben-Gurion considered that values find their expression chiefly in the actual political activity which is based upon them.[13] At the Mapai Center session in which his confrontation with Goldmann took place, he expressed this in another context. Polemicizing with Prof. Nathan Rotenstreich, who spoke of the state as an idea that had turned into reality, Ben-Gurion refused to accept the distinction:

> Professor Rotenstreich states: The state is not only an idea but an actuality. To some extent this is true, but not entirely. Since one can be precise with you about concepts, the state is also an idea, because it is a reality that differs from the reality of Jews throughout the world. It is different and this difference constitutes the idea.[14]

For Ben-Gurion, the idea of the state was expressed in its daily activity: agriculture, industry, science, etc. Thus historical justice, in his opinion, would reach fruition through activity at a given time and place, in Jerusalem's Bet Ha'am auditorium, where Eichmann was being tried. While Goldmann contended that he did not require any counseling from Ben-Gurion regarding the feelings of the people and the honor of the state,[15] Ben-Gurion posed the question of the Eichmann trial in a formal manner before the government of Israel, which authorized his decision to place Eichmann on trial before an Israeli court.

Some prominent Diaspora Jews opposed to the trial brought pressure to bear on Ben-Gurion. One American Jewish leader, Joseph Proskauer, sent the prime minister an editorial from the *Washington Post* which questioned Israel's right to try Eichmann. Proskauer begged Ben-Gurion to have Eichmann extradited to West Germany or brought before an international tribunal, so as to spare the Diaspora Jews the possible consequences. He feared widespread anti-Semitism as a result of the trial. He recognized "the great emotional urge to bring this wrong-doer to justice," but he believed that "emotional urge is not a valid reason for taking a false public relations step."[16]

Ben-Gurion did not view the exercise of sovereign rights in terms of public relations. In his reply to Proskauer, he set forth in five crammed pages what he termed "the attitude of the Jews in their independent country which acts according to its conscience." Initially Ben-Gurion replied to the argument of the *Washington Post* that Israel was not entitled to speak in the name of what it called "an imaginary

Jewish ethnic unit." He noted that despite the difference of opinions regarding the existence of such a unit, the six million Jews who had been killed in Europe "believed and felt with every fiber of their being that they belonged to a Jewish people and that there is such a thing as a Jewish people in the world." He added:

> The Nazis also murdered members of other peoples; Poles, Russians, Czechs, and so forth. These nations fought against the German Nazis and crushed and subdued them. Only the six million Jews had no state to champion them until the state of Israel was established.

Hence, although the Eichmann trial did evoke powerful emotions, they were in themselves not the justification for holding the trial. The real justification lay elsewhere:

> The Jewish state (which is called Israel) is the heir of the six million who were murdered, the *only* heir. For these millions, in contrast to the opinions of the *Washington Post*, regarded themselves as the children of the Jewish people and only the children of the Jewish people. If they had remained alive, the great majority of them would have come to Israel. The only *historic* prosecuting attorney of these six millions is Israel, and for reasons of *historic justice, it is the duty of the Israeli government, as the government of the Jewish state whose foundations were laid by millions of European Jews, and whose establishment was their dearest hope, to try their murderers.*

Ben-Gurion believed that the Jewish people had an obligation to realize the vision of the return to Israel. But conversely, he recognized that the raison d'être of the state of Israel was the fulfillment of a historic obligation toward the Jewish people:

> You ask what we shall gain from the Eichmann trial. We shall gain nothing, but we shall be fulfilling our historic duty toward six million of our people who were murdered. We cannot ignore this duty, otherwise we should not deserve to be what we are.[17]

These ideas were central to the interview which Ben-Gurion gave to the *New York Times Magazine* a few months later. He stressed the subject of sovereignty even more in this interview, which was intended to be widely circulated. Here he confronted the argument, voiced by a number of Western intellectuals, that even if Israel possessed a legal right to try Eichmann, it should not do so for ethical reasons. Eichmann's crime, they reasoned, was against humanity and the conscience of humanity, rather than against Jews as such.[18]

This contention stemmed from a serious attempt by philosophers to grapple with the enormity of the Nazi crimes against the Jews. They were so terrible that thoughtful people could not absorb them, and philosophers made attempts to endow the criminal acts with a significance that transcended their boundary. It was not merely the murder of Jews, but acts against the human conscience. However, Ben-Gurion disposed of these arguments in short shrift: "Only a Jew with an inferiority complex would say that. Only one who does not realize that a Jew is a human being." He believed that one could not divide a person's Judaism from his humanity, especially when others didn't engage in such niceties when they murdered Jews. "The Jews in Hitler's Germany were not murdered because they were human beings, but because they were Jews."[19]

The Boundaries of Sovereignty

Ben-Gurion denied that vengeance was a motive in the trial. Similarly, there was no consideration of retribution in Israeli-German relations, for no vengeance was possible for the murder of six million. Instead, he viewed the education of the young as the main purpose of the trial. But educating them to what purpose? Ben-Gurion did not view the trial as a means of recalling the Holocaust or of emphasizing the element of Jewish bravery during the Holocaust. He believed that young Israelis would recognize the one conclusion that he believed emerged from the Holocaust: the need to maintain sovereign lives in an independent state. Jewish youth, he stated, "should be taught the lesson that Jews are not sheep to be slaughtered, but a people who can hit back, as Jews did during the War of Independence." [20]

As the astonishing latter portion of this sentence reveals, for Ben-Gurion, the War of Independence a few years after the Holocaust was the real response to it and a guarantee for the prevention of a new Holocaust. Jewish sovereignty in the state of Israel was therefore not only a historic solution, but an ethical imperative.

The sovereign state that fulfills an ethical imperative is justified at times in departing from formal law in the name of this imperative. Thus Ben-Gurion justified the kidnapping of Eichmann from Argentina, an action that contravened international law and the laws of another sovereign country. As he wrote to President Frondizi of Argentina at the time:

> I don't take lightly the formal injury to the laws of your country which was inflicted by those who found Eichmann, but I am certain that only a few persons in the world will not understand us and will not respect the supreme moral force of their action. This is an event that one cannot approach, Mr. President, solely with a formal measuring stick. [21]

Ben-Gurion's letter was not a request for mercy before the law, but a claim for justice, and he had proven himself willing to use the resources of the sovereign state and its secret services in the process.

The response in the *New York Times* after the publication of the interview focused on the contradiction between the claim for justice on the one hand and the damage to Argentine sovereignty on the other. One writer asked in an ironic vein: "Suppose the Roman Catholic Church began kidnapping people and taking them to the Vatican for trial?" [22] Ben-Gurion himself was probably aware of this contradiction, but he also knew that in the dialogue between states one could find various means for avoiding its sting. Indeed, after a short period of tension in relations with Argentina, the dispute between the two states was officially forgotten.

This was not the case with regard to the fundamental problems inherent in the legal process against Eichmann. Ben-Gurion stressed Israeli sovereignty as a value. But what were the bounds of this sovereignty? And to what degree did Israeli sovereignty touch upon the entire Jewish people? These questions could not be answered with the aid of diplomats, if only because world Jewry, and particularly the Jews of the United States, did not readily support Ben-Gurion's attempt to appoint Israel as Eichmann's sole judge. They were certainly not convinced by the argument that if the six million were still alive they would have immigrated to Israel.

The question of the extent and bounds of Israeli sovereignty vis-à-vis the Jewish people arose repeatedly. The American Council for Judaism took umbrage at Ben-Gurion's claim that Israel had the "right to try Eichmann on behalf of the Jewish people." Calling the trial a show trial, this anti-Zionist organization claimed: "Many Jews in the United States, Great Britain and elsewhere have regularly denied that Israel, or its officials, can speak for all Jews in the world."[23] This question surfaced with redoubled intensity in connection with the notes sent by the Israeli government some time previously, to various governments around the world, regarding the swastikas daubed on synagogues and other Jewish buildings in a dozen countries in 1959. Ben-Gurion justified Israel's intervention, employing an argument of spurious logic. "Theoretically it is so: We always say we are responsible only for the Jews of Israel. But practically, Israel belongs to the Jewish people. We know in a way that we represent the Jewish people."[24]

However, many Diaspora Jews did not agree. When the issues were sharpened by the Eichmann trial, the American Jewish Committee responded. Its president, Herbert Ehrmann, sent a harsh letter to Ben-Gurion in which he noted that his organization had recently given careful consideration to the matter of the relationship between Israel and Jews of the United States and other countries. He viewed it as unfortunate that this question "has again become the subject of wide public discussion and controversy." Ehrmann argued that the belief of "Israeli officials ... that Judaism could not flourish elsewhere but in Israel" seriously weakened Jews everywhere. The Israeli attitude was drawn from "Jewish experience in other lands and other situations, not relevant to our lives, offensive to our countrymen and injurious to our position in the United States." Ehrmann's principal concern was that an impression was created in the United States during the swastika affair that "Israel was speaking on behalf of Jews who are citizens of the United States." He declared forcefully that "Jews have been an integral part of American life for more than three hundred years" and that American Jewry was "free to live purposeful and satisfying lives."[25]

Ben-Gurion said in reply:

I can appreciate the United States, its culture, its freedom and its place in the world. But I regard myself as a son of the Jewish people, which has a land of its own, a language of its own, a great past of its own, longer and more illustrious than that of the American people.

He added that for him "Jewishness" meant a Jewish field, a Jewish road, a Jewish port, Jewish scientific institutions, and so on, as well as Jewish membership in the world family of nations. The ability of the Jews to play a role within the framework of the community of nations stemmed from the fact that in 1948 a sovereign state was created. This point was stressed emphatically throughout Ben-Gurion's reply:

I do not believe, nor does any responsible person in Israel, that the government of Israel speaks in the name of the Jews of the world. It speaks only in the name of its citizens, Jewish and non-Jewish, for we also have non-Jewish minorities.... Just as you are interested in the fate of Jews in other countries, so are we. In one respect, however, we are different from the American Jewish Committee. You are one of many organizations of American citizens. We are a government, and we are entitled to approach any [other] government on matters affecting the rights of Jews wherever such rights are threatened, because we are a Jewish state.[26]

The State and the Historical Demon of Anti-Semitism

As the date of the trial opening in April 1961 approached, various problems related to it became clearer. It is interesting to note today the extent to which public discussion revolved around the issue of how anti-Semites around the world would react. This question preoccupied Israelis and Jews to such an extent that the Prime Minister's Office asked the Mossad (Israeli intelligence) to monitor anti-Semitic incidents worldwide during the trial.[27] The Mossad's three dry reports which deal with the period from the beginning of April until the end of July 1961, constituted an interesting answer to these apprehensions. The instrument of the state was applied in order to contend with the historic demon of anti-Semitism. Mossad agents arrived at the conclusion that during the period of the Eichmann trial, there were relatively few manifestations of anti-Semitism and these were devoid of any more widespread significance.[28]

Not everyone concurred. Richard Crossman, the chairman of the British Labour Party's Executive Committee and an international columnist, published an article in the *New Statesman* in March 1961, in which he wrote: "As the Eichmann trial approaches, I feel more and more uneasy—and so I find do quite a number of my Jewish and Israeli friends." According to Crossman, the political framework within which Ben-Gurion had decided to set the trial "is such a perturbing combination of Old Testament ethics and modern sensationalism that though what is done will no doubt be justice, what is *seen* to be done, may well look more like an act of tribal vengeance."[29]

It was impossible to ignore this contention. Since the Eichmann trial aroused strong feelings throughout the world, there were grounds for the fear that, as Crossman put it, "if the trial of Eichmann creates the impression of a Biblical act of vengeance, its net effect in the West will be to ferment a great deal of suppressed but real anti-Jewish feeling."

But was there a basis for viewing the trial as an act of vengeance on the part of the Jews of Israel? Interestingly, organizations of Holocaust survivors did not view it this way. They generally regarded the trial as important in bringing a mass murderer to justice, and mainly as an act of educational significance. They also attached great importance to the opportunity that the trial gave them of recounting the events of the Holocaust before the world.[30]

However, there were groups that were primarily concerned with retribution. "In order to judge Eichmann, we don't even require the Nuremburg Laws," wrote Dr. Israel Eldad, a prominent right-wing figure in Israel. "There is a law of the Torah regarding Amalek, which is both a law of justice and a law of vengeance, since vengeance is also justice." This was the approach of a person who grasped the sovereign status of Israel as primarily a symbol of the victory of the Jews over the Nazis:

> Placing Eichmann on trial in Jerusalem, the capital of the state of Israel, is a victory for the historic Jewish people whose capital was Jerusalem from the time of David and Solomon. This very fact is a sign as to who won this war between Nazism and Judaism.[31]

Yitzhak Y. Cohen wrote an article expressing the view that the Eichmann trial could have been conducted and concluded in an hour. On the basis of biblical citations, he concluded that a trial meant weighing the evidence, inspecting and cross-examining the witnesses, but only when dealing with an accused whose guilt was not sufficiently clear. This was not the case regarding Eichmann, he argued. When Agag, King of Amalek, was brought before Samuel the Prophet, his trial lasted as long as was required to enunciate a single sentence: "As your sword has rendered many women bereaved so shall your mother be bereaved among women." If Israeli agents had treated Eichmann in such a manner, Cohen wrote, they would have won eternal glory, whereas bringing him to trial was a political and historic mistake which harmed Israel and the Jewish people.

The world-view expressed in this article can clearly be defined as tribal. The Jewish people stand alone and confront a hostile world that, for historical and cultural reasons, will not forgive them this trial, even if it was a just one. An example, which Cohen finds proper to cite, was the trial of Jesus Christ, for which the Jews were never forgiven. He provided an exhaustive description of international anti-Semitism, stressing Israel's isolation, and noting that while the world would have accepted the verdict of an international tribunal, the Eichmann trial would turn the accused into a martyr and would cause problems for Jewish communities around the world.[32]

Ben-Gurion responded to this article. He pointed out that Britain, Poland and Czechoslovakia had tried Nazi murderers, and only a Jewish inferiority complex, in his words, could find fault with a Jewish trial for a murderer of millions of Jews. Here he submitted an alternative viewpoint to the one that saw the Jew as standing alone against the anti-Semite. With the establishment of the state, the status of the Jew changed, and thus:

> It was not for the sake of vengeance that the Israeli volunteers labored to reveal Eichmann's hiding place, and it was not for the sake of revenge that the government of Israel placed Eichmann on trial in a Jewish courtroom in the state of Israel. We, the sovereign Jewish people in Israel, are the avengers of the six million who were murdered solely because they were Jews. We will redeem their blood not so much through vengeance, as through a just trial.[33]

Ben-Gurion attempted to endow the Eichmann trial with the significance of a trial conducted by the sovereign Jewish people. He aimed to accomplish this not only on the theoretical plane, but also on the practical one. He was very much involved in formulating the concept of the trial. The opening address of the prosecutor Gideon Hausner, was submitted for him to study before it was delivered in court.[34] On the other hand, as far as can be discerned, Ben-Gurion, as head of the government, did not intervene in the actual judicial procedure. He took pains to ensure that the trial would be conducted in accordance with all the details of correct procedure.

One of the most severe critics of the Eichmann trial, Hannah Arendt, found words of praise for its procedure. As she wrote of the Chief Justice: "The trial is presided over by someone who serves justice as faithfully as Mr. Hausner serves the state of Israel."[35] But Arendt could not understand that for Ben-Gurion this was not a contradiction. The realization of legal justice in all its fine points abutted the real interest of the state of Israel. From Ben-Gurion's standpoint, Chief Justice Landau and his associates served the interests of the state of Israel no less than Hausner. This was also the reason why, notwithstanding the fact that a sensational public trial was under way, the elements of fanfare that could have accompanied it, such as during the execution of the sentence, were absent.

The Universal Message

Before and after Eichmann's execution, the question of carrying out the verdict was debated. Here the universal viewpoint found its fullest expression. No one doubted that Eichmann deserved the death sentence. But it seemed that it was precisely because the justice of the verdict was so readily recognizable and also perhaps because of the difficulty of associating the man in the glass booth with the terrible crimes recounted in the courtroom, that many grappled with the question. A U.S. Representative, James Roosevelt, son of the late President, announced at a Zionist meeting that Eichmann should be freed after he was convicted.[36] Others adduced reasons of realpolitik, such as the fear of turning Eichmann into a martyr in the eyes of neo-Nazi groups.[37] One interlocutor from El Salvador wrote to Ben-Gurion in order to advise him to avail himself of the opportunity to refute the charge that the Jews asked an eye for an eye and a tooth for a tooth.[38] Ben-Gurion's response touched on the major issues related to the trial:

> Many, to my sorrow, have still not accustomed themselves to view the Jewish people as a people having equal rights and equal status to any other free nation. The Jewish people do not require self-exculpation. The murder of millions of Jews is no lesser crime than an American or English act of murder, and no one comes with any complaints to the Americans or the English because they hang a murderer, and they don't constantly remind them of the "sin" of an eye for an eye.[39]

Walter Kaufmann, a Jewish philosopher from Princeton University, saw a different aspect in the Eichmann trial:

> Eichmann's trial represents a unique opportunity for impressing the world with a morality higher than it now accepts.... Our prophets gave the world a higher ethic than it had before. Now the new Israel could go a step beyond even that ethic and transcend retributive justice altogether.[40]

Kaufmann was not the only one who viewed the Eichmann trial as a basis for a new moral code, and who was entranced by the idea of determining his punishment not in accordance with the law for meting out justice to the Nazis and their collaborators, but according to some sort of transcendental code. Heading the intellectuals who demanded not implementing the death sentence was Martin Buber, the aged philosopher, whose philosophical method undoubtedly facilitated the concept that decisions taken in Israel could serve as the basis for a universal dialogue between man and man and between man and his God. Buber, who even met the prime minister personally in order to persuade him to attempt to rescind the execution, saw the punishment as a "mistake of historical dimension." In his opinion, "it may serve to expiate the guilt felt by many young people in Germany, and hence be an obstacle to the resurgence of humanism in them and in the world." Buber made it clear that he did not oppose the execution simply because of his objection to the death penalty, nor was he motivated by feelings of pity or by doubts about the severity of the sentence. He was not against the trial itself, although he preferred an international court "with a certain representation of humanity to give it the right kind of horizon." His opposition stemmed from the belief that it was pointless to seek retribution through the execution of Eichmann, for there can be no retribution for crimes of such magnitude. The crimes were so monstrous that they fell beyond the ordinary realm of punishment, and the death of Eichmann served none of the accepted purposes of punishment.[41]

This point was brought up with renewed vigor after the execution. The noted scholar, Gershom Scholem, addressed himself to the public and historical aspects of the trial and not to its legal aspects. He grasped the trial as geared to "a different sort of national and human education, a different human consciousness." He termed Eichmann himself "an impotent," a portrayal that aroused criticism from his colleagues, who reminded Scholem that Eichmann was a far cry from this image both in his deeds and in the way he grappled with the indictment. Scholem saw Eichmann principally as an example of the systematic liquidation of the image of God in man and the dehumanization of an entire nation. The verdict was an incorrect solution, he felt. It corrupted the historical significance of the trial by creating the illusion that it was possible to conclude something in this affair by hanging a single person. It would have been better, he wrote, if the hangman would not intervene between us and the reckoning which we had with the world.[42]

It is not surprising that the universal position that sought to annul carrying out the verdict, for reasons of principled philosophy, encountered cascades of anger and derision on the part of those who sustained the tribal position. In an open letter to Buber that appeared in the right-wing newspaper *Herut*, one person contrasted the spirit of revenge he felt as a moral alternative to the professor's stance of purifying the world. "Alas, I can already envision your derisive gesture with your hands. I can already hear you grunt, 'There is the bestial feeling of revenge. When will the world be cured of this base feeling?'"[43]

Alterman did not spare his criticism of Buber. He warned that Buber's abstract arguments could awaken a desire for that very tone which was to be kept from the courtroom:

> This tone denotes a burning feeling for revenge, a burning desire to punish and a
> hatred toward the crime and the criminal that serves no practical purpose. Perhaps it

hinders the revival of the sparks of humanism in Germany, but it is the source nonetheless from which the drive for justice and the drive for righteousness in the world emanate.

Alterman wanted to stress through hyperbole that a theoretical analysis which totally detaches the discussion from tribal instincts of hatred for the crime and desire for retribution, could undercut the basis from which justice sprang. His true position was closer to that of Ben-Gurion. According to this stand, the historic significance of the trial resided in resorting to regular criminal proceedings, despite or perhaps because of the dimension of the crime. As was his wont, Alterman addressed the topic in dramatic language:

> The crime of murdering a solitary Jew was ... hitherto a matter that could have been encompassed in the realm of criminal law. But the murder of many Jews was, for many hundreds of years, since the Jewish people went into exile, a matter that belonged to the realm of social historical processes and a topic for research into the causes and sources of hatred for the Jews. The Jerusalem trial, for the first time in Jewish history, lifted and shunted the murder of the Jews and the decrees and laws involved in it, from the realm of history and research to the realm of criminal law.

In addition, Alterman argued that a practical purpose was also served by the trial. Following the verdict, the murder of Jews could arouse in the hearts of those who yearned for it not only a feeling of revelry in these vile deeds, but also a sense of the bitter taste provided by being seized from a country of refuge and by the awaiting gallows.[44]

Conclusion

In the Eichmann trial, Ben-Gurion's concept of the place of the state of Israel in history and in the fate of the Jewish people, found expression. The response to the persecution of Jews in history resided in the real-life state and in its day-to-day activities. It was incumbent upon the state to act in a practical manner to avoid a new holocaust. It also possessed the tools for this purpose, since it was a member in the community of sovereign states with all the power accompanying this status.

Ben-Gurion believed that the Eichmann case had an educational significance, not only in the sense that it provided an opportunity to unfold the history of the Holocaust before the world, but also as an occasion to impart to a people that had not experienced sovereignty and was as yet unused to it, the feeling of power and independence that the judicial process imparted. For Ben-Gurion's purpose, the opening of a criminal file for a historically despicable murderer of Jews was the sole possible answer to the murder of Jews and also a way of deterring similar acts in the future.

During subsequent debates surrounding the Lavon Affair, a political crisis which unfolded at the same time as the Eichmann case, Ben-Gurion, as prime minister, was accused of overstressing the trappings of the sovereign state, at the expense of the spontaneous social forces operating within it.[45] The stance adopted in questions involving the Eichmann case reveals that he indeed stressed sovereignty and its symbols but also that his concept of sovereignty was not detached from its social and normative context.

In all his statements at the time of the trial, Ben-Gurion wrestled with two concepts of justice: the tribal and the universal. He positioned the sovereign state between them. For Ben-Gurion, the state could not act as a tribe, activated by instincts alone, nor as an intellectual who attempts to base political behavior on a rational analysis of the world. On the other hand, the state has to take account of both networks of imperatives simultaneously: that which emanated from society's needs for survival and that which was formulated according to universal values which transcended the state.

During the period of the Eichmann trial, Ben-Gurion contended with the topic of the state and its status vis-à-vis the tribal and universal imperatives, not only within the framework of his political responses to the trial, which were surveyed here, but in the actual theoretical plane. On December 2, 1961, the Bible study circle met in the prime minister's home. Supreme Court Justice Moshe Zilberg, a member of the group, sought Ben-Gurion's opinion on whether the prophetic concept or the royal concept was prevalent in Judaism. In the following weeks Ben-Gurion dealt with this topic, and in prolonged correspondence with Zilberg, he attempted to prove that the aforementioned dilemma was not a dilemma at all in the words of the prophets of Israel. The prophets' moral call was always accompanied by a profound view of reality. They understood that the demands for universal justice upon a single state had no significance, unless the entire world obligated itself to their fulfillment. But while a single state alone could not live in accordance with the demands of total prophetic justice, neither could it act as a tribe. Ben-Gurion summarized this in the following manner:

> In the regime of tribes, when the state is nonexistent, blood vengeance is dominant. The relatives of the murdered person avenge the blood of their tribesman. In a civilized country, this is forbidden. The state judges and the relatives of the murdered person are forbidden to touch the murderer. But this is only the first and by no means the final stage of imposing justice. For as long as any state is permitted to do what it wants, and what it can do, justice will not reign in the world. And the rule of justice will not arise, if it does not embrace the entire human race. Hence the prophetic concept, by its very essence, must be universal, embracing all of humanity. Whoever contemplates with open eyes what is transpiring in the world—the Cold War, the anarchy in the Congo, the events in Laos, the quarrel surrounding Berlin, the situation in our region, must perforce reach this universal conclusion.[46]

Notes

* Unless otherwise stated, all documents are housed at the Ben-Gurion Research Institute and Archives in Sedeh Boker, Israel. The author wishes to thank the Institute's staff and especially its director, Professor Ilan Troen, for access to the previously unpublished material as well as for a research grant which made this study possible.

1 On the Eichmann Trial, see especially Gideon Hausner, *Justice in Jerusalem*, New York, 1964; Hanna

Arendt. *Eichmann in Jerusalem: A Report on the Banality of Evil*, New York, 1964; [anon], *Die Kontroverse: Hanna Arendt, Eichmann und die Juden*, Munchen, 1964.

2 On tribalism and universalism, see Mulford Sibley, *Political Ideas and Ideologies*, New York, 1970, especially pp. 212-213.

3 This was already understood by Jean Bodin when he developed the concept of sovereignty in the sixteenth century. See especially his *Method for the Easy Comprehension of History*, published in 1566.

4 *Ma'ariv*, May 23, 1960.

5 Ben-Gurion to Frida Sasson, May 24, 1960.

6 *Ha'aretz*, May 24, 1960.

7 *Haboker*, May 31, 1960.

8 Ibid.

9 *Yediot Aharonot*, June 3, 1960.

10 Ben-Gurion to Nahum Goldmann, June 2, 1960.

11 Nahum Goldmann to Ben-Gurion, June 2, 1960.

12 "What Are People Saying?" (Hebrew), *Lamerhav*, June 3, 1960.

13 On Ben-Gurion's phenomenology, see Michael Keren, "Ben-Gurion and the Intellectuals: A Study of Elite Interaction," in *Political Elites and Social Change*, ed. Moshe Czyudnowski, Illinois, 1983.

14 Mapai Party Center meeting, June 2, 1960, Beit Berl, Labor Party Archives, 23/60.

15 *Lamerhav*, June 5, 1960.

16 Joseph M. Proskauer to Ben-Gurion, May 31, 1960.

17 Ben-Gurion to Joseph M. Proskauer, July 7, 1960.

18 See Hannah Arendt, *Eichmann in Jerusalem: A Report on the Banality of Evil*, New York, 1964, passim.

19 "The Eichmann Case as Seen by Ben-Gurion," *New York Times Magazine*, December 18, 1960.

20 Ibid.

21 Quoted in Ben-Gurion, *The Restored State of Israel* (Hebrew), Tel Aviv, 1969, vol. 2. pp. 654-655.

22 "Letters," *New York Times Magazine*, January 8, 1961.

23 Ibid.

24 Quoted in Michael Brecher, *The Foreign Policy System of Israel: Setting, Images, Process*, New Haven, 1972, p. 237.

25 Herbert B. Ehrmann to Ben-Gurion, February 28, 1961.

26 Ben-Gurion to Herbert M. Ehrmann, March 13, 1961. The quotations are from the Hebrew version written by Ben-Gurion.

27 Three reports submitted with covering letter addressed to Yitzhak Navon, August 17, 1961.

28 Ibid.

29 R.H.S. Crossman, "The Faceless Bureaucrat," *New Statesman*, March 31, 1961, pp. 503-504.

30 Josef Rosenzaft to Dov Joseph, undated telegram, file no. 2210.

31 Israel Eldad, "The Nazi Argument..." (Hebrew), *Haboker*, August 18, 1961.

32 Yitzhak Y. Cohen, "A Political and Historical Mistake" (Hebrew), unpublished, Ben-Gurion Archives, file 538.

33 Ben-Gurion to Yitzhak Y. Cohen, April 10, 1961.

34 Gideon Hausner to Ben-Gurion, March 24, 1961, and Ben-Gurion to Hausner, March 28, 1961.

35 Arendt, *Eichmann in Jerusalem*, p. 5.

36 Reported in *Ma'ariv*, May 12, 1961.

37 Nachman Ben-Shalom to Ben-Gurion, February 6, 1962.

38 W.T. Deninger to Ben-Gurion, May 20, 1962.

39 Ben-Gurion to Deninger, June 6, 1962.

40 Walter Kaufmann to Ben-Gurion, May 3, 1962.

41 "Buber Calls Eichmann Execution Great 'Mistake,'" *New York Times,* June 5, 1962.

42 Gershom Scholem, "Eichmann" (Hebrew), *Amot* 1 (August-September 1962), pp. 10-11.

43 A. Axelrod, "An Open Letter to Martin Buber" (Hebrew), *Herut,* March 21, 1962.

44 Nathan Alterman, "On Taking Responsibility" (Hebrew), *Davar,* June 7, 1962.

45 See Michael Keren, *Ben-Gurion and the Intellectuals: Power, Knowledge and Charisma*, Illinois, 1983.

46 Ben-Gurion to Moshe Zilberg, January 8, 1962.

The Early Years

BEN-GURION AND PO'ALEI ZION IN THE US DURING WORLD WAR I

At the start of World War I, in August 1914, both David Ben-Gurion and Izhak Ben-Zvi were in Palestine. From both the Jewish and the nationalist points of view, their basic reactions to the war were dictated by the political and ideological orientation they had adopted in the years following the Young Turks' revolution in 1908. They considered it a bourgeois democratic revolution that by its very nature would encourage the modernization of Turkey and thereby help the country withstand the internal and external political pressures that were then tearing it apart. The view that the Zionist movement stood to gain from the disintegration of the Turkish Empire was no longer considered realistic or even desirable. According to the new prognosis, a democratic Turkey could anticipate a more stable future. Zionism merely had to find the conditions for a *modus vivendi* within the democratic political ambience henceforth attributed to the Ottoman state. Up to this point, Zionism may have appeared as a movement leading to the development of Palestine along capitalist lines, which meant that it would inevitably find itself in military and political confrontation with the feudal Turkish Empire,[1] but which no longer seemed likely after the events of 1908. The modernization which Zionism was destined to bring with it to the Near East was perceived as readily compatible with the social program of the new Turkey.

The solution of the Jewish national question was no longer predicated on severing Palestine from the Empire. The solution would not be a territorial-political one realized by an alliance with a power seeking to violate Turkey's territorial integrity. Rather, Jewish aims could be attained by preserving Turkish sovereignty. The autonomy enjoyed by the Jewish community of Turkey for hundreds of years might be expanded to also encompass the Jews of Palestine.[2]

Espousal of the same political rights enjoyed by Turkish Jewry for the benefit of Jewish settlement in Palestine was not seen merely as a preparatory stage in the struggle for independence, but as an end in itself. It was believed that an increase in the number of Jews in Palestine would strengthen the communal autonomy of Turkish Jewry. A Jewish national region under Ottoman rule, similar to that of the Armenians and Greeks,[3] would add support to the religious autonomy Turkish Jews enjoyed.

There can be little doubt that the heads of Po'alei-Zion in Palestine, as well as other Zionist leaders, were fully aware that the Turkish Vilayet Laws were hardly an exhaustive expression of personal national autonomy as formulated in Russia at the beginning of the century. They assumed, however, that practical application of these laws and their formulation in modern legal terminology would reveal that they more than corresponded with the original concept's implications. Ben-Gurion expressed his certainty of this in a series of articles he wrote for *He'ahdut*, Po'alei-Zion's weekly journal in Palestine. He later returned to the subject, adding further comments, in an article in *Hatoren*, a Hebrew monthly published in New York:

> From the fifteenth century until today Jews in Turkey have enjoyed a special kind of national autonomy which, despite all its organic drawbacks and imperfections, has not only local import but also is of overall value in principle. The importance of our national rights in Turkey derives from the special principle...of the individual. It is not language or territory, but *individual nationality* that is officially, legally, provided for and accepted. It is the individual who is *granted rights*. We Jews, who have been endowed with numerous tongues and are dispersed among all countries of the world, are a national minority everywhere. We can enjoy national rights only if they do not depend on a territorial foundation but on a personal, individual basis, whatever the place or language may be.[4]

On the operative level, the shift to a pro-Turkish orientation evoked what contemporaries then called "Ottomanization." This was conceived as the only means by which increasing numbers of Jews in Palestine could add their weight to Jewish political power that had already been garnered and unified by virtue of the recognized Jewish establishment in Turkey. Only thus could those Jews become an integral part of the effort to introduce democratic forms to the country and advance Jewish national interests from within.

Furthermore, Ben-Gurion, Ben-Zvi and Israel Shochat[5] all understood that, paradoxical though it might seem, the Turkish Parliament could well become the scene of the main struggle for Jewish rights granted by the laws of democratic Turkey, and consequently the venue for realizing Zionist endeavors in Palestine. Hence, any clear-thinking person who wanted to exert influence in this sphere had to acquire the linguistic, cultural, legal and political skills that would enable him to represent the interests of the Jewish people before the Turkish public and its national institutions. This implied learning Turkish and obtaining legal training at Ottoman universities, which was the path these future Zionist labor leaders chose.

When war broke out it was therefore quite natural for Ben-Gurion and Ben-Zvi to identify with Turkey. As a result they increasingly adopted pro-German positions. They accepted Turkey's alliance with Germany as a political fact that need not be questioned. They urged rapid "Ottomanization" of Russian Jews in Palestine, both to secure their right to remain in the country and to facilitate their recruitment into Turkish and German military forces.[6]

Even when their attempts to negotiate with the heads of the Turkish regime in Palestine were obstructed and they were exiled to Egypt, Ben-Gurion and Ben-Zvi remained true to their convictions. They interpreted their exile as the result of local obstinance and assumed that matters could be resolved by intercession in Constantinople, which could be most effectively accomplished by the German Zionist Federation in Berlin.

This approach explains why they were so critical of the efforts of Yosef

Trumpeldor and Ze'ev Jabotinsky who favored an alliance with the British against the Turks. They obviously rejected Pinhas Rutenberg's initiative to form volunteer Jewish brigades that would fight with the Allies against Turkey in return for a commitment to endorse Jewish sovereignty in Palestine. In April 1915, they refused to meet with Rutenberg in Italy to discuss his political program, preferring to go directly to the United States.[7]

Ben-Gurion and Ben-Zvi were already in the United States when Rutenberg reached New York on May 22, 1915.[8] His arrival precipitated harsh ideological and political confrontations within the Po'alei-Zion Party and related circles.

Essentially, Rutenberg's program was intended as a shortcut to secure the political status of the Jews in Palestine. Its point of departure was the assumption that as a result of the war the political status of Palestine itself would very likely change. To bring about such a development, Rutenberg said the Jews must participate in the fighting. They could then expect a form of Jewish sovereignty in Palestine in recognition of this participation. In practical terms, Rutenberg's program was based on the conviction that the Allied powers would win the war. As a result, Turkey would be forced to secede territory or would otherwise be divided up so that Palestine could become politically independent. The projected bond between an independent Palestine and the Jewish people had to be based on an agreement between the Allies and authorized Jewish representatives. For their part, the Jews would have to recruit units from among Jewish immigrants from Russia, in return for an explicit undertaking granting the Jewish people political rights in Palestine. The demand for political rights, although expressed as the desire for a Jewish National Home in Palestine, in fact meant striving for the establishment of an independent Jewish republic there.[9]

Rutenberg's Jewish nationalism and the changes in his ideological outlook were the consequence of his reaction to the outbreak of World War I. Being politically aware, he was obviously cognizant of the difficult position the war created for both Russian and Polish Jewry. Rutenberg aligned his goal with a broader effort on the part of both patriotic and liberal circles in Russia. These circles sought to reconcile the masses of Russian Jewish emigrés, particularly those in the United States, with Russian democracy. This move would guarantee their support for the Allied war effort. Support for the national aspirations of the Jews in Palestine was considered an effective instrument for achieving this end.

On the operative level the plan called for establishing committees to advance the Jewish cause in every Allied and neutral country. These committees were to include Jews, both Zionists and non-Zionists, as well as non-Jews. They were to be considered as representing Jewish interests, with authority to conduct diplomatic negotiations during the war, and after the end of hostilities, to secure the national rights of the Jews in Palestine.[10]

This program implied a drastic deviation from the declarations of political principles that characterized the Zionist movement's tactics during the years 1908-1914. Rutenberg's ideas were not received positively by all of the leadership of the American Po'alei-Zion, and particularly not by the non-American members who were in New York at the time.[11] Before Rutenberg's arrival, Nachman Syrkin, one of the party's leaders, had already published articles supporting the Allies. He became enthusiastic about the idea of an American Jewish Congress or a Committee for Jewish Affairs, and he was not deterred by the proposal to form Jewish military contingents.[12]

Ber Borochov, leader of the Russian Po'alei-Zion, had become familiar with Rutenberg's ideas while they were in Milan from August to October, 1914. He too became an enthusiastic advocate of the plan.[13] However, he carefully extricated the concept of the Jewish Congress from Rutenberg's package, and in the long run made this the decisive issue of the forthcoming political struggle. Borochov saw the Congress as an end in itself, a tool for the national organization of Jews in the Diaspora, and not only for the formation of Jewish legions as Rutenberg visualized. This heightened Borochov's concern about the organization's democratic image as well as the principle of mass participation. In other words, unlike Rutenberg who wanted to create an impressive national representation of influential people as quickly as possible without undue concern for how it was done, Borochov sought to combine this representative body with the momentous project of organizing the Jewish people around the world into a political force that would be as democratically and geographically representative as possible.

Rutenberg's ideas were wholeheartedly supported by some influential Po'alei-Zion members in the US, but other leading members were not enthusiastic.[14] In the initial stages, the opposing faction was decisive. This group included Shlomo Kaplansky, a founder of the World Confederation of Po'alei-Zion parties, who managed to talk privately with Rutenberg before he left for Europe.[15] The recently arrived Palestinians naturally took strong exception to Rutenberg, while Baruch Zuckerman and other founders of the American branch of the party rejected the program.

The opposing view is best illustrated in articles written by Ben-Gurion. The first of these, "Toward the Future: On the Question of Palestine," was published in the fifth issue of *Hatoren* (August 1915).[16] It was a programmatic article that clearly reflected the ideological controversy that had disrupted the party ever since Rutenberg made his appearance. The key to the article lies in Ben-Gurion's statement that "Palestine belongs to Turkey—this fact determines the political attitude and position of the Yishuv in Palestine. *The principle of the strengthening of Turkey and its indivisibility* has always been a central tenet of Jewish settlement activity" and therefore the Yishuv remained "as always, loyal and faithful to Turkey":

> At this difficult hour when Turkey is fighting a life and death struggle, Ottoman Jewry and Palestinian Jewry as part of it, fulfills its *citizens' duty to the homeland* [Turkey]....It is *the first* land to have recognized the principle of free national self-determination, the first that has given all nations [including Jews] cultural-national autonomy....The coming peace conference must recognize the right of the Hebrew nation to establish its own homeland in Palestine. This crucial question is central to our lives....Around this objective all Jewish forces desiring to renew life in our national homeland must unite.[17]

Opposing Rutenberg's desire to take shortcuts to secure political rights for Jews in Palestine, Ben-Gurion wrote:

What we want in Palestine cannot be established in one moment, even if it is as great, decisive and opportune a moment as the present....Zionism is a *lengthy process* which by its very nature will be realized only over an extended period of time. The striving to root the Jewish people in its homeland, to return the land to the nation—which is the spirit, the inner significance and core of Zionist aspirations—may assume any of several forms as it is being realized: autonomy, federation or even sovereignty. But the external form cannot change the content.

Zionism will not be realized through political rights and *diplomatic guarantees* bestowed by others, but by continuous settlement activity, by entrenchment in the soil, by labor and commerce, by enhancing our spiritual and material assets, by increasing the population until [the Jews] have become a decisive majority in Palestine.

Ben-Gurion argued that:

There is no need to "reexamine our tactics" at this crucial time for the whole world, or to propose devious ways of achieving Zionism's objectives by "revolutionary" means.[18]

This was clearly hostile to Rutenberg's entire program. Despite his earlier stand, Ben-Gurion was unwilling to make the continuation of Zionist work in Palestine completely dependent on an internal Ottoman Turkish-Jewish consensus. He hoped that events would force Turkey to undertake a formal obligation with respect to the Jews of Palestine or, alternatively, would take the matter out of Turkey's hands altogether. Such a possibility was implicit in an article Ben-Gurion wrote in September 1915.[19] The very title—"Who Will Give Us the Country?"—centers around this point. The article is filled with reservations concerning any sort of intervention of a diplomatic or economic nature:

The land will not be given to us for money, through rights or by *a peace conference*. The Jewish worker who will come to the country and make himself at home there, who will settle in it and bring it new life, is the one who will give us the country. The Land of Israel will be ours if we are its workers. The historic task of the *pioneers* who are building and redeeming the Jewish homeland is actually to conquer it through their labor.[20]

It is clear that while Ben-Gurion did not completely reject the possible benefits of diplomatic endeavors at a future peace conference, he cautioned against focusing the political activity of world Jewry on such a conference. He wrote:

A [national] home will not be given as a gift and will not be taken away ...it will not be attained by political documents, by money or by force. A home is built, it is created. It is the sum total of the *historic creativity* and collective action of the nation, the cumulative product of the nation's moral, spiritual and material endeavors *throughout the centuries*.[21]

Ben-Gurion wanted to encourage the members of the Hehalutz movement in America, to which purpose he and Ben-Zvi directed all their activities and propagandizing. Because of the political configuration and internal developments in the party, the plan for creating a semi-military organization of *halutzim* who would go to Palestine as soon as it was legally possible became an alternative to Rutenberg's plan.

Ben-Gurion's article "Who Will Give Us the Country" appeared prior to the Cleveland Convention of Po'alei-Zion in September 1915. At the Convention itself, a crucial confrontation took place between Ben-Gurion, supported by the rest of the Palestinians, and his opponents.[22] Ben-Gurion now defined his position as a "historical conception" as opposed to the "political conception" held by the other side.

Immediately after the Convention, Ben-Gurion wrote an article entitled "The Historic Conception," in which he seemed bent on interpreting the Convention's resolutions in a way that would conform with his own views.[23] The resolutions, however, had been hammered out in a committee that included representatives of both points of view and were therefore the result of ideological compromise.

Commenting on the ideological confrontation between the "historical" and the "political" conceptions of the Convention, Ben-Gurion wrote:

> Realization of our hopes for Palestine...is not a matter of the accessibility of an opportune political moment....The possibility is historic; it is associated with the historic process by which the Jewish people is building the country. Po'alei-Zion does not ask to be given Palestine at a peace conference or expect to receive it...as recompense for a grave injustice the world has inflicted...upon our nation. The nation itself wants to build its own home. A country of your own has to be...won over by labor, capital, culture, civilization....It is a historic creation of the nation, a collective endeavor of generations.[24]

With the opposing "historical" and "political" positions published in advance, the notion of a future international Jewish Congress was debated at the Convention at some length.[25] Ben-Gurion and all those who identified with his "historical conception" had no great expectations from the Jewish Congress and naturally withheld all support for Rutenberg. This meant total rejection of the idea of Jewish brigades and of active participation in the war alongside the Allies. Hence those promulgating Ben-Gurion's view were prepared to accept minor political achievement, or none at all, since they did not consider it vital for furthering a process that was in essence historical.

At the Convention, the lines were drawn concerning both the Congress and the results of World War I. On one hand, the "political conception" considered the struggle for a Congress to be important in itself, as well as an instrument for strengthening world Jewry's international political position after the war. On the other hand, Syrkin admitted that it was necessary for Jews to engage in settlement activity in Palestine, although he could not agree with concepts such as the "historical process," and was quick to attack any arguments that bore traces of Borochov's ideas. Nevertheless, he was far from ignoring the importance of practical Zionism.

As opposed to Syrkin, Borochov was an outright protagonist of the historical conception. So too was Reuven Kendzhersky. Those who advocated the political approach, however, attributed considerable importance to arriving at a definition of the postwar political status of Palestine. They did not deny or obscure the legal difficulties the Turkish rulers placed before Jewish immigration to and settlement in Palestine, even after the Young Turks' revolt. Nor did they ignore the conflict of interests with the ruling power over the status of the Jews in Palestine during the war. They saw the war as a great opportunity for creating a situation in which no foreign power could hamper Jewish settlement in Palestine. They assumed that the war and the creation of Jewish brigades might give world Jewry a political foothold without which the historical process would come to a halt. The very presentation of the debate between "historical" and "political" conceptions seemed to them something of an anachronism, not reflecting fundamentally different approaches. It was intended as a tactic designed to avoid becoming too closely linked with the Allied cause, even though the future Jewish Congress would be used as a political tool for that very purpose.

The question of convening a Congress must be seen in relation to Ben-Gurion's political and ideological objectives. The idea of an international Jewish Congress was mooted in the United States almost immediately after the outbreak of hostilities, with the first news of the suffering the war brought to Europe's Jews.[26] From the outset, the Congress was intended to establish an authoritative Jewish representative body to assist Jews in distress and protect them against arbitrary action by governmental elements. Another objective was to crystallize a program for the postwar peace conference, including demands to change the legal status of the Jews in Eastern Europe. When Rutenberg appeared at the Po'alei-Zion Convention in Cleveland, he was privately led in this direction by those who opposed the program he brought with him. Against his will, he had to find a way of going along with the Congress supporters.

The Congress proposal naturally elicited a hesitant response. With respect to deterrent action directed against any force that threatened the personal or civil status of Jews, such a Congress would probably make Russia the target of its criticism. Traditional Russian denial of Jewish rights and Russian attacks on Jews became more apparent as the fighting intensified and the Russian army suffered greater losses.

Both Rutenberg and Jabotinsky, leaders of the "political" camp, were aware of the danger of singling out Russian oppression and expressed their disapproval of the platform. They maintained that a change in the status of the Jews in every country would come about only as a result of internal political changes, not through external intervention. A split Congress based on this platform would in fact work against Allied interests in America and encourage pro-German sympathy.

The same held true for any positive program, even if it were to be restricted to struggling for equal civil rights, ethnic-group status or national rights. Obviously this would have been directed against Russia and Rumania which were among the few countries that deprived the Jews of all civil rights, to say nothing of ethnic or national rights. It is therefore not surprising that this constellation of ideas gave rise to much deliberation in concerned Jewish circles. They sharply debated whether there was a necessity for a Congress movement which in effect would be critical of the Allies and supportive of Germany through propaganda disseminated among American Jewish groups.[27]

Those who harbored such doubts — including members of the America Jewish Committee (A.J.C.) and others — advocated a modest preliminary conference that would maintain a low profile and defer forceful action and lobbying until after the war. At that point, they did not want to rally the Jewish public around a Congress slogan which would only unify diverse Jewish groups on the basis of powerful propaganda that would, in turn, be detrimental to the Allies and expose the fact that the Jews were not neutral.

Rutenberg was naturally a partner to these deliberations. He wanted to focus his efforts on establishing a small representative Jewish body rather than on a concerted appeal for a large, vigorous mass movement. But his objection to such a movement was in conflict with the program of Po'alei-Zion, which had previously rallied to his assistance. Po'alei-Zion, together with other Zionist groups, condemned the hesitant stand of the A.J.C. as representing an anti-national, assimilationist position. Unlike the A.J.C., the Zionists wanted to foster the organization of Jews nationally in the framework of the Congress movement. Through it they could also press for improving the situation of Jews in countries where they were discriminated against, while simultaneously insuring that the peace conference would guarantee Jewish national rights after the war.

In principle, the Zionists' expectations of the Congress movement should have been satisfied first and foremost by a series of demands bound up with the rights of Jews in Palestine. Jewish rights, of course, were understood generally to refer to establishing the status of the Jewish people in terms of whatever political solution was found for Palestine. This notion was interwoven with the question of Palestine's political future in regard to remaining a part of the Ottoman Empire. With the outbreak of war, this issue was a subject of frequent debate at the highest levels of the Zionist movement.

Shortly after the start of the hostilities, a Provisional Zionist Executive was established in the United States. Its members, some of whom were from Europe, tended to follow the line taken by the German Zionist Federation which for the first three years of the war maintained its leading position and continued to formulate worldwide Zionist policy. Although an office existed in Copenhagen that ostensibly symbolized the movement's intention to remain neutral, the orientation of the Zionist institutions was essentially pro-German. Consequently, policy avoided anything that implied early submission of political demands relating to Palestine. By the nature of things these would have had an anti-Turkish bias as they would have pressed for a change in the Palestinian Zionist movement's formal status. The failure of such a move would have been damaging to Germany. Protagonists of this trend preferred quiet intervention that would lead to discussions with Germany and, under its auspices, with Turkey as the ruler of Palestine.[28]

The item on the Congress agenda designed to counter attacks on Jews in Europe in addition to demanding national rights for all Jews was received differently. Its purpose was considered desirable among pro-Congress forces. But stopping at this point would have created confusion within the World Zionist Organization, which could not advocate a struggle for civil and national rights for the Jews in the Diaspora while refraining from making similar demands vis-à-vis the Yishuv. Otherwise it would have been like the Bund and the *Jewish Daily Forward*, whose interests such a program served perfectly. It required agile maneuvering for the Zionist movement to extricate itself from this dilemma.[29]

The basic differences within the Zionist camp were between those who objected to immediate action and those who were enthusiastic about the Congress program. Its supporters recognized the possibility it offered for involving broad segments of the Jewish public, whether in the struggle for minority Jewish rights wherever they might be attained, or in the struggle for a Jewish homeland in Palestine. General emphasis was shifted to the educational, propaganda and organizational value of American Jewry's identification with the distress of European Jewry and with the demand for a national solution—either through acquiring national rights for Jews everywhere or by establishing a Jewish National Home in Palestine. The effect of this tactic was conspicuously enhanced as the A.J.C. and the *Jewish Daily Forward* became increasingly hostile to the Congress program. Indeed, the influence of the Zionist movement in the United States had never before been so widespread.[30]

However, as the pressure for a Jewish mass movement increased, and opposition circles appeared ready to submit to it, the Zionists began to retreat. They were ready to discuss a compromise with their opponents—one that could have been achieved long before—which, in actual fact, put a stop to any further progress.

Two issues, in both of which the Jewish Congress Organizational Committee played a decisive role, in the name of the Zionist Organization, illustrate this point. The first issue was the Assembly, initiated by the Committee, that was held in Philadelphia on March 26, 1916. The decisions taken there had far-reaching implications: no further negotiations would be conducted with opponents of the Congress movement; if such opponents changed their minds, they could join only on the basis of the platform that was formulated by the Assembly, according to which their number could not exceed twenty percent of the total constituency (70 delegates); the Congress must be convened between September and December 1916. Postponement for special reasons could be decided upon only by a three-quarters majority of the members of the Executive Committee.[31]

These unequivocal decisions were approved, even though on the eve of the Philadelphia Assembly the A.J.C. put out feelers with respect to negotiations, and indicated that it was prepared to accept the national program of the Jewish Congress Organizational Committee. It also agreed to a convention of democratically chosen delegates "as quickly as possible." Furthermore, it proposed that the convention appoint the Executive which would be authorized to embark immediately on "political and organizational action here in America and in Europe as well." This Executive would be responsible to the second convention of democratically chosen delegates, which would be held at the end of the war. But when Judah Magnes, a leading Reform rabbi who later immigrated to Palestine, presented the proposal, he added an ultimatum: the name "Congress" was not to be used.[32]

Negotiations broke down over this point. With the approval of the Zionists, another unexpected resolution was passed in Philadelphia: only American citizens were permitted to participate in elections to the Congress or represent political bodies. This meant curbing the participation of an entire category of politically active people who had arrived in America and had united around the Congress movement. With good reason, Rutenberg fumed that "in Jewish life here in America we are all equally important."[33] But his protest was to no avail, and Po'alei-Zion also accepted this limitation.

Despite their mandate to act, the Zionist movement and the Congress Committee that it controlled did nothing to bring the Congress into being. Instead, the whole matter remained alive but in the background.

The second decisive issue was the appearance of a delegation of the Jewish Congress Organizational Committee, headed by Judge Louis Brandeis, at the conference of the A.J.C. and the National Workers' Committee held at New York's Hotel Astor on July 16, 1916. In private discussions, Brandeis, who had just been confirmed as a justice of the US Supreme Court, and led the Zionist delegation to the conference, suggested that they join the Executive Committee that had been chosen in Philadelphia. Magnes approved, but demanded parity. Brandeis tried to object, citing the irrevocable Philadelphia decision providing a ceiling of twenty percent of the delegates for new participants. Magnes angrily rejected this explanation.[34]

After lengthy arguments, a preliminary agreement to negotiate was reached. Contact was initiated between the two groups—the Philadelphia Committee and the Astor Committee (of non-Zionists)—almost immediately after the Hotel Astor Conference closed. By August 16 both sides could produce an agreement that each executive soon approved.[35]

At the time, people were surprised to find the agreement more in keeping with the spirit of Astor than with the nationalist spirit of Philadelphia. It refrained from giving the Congress discussions a permanent character, defining its purpose as a council "for the sole objective" of securing the full rights of Jews in all countries. "Full rights" was interpreted by those who formulated the document as referring to civil, political and religious rights. "Group rights" for Jews were to be guaranteed in those countries that normally granted them to other ethnic groups. In addition, it was stated that the Congress would strive to "guarantee and preserve the rights of the Jews in Palestine."

A joint executive was eventually formed. In general, it appears as if the Zionists, outside of gaining a peaceful "reconciliation" that made it possible to talk with the Congress movement and a vague commitment to include a point about Palestine, yielded on all operative issues, and in effect neglected the task of convening the Congress.

The Zionists' behavior was motivated by the same hidden agenda that guided the action of the Provisional Executive Committee of the World Zionist Organization (guidelines that were formulated by Shmarya Levin, the Russian labor Zionist leader),[36] when its members sought to impede the practical preparations to convene the Congress. They nevertheless took advantage of the struggle for the Congress to strengthen the American Jewish public's national consciousness and organize it into a bloc within the Zionist movement. Obviously, tension occasionally resulted from the conflicting needs of the two objectives, and skillful handling was essential in order to deal simultaneously with both. A similar purpose was served by the ultimatum formulated at the Philadelphia Assembly in March 1916, and above all, by the recommendation to neutralize pro-Congress forces among recent arrivals in the United States, the "greenhorns" who were the guiding spirits and intellectual elite of the Congress movement. The "reconciliation" achieved in August 1916 also placed additional obstacles in the way of the Congress and made its convening uncertain. Moreover, even acceptance of a meaningless statement about Palestine did not conflict with the World Zionist Organization's operative perspectives, because under all circumstances the Zionist leadership in Copenhagen, to say nothing of that in Berlin, advocated political immobility.

These issues have been discussed in some detail as essential background for an understanding of the American Po'alei-Zion and the specific position taken by Ben-Gurion who was serving as secretary of the National Socialist Workers' Committee[37] in the months following the Philadelphia Assembly.

As for the American Po'alei-Zion's reactions to these developments, the party was not prepared to go all the way with Rutenberg, although his views were quite favorably received. But the prevailing opinion was that when the Jewish Congress really gained momentum, it would be divorced from the special tasks Rutenberg wanted it to fulfill. Nevertheless, Po'alei-Zion's support of the call for a Jewish Congress was more than mere lip-service. Its target was not only the educational and instrumental aspect implicit in unifying the American Jewish public under Jewish national leadership. Po'alei-Zion also considered the American Jewish Congress and the World Jewish Congress as legitimate and exclusive instruments for furthering recognition of Jewish national rights in those countries where the struggle for minority rights was necessary and feasible. The party was also satisfied that the Congress would press for recognition of Jewish demands in Palestine by the international authority of the peace conference, and advocated public discussion of these problems, irrespective of the war. This approach also meant that it was not essential to convene the Congress at once, as decision-making on crucial issues had to wait until after the war was over.[38]

It is true that Po'alei-Zion reacted negatively to the understanding, known as the "reconciliation," reached between the Jewish Congress Organization Committee and the representatives of the Astor Conference, and it initiated a protest action.[39] But it appears that Ben-Gurion did not agree with this and even found it necessary to resign from his position as secretary of the National Socialist Workers' Committee. His approach was reflected at the 10th Party Convention held in Boston in October 1916. He delivered a programmatic speech about the passage on Palestine included in the "reconciliation" agreement. He wanted to focus his audience's attention on two points, the first involving tactical orientation in light of the Congress discussions.[40]

> Our tactic concerning the issue of Palestine must not draw us into advocating one of the two accepted political orientations: pro-German or pro-Ally. We must be wary of irresponsible [military] adventures with legions, as certain individuals have suggested....Would that the Jewish people were in a situation in which they could defend their national rights with arms, but that is not the case. The purpose of our struggle is not to liberate our land but first to build it. And therefore it is incumbent on the Jews to remain neutral...to conduct an independent Jewish policy with respect to Palestine and not a German or an English policy.

When presenting his second point, Ben-Gurion returned to his main tenet, the "historical conception":

> We do not demand a Jewish state, for we do not wish to rule over Arabs. We do not even demand a Jewish [national] home, for a home is not given, nor can it be created for us. The Jewish people itself must build its home. We therefore demand the right to freely work the land in Palestine, the right to make it blossom, the right to settle in the country, and this no one can refuse us.

His words, then, stressed two salient points: the rejection of an orientation favoring one of the belligerents and the idea of legions, and making no claims on Palestine that could be interpreted as explicitly political—such as the demand for a state or a National Home.

Close scrutiny of these two points reveals that they contain an implicit refutation of the need to convene the Congress quickly and to establish it as a permanent institution. As a natural outgrowth of this, there was a tacit agreement with the concessions made by the Philadelphia Committee to the Astor Committee with respect to the Palestine question. It is interesting to note that in the issues discussed here, the Po'alei-Zion Party on the whole was less yielding than Ben-Gurion.[41]

Thus, Ben-Gurion's historical conception, aside from its political and theoretical aspect, actually brought him closer to those Zionist circles in the United States which were responsive to considerations prevalent in Copenhagen and Berlin. In this regard his position was similar to that of Kaplansky[42] and Ben-Zvi.[43]

In 1917 Ben-Gurion, Ben-Zvi and other prominent leaders of the Yishuv were forced to change their views as the British conquest of Palestine radically altered the context of Zionist policy.

Notes

* Few studies of Ben-Gurion have discussed the question I deal with here. In *David's Jealousy*, Shabtai Teveth focused at length on the attitudes of both David Ben-Gurion and Izhak Ben-Zvi toward Palestine, Jewry and Zionism, during World War I, but failed to avail himself of literary or other sources that could have afforded more concrete elucidation. In his two-volume biography, Michael Bar-Zohar skims over the period, making do with lengthy quotations of Ben-Gurion's own words, but sidesteps the essential issues. In his own memoirs, Ben-Gurion himself paid little attention to the subject, simply reprinting in its original form the article "Toward the Future," which he had published in *Hatoren* in August 1915. He thus refrained from transmitting a comprehensive picture of the direction his thinking took during the war years. See Teveth's *David's Jealousy* (Hebrew), Tel Aviv, 1978; also his English version covering the years 1886-1948, *Ben-Gurion: the Burning Ground, 1886-1948*, Boston, 1986. Bar-Zohar's *Ben-Gurion* (Hebrew), Tel Aviv, 1975, and Ben-Gurion's *Memoirs* (Hebrew), vol. 1, Tel Aviv, 1971.

1 See Matityahu Mintz, "Borochov and the Lessons of the 1905 Revolution in Russia" (Hebrew), in *Proceedings of the Fifth World Congress of Jewish Studies*, II, Jerusalem, 1972, pp. 239-255.

2 Izhak Ben-Zvi, "Our National Demands in Turkey" (Hebrew), *He'ahdut* II, no. 7, November 11, 1910, pp. 1-8; Ben-Gurion, "In Clarification of Our Political Situation," *ibid.* I, no. 3, September 1910, pp. 87-93; "Self-rule in the Vilayet," ibid. V, no. 12, January 4, 1914, pp. 1-4; no. 13, January 9, 1914, pp. 8-12; no. 14, January 16, 1914, pp. 9-11; nos. 17-18, February 13, 1914, pp. 10-15; no. 19, February 20, 1914, pp. 1-4; no. 20, February 27, 1914, pp. 6-9; no. 21, March 12, 1914, pp. 1-5; nos. 22-23, March 22, 1914, pp. 16-20.

3 David Ben-Gurion, "A National Speaker or a Religious Functionary" (Hebrew), *He'ahdut* I, no. 1, July-August 1910, pp. 25-28; "In Clarification of Our Political Situation" (Hebrew), *ibid.*, no. 3, September 1910, pp. 87-93; "Self-rule in the Vilayet" (Hebrew), *ibid.* V, nos. 17-18, February 13, 1914, pp. 10-15.

4 *Hatoren*, no. 14, June 2, 1916, p. 8. Appeared in Yiddish in collection *In the Struggle for Rights*, edited by Ber Borochov, New York, 1916.

5 Shochat studied law with Ben-Gurion in Turkey, was a founder of Hashomer and cofounder of the World Confederation of Po'alei-Zion parties.

6 Teveth, *David's Jealousy*, pp. 256ff.

7 Ibid., pp. 296ff.

8 About Rutenberg's objective, see Matityahu Mintz, "Pinchas Rutenberg and the Establishment of the Jewish Legion in 1914." *Studies in Zionism* 6, no. 1, 1985, pp. 15-26; Ze'ev Jabotinsky, *Autobiography* (Hebrew), vol. I, Jerusalem, 1947, pp. 108ff. Concerning the refusal of Ben-Zvi and Ben-Gurion to meet with Rutenberg, see David Goldstein's letter to Izhak Ben-Zvi, Central Zionist Archives, Jerusalem (hereafter C.Z.A.), A116/40/2.

9 See Montz, "Pinchas Rutenberg and the Establishment of the Jewish Legion," *ibid.*

10 Ber Borochov, "The Local and Foreign Jews in Italy" (Yiddish), *Warheit*, May 22, 1915 and also "The Chronology of the Jewish Congress" (Yiddish), *Der Yiddisher Kemfer*, December 30, 1916. Rutenberg himself in his article "A Response to Zion" (Yiddish), *Der Yiddisher Kongres,* September 4, 1915. Cf. also the long article by Alexander Valentinovich Amphiteatrov in *Ruskoye Slovo*, no. 9, March 22, 1915.

11 Rutenberg tried to bring his message to all circles. For our purposes here we deal only with the Po'alei-Zion sector.

12 Teveth, *David's Jealousy*, p. 374.

13 See Matityahu Mintz, "Ber Borochov at the Beginning of World War I" (Hebrew), *Shorashim*, 3, (1982), pp. 191-212.

14 Letters of Zvi Ehrenreich to S. Bonchek dated June 11, 1915, and June 17, 1915, Labor Movement Archives, Lavon Institute; Archives, of Po'alei-Zion in America, vol. 3, 24 (73), files 117, 118.

15 Kaplansky intended to sail for Europe on May 21, 1915, but his ship collided with another vessel while still in port and his departure was delayed until May 24. Rutenberg arrived in the United Sates on May 22, 1915. See Kaplansky's letter to Ehrenreich, ibid., file 117.

16 *Hatoren*, August 1915, p. 171. Author's italics.

17 Ibid., p. 168.

18 Ibid., p. 169.

19 David Ben-Gurion, "Who Will Give Us the Country?" (Yiddish), *Die Kemfer Stimme*, no. 27, September 1915. The issue came out in preparation for the party's Cleveland Convention (the ninth). Author's italics.

20 Ibid.

21 Ibid.

22 The reference is to Nachman Syrkin, Yitzchack Zar, Reuven Kendzhersky, even Borochov, with Rutenberg, who was not a member of the party, supporting them. It was at this Convention that Ben-Gurion began his political career, which was to result in his assuming a major role in the labor Zionist movement.

23 David Ben-Gurion, "A Historical Conception Concerning the Resolution about 'Eretz-Israel in the Pending Moment' Accepted by the Po'alei-Zion Convention" (Yiddish), *Der Yiddisher Kongres*, October 8, 1915.

24 Ibid.

25 In the third point of the Cleveland Convention resolutions.

26 Jonathan Frankel, "The Jewish Socialists and the American Jewish Congress Movement," in *Yivo Annual of Jewish Social Science*, vol. 16, New York, 1976, pp. 202-341.

27 This consideration led German sympathizers to support the Congress. Letter from Louis Marshall to Judah Magnes, May 24, 1915, Louis Marshall Papers, American Jewish Archives, Cincinnati.

28 See study by Isaiah Friedman, *Germany, Turkey and Zionism 1897-1918*, Oxford, 1977, pp. 228-267.

29 For a full description of the negotiations, manipulations, tactics and tacit agreements reached by the various groups at the convention, see Frankel, n. 26 supra.

30 See Shmarya Levin's letters of July 12 and 15, 1915 to Dr. Hantke in Berlin. Shmarya Levin, *Letters* (Hebrew), Tel Aviv, 1966, pp. 336ff.

31 Cf., "Report from the Philadelphia Conference" (Yiddish), *Warheit*, March 29, 1916, and also his article "What Was Decided in Philadelphia" (Yiddish), ibid., April 1, 1916.

32 Condensed from the article by Pinchas Rutenberg, "The Rebellion Against the Peace Agreement" (Yiddish), *Warheit*, September 5, 1916. Louis Marshall was behind the Magnes proposals. On this subject, see also Frankel, n. 26 supra, p. 251. Borochov was enthusiastic about the decisions that were taken. Rutenberg and David Pinski were not. See Pinchas Rutenberg, "On Guard at the Congress" (Yiddish), *Warheit*, April 6, 1916, and David Pinski, "I Was Not Satisfied" (Yiddish), ibid., April 8, 1916.

33 Rutenberg, ibid. It is worth noting the hint included in the letter of Shmarya Levin, member of the Provisional Zionist Executive Committee, written on October 27, 1915 to Victor Jacobson and his colleagues in Berlin, to the effect that the American comrades would prevent an inappropriate delegation. C.Z.A., Z3/396.

34 Frankel, "The American Jewish Congress Movement," p. 277.

35 Ibid., p. 280.

36 See Shmarya Levin's letter of July 15, 1915 to Hantke, in *Letters* (cf. note 30 above), as well as his letter to Victor Jacobson (cf. note 33 above).

37 Teveth, *David's Jealousy*, p. 354. On the entire subject, see Baruch Zuckerman, "The New Agreement in the Congress Movement" (Yiddish), *Der Yiddisher Kemfer*, October 11, 1916.

38 Ben-Gurion to Ehrenreich, January 17, 1916, Archives of Po'alei-Zion in America, file 142.

39 Frankel, "The American Jewish Congress Movement," p. 281. Statement in *Der Yiddisher Kemfer*, August 18, 1916, and also Borochov's article "We Will not Allow" (Yiddish), *Warheit*, August 21, 1916.

40 "Report on Convention" (Yiddish), *Der Yiddisher Kemfer*, August 18, 1916.

41 Its criticism of the understanding in the protest declaration appeared in *Der Yiddisher Kemfer*, August 18, 1916.

42 See his article "Wartime Zionism" (Yiddish), *Der Yiddisher Kemfer*, December 22, 1916; December 29, 1916; January 5, 1917.

43 Izhak Ben-Zvi, "After the War" (Hebrew), *Hatoren*, no 2, March 10, 1916; no. 3, March 17, 1916; and no. 4, March 24, 1916. Also appeared in Yiddish as "Our Prospects in Palestine" (Yiddish), *Der Yiddisher Kemfer*, May 1916 issue.

IDEOLOGY, NAIVETE OR PRAGMATISM ?

SHABTAI TEVETH

I

The Arab policy of Ahdut Ha'avoda, in which Ben-Gurion played a central role, is sometimes described as naive.[1] It is tacitly agreed that in the 1920s this naiveté expressed itself in Ben-Gurion's belief that the Arab problem would be solved by the successful outcome of the class struggle. Ben-Gurion based his class approach to the Arab question on the assumption that the Bolshevik Revolution would spread rapidly throughout the world. With the liberation of the Arab fellah and worker from subservience to the effendis and religious leaders, working-class brotherhood would elicit cooperation of the Jewish and Arab peoples.

Ben-Gurion himself gave credence to the claim of ingenuousness. He wrote:

> The general assumption then prevailing in the Zionist movement was that our settlement enterprise would prove a benefit to the Arab community, and the same view was current among the Jewish labor movement in Palestine. It was therefore believed that the Arabs would welcome us with open arms....[2]

On the basis of this and other statements he wrote and said, scholars have constructed seemingly incontestable proof of the naiveté of his approach.

After all, Arab stevedores carried Ben-Gurion in their arms — as they did other immigrants — and set him down bodily on the soil of Palestine. How could it even occur to him that those same Arabs objected to Jews and Zionism? But even before they carried him ashore at Jaffa on September 7, 1906, Ben-Gurion considered the Arabs as peaceful, understanding copartners. The first time he met them was on board ship and he described them to his father as having "made a very good impression on us. Almost all of them are warmhearted. They are easy to befriend and associate with. One may say that they are big children."[3]

The foundations Ben-Gurion created for a joint trades union organization also testify to his naiveté, stemming from a conviction that under socialism the two nations — Jews and Arabs — could live side by side in harmony. This ingenuousness was demonstrated even more forcefully because of the timing of his initiative. Ben-Gurion chose to make his views public while the labor movement was still mourning the deaths of Joseph Trumpeldor and his comrades in 1920, and only a few days after the riots of 1921, in which Y.H. Brenner fell. With unseemly, apparently insensate haste, Ben-Gurion issued a six-point program which he called "Relations with Our Neighbors." It is not hard to imagine the chagrin felt by the grieving Ahdut Ha'avoda membership at the sight of the opening lines of the message he published in *Kuntress*:

> Establishing comradely relations between the Hebrew laborers and the masses of
> Arab workers, on the basis of common social, political and economic action, is a
> prerequisite for our redemption as a free working nation and for the liberation of the
> Arab laborers from the exploitation, oppression and enslavement of the ruling
> property-owners.
> Laying the foundation for such joint action devolves on the informed, cultured
> Hebrew worker, whose historic task in the building of a free labor society in
> Palestine is to stand at the forefront of the movement for rebirth and liberation of the
> peoples of the Near East.[4]

In other words, Zionist-Jewish workers, together with Arab workers, would create a
movement of rebirth and liberation for the peoples of the Near East. Ben-Gurion
even thought of founding joint Histadrut and Arab labor organizations. He spoke of
the Hebrew labor movement's historic mission to educate the Arabs to
socialist — working-class consciousness while they labored side by side with Jews on
public works that would be contracted out to the Histadrut. He was prepared to take
the burden of this educational task upon himself. He suggested that representatives
of the Histadrut and of the Arab workers form a joint "working executive" that
would establish a sick fund affiliated with the Histadrut sick fund (Kupat-Holim)
and also workers' kitchens to be associated with the Histadrut's cooperative
restaurants. The same held true for cultural activities: "During the Arab workers'
free time, pleasant simple lectures will be arranged to discuss the labor movement,
life in the *kvutza*, Arab and general history, health care, etc." In his opinion "The
major target of working together must be to educate the Arab worker to an orderly
and cooperative life of labor and accustom him to [class] discipline and mutual
responsibility."[5] The Histadrut would also manage to organize the Arab workers
into their own Histadrut-affiliated trade unions.[6]

Ben-Gurion saw socialism as a means of achieving conciliation with the Arabs
both in and out of Palestine. The socialist awakening would open the Arabs' eyes to
the justice implicit in the very conception of Zionism — the right of the Jews to return
to their country — as well as to the dual blessing inherent in socialist Zionism.

Those who maintained that Ben-Gurion was naive cited as a consummate example
his insistence that the Histadrut publish an Arab newspaper. Through this
publication he hoped to imbue the Arab worker with class consciousness and a
recognition of the importance of organizing his own trade unions' federation. The
initial attempt to publish such a paper was made with the railroad workers. Their
trade union was the only one at the time that included both Jews and Arabs, and was
the basis of Ben-Gurion's plans to create a joint organization. Preparations for the
publication, to be edited by Izhak Ben-Zvi, began early in 1925, and in April it
started to appear once every two weeks, under the name *Ittihad al-Amal*. The issues
contained installments of Ferdinand Lassalle's *Program for Workers,* the play "The
Weavers" by Gerhart Hauptmann, and stories by Maxim Gorky, Oscar Wilde and
Abraham Reisin; thus it included translations from German, Russian, English and
Yiddish. The appearance of the biweekly was followed in July 1925 by the
foundation of the "General Workers" Club in Haifa; similar clubs were later formed
in other cities as well.[7]

The riots of 1929 dealt this effort a deathblow. Following the disturbances, Ben-Gurion considered these educational and indoctrinating activities all the more essential. He gave them even more time and energy, and tried to expand them to reach the fellaheen who represented the largest segment of the Arab community in Palestine. In September 1929 he began to plan comprehensive, diversified instructional activities designed to clarify the just and advantageous nature of socialist-Zionism for both fellaheen and workers. The Arab biweekly would be the medium for disseminating Zionist truths, as would the joint clubhouses where Jews and Arabs would meet and become acquainted with one another. There would be further opportunities for interaction at the evening courses in Arabic and Hebrew, at vocational courses, lectures, and sessions on health care, mutual aid institutions, sick funds and loan funds.

Ben-Gurion's naiveté again manifested itself in a discussion about the journal that was held at a session of the Histadrut Executive. When he explained his vision of a popular paper for the Arab worker and fellah, the "Arabists"—Jews who maintained close contact with Arabs—had no difficulty in making him look ridiculous. They pointed out the simple fact that Arab workers and peasants are, for the most part, illiterate, and therefore nothing at all would be gained by Ben-Gurion's publishing a paper for them, even if it were of a popular nature.

When Michael Assaf asked what language would be used in the journal—literary, intermediate or spoken Arabic, Ben-Gurion answered that he would prefer spoken Arabic. To him the fact that no periodical appeared in spoken Arabic was further proof of how oblivious the effendis and the Arab intelligentsia were of the needs of the Arab working class; labor Zionism was thus offered an opportunity to fill this resultant vacuum. But the question was again raised of how people who were illiterate would be able to read the paper, no matter in what language it appeared.

Ben-Gurion had a ready answer: the Arab village schoolteacher would gather the fellaheen around him and read them the message of the Histadrut. The "Arabists" were not convinced. David Avissar, for example, commented that it was the Arab teacher who incited to murder and riots in Hebron and Safed, and on occasion even took an active part in the depredation. But Ben-Gurion was adamant, insisting that it was within the power of the labor movement to convince the Arab worker and fellah not only that labor Zionism was advantageous for them, but that if there were 300,000 Jewish workers in the country—and eventually three million—"and we will become a great force, then we will be able to help the Arab workers; we will raise the Arab masses from the depths of humiliation and we will be a tremendous factor in the development of the neighboring countries....This is Zionism." This was the faith that supported Ben-Gurion when he assigned labor Zionism the task of participating in the awakening and revitalization of the East.[8]

This naiveté was closely related to, perhaps even generated by, the denial of a conflict of interests between Zionism and the Palestinian Arabs, a denial prevalent among Zionist and labor Zionist leaders. They also totally ignored the existence of a Palestinian people and an Arab national movement. An outstanding expression of this was manifested in Ben-Gurion's claim that the Arabs of Palestine were but a small part of the Arab nation, lacking a national movement of their own. This was also a basic tenet of Ahdut Ha'avoda.

As early as 1915, when Ben-Gurion was in exile in the United States, he denied the inevitability of a conflict of interests, claiming that it did not exist. "Our objective does not stand in conflict with Palestine's Arab community," he maintained in his well-known article "Toward the Future." He declared that the Jews were returning to Palestine "not for the sake of domination or exploitation...it is not our intention to encroach upon the Arabs, dispossess them and take their place. There is enough room in the country for both of us." Since there had been four million inhabitants in the country at the end of the Second Temple period, there was no doubt in his mind that it could again support three to four million. As proof of his hypothesis that the population could be increased sixfold, he roughly divided the country in two: the desert lands and the inhabited, cultivated lands. The Jews would settle in the desert, which covers 80-90 percent of the land, and make it green, "and the desolate land would become like the Garden of Eden." Until the desert bloomed, the Jews would have to make use of other parts, the cultivated ones, but even there the Arabs would not be hurt, on the contrary they would stand to gain. For the inhabited parts too could support a larger population: "Nor is the cultivated area as productive as it might be because the Arabs are not trained for modern skills...their primitive methods are obsolete, they deplete the land and impoverish the soil so that it yields poor returns." The Jews, on the other hand, as their agricultural settlements had already proven, would introduce advanced machinery, modern methods of farming and irrigation; they would construct drainage and transport systems. In brief, the Jews would make every plot of arable land produce twice and three times as much as it had yielded before. This, then, was Zionism's moral rationale: it had no intention of depriving or exploiting the Arabs; on the contrary, it brought them benefits. "We are building and reviving the country," Ben-Gurion wrote, "and this is the moral and humane basis of our goals, inherent in our work and settlement in Palestine."[9]

The argument that there was no conflict between the Arabs and Jews in Palestine was put to the acid test during the riots of 1920 and 1921. Ahdut Ha'avoda maintained that the riots were perpetrated by savages, thieves and riffraff—mobs incited by effendis and religious leaders.[10] An outstanding example of the refusal to recognize the national aspect of the riots is the "In Memoriam" written by Berl Katznelson after Trumpeldor and his comrades fell in defense of Tel Hai. Katznelson's words etched themselves into the collective memory and became the foundation stone for the education of an entire generation:

> Let Israel remember the pure souls of its sons and daughters ...courageous and true, people of toil and peace who followed the plowshare and sacrificed their lives for the honor of Israel and for its land. Let Israel remember and be blessed in their seed, and mourn for the bloom of youth and joy of valor, for the dedicated will and spiritual devotion of those who fell in the fierce struggle. Let none rest, let none be consoled or cease mourning until the day when Israel returns to redeem its pillaged land.[11]

The identity of the enemy in this "fierce struggle" is not even hinted at. Instead Katznelson stressed the noble qualities of the fallen: they were pure of heart, they were people of toil and peace, and they were brave, honorable men who followed the plowshare. The enemy was by implication the opposite—lawless individuals or gangs, thieves, the dregs of society—never the Arab nation.

Ben-Gurion personally took no part in Ahdut Ha'avoda's reactions to the riots of 1920-1921. As secretary of the party he signed his name to documents and telegrams wherein the party's line was repeated, i.e., the rioters were only a marginal group of criminals thirsty for slaughter and pillage. But he did not write a word in his own name. During this period *Kuntress* printed nothing under his by-line. Ordinarily it was Ben-Gurion's custom to express his opinions boldly, in speech and in writing, which makes his two-year silence the more surprising.It was not until after the November 1921 riots that he wrote an article bearing only his initials. It coincided with the declared position of Ahdut Ha'avoda and placed the blame on the British administration. The rioters were savages and thieves who had been incited, and responsibility for what they had done rested entirely with the government. From the fact that the pogroms (the Russian word was used for "riots") began in Palestine only after the British conquest, Ahdut Ha'avoda and Ben-Gurion concluded that it was not the Arab people who were behind them, but only the "dregs of humanity," putty in the hands of "overt and covert provocateurs, evildoers and wicked rulers." These were the words he used to describe the military government officials whom Ahdut Ha'avoda demanded be replaced. Herbert Samuel was guilty in that he had not fired all the "provocative administrators" who continued to foment war between the Jews and Arabs. Outstanding among them was Ronald Storrs, governor of Judea and Jerusalem, "one of the leading criminal, blood-stained officials" whom Ben-Gurion named Pontius Pilate. Was it any wonder that there was a pogrom in Jerusalem in 1921 when Storrs was still at his post? The Arab people were not responsible for the riots of those years, but the British rulers and the effendis.[12]

Obviously, this was the stand that had to be taken by anyone who argued, as Ben-Gurion did, that there was no inherent conflict between Zionism and the Arabs in Palestine. Were they to have admitted that the rioters represented the Arab people, how could they possibly have simultaneously maintained that no conflict existed? No trace of this inherent contradiction remained the moment one applied the class formula: not the people, but their oppressors and exploiters. The effendis and the Imperialist government, those who avidly pursued their own advantage, were the ones who fomented the bloody contention between the Jews and Arabs.

Ahdut Ha'avoda and Ben-Gurion derived from the foregoing a moral prohibition against holding a dialogue with a movement headed by effendis and clerics that professed to be a national movement, the more so in that no political gain could be expected from such negotiations. Cooperation and mutual discussion could be undertaken only with an Arab labor movement, when such a movement would emerge.

At the Ahdut Ha'avoda conference held in Ein Harod in 1924, this approach was called in question. Shlomo Kaplansky, a founder and leader of the World Union of Po'alei-Zion, demanded immediate negotiations with the Arabs. Since 1920 he had been advocating recognition of the Arab national movement and support of its program to establish a national government and Palestinian parliament. Kaplansky was among those who had joined Ahdut Ha'avoda despite serious reservations as the movement was not sufficiently Marxist for his taste. Now he, of all people, questioned the class approach and claimed that a democratic parliament should be established in the country; that an agreement must be reached with the Arabs to fight together to establish broad authority for a parliament and an independent government formed jointly by the Jews and Arabs. To safeguard the rights of the Jewish minority, Kaplansky envisioned a parliament composed of two houses: an assembly whose members would be elected at general, universal, proportional elections; and a senate in which Jews and Arabs would have equal numbers of delegates. The senators would be named by Jewish and Arab autonomes respectively. In effect, this meant laying the cornerstone for the binational state advocated by Brith Shalom, formed in 1925, and by other groups that emerged subsequently.[13]

Ben-Gurion countered Kaplansky's proposal with a program of his own: separate autonomes for the Jews and for the Arabs, with cooperation on the governmental level. He remained loyal to the class solution: there would be cooperation only with the Arab workers within the framework of an international workers' alliance. That is, there would be two separate national trade union federations which would cooperate only at the top level. This was the joint organization that later was to become the "Union of Workers of Palestine." Ben-Gurion absolutely rejected Kaplansky's policy. Before discussing the type of regime, he maintained, the true content of the national government desired by the effendis had to be thoroughly clarified. Their intentions were not to establish a parliamentary democracy or democratic government. They wanted power to enable them to control, to determine the fate of Palestine and deny the Jews the right to build the country and settle on the land.

> We will not seek any agreement with leaders of such a movement. A way must be devised to reach the Arab worker who has yet to become a social force and a political factor. But this situation is bound to change, and we will play a decisive role in bringing about this change. We must be aware that without improvement of the standard of living of the Arab worker, we will not fulfill our historic mission. The fate of the Hebrew worker is tied to that of the Arab worker. We will rise or fall together. Our historic task—one that will devolve upon coming generations as well—is to improve the standard of the Arab workers.[14]

II

As discussed above, scholars have found ample proof that Ben-Gurion's ingenuous approach was at the root of his policy on the Arab question and spawned his denial of a conflict of interests—a denial that inevitably resulted in a clash. But is this true? Are not the naiveté and oversight too transparent for us to unquestioningly accept them at face value? Should one really attribute to Ben-Gurion an artless disregard of such a crucial problem whereas with respect to all other issues his thinking was highly complex, the very opposite of simplistic? Moreover, he did not always state in public what he said in inner circles, and he did not always say in inner circles what he entered in his diary—nor did he always confide to it everything that came into his mind. There is strong evidence that Ben-Gurion was very much alive to the conflict and aware of it.

In March 1908, soon after his arrival in the country and twelve years before the founding of Ahdut Ha'avoda, Ben-Gurion was shaken out of his naiveté. The "Purim Incident" in Jaffa roused him to an awareness of the conflict of interests between Jews and Arabs; he understood that the outbreak had occurred against a nationalist background. This statement is based on a comparison of two letters he wrote to his father. The first, like all his early letters, lauded the country and its conditions. Reassuring his family in Plonsk, he described the incident as a part of everyday life, as if attacking a Jew was not necessarily an expression of national Arab hostility. But from a later letter on the same subject it becomes clear that he had previously hidden his profound concern that the incident was perpetrated against a distinctly nationalist background.[15]

Moreover, Ben-Gurion was acquainted with Negib Azoury's book *Le Réveil de la nation arabe dans l'Asie turque*, published in 1905 in Paris. According to Azoury, he had founded, in 1904, the "Ligue de la patrie arabe" with the express purpose of opposing Jewish aspirations in Palestine, using as his motto "Arabia for the Arabs." In his introduction to the book, Azoury said: "Both of these movements [Arab and Jewish] are destined to fight each other constantly, until one of them triumphs." Ben-Gurion noted that this was a "book about the Jewish peril in Palestine," an impediment to "the creation of a great Arab empire," advocated by Azoury. Ben-Gurion regarded Azoury's book itself as "the work of an individual who is appealing to the great powers." However, after the 1908 *Huria* (the restoration of the Constitution) Ben-Gurion said at the Po'alei-Zion Party Council held in October 1910 that anti-Jewish propaganda in Palestine was no longer the work of one individual:

> The moment freedom of speech was permitted and newspapers could write whatever they wished, the Christian press embarked on an intensive propaganda campaign against the Jews. In the Christian Arab press propaganda against the Hebrew Yishuv in the country is particularly acrimonious. Today we see many newspapers in Palestine, Syria and Egypt opposed to us, and the disciples of Negib Azoury no longer appeal to foreign governments, but direct their propaganda toward the Arab people and the Turkish government.

This development in itself was bad enough, but for Ben-Gurion there was something even worse: "Even more saddening is our Arab neighbors' hatred for us." It was this hatred that led to the series of raids on villages in Judea (he named each village separately), and engendered "a much worse situation" in the villages of the Galilee. "Immediately after the Constitution was restored the attacks on the villages [in the Galilee] began, and they have not let up for two years." As they continued, "young lives are snuffed out, young Jews are being cut down by Arabs." It is quite obvious that he was familiar with the Arab press, particularly *Al-Karmil* which appeared in

Haifa and was known for its unbridled hostility to the "Zionist enemy" who "aimed to conquer Palestine." Arab newspapers, stated Ben-Gurion; "on the one hand spread in government circles groundless, libelous tales about the Hebrew Yishuv in Palestine, and on the other, they plant seeds of hatred for the Jews within all walks of the Arab people." Under their influence, he said, "the government has recently been looking unfavorably upon Jewish settlement in Palestine."[16] At the Third World Conference of the Po'alei-Zion held in Vienna in 1911, he also spoke of "the Arabs' growing hatred."[17]

While studying law at the University of Constantinople from 1911 to 1914, Ben-Gurion spent much time on the new, 1913 *Vilayets* law. As it turned out, his entire reading of Ottoman attitudes toward autonomy was based on his misunderstanding of the 1913 law for provincial reorganization. It was his belief that this reform had been introduced to bestow greater freedom of action on provincial governors:

> A severe struggle will ensue and there will be fierce rivalry among the various national groups. Each will try to fortify its own position in industry, commerce and labor, expand its political sphere of influence, increase its strength and power, and outdo all the others.

The Jews would have the right to declare autonomy for themselves in Palestine, but he had misgivings, predicting that the Arabs in Palestine and its vicinity would also claim the right to autonomy. They and the Jews would be adversaries in the same arena, and the question was which of them the Turks would prefer. That is to say, for him the struggle between the Jews and Arabs would be decided by a third party, the Ottoman state. With this he may have laid the foundation of what might be called his "Dominant Power" principle. In other words, Zionism would achieve its goal not by a dialogue and understanding with the indigenous Arabs, but rather through a third party, the Dominant Power that controlled the region. At first this was Turkey; then—almost simultaneously—there was the Bolshevik Revolution that was expected to spread throughout the world, and the British Empire that took over Palestine and became the Dominant Power throughout the Middle East. Incidentally, this principle, conceived by Ben-Gurion more than 70 years ago, is still valid today. Ben-Gurion envisioned that in the struggle among the smaller nations, the nation that is "better organized and united and can forcefully and consistently pursue its case and defend its rights, will win." He therefore called for political action that would unite the Jews in the Ottoman Empire, and above all, those in Palestine. As this thesis was published in *Ha'ahdut*, Ben-Gurion's conclusion that it was the Arabs against whom the Jews in Palestine would be pitted, reached a wider public.

When Ben Gurion returned from Constantinople in August 1914 he told his party that in order to be victorious in the struggle for autonomy in Palestine, the Jews would have to engage in intensive political action. The condition for such action was "Ottomanization." This meant that the Jews of Palestine should become Ottoman citizens so that they could participate in the political life of the Empire and have their own representatives in the Majlis and at court. Ben-Gurion himself hoped to be a representative to the Majlis and even a minister in the Turkish government. His aim was to win over Ottoman sympathy and understanding. To achieve this, Palestine's

Jews had to harness themselves to Turkey's war effort. If the Ottomans were weak the only ones to benefit would be the Arabs and "is there anyone who hates us as they do?" He was unable to do much to advance such policy, as in March 1915 he and Ben-Zvi were banished to Egypt.[18]

While being held by the authorities in Jerusalem, Ben-Gurion met Yihia Effendi, an Arab who had been a fellow-student in Constantinople. Hearing that he had been ordered to leave the country, Yihia said to him: "As your friend, I regret it. As an Arab—I am glad." In the course of time the importance of this chance encounter acquired weight until it became a significant signpost in Ben-Gurion's political life. He said that Yihia's words had hurt him more than the murder of his two comrades at Sejera in 1909. Until then he had considered Arab attacks on Jews as caused by events and circumstances, whereas "this was the first time I met an expression of *political hostility* [my stress, S.T.] on the part of an Arab." Already then, to believe his memoirs, he envisioned a future of unrest and riots in Palestine.[19]

Thus before World War I, Ben-Gurion explained the cause of the riots and the composition of the rioters differently than he did after it. In 1910 he spoke of a general Arab hatred. By the 1920s he was more specific, attributing the riots to "rabble", "thieves" and "savages", and he considered those responsible for spilling Jewish blood to be the effendis, religious leaders and government officials.

Finally, on a long, sleepless January night in 1916 in Omaha, living as an exile in the United States, he recorded his views on Zionist policy during and after the World War. Writing on scraps of paper, for the first time he revealed his talent for pragmatic, dialectic thinking, and for revealing in public only those ideas that would advance Zionism toward its goal. Among other things, he wrote:

> The Arabs oppose Jewish settlement. Yes, to some extent, such objection exists. But this cannot stop us....It is possible to come to terms with the Arabs too. For the Jewish community this is a question of *tactics* [my stress, S.T.].[20]

Thus in his opinion coming to terms or going to war, overcoming the opposition or taking cognizance of it, was a question of tactics. It should be borne in mind that he wrote these words to himself and for himself, only half a year after he had published his article "Toward the Future" in which he stated that there was no Jewish-Arab conflict.

III

It may therefore be assumed that what Ben-Gurion said and wrote in 1921 was part of the same strategy. Perhaps this also explains his two-year silence. It might have resulted from some difficulty on his part to find tactical solutions or he may have been at an impasse caused by the conflicting demands in his own mind. Indeed, while blaming the riots on Storrs, rabble, "savages" and the effendis, he was closely observing the Arab commercial strike organized by the Supreme Muslim Council. They put a stop to all business activities on July 12 and 13, 1922, as an advance protest against the League of Nations' approval of the British Mandate. This action led Ben-Gurion to write in his diary: "The success of the Arabs in organizing the closing of the shops shows that we are dealing here with a national movement." This recognition of an Arab national movement brought him very close to formally/officially acknowledging that there was indeed a conflict. In December, half a year later, he covered the short remaining distance when he said at the Third Conference of Ahdut Ha'avoda: "The Arab question is our central political question. We are faced with conflicting national goals. A national war is being waged against us." [21] But this discussion was still an internal movement debate, like his private internal debate over strategy . Publicly he continued to ignore and deny the conflict, remaining true to Ahdut Ha'avoda's position of which he himself had been perhaps the most important architect.

At the conference in Ein Harod in 1924, Katznelson and Yitzhak Tabenkin maintained that no Arab national movement existed since a true national movement must have positive content. Such a movement must show concern for the people's education and development, must strive to enhance their common weal. It should be recalled that Ben-Gurion supported this stand at the conference. If he did so as a tactical move, then it follows that he was again employing a tactic when, after the August 1929 riots, he recommended that his party drop the class approach and recognize the fact that an Arab national movement did indeed exist in Palestine. In the course of responding to Katznelson and Tabenkin, he proposed a different criterion by which to judge a political movement:

> It is true that the Arab national movement has no positive content. The leaders of the movement are unconcerned with the betterment of the people and provision of their essential needs. They do not aid the Fellah; to the contrary, the leaders suck his blood, and exploit the popular awakening for private gain. But we err if we measure the Arabs and their movement by our standards. Every people is worthy of its national movement. The obvious characteristic of a political movement is that it knows how to mobilize the masses. From this perspective there is no doubt that we are facing a political movement, and we should not underestimate it.[22]

Subsequently, at a "clarification" with Ahdut Ha'avoda and Histadrut "Arabists" in October 1929, Ben-Gurion revealed his stand clearly: "in the political sense" the Arabs in Palestine had "a national movement," and the riots of 1929 were the physical and spiritual creation of this national movement. But this admission was for internal consumption, directed at Ahdut Ha'avoda. A comparison with what he wrote in a memorandum he sent only a day or two later to the Trade Union International and the Socialist International illuminates Ben-Gurion's method of marshalling his arguments to fit his audience.

In the memorandum, Ben-Gurion repeated some of the things he had said at the meeting with the Arabists, but omitted his new criterion (for a political movement) and his statement that an Arab national movement existed. The title "Concerning Arab Unrest Because of the Western Wall" immediately implied a religious rather than national aspect. It was not a national movement that had brought about the riots, Ben-Gurion wrote, but "attackers ...incited masses, intoxicated with the flame of religious fanaticism" and "rabble goaded to plunder." Ben-Gurion devoted a lengthy section of the memorandum to data proving the benefits Zionism brought to

Palestine and the Arabs. Most of the Arabs, he maintained, were aware of these advantages. The riots were not a national protest against the Mandate, the National Home or Zionism. But "the strongest and most reactionary" effendis could see no other way of uniting and reinforcing their control over the Arab population "than to rouse religious hatred, which has a most powerful hold over the Oriental masses." They had sought a pretext to foment religious dispute between Jews and Muslims, through which they would strengthen their own position. And indeed the "natural" allies of the effendis, Ben-Gurion wrote, were "the Muslim religious leaders in Palestine." They also had direct economic interests in fanning hostility "to unite the Muslim religious institutions around the institutions that were already under their own control." Thus, when addressing himself to overseas socialist bodies, Ben-Gurion returned to the "class solution" and again employed the old formulations used by Ahdut Ha'avoda and himself to explain the outbreak of the riots.[23]

Just as after the disturbances of 1921, Ben-Gurion advanced the idea of a joint Jewish-Arab organization, so after the 1929 riots Ben-Gurion published his famous "Guidelines" for a constitutional change in Palestine, which will afford the Jews and Arabs an administrative parity. By then he was already considering the plan of a federation of two autonomes, Jewish and Arab, and advocated contiguous Jewish settlement, to make for the territorial contiguity of the Jewish autonome.[24] This approach called for negotiating with the Arab national movement, whose leaders—the effendis, clerics and others—instigated the spilling of Jewish blood. Later he announced his intention to meet with the Mufti, Haj Amin al-Husseini, who in the eyes of the Jews carried the largest share of blame for the 1929 riots and was held responsible for the slaughter in Hebron, Motza and Safed.

From late 1929 he was ready for steps toward a dialogue between the Jewish national movement and its Arab counterpart. To many Zionists, his project resembled a blueprint for a binational state. This too was a tactic and its objective was to gain time, to enable the Jewish community to grow stronger. But his party silenced him. Under the influence of Katznelson it even forbade him to publish his book *Our Neighbors and Ourselves* which he had prepared as a "passport" for the negotiations he hoped to initiate with representatives of the Arab national movement headed by the Mufti. The ban on his book was lifted only in 1931.

In August 1933, Ben-Gurion was elected to the Jewish Agency Executive. Between 1932 and 1936 the Jewish community in Palestine doubled in size and strength. By 1936 it was more than 400,000 strong as compared with 170,500 in 1931. With the change in circumstances Ben-Gurion changed his tactics. On the eve of and during the 1936 riots he spoke openly of the conflict, calling the riots an Arab "revolt" and "uprising." He harshly criticized his comrades Katznelson, Tabenkin and Moshe Beilinson for their "blindness," their inability to see that there was an Arab national movement and that these were not merely "disturbances" but a virtual revolt of Palestine's Arabs. It was then when he came out with his famous motto: "Immigration before peace,"[25] unquestionably a belligerent slogan.

Ben-Gurion chose his tactics not only to suit his political strategy but also to placate the allies whose support he sought. Each tactic had its particular address.

Before World War I, when he admitted the existence of a conflict, the address was the Ottoman government. Turkey should know that the Zionist Yishuv was allied with her against the Palestinian Arabs and it was to her advantage to support the Jews. Following the Bolshevik Revolution, when the Po'alei-Zion Party anticipated with confidence that it would spread to the east, Ben-Gurion directed his tactics to Moscow which, he hoped, would regard Zionism as the spearhead of the revolution in the Middle East. In 1920 he was prepared to join the Comintern if it would recognize Zionism; in 1923 he even went to Moscow with a view of convincing its leaders (apparently Leon Kamenev) that they had no better ally in the Middle East than Labor Zionism.

When he held the class approach and denied the conflict, and as general secretary of the Histadrut promulgated the idea of a joint organization, his tactics were directed to the British Labour Party, the Socialist International of which Ahdut Ha'avoda was a member, and the Trade Union International in Amsterdam, with which the Histadrut was affiliated. These were important auxiliary elements for him — socialist public opinion in particular — and he wanted to portray Zionism to them not as a discriminatory movement that would try to dispossess the Arabs, but as a movement portending social justice and progress to the Arab worker as well. The class struggle tactic was well received by these bodies, which fully agreed that Zionism need not or could not negotiate with feudal-clerical-imperialistic elements. In each case it was important to Ben-Gurion that Zionism should not be viewed as the cause of international dispute — something that would deter not only potential supporters, but also young Jews tending to the left. More than once he said that only a Zionism aspiring to justice would attract Jewish youth to take part in the Zionist enterprise in Palestine. Recognition of the Arab national movement and its revolt, as well as the readiness to negotiate with its leaders, was aimed at British opinion and British government. This tactic implied recognition of the true state of affairs and a search for accommodation — an approach congenial to the British, hence making it easier for them to support Zionism.

As if seeking to drive home this new tactic, tailored to fit his belligerent motto "Immigration before peace," Ben-Gurion took an uncharacteristic step. He admitted that he had been wrong. In June 1936 he wrote to Mapai's Central Committee: "At the Ahdut Ha'avoda Conference in Ein Harod, I said that we must have nothing to do with Arab effendis. I would not say that now."[26] As if that was not enough, at the Histadrut Council in February 1937 he stated:

> I want to point out a mistake which I made...thirteen years ago...in Ein Harod....Today I would not say that the only way to an understanding is through the Arab worker. We must find a way to the whole Arab people...by contact and negotiations with its representatives, whoever they may be.[27]

This statement, too, was directed to a supporting power, Great Britain. In 1936 Ben-Gurion called for "initiating the policy of a Jewish State."[28] He knew that he needed the active support of Great Britain for such a policy, support that he was convinced would be forthcoming only if Zionism took steps to achieve peace with the Arabs. British public opinion would support aid to peace-seeking Zionist endeavors. The policy of "self-restraint" during the riots was directed toward the same end. True, in the days of Ahdut Ha'avoda he had said that Zionism would not be implemented by the force of British gunships and bayonets, but in 1936 he changed his mind; he was ready to use such help.

In 1936, Katznelson, Tabenkin, Beilinson and others were still faithful to Ahdut Ha'avoda's class doctrine of the 1920s, refusing to acknowledge the existence of an Arab national movement and insisting that a movement for national liberation was inconceivable without a vision of social redemption and liberation. Ben-Gurion, however, described the riots in Palestine as a revolt against Great Britain and an Arab war against the Jews. He maintained that all the Arabs supported the rioters, and he designated Izz al-Din al-Qassam the "Arab Trumpeldor." While he was impressed by Arab show of self-sacrifice (some 3,000 Arabs were killed in the riots of 1936-1939), Katznelson and Tabenkin continued to attribute the "disturbances" to hatred incited by an exploitative feudal regime that oppressed the working class and discriminated against women and children.

Nevertheless, Katznelson and Tabenkin too were not naive; their stand differed from Ben-Gurion's because they advocated different tactics, and tactics were needed more by socialist Zionism than by General Zionism. Just, democratic, liberal Zionism could not explain why it did not incorporate into its own policies the principle of majority rule and why it denied the right of Palestine's Arabs to self-determination. Socialist Zionism had additional difficulties due to the impossibility of applying the principle of class solidarity to the realization of Zionism. It had to justify its insistence on "Hebrew labor" and exclusively Jewish trade unions (the Histadrut). Ahdut Ha'avoda could not explain why it did not apply the principle of "workers of the world unite" on its home territory, and why it discriminated on a national basis between worker and worker when it came to trade unions, the sick fund and other Histadrut institutions. Only strategic-tactical considerations could explain away these contradictions. The most important tactic used by Labor Zionism as well as General Zionism was the delay: there was need to gain time, in order to enable the Jewish community to grow as rapidly as possible. When Jews were the majority they would rule the country in accordance with democratic principles.

The main tactic employed was evasion, or denial. Thus it was argued that to the extent that Zionism represented the entire Jewish nation, it was obliged to talk with the entire Arab nation and not with its droplet that lived in Palestine. Until the emergence of a united Arab nation, Zionism had time. This applied to Ahdut Ha'avoda's class approach as well. Negotiations with the Arabs could take place only after the Arab laborer had developed and progressed, was organized in his own trade unions, and stood at the forefront of the Arab national movement—which would not happen for a long time to come. Katznelson and Tabenkin could not accept Ben-Gurion's changing tactics and at the same time remain loyal to socialist-Zionist theory. Were they to have accepted his thesis that there was an Arab national movement and an Arab "revolt," they would have had to admit the existence of Palestinian Arabs. If there were indeed Palestinian Arabs, their principles would oblige them to support the Arabs' right to self-determination. If they recognized the existence of a Palestinian Arab nation that constituted the majority in the country, how could they present socialist Zionism as a liberating, just movement seeking democracy? How could they rationalize the Histadrut's contravention of the principles of solidarity and mutual assistance that were its most basic tenets and the very foundation stones of all progressive workers' organizations throughout the world?

Notes

1 Anita Shapira, "Zionism and Power," Annual Chaim Weizmann Lecture at Beth Hatefutsoth (Museum of the Diaspora), November 18, 1986.

2 David Ben-Gurion, *My Talks with Arab Leaders,* Jerusalem, 1972, p. 6.

3 David Ben-Gurion, *Letters of David Ben-Gurion* (Hebrew), Tel Aviv, 1971, vol. 1, p. 71.

4 David Ben-Gurion, *Our Neighbors and Ourselves* (Hebrew), Tel Aviv, 1931, p. 61.

5 Report to Third Histadrut Convention, published by the Histadrut Executive Committee, July 1927.

6 See note 4.

7 Archives and Museum of the Israel Labor Movement (hereafter L.M.A.), IV/208, file 320.

8 Protocols of the Histadrut Executive Committee, September 5, October 27, 1929; protocols of the Histadrut Council, September 10 and October 10-11, 1929, Archives of the Executive Committee of the Histadrut.

9 David Ben-Gurion, "Toward the Future" (Hebrew), *Hatoren* No. 5 (1915); idem, *Our Neighbors and Ourselves*, p. 1.

10 *Yalkut Ahdut Ha'avoda*, vol. 1, p. 214, 1929.

11 *Kuntress* 29 (March 1920), p. 1.

12 *Kuntress* 100, November 11, 1921. The article is signed "B.G."; "Decisions of the Third Histadrut Council," Jaffa, November 8, 1921, *Pinkas A.*, January 1, 1922, L.M.A.

13 Proceedings of the Fourth Ahdut Ha'avoda Conference, Tel Aviv, 1925, pp. 10ff.

14 Ben-Gurion, *Our Neighbors and Ourselves*, p. 72.

15 Y. Slutzky, ed., *The History of the Haganah* (Hebrew), Tel Aviv, 1971, vol. 1, pp. 120, 208; Ben-Gurion, *Letters*, letters 48, 49.

16 David Ben-Gurion, *Ha'ahdut* 1 (August 1910) and 2-3 (September 1910); David Ben-Gurion, *First Writings* (Hebrew), ed., Y. Erez, Tel Aviv, 1962, pp. 23ff.

17 "Report on the Third World Conference in Vienna" (Hebrew), *Ha'ahdut* vol. 2, no. 43 (1911).

18 *Ha'ahdut*, 1913-1914, nos. 12-14, 17-24, 30; Ben-Gurion, *First Writings*, pp. 23ff.

19 David Ben-Gurion, *Memoirs* (Hebrew), vol. 1, Tel Aviv, 1971, p. 71.

20 Omaha Notes, Central Zionist Archives, A116/40/1; Shabtai Teveth, *David's Jealousy* (Hebrew), vol. 1, pp. 590-591.

21 Third Conference of Ahdut Ha'avoda, Haifa, December 17-20, 1922, *Kuntress* 119, January 19, 1923.

22 Ben-Gurion, *Our Neighbors and Ourselves*, p. 179.

23 "On the Arab Riots Over the Western Wall," Memorandum to Socialist International from Ahdut Ha'avoda. Ben-Gurion, *Memoirs*, vol. 1, pp. 740-750; two versions of minutes of "The Meeting on the Arab Question," October 10-11, 1920, L.M.A. IV/208, file 241; Ben-Gurion's diary, October 10-11, 1929, Ben-Gurion Archives, Sedeh Boker (hereafter B.G.A.).

24 David Ben-Gurion, "Guidelines for Establishing a Sovereign Regime in Palestine" (Hebrew), *Hapoel Hatzair* 22, March 20, 1931; David Ben-Gurion, "Memorandum on Security of the Yishuv," September 23, 1929, Weizmann Archives (see also *Memoirs*, vol. 1, p. 362); idem, *Our Neighbors and Ourselves*, p. 179.

25 Ben-Gurion's diary, March 11, 1936, B.G.A.; Protocol of Mapai Political Committee, March 30, 1936, Israel Labor Party Archives, Beit Berl (hereafter L.P.A.).

26 Ben-Gurion's letter to Mapai Central Committee, June 18, 1936, B.G.A.; Ben-Gurion, *Memoirs*, vol. 3, Tel Aviv, 1973, p. 281.

27 Protocol of the Histadrut Council, February 8, 1937, L.M.A.

28 Protocol of the Mapai Political Committee, March 9, 1936, L.P.A.

The Challenge of World War

BEN-GURION AND WEIZMANN DURING WORLD WAR II

YOSEF GORNY

> *I view him as an important instrument for our enterprise —*
> *and the enterprise, and only the enterprise, interests me.*
>
> [*David Ben-Gurion to Paula, October 7, 1937*]

From the time their paths first crossed after World War I until their dispute at the 22nd Zionist Congress following World War II, relations between Chaim Weizmann and David Ben-Gurion were charged with personal tension and political contradiction. Their respective positions in the Zionist movement were in disequilibrium. Weizmann was a recognized scientist, a personality of repute in the international arena, and a respected national leader. Although Ben-Gurion had served as secretary-general of the Histadrut, he was almost unknown in the Zionist movement and among the Jewish people.

The initial friction between them was socioeconomic in origin. Like other leaders of Ahdut Ha'avoda, Ben-Gurion criticized Weizmann for inadequate constructive actions in Palestine on the part of the World Zionist Organization (hereafter the WZO). In his characteristic way, however, Ben-Gurion surpassed all his colleagues in the tone of his criticism, and gave public notice more than once to "ruminations of resignation" from the Zionist Organization, for the purpose of founding a parallel organization of "fulfillment Zionists," in accord with the labor movement.[1]

The 1930s were characterized by mutual dependence between Weizmann, whose strength in the Zionist Organization had waned, and Ben-Gurion, who understood that the labor movement had not yet acquired the maturity in public affairs necessary for domination of the Zionist Organization without Weizmann's patronage. Thus Ben-Gurion, who had opposed the renewal of Weizmann's tenure as president in 1931 and expressed reservations about his candidacy in 1933, enthusiastically supported his return in 1935.

Relations between the two during these years were typified by disputes on minor political and practical issues and unanimity on questions of principle, such as the partition of Palestine and the establishment of a Jewish state.

During World War II, Ben-Gurion and Weizmann engaged in an uncompromising struggle for leadership of the Zionist Organization, during which the boundaries between principles, political tactics, and personal relations were blurred. The struggle was waged in three dramatic clashes, with the circle of participants widening in each. The first, enacted in the United States in 1942, involved a direct confrontation between the two. The second struggle occurred in Palestine in 1943, with disputes raging between Ben-Gurion and his party. The third, at the 22nd Zionist Congress in 1946, engulfed the entire movement.

This article focuses on the first act of the Weizmann—Ben-Gurion struggle: the 1942 clash and the events leading to it. The confrontation incorporates most of the differences in political outlook and personal motivation that typified Weizmann— Ben-Gurion relations. Moreover, it marks the point of transition from political differences to the struggle for leadership of the Zionist movement.

It is difficult to identify Ben-Gurion's attitude toward Weizmann with certainty. Sweeping declarations of admiration appear with expressions of anger and resentment. Although Ben-Gurion publicly praised Weizmann, privately he warned that Weizmann was a menace to Zionism. This ambivalence was shared by all Mapai leaders.[2] Ben-Gurion was a man of principle and a cunning politician, a daring national leader and a cautious statesman, a consistent idealist and a pragmatic compromiser. He was simultaneously Weizmann's admirer and opponent.

The conflict between them may be viewed in the light of personal competition. But there are several difficulties in the theory that Ben-Gurion wanted Weizmann expelled from the leadership so that he could succeed him. Why did Ben-Gurion agree to Weizmann's return as WZO president in 1935? If domination were his aim, he would have achieved it under Nahum Sokolow's presidency. Under the authoritarian leadership of Weizmann, by contrast, he must have known that his freedom of action would be limited. On this occasion, Ben-Gurion was clearly acting on the movement's behalf and not his own.

A more pointed question concerns Ben-Gurion's choice of timing and venue for the confrontation. The United States was a neutral arena, far from Ben-Gurion's party and sympathetic public in Palestine, and from Weizmann's inner circle of associates in England. And 1942 was hardly an appropriate time to initiate an upheaval in the Zionist movement. The world was engulfed in crisis and the outcome of the war was unresolved while the future of the Jewish people and the Zionist movement were shrouded in tragedy and uncertainty. Did Ben-Gurion fail to understand that the WZO would not risk deposing Weizmann as president at such a critical period? Did he not grasp that Weizmann was not an elected prime minister like Chamberlain, who could be unseated by Parliament for misconduct of the war, but rather a true national leader? Moreover, why did Ben-Gurion continue to oppose Weizmann when he became aware that his anti-Weizmann campaign was generally opposed both in the United States and in Palestine, and that he had no chance of success?

The last question proves even more troublesome in light of the historical context in which the struggle was waged. In 1943, as the Warsaw Ghetto erupted in flames, and as thousands of Jews were being murdered in Europe every day, Ben-Gurion chose to drag his party into an eight-month tumult over Weizmann's leadership. Did Ben-Gurion's personal ambition distort his sense of perspective? Or did the seriousness of the events of the time convince him that Weizmann's leadership threatened the Jewish people?

Only a conjectural explanation is possible. Ben-Gurion and Weizmann could not always distinguish between their personal desires and the cause they represented. Both men, over a period of years, came to identify totally with the Zionist movement. Such identification perhaps explains the overbearing personal attitude they displayed toward their colleagues and the entire movement when at the peak of their power.

It may also be the case that this identification originated in their great self-confidence. This trait led to an almost unquestioned faith in the compatibility of the subjective interpretation they gave to political and historical developments and the objective truth. They identified their own interests as national interests. They believed that their opponents imperiled the nation's future. The harsh and unrestrained language which the two leaders used in their dispute also becomes more understandable: in their eyes, they were struggling over the fate of the people and land of Israel.

Weizmann knew how to bear a grudge as well as how to rise above momentary passions and forget an insult.[3] Ben-Gurion's attitude toward him since 1931; his comments to Weizmann after the latter's election as WZO president in 1935; his stinging attack on Weizmann in 1935 for having indicated that he might favor a temporary halt to Jewish immigration; the tension in the Zionist Executive on the issue of testifying before the Peel Commission—all these certainly left deep scars in the psyche of a man as sensitive as Weizmann.[4]

Although both men reached the 20th Zionist Congress in 1937 in favor of the partition plan and establishment of a Jewish state, Weizmann found an opportunity to exact public revenge on Ben-Gurion. His method was both original and offensive. In his address at the closing session of the Congress, he showered praise on Moshe Shertok and deliberately ignored Ben-Gurion. After basking in Weizmann's compliments, Shertok soon found himself in the "miserable" situation, as he put it, of having been the subject of exaggerated praise. The audience understood this; Shertok felt that "to be placed on a pedestal so that your greater counterpart may be humiliated ... is unbearable torture ... Ben-Gurion was greatly insulted ... and I myself was miserable."[5] Ben-Gurion, however, commented: "I am not at all interested in how he relates to me. I do not depend on him, and I don't need his attention. I view him as an important instrument for our enterprise—and the enterprise, and only the enterprise, interests me."[6]

Ben-Gurion undoubtedly did care about Weizmann's attitude toward him, but he constructed a personal barrier between them. Just as he habitually secluded himself from colleagues at times of "hard thinking," he also failed to establish an intimate dialogue with Weizmann. Vera Weizmann described this phenomenon in her memoirs when discussing Ben-Gurion: "I always treated him with full honor. I grew excited as I heard him speak .... But for some reason I felt that he lacked a certain element of human contact; a certain 'something' was lacking in our relations with him .... He is one of the few people with whom I never succeeded in feeling at home."[7]

As early as 1937, Weizmann had expressed concern that he could not discern a young leadership in the labor movement in Palestine which would eventually be able to replace Ben-Gurion. Weizmann blamed the collectivist nature of the labor movement for this shortcoming, as it stifled the personalities of its leaders. He did not consider Shertok capable of succeeding Ben-Gurion. The latter was, he believed, a statesman of great intellect, but he lacked the hypnotic intensity of the true leader.[8]

The tension between the two resumed a year later. In September 1938, the Zionist Executive heard rumors of Britain's intention to withdraw its earlier support of the Palestine partition plan. Weizmann adopted a forceful stand, telling a Jewish Agency Executive meeting in London that he despaired of British Government policy and that the Yishuv had to prepare for a possible confrontation with the Mandatory Government. He agreed that this was not the moment to declare a split with the government; personally, however, he would conduct no further negotiations with it. Ben-Gurion agreed with Weizmann's analysis of the situation but objected to his conclusions. Negotiations, he insisted, must continue and be pursued to the end.[9] Shertok finally effected a reconciliation between the two, as he recorded in his diary: "In recent days a certain cooperation has also resumed between Weizmann and Ben-Gurion—they went to Malcolm MacDonald together ... and took each other's counsel about several matters."[10]

The discord that surfaced between the two in late 1938 indicates that their political perceptions and methods were not dissimilar. Both men adopted positions that were contrary to established views. Weizmann accepted Ben-Gurion's view of the Yishuv as a decisive instrument in the political struggle, while Ben-Gurion agreed with Weizmann's method of conducting patient negotiations with the British. Weizmann's forcefulness and Ben-Gurion's moderation, considered together, help explain their agreement regarding the preferred negotiating style in the St. James Conference of 1939 and the proper response to the White Paper that year.[11]

In late 1939 Ben-Gurion, reporting to the Mapai Political Committee on his talks with Weizmann in London, expressed satisfaction with the realism of Weizmann's political assessment. Weizmann, Ben-Gurion explained, had been doubtful of the extent to which the Zionist movement could expect help from the United States, as the US would probably stay out of the war and would therefore have little influence on the shaping of the postwar international order. At war's end, Weizmann believed, the British dominions—especially Canada and South Africa—would grow stronger in political status. Zionist policy should therefore be directed at fostering relations with these states. Weizmann felt that the Zionists' postwar political demands had to be formulated in advance, even though the outcome of the war was still uncertain. These demands were: 1) reaffirmation of the national rights of the Jews worldwide; 2) establishment of a Jewish state in western Palestine; and 3) monetary compensation from Germany to the Jewish people. Apart from noting his satisfaction with Weizmann's consistent advocacy of a Jewish state, Ben-Gurion had no further comment about the program.

When Weizmann was about to depart for the US, the two agreed that it would be inappropriate to engage in intensive political activity in America. They also agreed, for political reasons, not to propagandize for a Jewish army. Ben-Gurion suggested that Weizmann concentrate on fund-raising for the Yishuv. Weizmann accepted this proposal.[12]

The two leaders' agreement on political affairs, especially those involving the role of the US, lasted only until that country entered the war at the end of 1941. Then their assessments changed and their relations deteriorated. Meanwhile, in late 1938, Ben-Gurion continued to express his customary ambivalence regarding Weizmann. Commenting on Weizmann's political activity in London, Ben-Gurion claimed that Weizmann served now, too, as the major instrument of Zionist action. An instrument whose possibilities are many, and which, in known circumstances, could be great, but an instrument whose value, direction, and ability to act depend on the presence of a guiding hand. However, Ben-Gurion did not believe that Weizmann's advisers in London were up to the task, which was particularly serious as England remained, to Ben-Gurion, the main arena of Zionist diplomacy.[13]

Both men visited the US in 1940. Each returned with vivid and encouraging impressions. Their encounters with American Jewry aroused hope as to the political possibilities these masses of Jews and their organizations could effectuate. For Weizmann, the visit was cathartic. The man who had moved about London depressed and disappointed, returned from the US exhilarated. His confidence in his personal power had been restored. The ambience of goodwill, the affection and appreciation that had enveloped him everywhere in America, renewed his faith in himself. Shertok, addressing the Mapai Center, described the change in Weizmann's spirits, and added that Weizmann had found the US to be a country "in which the Jews have great potential power, but a power that is not utilized in the furtherance of Jewish policy."[14]

Ben-Gurion also was encouraged by his visit to America. However, he adopted sweeping maximalist programs. He became convinced that the key to establishing a Jewish state in Palestine after the war, and transferring millions of Jews from Europe to that state without delay, was the application of organized political pressure by American Jewry on the US Government.[15]

Upon learning in early 1941 that Weizmann intended to visit the US again, the Zionist Executive in Jerusalem asked him to travel via Palestine first for consultation regarding future policy. Weizmann was also advised that a stay in Palestine for an exchange of views and an encounter with the Yishuv would enhance his mission and impart greater authority to his talks in the US[16] However, Weizmann chose to travel directly to America. The request that he visit Palestine had been issued on Ben-Gurion's initiative, and when Weizmann returned to London in the summer of 1941, Ben-Gurion was furious. His concern that Weizmann was unwilling to accept the movement's collective leadership reawakened.

The failure of Weizmann's negotiations with the British for the establishment of a Jewish unit in the British army confirmed Ben-Gurion's fears. Ben-Gurion considered such a unit an instrument to defend Palestine in the event of a German invasion (German armor was then sweeping across the Western Desert), as well as a political device for the future. He accused Weizmann of having mismanaged the talks and demanded that Weizmann include him in all future political negotiations. Weizmann saw Ben-Gurion's demand as an insult, and the episode remained unresolved.[17]

Ben-Gurion returned to America in late 1941, a few months before Weizmann arrived in April 1942. He came in a combative mood, with the intention of mobilizing American Jewry to the Zionist cause. As chairman of the Jewish Agency Executive, he pressed adamantly for primacy and supreme authority in American Zionist institutions. This demand generated constant tension between himself and Weizmann's followers, who headed the Emergency Committee Weizmann had founded in 1939.[18] Weizmann, in contrast, reached the US in mourning. Just before his arrival, he had learned of the death in action of his son Michael, an R.A.F. combat pilot.

Ben-Gurion fought to make the Jewish Agency Executive the promulgator of Zionist policy, and to confer prestige rather than authority on the president, who, although an integral member of the Executive, would nonetheless remain subordinate to its decisions. As chairman of the Executive, Ben-Gurion considered his authority to be at least equal to Weizmann's as the movement's president.

By extension, Ben-Gurion continued, the president's aides were subject to the Executive as well. His reference, of course, was to the leaders of the Emergency Committee, all of whom were Weizmann confidants. Weizmann and his supporters held the opposite view: as movement president, Weizmann was accountable to the Zionist Congress alone, not to the Executive. He was willing, of course, to consult with the Executive and involve it in his political activity but he could not be considered subordinate to that body. His aides, by inference, were answerable directly to him, and not to the Executive or its chairman.

Even before Weizmann landed, Ben-Gurion argued that the Emergency Committee had no authority to conduct political negotiations with Jewish and non-Jewish personalities without authorization of the Executive in Jerusalem. He sharply rejected any attempt to enter into dialogue or cooperation with the Revisionist-founded Committee for a Jewish Army.[19] The Revisionists, he consistently asserted, had rendered themselves unfit by having withdrawn from the WZO, and must not be rehabilitated by being allowed to negotiate until they returned to the legitimate Zionist umbrella body.

When Weizmann reached the US another controversy broke out. He proposed the establishment of a political bureau in Washington under the auspices of the Emergency Committee. Ben-Gurion, while agreeing to the establishment of a political representation in the US capital, fiercely opposed its personal composition and its subordination to the Emergency Committee. He insisted that such a body be the representative of the Jewish Agency Executive; its leader must be Palestinian. Ben-Gurion's intent was clear, and Weizmann and his backers tried to counter it.

The final split between the two was stimulated by the exacerbation of their personal relationship. Weizmann, Ben-Gurion charged, excluded him from political contacts he was pursuing in the US. Although the two conducted talks, and Ben-Gurion had written to Weizmann concerning his desire to participate with him in common counsel in the political domain, Weizmann appears to have deliberately ignored Ben-Gurion's repeated appeals for involvement in political contacts with representatives of the American and British governments.[20]

The tension between the two increased until it finally surfaced in June 1942, when Ben-Gurion wrote to Weizmann charging that the latter was excluding him from his activities, surrounding himself exclusively with cronies, and treating matters of Zionist policy as his personal domain. These practices were detrimental to the cause and contradicted proper democratic procedure. With regard to the cause itself, Ben-Gurion claimed that Weizmann had failed in his attempt to mobilize American Jewry as an instrument of political influence on the US Government. With typical abrasiveness magnified by rage, Ben-Gurion asserted that Weizmann was not qualified to conduct Zionist policy. Ben-Gurion closed his letter by unequivocally announcing that, despite his appreciation of Weizmann's efforts, he saw no possibility of cooperation between them until procedures were established to define the powers of the president and chairman of the Executive.[21]

Weizmann's reply was no less blunt. He categorically denied Ben-Gurion's accusations of dictatorial conduct, claiming he had undertaken no action without prior consultation with Emergency Committee leaders and without then reporting to the Executive. He had always been fully accountable for his actions. He expressed astonishment at Ben-Gurion's absence from the consultations he had conducted with the Emergency Committee. He wondered at the very fact of Ben-Gurion's mission to the US, which Ben-Gurion had undertaken without informing Weizmann and against his standing advice.[22]

In Ben-Gurion's reply, the Mapai leader admitted that foreign matters had been entrusted to the president of the movement, but not to him alone. Furthermore, he maintained, it was believed both in the movement in general and in Palestine in particular that Weizmann's status as sole caretaker was not good for the cause. Weizmann parried by announcing that there would be no point in further correspondence between them.[23]

Following this break in their communications, Ben-Gurion turned to Stephen Wise, chairman of the Emergency Committee, with a request to convene an informal meeting of American Zionist leaders in order to resolve the conflict with Weizmann. This request was accompanied by the explicit threat that if Weizmann did not alter his personal policy, Ben-Gurion would turn to the Jewish Agency Executive in Jerusalem and demand that Weizmann be removed from the presidency of the movement.[24]

Wise swiftly responded to Ben-Gurion's appeal to mediate and invited Weizmann to his office for the meeting Ben-Gurion had requested. In his written reply, Weizmann did not reject the invitation but explained to Wise the nature and motivation of Ben-Gurion's demands. According to Weizmann, Ben-Gurion's offensive attitude stemmed from personal frustration; unable to promote the cause of the Jewish army while in London, Ben-Gurion hurriedly pinned the blame on Weizmann. As for the caution that governed his own political moves in the US, Weizmann explained, the situation in that country was most delicate. As president of the Zionist movement and a British national, he had to be careful to avoid the suspicion that he intended to damage the relationship between the U.K. and the United States. In this respect, Ben-Gurion, free of Weizmann's commitments, would have found the going easier. Weizmann explained that he had to maintain amicable relations with British prime minister Winston Churchill, the greatest friend of Zionism in Great Britain, just as American Zionist leaders took care not to alienate their president. Rash declarations and actions against the British Government in the US could negate that favorable bias. Despite the resulting need for caution and responsibility in his political action, he had not foresworn action and had maintained ongoing contact with various officials in the American and British governments.[25]

Wise convened the two leaders in an atmosphere full of suspicion and distrust. The disputants proceeded to infuse their discourse with dramatic flourishes and appeals.[26] The forum gave their words new gravity. Weizmann and Ben-Gurion had been acquainted for more than twenty years, a period during which they had displayed sharp differences of opinion and had clashed personally. Never before, however, had they confronted each other with such animosity.

Ben-Gurion expressed doubt as to Weizmann's ability to handle the political front without the support and counsel of a determined adviser. The reason for this, Ben-Gurion explained, was that Weizmann, although "a great statesman," was very naïve, was often ruled by emotion, and confused subjective and objective situations. The result was a periodic failure to comprehend historical reality in all its complexity, leading in turn to a general tendency on Weizmann's part to err in political judgments.

Weizmann's reply was no less harsh. If Ben-Gurion charged that Weizmann's policy was flawed by excessive subjectivity, Ben-Gurion's policy was ill-considered. All Ben-Gurion's accusations were based on nothing but "a sick imagination — the imagination of a man suffering from insomnia and anxiety. In my opinion, he's on the wrong path. He sees demons and spirits and creates a picture which has led him to the conclusion he has brought before you." Weizmann then accused Ben-Gurion of adopting "fascist" tactics of struggle against him, tactics based on character assassination.

Despite the vituperative tone, the discussion allowed both men to clarify their differences regarding the movement's future political line. Ben-Gurion told the meeting:

> One might ask why I have raised the question at this time. Is the situation more serious? Don't we have enough troubles? I have tossed in my sleep many a night because of these thoughts. My view — perhaps I'm wrong — is that the United States is even more important than England, although I do not think we should forgo England. England will no longer fit the definition of a great power after this war. We can work in England. But the United States is different: it is a decisive power, and our work there is of decisive importance for the army. If the United States gives its word, it will have to honor it.

Weizmann deflected this contention by saying:

> I have never thought — and I think Ben-Gurion expressed this with greater restraint today — that the world begins and ends with the United States. I think we must do our best to induce England and the United States to cooperate with regard to our problem.

Ben-Gurion, influenced by the decisive impact of organized political groups in American democratic practice, believed that a more assertive Jewish political policy was crucial for the movement. Weizmann, by contrast, remained faithful to the method of quiet personal diplomacy and focused mainly on averting a split between the US and Great Britain on the Palestine question.

The two leaders summed up their comments with dire warnings. If Weizmann did not desist from his futile, autocratic methods, Ben-Gurion asserted, he would demand Weizmann's resignation in the appropriate forums. Weizmann, in turn, explicitly warned that, if the movement institutions supported Ben-Gurion in restricting the president's freedom of action, he would consider resignation from all political activity.[27]

What had Ben-Gurion hoped to obtain from the meeting with Wise? The forum in which the exploratory session was held, after all, had no authority to coerce Weizmann. Even had it such authority, most of the attendants were friends of Weizmann and agreed with his views. It is possible that Ben-Gurion simply wanted to dramatize his dispute with Weizmann. Weizmann became ill shortly after the dramatic meeting and was confined to bed for several weeks. Meanwhile Ben-Gurion persisted in his efforts to organize American Jewry into a political body capable of action. He met with the leaders of various groups, Zionist and non-Zionist, relentlessly attacking Weizmann's policies. By the time Ben-Gurion had left the United States, in the fall of 1942, and returned to Palestine, Weizmann's fear of him had grown. Reports from Palestine convinced him that Ben-Gurion had succeeded in infecting moderate circles with his activist views.

Weizmann's concern was not misplaced. In October and November 1942, Ben-Gurion succeeded in aligning Mapai and Zionist Executive Committee support for the broad maximalist interpretation he gave to the resolutions adopted at the May 1942 Biltmore Conference.

American Zionists had convened at the Biltmore Hotel, with the participation of Weizmann and Ben-Gurion, at the initiative of Meyer Weisgal. The Conference considered a solution to the problem of homeless Jews an inseparable aspect of the new world order destined to emerge at war's end. Such a solution required the fulfillment of three demands: a) the possibility of mass Jewish immigration to Palestine; b) the transfer of supervision of Jewish immigration to Palestine and the requisite authority for the country's development to the Jewish Agency; and c) the establishment of Palestine as a Jewish Commonwealth integrated into the new democratic structure of the world.

Ben-Gurion, interpreting this program as an activist, demanded the resettlement of two million Jews in Palestine. Weizmann, by contrast, was consistent with his doctrine of gradual and continual immigration, at a level of about a hundred thousand per year. Ben-Gurion's program, although unrealistic during the Holocaust, in effect would have established a de facto Jewish state. By force of its intrinsic logic, Ben-Gurion's activist interpretation led to a confrontation with Great Britain and the Arabs.

Weizmann had supported the convening of the meeting,[28] and the resolutions which were adopted suited his own political outlook. His more cautious reading of the Conference resolutions left room for a range of political options, such as extending the Mandate, partitioning Palestine, or integrating it into either the British Commonwealth or a confederation of Middle Eastern nations. Weizmann characterized Ben-Gurion's proclamations as dangerous manifestations of "mock-heroism,"[29] and in a letter he wrote to a British gentile friend, Blanche Dugdale, he minimized the value of the convention itself.[30] Ben-Gurion's interpretation of the Biltmore Resolutions, he wrote, was liable to create the mistaken impression that they were a new Basle Program. In fact, this package of resolutions was merely one example of the hundreds of resolutions or declarations every American assembly adopted to magnify its importance. He had expressed similar views half a year before, in an article he had published in *Foreign Affairs* in January 1942, advocating postwar Jewish independence in Palestine, and the Biltmore Resolutions added nothing.

Weizmann justified his choice of the term "commonwealth," due to its acceptability in US public opinion compared with the term "state." It was also a far more flexible term, one that accommodated a variety of political solutions for Palestine, including membership in the British Commonwealth, United Nations patronage, etc. Final interpretation, in any event, would depend on political developments in Asia at the war's end, and on the future political-national structure of the area. While Ben-Gurion predicted intensive American intervention in international policy after its entry into the war, Weizmann discerned isolationist tendencies in American public opinion. He based this conclusion on the outcome of the 1942 US congressional elections, in which the Republicans registered significant gains. These election results, Weizmann believed, were a warning for the future. America's will to become the determining force in international policy was not self-evident. Neither was Ben-Gurion's assertion that British influence in the Middle East would diminish after the war.

Weizmann believed that British interest in Palestine would grow precisely because Britain would be forced to relinquish its Far East and Middle East colonies. He predicted the granting of independence to postwar India and the change this would precipitate in British status in the area. The British Empire, he asserted, would be compelled to find an alternative base and ally in Africa. Notwithstanding its declarations to operate in concert with France and Belgium in Africa, Britain would be the dominant power on that continent. The nature of postwar colonialist policy, however, would change as well. No longer would Britain be able to focus exclusively on the economic exploitation of the colonies; it would need to invest thought and capital in economic development of the colonies as well. This would lead to a close affinity with the Yishuv. A Jewish national entity with a population of several million, founded on the finest accomplishments of Western civilization, would allow large-scale cooperation between the British and the Jews. Weizmann, who had first proposed political cooperation between Britain and the Zionists during World War I, believed that World War II offered another opportunity to link the two peoples, this time on a constructive economic basis.[31]

The sweeping program Weizmann sketched for Dugdale is important for understanding his personality as a statesman. Although elderly and ailing, Weizmann remained able to embrace massive, far-reaching political programs that spanned continents and affected millions of people. He was proud of his political realism, which he juxtaposed to Ben-Gurion's fantasies. Nevertheless, only some of his predictions came true. India did win its independence at the end of the war, and Great Britain relinquished its empire in the Middle East. But Britain did not build an alternative colonial regime in Africa. Isolationist tendencies did surface in the US, and American unwillingness to become involved in Middle East was evident. In the end, however, America became the dominant actor on the world stage and an important source of assistance in the establishment of the State of Israel.

After Ben-Gurion returned from the US to Palestine, the conflict between the two men continued. The Executive invited Weizmann to Palestine for "consultations," but he declined to attend, citing poor health. In his reply, Weizmann inserted a strong attack on Ben-Gurion, describing him as a "petty dictator," a "thin-lipped" and "humorless" person, whose dangerous aggressiveness originated in the frustration of his uninhibited ambition. Ben-Gurion's methods in conducting the struggle, he added, were even more tyrannical than Jabotinsky's.[32]

The dispute resumed in 1943 in Mapai forums in Palestine, and at the 22nd Zionist Congress in Basle late in 1946. Although circumstances in both of these venues differed, motivations remained intact. Ben-Gurion through the years tried to limit the WZO president's powers in the conduct of foreign policy. He persistently challenged Weizmann's authority in this field in 1942, demanded Mapai backing on the issue in 1943, and tried to reduce Weizmann to an honorary president in 1946. When it became clear that these proposals were not acceptable either to Weizmann or to his ally Abba Hillel Silver, Ben-Gurion tried relentlessly to expel Weizmann from the leadership, even against the will of the Mapai Party. Here he succeeded.[33]

During the early 1940s, Ben-Gurion emerged as the leader of the activist line in Zionist affairs. In 1942 he called for the mobilization of American Jewry to influence Great Britain, and he was willing to risk armed struggle with England in 1946. Admittedly, unlike the I.Z.L. and Lehi, he favored—and practiced—a controlled struggle subordinate to political considerations. In no way, however, was he willing to relinquish the right to use force, as Weizmann demanded in their political debate at the Zionist Congress.

In the turmoil following the King David Hotel incident, Ben-Gurion rejected the renewal of armed struggle and extricated himself from the alliance with the I.Z.L. and Lehi. At the 22nd Zionist Congress, the advice of Ben-Gurion and Silver to reject negotiations with England on the basis of the Morrison—Grady Plan prevailed. Nevertheless, immediately after the Congress, Ben-Gurion, as chairman of the Jewish Agency Executive, initiated discussions with British Foreign Secretary Ernest Bevin.

Finally, both men had consistently supported partition. Agreement on this main political issue casts doubt as to the significance their conflict may have had. Excluding their political disagreements and beyond their interpersonal tension—

with its residue of undying personal resentment and unhealed wounds of past insult—Ben-Gurion and Weizmann belonged to different leadership types. Ben-Gurion was a leader who emerged from a political organization, Mapai and the Histadrut. In Ben-Gurion's view, the distinction between an organization's utility and essential value was of little consequence. At various times, Ben-Gurion regarded the party, the Histadrut, the WZO and, of course, the State itself as inseparable from the national and social goals he set for himself. By his very act of putting Weizmann at a distance, Ben-Gurion gave the movement a "fighting" image that was of intrinsic, and positive, political significance.

Weizmann, on the other hand, was fundamentally an individualist. He was captivated by the charm of his own personality; by nature he shunned self-serving political power structures, viewing them as somehow dishonorable.[34] Even near the end of his life, Weizmann appears to have been unable to grasp his inherent tragedy, in which Ben-Gurion's accumulation of political power ultimately vanquished Weizmann's fading personal charm. Ben-Gurion was primarily a "territorial" leader who drew his power from the Palestine-based institutions of the Zionist movement, while Weizmann, who considered the Jewish world his arena, had no power base at all.

Both were egocentric leaders who treated those close to them largely as instruments. Both were subject to extreme moods that constantly fluctuated. Predominant, however, was Ben-Gurion's aloof alienation and Weizmann's intimate openness. Outgoing Chaim Weizmann disclosed his fears and weaknesses in public; Ben-Gurion kept his anxieties strictly to himself, thus creating the image of a stronger leader. Weizmann symbolized the Zionist tradition; Ben-Gurion the revolution that had engulfed it.

Notwithstanding their great differences, each of these men, even in the midst of their struggle, knew he needed the other. Weizmann was aware of the fact that Ben-Gurion had no peer as a Zionist leader; Ben-Gurion acknowledged Weizmann's indispensability at fateful historic moments. In the final analysis, their conflict did not effect any decisive change in the Zionist enterprise. Both knew that a movement operating in historical reality must adapt itself to that reality. Practical considerations do not necessarily contradict principles, and compromises do not always negate aspirations. On the contrary, compromise usually enables their realization.

Notes

This article is an adaption of a chapter of the author's *Partnership and Conflict: Chaim Weizmann and the Jewish Labor Movement in Palestine* (Hebrew), Tel Aviv, 1976.

1 Yosef Gorny, *Ahdut Ha'avoda, 1919-1930: Ideological Principles and the Political System* (Hebrew), Ramat Gan, 1973, Chap. 10.

2 Yosef Gorny, *Partnership and Conflict*, Chapter 3.

3 Tape-recorded memoirs of B. Locker.

4 Blanche Dugdale, *Baffy. The Diaries of Blanche Dugdale, 1936-1947*, London, 1973, p. 40.

5 Moshe Shertok (Sharett), *Political Diary* (Hebrew), Tel Aviv, 1971, Vol. 2, pp. 279-280.

6 David Ben-Gurion, *Letters to Paula and the Children* (Hebrew), Tel Aviv, 1968, p. 215.

7 Vera Weizmann, *My Life with Weizmann* (Hebrew), Tel Aviv, 1967, pp. 175-176. A rare episode of intimate communication between Weizmann and Ben-Gurion is related in an anecdote of M. Shenhavi. In 1950, Weizmann and Ben-Gurion found themselves in the same hotel in Tiberias. There was a rare snowfall, leaving the two imprisoned in the hotel for a full day—whereupon they conversed for hours. Weizmann later told Shenhavi he had discovered a new Ben-Gurion: an erudite man who took interest in philosophy, knew Greek, etc.

8 See Dugdale, *Diaries*, p. 62.

9 Ibid., p. 101.

10 Shertok, *Political Diary*, Vol. 3, p. 334.

11 See Yehuda Bauer, *Diplomacy and Resistance. A History of Jewish Palestine*, New York, 1973, pp. 16-51.

12 Political Bureau session, November 27, 1939, Labor Party Archives, Beit Berl, (hereafter L.P.A.), bloc 23/29.

13 See Bauer, *Diplomacy and Resistance*, p. 51.

14 Mapai Central Committee, April 1940, L.P.A., bloc 40.

15 Bauer, *Diplomacy and Resistance*, pp. 230-232.

16 Mapai Central Committee, March 19, 1941, L.P.A., bloc 23/41.

17 See Bauer, *Diplomacy and Resistance*, pp. 233-234.

18 In full: The American Emergency Committee for Zionist Affairs.

19 The Committee for a Jewish Army (1941 - 1943), initiated by Hillel Kook (Peter Bergson).

20 Ben-Gurion to Weizmann, April 16, 1942, Central Zionist Archives (hereafter C.Z.A.), Z5/1361.

21 Ben-Gurion to Weizmann, June 11, 1942, estate of Berl Locker, L.P.A. An excerpt from the letter follows: "I wish I were convinced that you could conduct our political affairs and guide the movement alone. I am sorry to say that I am not."

22 "...I must reject *in toto* your conclusion as uncalled for by the circumstances, and regard the whole incident merely the result of a temporary mood, dictated not by calm judgement but rather by imaginary grievance caused undoubtedly by the many heartbreaking disappointments which all of us must face in this crucial hour." Weizmann to Ben-Gurion, June 15, 1942, Weizmann Archives (hereafter W.A.).

23 See Ben-Gurion to Weizmann, June 16, 1942, W.A.; Weizmann to Ben-Gurion, June 17, 1942, W.A.

24 Ben-Gurion to S. Wise, June 19, 1942, C.Z.A., Z5/1361.

25 Weizmann to S. Wise, June 20, 1942, W.A.

26 The meeting was held on June 28, 1942. In addition to Weizmann, Ben-Gurion, and Wise, participants included Nahum Goldmann, Robert Szold, Louis Lipsky, Hayyim Greenberg, Meyer Weisgal, and others.

27 Weizmann probably never intended to carry out his threat to resign from the WZO presidency. He portrayed himself as a sacrificial lamb in the movement's hands. Several days after the meeting in Wise's office, Weizmann wrote to B. Locker: "I was really furious, and if it were not for the critical situation, the best thing one could do is to leave the whole thing alone and let those who can do better try to do it, but unfortunately one is a prisoner." (Chaim Weizmann to B. Locker, July 1, 1942, W.A.)

28 M. Weisgal's letter to the Zionist Executive in London, January 8, 1943, C.Z.A., Z5/1385; and to B. Locker, February 2, 1943, ibid.

29 Weizmann to S. Wise, October 21, 1942, W.A.: "All these mock-heroics are disquieting, most harmful and demoralizing."

30 Weizmann to B. Dugdale, June 1, 1943, C.Z.A., Z5/1385.

31 Weizmann concluded: "You see from this short statement that I believe as I always do in that respect, that our fate is again bound up with England. They will have to develop Africa to the maximum, just as we would have to do the same in Palestine, and here both sides meet." (ibid.)

32 Weizmann to the Zionist Executive in Jerusalem, October 22, 1942, C.Z.A., Z5/1385. "I have watched Mr. Ben-Gurion carefully during his stay here. His conduct and deportment were painfully reminiscent of the petty dictator, a type one meets with so often in public life now. They are all shaped on definite patterns, they are humorless, thin-lipped, morally stunted, apparently frustrated in some ambition, and nothing is more dangerous than a small man nursing his grievances introspectively. Mr. Ben-Gurion is in a constant state of exaltation and moral tension, obsessed by a mission in life."

33 See Gorny, *Partnership and Conflict*, Chapters 5-6.

34 Norman Rose, "The Chief: A Pen Portrait of Chaim Weizmann," *Studies in Zionism,* Vol. 6, No. 2 (Autumn 1985), pp. 171-197.

IMMIGRATION AND REVOLT: BEN-GURION'S RESPONSE TO THE 1939 WHITE PAPER

YITZHAK AVNERY

In December 1938, David Ben-Gurion proposed a direct confrontation with the British by means of the open and illegal immigration to Palestine of thousands of young Jews from all countries of the globe. He elaborated on the scheme and attempted to secure support for it until the outbreak of World War II nine months later, despite the opposition of members of the Jewish Agency Executive, of the leadership of the Yishuv (Jewish community in Palestine), and even of some Haganah commanders and activists involved in organizing covert illegal aliya.

The concept of an open "immigration rebellion" marked a reversal of Ben-Gurion's previous position on illegal immigration. Until the end of 1938 he had been one of its staunchest opponents, due to his desire to maintain good relations with the British Government. It was very important for him to increase "the cooperation and friendship with the Mandatory Government."[1] He knew that "we need aliya and for this aliya we require the assistance of the English."[2] Ben-Gurion did not believe that such immigration would succeed in forcing a change in the Mandatory Government's policy, nor would it significantly increase the size of immigration to Palestine. He was also concerned that such a mass movement would raise the level of unemployment. Ben-Gurion had been stridently critical of the two sailings in 1934 of the first illegal immigration ship, the *Velos,* and was equally opposed to the renewal of such traffic in 1937 and at the beginning of 1938 when the *Poseidon* anchored off the coast of Palestine.

Beyond his concern for relations with the British authorities, Ben-Gurion was also apprehensive of the inevitable contact and cooperation with smugglers and criminals that the organization of the illegal traffic required. Its high cost was yet another factor that influenced his negative stand. It seemed that there was no justification for the effort and risk connected with organizing an illegal influx, while opportunities for legal immigration remained open at least in principle. Furthermore, the latter was subject to the supervision of the Jewish Agency, whereas the possibility of exercising such supervision was dubious under conditions of illicit traffic. Illegal immigration, he then believed, would have undermined legal aliya.[3]

Until September 1938, Ben-Gurion still hoped that the British Government would implement the partition plan in accordance with the recommendation of the Peel Commission, and that a Jewish state would soon be established, to which Jews could come without any restrictions. He also was not confident that "we by ourselves, without the knowledge of the government and without its permission, will be able to arrange large-scale immigration."[4] And indeed, judging from the results, the experience of the first ten months of 1938 was very disappointing. The activists of Hakibbutz Hameuchad and Hehalutz had managed to bring in four small ships carrying only 415 illegal immigrants.

However, when he became convinced, in October-November 1938, that the British Government did not intend to implement the partition plan, and in view of the deteriorating situation of the Jews in Europe, Ben-Gurion called for an aggressive Zionist policy, including a "rebellion" against the immigration restrictions. Mass illegal entry, with resort to force if necessary, would be an essential political tool in the struggle against the new British policy. He now advocated "a different drive, a different tempo, different efforts, and new methods of war and action."[5]

Britain's retreat from partition ended any hope of solving the refugee problem by establishing a Jewish state in part of Palestine. Ben-Gurion emphasized that it was precisely on the question of aliya that the Jewish Agency could not compromise. Thus, both political considerations and the desire to save Jews merged in the campaign which he initiated to implement his plan regarding mass illegal immigration.

At the beginning of December, Ben-Gurion returned to Palestine from London after a prolonged stay there. On December 10, 1938, he wrote down the thoughts and proposals that he would present at the Jewish Agency Executive meeting on the following day. He called for

> an immigration rebellion, a declaration of war on England—not with guns and bombs, not by terror and murders like the Arabs, but by internal organization of mass immigration to Eretz-Israel, and the transport of thousands of refugees, irrespective of the government's prohibitions, to the shores of Eretz-Israel—an act which would again tie the question of the refugees to Eretz-Israel.[6]

In order to launch this rebellion, Ben-Gurion knew that it was necessary to make large-scale preparations. Ships would have to be purchased, contacts established with smugglers, and networks organized in Europe to deal with transport. The Yishuv would have to be prepared for their absorption. Ben-Gurion was ready to bring to Palestine, openly or secretly, thousands of youths and to force the British "either to fire upon the refugees or return them"—a matter which would, in his opinion, disturb the international community as well as arouse public opinion in Britain.[7]

The authorities in London planned talks between His Majesty's Government, Arabs and Jews in the hope of finding a solution to the Palestine conundrum. Ben-Gurion was convinced that the negotiations would fail. When this happened, he noted, it would be necessary to convene a world Jewish conference in America and announce that "the Land of Israel is our country" and that the Jewish people "would organize a mass return" there. The conference would elect "a committee for the salvation of the people and the homeland" and would raise the funds necessary for the projected activities. The Jewish Agency Executive would resign and "would announce the cessation of political cooperation" with Britain. A similar declaration would be issued by institutions of the Yishuv. A passive revolt would be organized in Palestine.

> No attack against the government would be permitted, but no contact with it would be maintained, save by compulsion. The municipalities and villages would not enter into discussions with the government, save under duress.

Likewise, "we will prepare to conquer Haifa by force and from Haifa we will announce the establishment of a Jewish state."[8] He believed that immediately after the conclusion of the talks in London and the announcement of the new British policy, a

> conference in America should be convened and the transport of masses of refugees to Eretz-Israel should begin openly, with all the efforts and means available to the Jewish people....If we should fulfill this plan, and have the strength to continue the immigration rebellion...England will be forced to surrender.[9]

On the following day, December 11, 1938, Ben-Gurion presented a comprehensive survey of the political situation to the Jewish Agency Executive. Britain, in his opinion, was interested in guaranteeing the friendship of the Arabs in Palestine and the neighboring states, in order to ensure their support should war with Germany erupt, even at the expense of the Jewish people. The "immigration rebellion" was intended as an appropriate reaction to such a situation.[10]

> This will be our political war for our Homeland....No other action will succeed...because pressure on the the Arabs is too strong and only the pressure of a rebellious immigration will be decisive against Arab pressure...an immigration rebellion openly organized by the entire Jewish people.[11]

At that meeting, Eliahu Dobkin, who was closer than all other members of the Executive to the problems and plight of the refugees from Eastern Europe, opposed Ben-Gurion's suggestion that ships with illegal immigrants should arrive openly and by day, serving as a public demonstration against the British Government. He did not view the illegal traffic as a political measure but as a method for saving thousands of refugees. In his opinion, it was essential that the immigrants be brought into Palestine secretly and not openly.[12]

In his reply, Ben-Gurion explained that there was little chance of bringing over a large number of illegal entrants secretly. Instead, he advocated something even more radical:

> A new method of political warfare—an aliya war, *not a war for aliya, but a war by aliya*...harass the government through open and public methods rather than clandestine aliya designed to increase the number of Jews in Eretz-Israel, aliya as a method of political warfare, that will provide the British Government with no respite, that will shake up public opinion in England and in the world. Only unceasing aliya, repeating and redoubling itself stubbornly and with unremitting sacrifices, bringing masses of youths from Germany, Poland, Rumania, Greece and other countries to the shores of Eretz-Israel—will not give the Government any rest and will force it to change its policy.[13]

If agreement on immigration was not reached during the course of talks with the British Government or by an accord with the Arabs (to which he himself gave little credence), Ben-Gurion believed that there was no alternative other than "organizing through the aid of the entire Jewish people a mass aliya on our own initiative."[14]

The next day, in his address before the Va'ad Haleumi, one could detect a different tone in Ben-Gurion's words. Then, as distinct from previous occasions, he emphasized an immigration of salvation.

> Faced with the situation in the world, faced with the decree of extermination pronounced against us in the land of Hitler...we have been placed in a position where on one issue we cannot speak of any concessions whatsoever, and that is the issue of immigration. We have one single interest—the immigration of hundreds of thousands of Jews to Eretz-Israel...at the soonest possible moment.[15]

At a meeting of the Mapai Central Committee which convened on December 15, 1938, Ben-Gurion stated that he conceived of a "pressure of immigration...not directed solely toward aliya itself, but as a political tool." He believed that "the organization of open aliya...has to be directed toward the transfer of hundreds of thousands of youths...and if it is decreed for them and for us to die, they will die here; and if it is decreed that they should fight—they will fight here, because this is the only place for our war."[16]

Early in January 1939, about a month before the convening of the St. James Conference, Ben-Gurion traveled to the United States in order to publicize his program, organize the world Jewish conclave, and win supporters for the program's implementation. Three weeks later, he admitted that his plan had not been received with enthusiasm in the United States:

> The conference met with objections on the part of the non-Zionists and lack of enthusiasm on the part of the Zionists. The former fear the conference, the latter fear the fears....As to the ships, nothing has been achieved till now."[17]

Ben-Gurion's journey to the United States was a total failure because of the opinion prevailing among the American Jewish leadership that it was impossible to contend with Britain while simultaneously arousing support for its opposition to Nazi Germany.

At the St. James Conference, the Jewish delegation was united in its approach to the basic issues, including the question of aliya. Ben-Gurion adopted a particularly aggressive position on this issue. During the session which took place on February 15, 1939, Colonial Secretary Malcolm MacDonald proposed an overall ceiling on Jewish immigration over a number of years, so that the Jewish community in Palestine might reach a specific level (about forty percent of the general population). That would be effected without prior consultation with the Arabs and without obtaining their consent. Only after some years would any additional immigration be dependent on Arab agreement. Ben-Gurion asked for the floor and declared:

> The Jews would never give up a land of their own. They immigrated to Eretz-Israel at the time of the Turks, as illegal immigrants....He himself was an illegal immigrant. He broke the Turkish law because of a superior law. Four hundred thousand Jews in Palestine would not recognize a law which conditioned the right of immigration to Eretz-Israel upon the consent of the Mufti.[18]

At a meeting that took place ten days later, Ben-Gurion made clear to members of the British delegation "that a cessation of Jewish immigration was out of the question...save by force of British bayonets, British police and the British navy."[19]

The final British proposals were presented to the parties on March 15, 1939. They constituted the basis of the 1939 White Paper on Palestine, published two months later. These were ultimative proposals, motivated chiefly by an attempt to secure the sympathy of the Arab national movement for the continuation of a British presence in the Middle East. The British statesmen were convinced that neither the Yishuv nor the Zionist Organization would be able to act against Britain, beyond protests and arousing public opinion. Further, they believed that due to political circumstances and the danger of a war against Germany, it was not possible for the Jews to support Britain's enemies.

The reaction of the Jewish delegation was particularly sharp. The British proposals were rejected by all the Jewish representatives, including the non-Zionists, and on the following day the delegation left the Conference.[20] Most of the Yishuv's leaders began to express a more aggressive stand against the new British policy. The need for illegal immigration was now agreed upon by all sectors of the Yishuv.[21] The moderates preferred it to other ways of fighting against the government's policy, because they hoped it might be implemented without violence.

There was, however, no consensus regarding the nature of this aliya, its scope, or method of implementation. The opposing policies of open, massive illegal aliya as a tool in the political struggle against the new British policy, or clandestine immigration, the sole purpose of which was to save as many Jews as possible from European countries, were clearly juxtaposed. How should armed clashes with the British police, army and navy be handled? The question of selecting candidates for aliya also became important. Was quality preferable to quantity? Should every Jew who desired to immigrate be allowed to do so, or should preference be given to members of the pioneering movements and the young? There was also the very serious aspect of funding to be considered.

. Within the leadership, opinions were divided between the moderates and the activists, although neither camp was unanimous in its stand. Some moderates opposed strikes and silent demonstrations, while others supported passive resistance. In contrast, there were activists who believed that one should not only cut off contacts and cease cooperation with the authorities, but initiate clashes involving force and weapons, even if such confrontations would endanger the lives of illegal immigrants and fighters.

In the forefront of the activists were Berl Katznelson, Ben-Gurion and Yitzhak Tabenkin of the labor movement; Eliahu Golomb, Dov Hoz, Shaul Meirov and Yisrael Galili from the Haganah leadership (also from the labor movement); Rabbi Meyer Berlin (Bar-Ilan) and Rabbi Yehuda Leib Fishman (Maimon), heads of the Mizrahi; many youths from non-affiliated groups; as well as members of the right-wing parties such as the Maccabee movement. The moderates included Chaim Weizmann, Eliezer Kaplan, David Remez, Yosef Sprinzak, the leaders of the left-wing Hashomer Hatzair, as well as Moshe Smilansky of the Independent Farmers' Union, and Israel Rokach of the General Zionists.[22]

Some leaders, including Ben-Gurion, believed that Britain would not adopt any strong measures against illegal immigration. If ships were fired upon, this would have negative repercussions in Britain and around the world, possibly leading to the fall of the government.[23] By contrast, Katznelson doubted whether clashes with the army and the police would yield political gains. He contended that incidents in which British vessels fired on illegal immigrant ships had already occurred, and the British and world press had not even reported them.[24]

At the 13th Mapai Conference, additional opinions were voiced. Although all were in support of the illegal traffic, they represented different perspectives. Rachel Yanait (Ben-Zvi) was the only speaker at the Conference who supported Ben-Gurion's position regarding open mass illegal immigration.[25] Ben-Gurion insisted that the implementation of clandestine immigration was impossible. He reiterated his political justifications for overt action, even if it were to result in the use of arms. Such immigration, he believed, could serve as the political means for toppling the regime which was curtailing legal migration.[26]

Clarification of a new Zionist course of action and reaction to British policy were widely debated in Palestine and abroad, both prior to and immediately following the issuance of the White Paper on May 17, 1939. Ben-Gurion contended, on the eve of its publication, that strikes and demonstrations would not suffice:

> When the White Paper is published, we must react, but not only with a strike which merely harms us. We don't have to imitate the Arabs....We don't have to make ourselves ridiculous, doing things that neither harm nor intimidate anyone else, but are liable to be injurious only to ourselves.[27]

He now stood at the head of the extremists and he planned to bring illegal immigrant ships to the shores of Tel Aviv. They would arrive openly on the date when the White Paper was to be issued. Members of the Haganah would provide armed defense against the authorities' possible intervention to prevent the disembarkation of the passengers.[28] Ben-Gurion wrote in his diary:

> In consultations among our friends, we discussed the arrangements for the approaching date of the White Paper's release. The new regime will be declared illegal and we will not obey it. We will continue immigration and we will not fear imprisonment or fines. Every Jew will provide shelter to the immigrants and if possible, ships will arrive on the very day that the White Paper will be published.[29]

At the session of the Zionist Executive on May 9-10, 1939, various members supported this position.[30] Implementation, however, was technically impossible, due to the lack of time.[31] Close to the actual announcement of the new British policy, Shura Oshrowitz, a member of Kibbutz Givat Brenner, was sent to Paris with instructions from the leading institutions for Aliya Bet activists regarding the planned open disembarkation of illegal immigrants, in order to hold up publication of the White Paper. Hundreds of members of the Haganah were to wait on the shore for the ship's arrival. If clashes between the police and military authorities and the new arrivals would ensue, the latter would brought ashore by force.[32]

The organizers of the clandestine immigration (Aliya Bet) in Paris opposed the plan, arguing that their goal was to save the maximum number of Jews from Europe within the minimum time and in total security, rather than to engage in the struggle against the British. Open and demonstrative aliya would endanger the lives of the newcomers by exposing them to possible clashes with the armed forces and the police. Further, the ships' crews, who at that time were non-Jewish, might transfer the illegal immigrants to lifeboats far from the Palestinian coast, so as not to risk arrest. Even worse, they might abandon them on the open sea. There was also the fear that the shipowners and the crews would cease their collaboration due to the implicit dangers.[33] They felt that it was improper to expose the refugees, whose sole desire was to reach Palestine, to such a dangerous test.[34]

In their opposition to Ben-Gurion's proposals, the European activists were supported by Katznelson, Tabenkin, Golomb, and Galili, who feared that clashes with the Mandatory authorities would doom the project.[35]

The decision to organize demonstrations on the day of publication of the White Paper was finally adopted due to pressure by the activists, who demanded a clear and open expression of the Yishuv's resentment against the authorities.[36] On May 17, 1939, a Sabbath of public protest was declared.[37] The following day, mass demonstrations took place in all parts of the country. In several localities there were violent clashes with the police.

Ben-Gurion was not content with such a mild response. On May 21 he informed members of the Jewish Agency Executive that Jewish immigration was the sole means of changing the situation: "There are among us people who are willing to risk their lives for immigration and only this weapon can save us." He suggested to the Mapai Political Committee a program that would provide immigration, with protection, of a thousand people a week.[39] He explained his views to a meeting of youth movements in Jerusalem. The Jewish people were, he declared, standing on the threshold of a new era,

> the era of fighting Zionism...the continuation of our Zionist activity will be possible only within the context of a war...we will be able to continue our activity, and also intensify and accelerate it, only within the context of an open and daring war that will not recoil from any obstacle and danger.

This was not a war against the English people and the British Empire but "a war against the policy of the British Government." Its goal was not to achieve independence for the Jews of Palestine,

> but to open the gates of the country to the Jewish masses, to the ingathering of the exiles, to Jewish settlement throughout the entire land....The first measure, both in time and in importance, is the war of immigration.[40]

Ben-Gurion's words are enlightening because he apparently felt that this was the most appropriate time for a struggle against the British policy. It seems that the possibility of an approaching world war was not considered.

On May 25, 1939, when the illegal immigrant ships *Atrato* (on its seventh voyage) and *Colorado* were approaching Cyprus, the *Atrato* received a cable apparently dispatched from the command headquarters of the Mossad L'aliya, containing an explicit detailed order in accordance with Ben-Gurion's policy. One hundred young men were to be equipped with life belts and disembarked in lifeboats during daylight a few miles off the coast of Tel Aviv. They were to resist with force if the British intervened.[41] The overall plan included directing the immigrants to Tel Aviv, and bringing the citizens to the beach at lunchtime. Ben-Gurion sought to dispatch an armed detachment from the Haganah to receive the immigrants. If a British police force appeared at the site, it would be up to this detachment to clear a way for the immigrants through the streets that led from the seashore to the city center. Another detachment would block the side streets by setting up roadblocks.[42]

Although the volunteers were found, the plan was cancelled because of opposition from within Ben-Gurion's Mapai Party.[43] Three days later, the *Atrato* was seized by the British near the coast at Shefayim (north of Netanya) where hundreds of members of the Haganah awaited its arrival. In the end, the ship was forced to sail to Haifa.

The activist approach was dubbed Aliya Gimmel.[44] It would differ from Aliya Bet in that it included both illegal entry and the possibility of armed rebellion or at least the element of immigration by force. Ben-Gurion's purpose was to bring about the annulment of the White Paper. He hoped that it would be possible to accomplish this when the public in Britain would become convinced that it was possible to implement the White Paper only through violent clashes, cruelty to refugees fleeing Nazi persecution, and total suppression of the Yishuv.[45]

However, the British did not provide a pretext for a bitter response on the part of the Yishuv. Indeed, they used force sparingly. Ben-Gurion believed that the policy of not returning the illegal immigrant ships and allowing their passengers to remain in Palestine, as well as the authorities' abstention from clashes, "stemmed from the government's fear that the Yishuv is ready to fight, and the government recoils from such a war."[46] The government was also aware, in his opinion, "that a clash with us in the sphere of aliya is not likely to be the beginning of our end...but rather the beginning of the end for the White Paper."[47]

At the next meeting of the Zionist Smaller Actions Committee, Ben-Gurion again raised the question of using force and the possibility of revolt:

> We must create a Jewish military force, which will be able to rebel if a need for such action should arise. I am sure that there will be no such a need, but the possibility of rebellion is essential to us....According to the present situation, there is nothing to prevent us from bringing over 50,000 youths to Eretz-Israel this year, if we will only have the necessary money, ships, techniques, and loyalty. This alone, perhaps, can destroy the White Paper.[48]

In July 1939, when the *Colorado* approached the shores of Palestine for the second time, it carried 380 illegal immigrants. Once again Ben-Gurion raised his idea of using force to protect them. He demanded that the ship sail to Tel Aviv and that its passengers be brought ashore with the assistance of armed members of the Haganah. However, this time, according to Ben-Gurion, both the members of the Jewish Agency Executive as well as those of the Mapai Political Committee rejected the idea.[49] As in the past, it was Golomb and Tabenkin who headed the opposition.[50] One should note that Golomb's objection to Ben-Gurion's plan did not relate to the use of force itself,[51] but to the bringing of illegal immigrants to Palestine at the risk of their lives, as if they themselves were combatants. This stand coincided with the views of Tabenkin, Katznelson, and the activists of Aliya Bet. The question was brought to a vote. Ben-Gurion, who was in the minority, threatened to resign, but in the meantime the ship was seized by the authorities. When the *Colorado* was brought to Haifa, Ben-Gurion suggested an alternative: to take control of the port, lower the immigrants from the ship, and then remove them from the port. This proposal was also rejected by the members of the Zionist Executive and of Mapai. Under the circumstances, it became clear to Ben-Gurion that he could no longer count on the support of his party for an extreme approach. Aliya Gimmel was finally set aside.[52]

The intensification of activities for illegal immigration, and the Zionist leadership's recognition of the need for such traffic, hastened the establishment of a special body, the Mossad L'aliya Bet, to coordinate it. Its membership consisted of the same activists who had previously organized it illegal immigration. Until 1939, it was run by left-wing groups and, in particular, by Hakibbutz Hameuchad and Hehalutz. The right-wing parties, such as the General Zionists and Mizrahi, were not partners to this activity. The changes in attitude that took place among the leadership of the Yishuv and the Zionist movement led, in the spring of 1939, to a planned reorganization of the newly established Mossad. The idea was to widen the organizational framework dealing with illegal immigration, in order to involve those who previously had not been engaged. The Jewish Agency Executive sought to intensify its control and supervision over this immigration and hoped to accomplish this by conducting a reorganization of the Mossad, introducing both workers who were loyal to it and efficient work methods.

The importance of this reorganization was that the program of illegal immigration would not be determined by the activists themselves, the majority of whom were members of Hakibbutz Hameuchad and personnel of Hehalutz. Henceforth, this would be the purview of the leadership of the Zionist movement and the Yishuv, based on their conception of the role of illegal immigration in the general struggle against the White Paper.

Ben-Gurion was interested that the Jewish Agency Executive should have the responsibility for and control over the activities of illegal immigration. He also wanted to involve the right-wing parties in this struggle, hoping that they would support his plan. However, they feared Ben-Gurion's assumption of control, in his capacity as head of the Jewish Agency Executive, over the Mossad, as had been the case with the Haganah.[53] The representatives of the right also sought to ensure that those associated with them abroad would be allotted places on the ships.

The reorganization plan aroused opposition among personnel of the Mossad who were concerned about the fragmentation into departments and the bureaucratic confusion that might emerge from this. They were also apprehensive about the recruitment of unsuitable and inexperienced people. Their objections were partly based on party considerations and on the competition that existed between the "Pioneering Left" and the right-wing, as well as the fear on the part of the activists that they would now be removed from key positions and would thus lose control.

There is no doubt that the reorganization would have placed Ben-Gurion, in his capacity as chairman of the Jewish Agency Executive in Jerusalem, in a strategic position regarding the possibility of implementing the plans for Aliya Gimmel.

However, the planned reorganization was never completed because of the opposition of the Mossad personnel, the lack of a budget, and the outbreak of World War II.

The cooperation between the Haganah and the Mossad was greatly strengthened when, in the spring of 1939, Shaul Meirov (Avigur) from the Haganah Command Council, was appointed to head illegal immigration activities. This appointment, made with Ben-Gurion's approval, led to a series of moves that were intended to aid the struggle for the illegal traffic.

On publication of the White Paper, problems arose within the Yishuv regarding the question of whether the Haganah organization, till then intended solely for the protection of settlements against Arab attack, should also serve as a military tool against the White Paper policy. The right wing was against it, whereas the decisive majority of the labor movement accepted the opinion of the Jewish Agency leadership that the Haganah must protect the rights of the people, not in a struggle against the British but only in a campaign against the policy of the White Paper.[54]

On July 3, 1939, the Haganah Command Council, in accordance with directives received from the political leadership, gave official recognition to the importance of illegal immigration.[55] Five days later, a two-month naval course was started within the framework of the Haganah's special detachments.[56] Its main purpose was "to prepare people for accompanying illegal immigrant ships and putting their passengers ashore at coastal settlements.[57]

Sabotage missions connected with the illegal immigration were also carried out in the course of the armed campaign. On the night of June 6, 1939 (still one month prior to the aforementioned directive to the Haganah Command Council) two bombs exploded near the Coastal Police station at Sidna Ali. On July 18, 1939, Ben-Gurion met with the senior commanders of the Haganah (Dov Hoz, Yochanan Ratner, Yaakov Dori and Yisrael Galili) and instructed them to prepare plans for a response in the event that the authorities would attempt to act against the illegal immigrants.[58] Three weeks later authorization was given by the High Command of the Haganah to sink the new ship of the Coastal Police, *Sinbad II*, which was used against the illegal traffic, with the explicit order to avoid loss of life as far as possible. On August 9, 1939, the vessel was indeed sunk, while it lay in ambush in the the vicinity of Netanya.[59] These actions, authorized by Ben-Gurion and the Haganah High Command and carried out by its special units, were intended as a signal to the authorities that the Yishuv was determined to fight for intensifying immigration to Palestine. Installations used by the authorities in their campaign against illegal immigration would be attacked.

It should be stressed that these activities and others do not attest to the acceptance of Ben-Gurion's plan for an "immigration rebellion," since they did not ensue from an *a priori* active cooperation of the illegal immigrants. They were guided by the policy of the commanders of the Haganah and the activists of the Mossad to do nothing that could endanger the lives of the immigrants themselves and perhaps even the very existence of the Haganah. Haganah units went to the assistance of the refugees from the *Parita* on August 21, 1939 and those on the *Tiger Hill* on September 1, and were present on the shore when they arrived. But the main response came from the citizens of Tel Aviv, without any resort to force or arms. These were spontaneous actions on the part of civilians which point to the fact that the psychological foundations for the implementation of the "immigration rebellion" were real and not a figment of Ben-Gurion's imagination.

Ben-Gurion's plans to bring large numbers of immigrants to Palestine openly and by force had no firm basis. The Zionist movement lacked the financial means and the organizational ability to realize such a project. As long as many leaders in Yishuv institutions were hostile to Aliya Bet, the paucity of resources influenced the scope of activity. Until late 1938, funding came almost totally from Hakibbutz Hameuchad and Hehalutz, from payment by the passengers, as well as from contributions of "friends" in various countries.[60] In Czechoslovakia, this immigration was also financed by the *Ha'avara* ("Transfer").[61] When the new policy was adopted, the financial problem should have been solved by the institutions, but this was not the case. Financial support remained a heavy burden on those engaged in the activities themselves. Indeed, there was still dim hope that, despite Ben-Gurion's failure to raise funds in the United States in January 1939, a "suitable appeal in America" would solve the problem.[62]

The Zionist leadership planned a massive fund-raising drive for April-May 1939. The money which would be collected was intended for both day-to-day work as well as for special campaigns (immigration, settlement, the Haganah and probably also Aliya Bet). Weizmann expressed his readiness to travel to North America during the first week of June in order to raise money there, but he was informed that the time was not appropriate for such a mission.[63] Ben-Gurion's approach, on May 24, 1939, to Rabbi Solomon Goldman, head of the Zionist Organization in the United States, to raise 7,000 Palestinian pounds on a weekly basis, to assist the immigration of 50,000 Jews (1,000 per week), elicited no reply.[64]

At a meeting of the Jewish Agency Executive on June 5, 1939, a resolution was adopted to conduct a special appeal in Palestine and abroad, for the purposes of immigration, and to provide £25,000 for Aliya Bet against the proceeds.[65] However, Eliezer Kaplan, Treasurer of the Jewish Agency, opposed the appeal and the idea was dropped.

The gap between the huge number of immigrants Ben-Gurion was talking about at the time and the sum of money which they thought of budgeting for the organization of this immigration shows that Ben-Gurion and, apparently, most of his comrades had not as yet formulated their thoughts regarding Aliya Bet and its dimensions. Without raising substantially larger funds there was no possibility that Ben-Gurion's plan for Aliya Gimmel could be realized.

The 21st Zionist Congress, which opened in Geneva on August 16, 1939, dealt mainly with opposition to the new British White Paper, and the plight of the Jews living under Nazi rule and of Polish Jewry. The deliberations at the Congress were shadowed by an atmosphere of crisis, confusion, and helplessness. This was the first Zionist Congress which discussed illegal immigration publicly. All the representatives from Palestine supported it fully. They were divided only on the desirable course of action to be taken. However, there were representatives from the Diaspora — chiefly from the United States—who totally opposed the concept of illegal immigration.

The World Labor Movement faction convened on August 15, 1939 to formulate a uniform position and a united stand at the Congress. An in-depth discussion which lasted several days revolved around the question of the use of force in illegal immigration.[66] Ben-Gurion opened the deliberations by posing a number of questions:

> With what means should we fight? For whom should we fight? What should be our course when a clash with the government becomes inevitable? What will happen when the authorities will attempt to return some or all of the immigrants?...There are Jews, myself included, who believe that if Jews display vigorous opposition, the White Paper will be annulled....This immigration is a political one.

Moshe Shertok (Sharett) agreed with Ben-Gurion's political analysis and conclusions, but opposed any conflict. He viewed the use of force as a measure to be employed only in special circumstances. Shertok attempted to bridge between the extreme position of Ben-Gurion and that of the moderates, whose chief protagonist was Kaplan. He tried to persuade his listeners of the dangers inherent in Ben-Gurion's proposals, which he feared would incur great expense, leaving the Zionist movement without means or sufficient resources to continue.

Berl Katznelson stressed that he

> attaches importance today to every ship...even from the standpoint of a political demonstration....The preparedness for war that surfaced during the recent period in the example of the Haifa demonstration [April 24, 1939] already brought us a number of important political achievements, for it was due to this that they stopped returning illegal immigrant ships from Eretz-Israel [to Europe].

Like Ben-Gurion, he viewed illegal immigration as part of the political struggle, but at that time he still opposed the deliberate employment of force and favored passive resistance only should the authorities attempt to forcefully block aliya.

Although a variety of opinions found expression in the prolonged deliberations of the labor faction, Aliya Bet was generally agreed upon as a suitable method for combating the White Paper and essential for saving Jews from Europe. Nevertheless, owing to pressure of time, no decision was reached. When Ben-Gurion presented his policy to a meeting of the Policy Committee on August 21, only Menachem Ussishkin gave his full support, while Nahum Goldmann offered a general endorsement. However, Professor Selig Brodetsky, representing British Zionists, echoed the reservations of other participants:

> Perhaps Ben-Gurion forgets that any day now war could break out....I am for a war against the White Paper and for an active war. I accept the principle that we must fight the White Paper with all the means at our disposal. The question is how to implement that war....What can we do right now, and do in such a manner that during the world war, England will never doubt, for a single moment, whether she can count upon the Jews.[67]

Special importance was attached to the words of Rabbi Abba Hillel Silver, chairman of the American section of the World Zionist Organization, in light of the resentment which they aroused in the plenum. Silver explained his opposition to "the Ben-Gurion Plan," which he felt was doomed to failure. He believed that the overwhelming majority of American Jews were not prepared to fight Britain, "the last remaining friend of the Jewish people." If, according to the spirit prevailing within the Congress, it would nonetheless be decided to organize illegal immigration on a vast scale, he sought permission to assure American Jewry that funds raised there would not be earmarked for such activity. In his opinion the Zionist movement did not possess, nor would it possess, the requisite financial means for implementing a program designed to bring forty to fifty thousand Jews to Palestine, thus quashing the White Paper.

In the final account, the 21st Zionist Congress proved a great disappointment. The question of the requisite budget for Aliya Bet was not finalized and the much awaited major impetus was not provided.[68]

* * *

Illegal immigration did not cease during World War II, and was renewed with greater intensity at its conclusion, at which time Ben-Gurion's plan for an "immigration rebellion" was realized. Tens of thousands of refugees attempted to reach Palestine in dozens of ships, occasionally resorting to the use of force. Indeed, the illegal immigration movement constituted a major factor in the political struggle against Britain in the postwar years, much as Ben-Gurion had proposed it would immediately following the publication of the White Paper in 1939.

Notes

1 Minutes of meeting of the Zionist Executive Committee, April 1934, p. 134, Central Zionist Archives, Jerusalem (hereafter C.Z.A.).

2 David Ben-Gurion, *In the Struggle* (Hebrew), vol. 1, Tel Aviv, 1957, p. 26.

3 At the 13th Conference of Mapai Ben-Gurion said: "I was against this [the *Poseidon* affair], I am not ashamed and I have no regrets. I was then opposed to Aliya Bet, because this would have undermined legal aliya" (protocol, 13th Conference of Mapai, April 16, 1939, Labor Party Archives, Beit Berl, Zofit, [hereafter L.P.A.]).

4 Ben-Gurion, *Letters to Paula and the Children* (Hebrew), Tel Aviv, 1968, p. 252; Ben-Gurion to his children, October 7, 1938.

5 Ben-Gurion, *In the Struggle*, vol. 2, pp. 80-90, in particular p. 86,(Ben-Gurion's address to the Va'ad Leumi [National Committee], December 12, 1938). See also M. Basok, ed., *The Book on the Illegal Immigrants* (Hebrew), Jerusalem, 1947, p. 61.

6 Ben-Gurion's diary, entry for December 10, 1938, Ben-Gurion Archive, Sedeh Boker (hereafter B.G.A.).

7 Ibid.

8 Ibid.

9 Ibid.

10 Minutes of meeting of the Jewish Agency Executive, December 11, 1938, C.Z.A. See also Yehuda Bauer, *From Diplomacy to Resistance*, Philadelphia, 1970, pp. 9, 20-22.

11 Minutes of meeting of the Jewish Agency Executive, December 11, 1938, C.Z.A.

12 Ibid.

13 Ibid.

14 Ibid.

15 Meeting of the Va'ad Leumi, December 12, 1938, C.Z.A., J1/7238.

16 Meeting of the Mapai Central Committee, December 15, 1938, L.P.A.

17 Ben-Gurion's diary, entry for January 24, 1939, B.G.A.

18 Moshe Sharett, *A Political Diary* (Hebrew), vol. 2, Tel Aviv, 1971 pp.55-58.

19 Ben-Gurion, *In the Struggle*, vol. 2, p. 90.

20 Regarding Weizmann's response and his great anger, see Meir Avizohar, *Militant Zionism* (Hebrew), Jerusalem, 1985, pp. 31-32 and footnote 52!

21 See for example the statement by Aharon Zisling at the Mapai Central Committee, March 22, 1939. "There is one matter on which everyone agrees, even Smilansky—the matter of immigration....I fear that if this immigration did not exist, they would not have decided upon it now or they would have decided and would have delayed execution. The existence of a fact made this [immigration] an agreed upon subject, at least as a course of action for them." L.P.A.

22 Y. Slutzky, ed., *The History of the Haganah* (Hebrew), vol. 3, Tel Aviv, 1972, part 1, p. 20.

23 Ben-Gurion's comments at the St. James Conference. See Sharett, *Political Diary*, vol. 4, Tel Aviv, 1974, p. 91, and Michael Bar-Zohar, *Ben-Gurion* (Hebrew), vol. 1, Tel Aviv, 1975, p. 400. Cf. also Ben-Gurion's diary, entry for December 10, 1938, B.G.A.

24 See his statement at the 13th Conference of Mapai, April 14, 1939, L.P.A.; see also Berl Katznelson, *Writings* (Hebrew), vol. 9, Tel Aviv, 1945, p. 45; Basok, *The Book on the Illegal Immigrants*, p. 198.

25 Protocols of the 13th Conference of Mapai, April 15, 1939, L.P.A.

26 Ibid., the session of April 16, 1939. He spoke in this vein also at a session of the Jewish Agency Executive on April 30, 1939.

27 Ben-Gurion, Zionist Executive Committee, April 24, 1939, C.Z.A., S25/1823.

28 Y. Braginsky, *A People Makes for the Shore* (Hebrew), Tel Aviv, 1965, p. 217.

29 Ben-Gurion's diary, entry for May 1, 1939, B.G.A. He said similar things at the meeting of the Zionist Smaller Actions Committee, on May 3, 1939, C.Z.A., S25/40.

30 Minutes of the session, C.Z.A., S25/1836.

31 Braginsky, *A People Makes for the Shore*, p. 216.

32 A. Abrahami, "Before the Curtain Falls" (Hebrew), *Lamerchav*, April 15, 1964.

33 See for example a letter from Meirov (who was residing in Paris) to David Nameri (who was responsible for the disembarkations on the shore), May 21, 1939: "None of these wagon [ship] owners will agree *to work by daylight. There is nothing to talk about.* If such a matter was decided, we will have to provide (that is to say, you in Eretz-Israel) all the workers and we will pay for the wagon, should it be lost" (Haganah Archives, David Nameri file).

34 See the testimony of Shaul Avigur (Meirov): "I knew these people with whom we were going to war, the illegal immigrants, and I believe that we cannot place them before too stern a test.... When you have to work with such an element, you have to know what it is capable of and what it is not capable of" (Haganah Archives, 3404/278).

35 Slutzky, *History of the Haganah*, vol. 3, part 1, p. 79. See also ibid., vol. 3, part 3, p. 1617 (footnotes).

36 The decision regarding a general strike was taken at a session of the Executive of the Va'ad Leumi, April 30, 1939, C.Z.A., J1/4027.

37 From a poster of the City Action Committee for the city of Tel Aviv's Day of Emergency, May 18, 1939, C.Z.A., J1/4027.

38. Minutes of meeting of the Jewish Agency Executive, May 21, 1939, C.Z.A.

39 Ben-Gurion's diary, entry for May 24, 1939, B.G.A.

40 David Ben-Gurion, "Lines of Action," C.Z.A., S25/59. Small passages are located in Ben-Gurion's diary, entry for May 24, 1939, B.G.A. Ben-Gurion read out this plan at a meeting of the Mapai Central Committee, which took place on May 28, 1939.

41 Braginsky, *A People Makes for the Shore*, p. 217, A similar version is cited by Bracha Habas, *The Gate Breakers*, New York, 1963, p. 80. Cf. also the *Atrato* file in the Haganah Archives.

42 Testimony of Yisrael Galili, Haganah Archives, 4283; Braginsky, *A People Makes for the Shore*, p. 217.

43 Ibid. It is possible that Ben-Gurion's words at a study day for activists of Hakibbutz Hameuchad on April 19, 1944 refer to this plan and its cancellation or to other similar schemes. Cf. Haganah Archives, Ben-Gurion series, File 277/12, May-June 1944. Cited in Slutzky, *History of the Haganah*, vol. 3, part 3, p. 1617 (footnotes). Galili relates that Ben-Gurion planned "to demonstratively convey a ship to the shores of Tel Aviv and protect with arms those illegal immigrants who would disembark, and the intention was to achieve a political effect." His fellow members in the party committee that was chosen to guide the special operations opposed Ben-Gurion's plan: "We stated that this would be a provocative act; that this would frighten the ship-owners and they would discontinue immigration. The political effect would supplant the real value of the illegal immigration." (Testimony of Yisrael Galili, Haganah Archives, 4283.)

44 Slutzky, *History of the Haganah*, vol. 3, part 1, p. 79. At a meeting of the Mapai Central Committee, on September 12, 1939, Ben-Gurion mentioned the concept of "Aliya Gimmel."

45 David Ben-Gurion, "On the Road to an Army and to the State of Israel: (10), Preparing the Younger Generation for Revolt" (Hebrew), *Davar*, October 4, 1963.

46 Ben-Gurion's diary, entry for June 16, 1939, B.G.A.

47 Ibid., entry for June 20, 1939.

48 Minutes of meeting of the Zionist Smaller Actions Committee, June 26, 1939, C.Z.A., S25/1835.

49 Bar-Zohar, *Ben-Gurion*, vol. 1, p. 400. I did not discover discussions on the subject in the protocols of the Zionist Executive. It is conceivable that even if the matter was brought before the Executive, it was not recorded in the minutes owing to its importance and secrecy. However, it is more plausible to assume that there never was a formal discussion on this issue in the Executive. Ben-Gurion apparently submitted his proposal to a few members of the Executive and it was they who rejected the idea.

50 See above, footnote 43.

51 Minutes of meeting of the Histadrut Executive Committee, Histadrut Archives, Tel Aviv, July 28, 1939 (Golomb).

52 Bar-Zohar, *Ben-Gurion*, vol. 1, p. 400. Ben-Gurion wrote in his diary on August 3, 1939: "Only Eliahu [Golomb] came. In my opinion, he opposes disembarking the immigrants. It is better that the ship should return and take on additional immigrants....I have mandated Yaakov [Dori] to immediately proceed to Haifa and bring a plan for disembarking the immigrants. Meeting of the Executive. Gruenbaum, Kaplan and Moshe [Shertok] oppose my suggestion. Final decision will be taken after we receive Yaakov's suggestion." The entry for the next day reads: "Yaakov brought from Jerusalem the negative response of Moshe and Gruenbaum to my proposal." This may be the meaning behind Shertok's handwritten note of August 4, 1939 in the Haganah Archives, Ben-Gurion file: "...1. An attempt should be make to lower the people. 2. Under no circumstances should the use of arms be permitted by our people. 3. For this reason, our people should go unarmed. 4. One should make all efforts to guarantee success by speed and dispatch. 5. If the opposite side will begin to fire, or will appear in great force, we should get out. 6. In the case of failure, the result can be only part of the people or few of them will succeed in escaping. 7. In the case of total failure, no one will succeed in escaping. In these two cases, the demonstrative value of the protest remains. 8. If it is your opinion or the opinion of our experts that one should not make such an attempt, save if our people are prepared for a bloody clash—then we are against the attempt" (B.G.A., document in chronological order, August 4, 1939). Braginsky, *A People Makes for the Shore*, p. 217, relates that a directive to lower the illegal immigrants on the shore by force was sent to the *Tiger Hill* as well at the end of August 1939, but in this case too the directive was canceled.

53 For more exhaustive details regarding reorganization, see Braginsky, *A People Makes for the Shore*, pp. 218-228; Z. Tzahor, "Mossad L'aliya Bet: The Source of its Authority" (Hebrew), *Cathedra*, no. 39 (1986), pp. 162-178. See also Haganah Archives, Ben-Gurion Series, June 12, 1939.

54 See Slutzky, *History of the Haganah*, vol. 3, part 1, pp. 38-44.

55 Haganah Archives, General Staff Files, July 3, 1939.

56 See Slutzky, *History of the Haganah*, vol. 3, part 1, pp. 42, 69; Bauer, *From Diplomacy to Resistance*, p. 57. The tasks of the special units themselves included, *inter alia,* training for illegal immigration projects, and their personnel took an active part in these operations.

57 Testimony of Aharon Leshevsky, Haganah Archives. See also Slutzky, *History of the Haganah*, vol. 3, part 1, p. 74 and part 3, p. 1616 (footnotes).

58 Ben-Gurion's diary, entry for July 18, 1939, B.G.A.

59 It is possible that this action was planned to thwart the expulsion of the illegal immigrants from the *Colorado*.

60 The pseudonym *yedid* (close friend) was bestowed on Bernard Cohen of London, one of the major contributors to the illegal immigration project, who preferred to remain anonymous. On the problems of finance, see Braginsky, *A People Makes for the Shore,* pp. 57, 108, 129, 134, 140, 167, 219-228.

61 See P. Metz, "The Czech Ha'avara: Salvation in Time of Trouble" (Hebrew), in Felix Volks, ed., *Prague and Jerusalem*, pp. 167, 168, 172, 173. The *Ha'avara* ("Transfer") was an agreement with the Nazi authorities regarding the transfer of the property and merchandise of private individuals who lived in lands under Nazi rule to other countries.

62 Letter from Meirov to Berl Katznelson, April 23, 1939, L.P.A., Carton no. 44, A1 file 7.

63 Sharett, *Political Diary*, vol. 4, p. 305.

64 See Slutzky, *History of the Haganah*, vol. 3, part 1, p. 78 and part 3, p. 1617 (footnotes).

65 Ben-Gurion's diary, entry for June 5, 1939, B.G.A.

66 The information provided below on the August 15-19, 1939 sessions of the World Labor Movement faction in Geneva appears in internal bulletins of the Secretariat of the Executive Committee of Hakibbutz Ha'artzi; the sessions of August 15-16, 1939—in issue 86 (August 23, 1939); the sessions of August 18, 1939—in issue 88 (August 30, 1939); and the sessions of August 19, 1939—in issue 89 (August 31, 1939). The papers are located in the Archives of Hashomer Hatzair, Givat Haviva.

67 Protocol of the Political Committee session at the 21st Zionist Congress. The protocols are not complete. The discussions apparently continued also after August 23, 1939, but that part of the protocol is nonexistent. Most of the participants mentioned in the existing protocol belonged to the moderates. C.Z.A., S25/441.

68 In the general budget that was presented, totaling 720,000 Palestinian pounds, only 150,000 were allocated to immigration and training. This was an especially small sum if we accept the fact that in the open budget it was impossible to include sums earmarked for Aliya Bet. There was apparently no additional "secret" budget.

THE SOURCES OF BEN-GURION'S AMERICAN ORIENTATION, 1938-1941

Allon Gal

The two years from the fall of 1938 to the end of 1940 encompassed a crucial turning point in Zionist history. Britain began pursuing a policy which threatened to destroy the whole Zionist enterprise, while in Europe the situation of the Jews under Nazi rule deteriorated dramatically.[1]

The outbreak of World War II sharpened the challenge to Zionist plans created by the new circumstances. The United States of America, where the largest Jewish community in the free world lived, remained formally neutral for more than two years. Britain's dependence on American military aid in this period created the opportunity, and the dilemma, of using American Jewish pressure as a leverage for fulfilling Zionist aspirations.

Chaim Weizmann, president of the World Zionist Organization, enjoyed tremendous influence in the Jewish and Zionist worlds, while David Ben-Gurion, chairman of the Jewish Agency since 1935, was less well known. The bases of Ben-Gurion's power were the Zionist labor movement and the Jewish community in Palestine (the Yishuv).

However, Ben-Gurion was the established leader of the Yishuv, a community whose weight and significance steadily increased, while Weizmann's World Zionist Organization was fragmented by the Nazi occupation of Europe. Under these circumstances, parallel to the strengthening of the Yishuv, the importance of the American Jewish community increased immensely. Support for Weizmann among American Jewry and its Zionist movement there was neither overwhelming nor self-evident. On the other hand, Ben-Gurion had a genuine American background. His growing prominence was largely the result of the new circumstances. Weizmann's exclusively British-oriented policy could not be effective in this situation,[2] while Ben-Gurion elaborated a political program during 1938-1941 that was responsive to the new developments.[3] Already in the fall of 1938, following the British retreat from the Peel Commission plan, Ben-Gurion started in a new political direction. This was characterized by the recognition of the growing importance of the United States and systematic efforts to influence its policy; an emphasis on the political potential of American Jewry; the belief that this community could realize its potential in a way that would shape American foreign policy; and a tendency to activate Jewish power, as well as sympathetic non-Jewish forces, in a broad democratic, public, and massive way.[4]

Since the outbreak of World War II, and especially after Roosevelt's victory in the elections of fall 1940, Ben-Gurion strove to have the American Zionist movement endorse the goal of Jewish sovereignty in Palestine at the end of the war. In

December 1940, the Po'alei-Zion Party in the United States adopted a resolution in support of the reconstitution of Palestine as a Jewish Commonwealth upon termination of hostilities, and in January 1941 the conference of the United Palestine Appeal adopted a similar motion. Ben-Gurion played a crucial role in both resolutions.

In juxtaposition to other leaders of the Yishuv, Ben-Gurion was distinguished by his direct experience of America and its Jewry. From May 1915 to May 1918, significant years in his personal life and political development, he lived in the United States. As his biographer Shabtai Teveth has noted, Ben-Gurion identified with the American pioneers. The Jews had been expelled from the Land of Israel as they had been expelled from England:

> We, who want to build a new country, amidst desert and desolation, should see how the expelled and persecuted Sons of England established a rich and powerful state, first in the world for its resources and creative powers.

He was attracted to the "busy, energetic ... and vigorous pulse of the modern and materialistic life of that most developed and democratic country."[5] Ben-Gurion married while in America, where he took the first steps toward becoming a leader of the Palestinian Po'alei-Zion movement.

His early years in America were successful and gratifying, and they undoubtedly had an impact on his later development. The growth and accomplishments of the American Jewish Congress, a movement in which Ben-Gurion actively participated, are very relevant. The movement began after World War I with Zionist initiative, demanded the assembling of a democratic Jewish congress in the United States, and eventually represented the American Jewish community at the Peace Conference in Paris (this version of the American Jewish Congress existed until 1920). One can surmise the lessons Ben-Gurion learned from the emergence of the Congress movement and its political achievements, including the power and political effectiveness of mass organization.[6]

When Ben-Gurion was not engaged in political activity and writing, he devoted his time to reading about American democracy and the ways of policy formation there. According to one account, the books he read in the New York Public Library included "history of the American parties, practical guidebooks on the technique of mass mobilization, textbooks for organizational work, etc."[7]

When Ben-Gurion led the Histadrut (General Federation of Jewish Labor), in 1920-1935, he was the architect of its intensive contacts with the Jewish and general labor movement in the United States.[8] He visited America frequently: from November 1930 to January 1931, and every two years from the time when he joined the Jewish Agency Executive in 1933 until the outbreak of World War II.[9] Nevertheless, Ben-Gurion's interest in America remained sporadic until the fall of 1938, when it became meaningful in the formulation of a new foreign policy.

Paradoxically, it was the emphasis on Palestine in Ben-Gurion's Zionism that ensured his openness and flexibility in international affairs. The basis of his power was the Yishuv, and the priority in his Zionist agenda was for the all-embracing advancement of Palestine as the center of Jewish life.[10] He saw the international alignments from a Palestinian vantage point. His flexibility is conspicuous when compared with that of Weizmann, whose personal and political career was based in Britain.[11] But even Ze'ev Jabotinsky, the Revisionist leader who moved to the United States in March 1940 and died there after several months, was confined to a limited international arena. Jabotinsky thought that pressure from Eastern European countries would impose a pro-Zionist solution on Britain.[12]

Ben-Gurion considered the United States to have an especially well-rooted and dynamic democratic tradition. When he spoke in January 1941 before the National Council of the Zionist Organization of America (Z.O.A.), he argued that "the real spirit of American democracy and of Jewish democracy ... are one."[13] He believed that the more sensitive American democracy would be to the plight of minorities, deprived social groups, and small nations, the better were Zionism's chances of gaining support. Also, the more pluralistic American political life was, the more successful Jewish policy could be. At a time when no effective Jewish public pressure had been mobilized, Ben-Gurion recognized that if Irish Americans could support the struggle for the independence in Ireland, then Jews could press for a state for themselves.[14] If America was "loyal to itself," Ben-Gurion believed, it would eventually support the Zionist cause.

In April 1941, Ben-Gurion lectured on "Zionist policy" to a Histadrut seminar, setting out the ideological elements of his foreign policy during the years under discussion:

> There is an *external* precondition for a Zionist policy — democracy. A Zionist policy is inconceivable under dictatorships ... in Russia, Germany and Italy ... Jews ceased to be a factor, and these countries ceased to be an address for Zionist policy.... Wherever you do not have free speech, free thought, free press, free communication, free entrance and free exit — there is no possibility whatsoever for the implementation of Zionist policy.... Zionist policy is based upon the action of the masses — upon Jewish masses and other nations' masses.... Zionism is built upon the fact that part of the world is democratic, that it is possible to act there via public information, that there is room for appeal, that it is possible to argue, to morally lecture and to morally criticize. That is, the moral factor is strong or weak, but it does exist, and the government is dependent on the people ... and must daily respond to questions and justify itself.[15]

Ben-Gurion sought an alliance with a democratic power not only because of the immediate interest which was vital as it was for the whole Zionist enterprise at the time, but also because of his far-reaching social perspective. He tended to assure the building up of the country, especially when the attainment of sovereignty became feasible, with the support of at least one world democratic power. He believed that interaction with nations of highly democratic culture was desirable to ensure the proper development of Jewish society. Consequently, he strongly opposed a struggle without partners, based on military power only, as the I.Z.L. in Palestine advocated. He saw this form of struggle as ineffective in attaining political goals as well as being internally destructive to Jewish society. In another lecture to the Histadrut, Ben-Gurion emphasized his view that "the framework of Zionist policy is not confined to the borders of Eretz-Israel" because the movement appeals to the "whole family of nations of the world.... Zionist policy is founded on the relationship of the Jewish people with the human race, with the community of the peoples of the world."[16]

Ben-Gurion saw an inherent connection between the concept of "Israel—a people that dwells alone" and the phenomenon of Jewish terrorism. His concern with the impact on Palestinian Jewish society of the strenuous effort to attain independence was one reason for his tireless efforts to cultivate a great power as patron, in lieu of Great Britain. He expressed his views on this issue clearly:

> The Jews in the Land of Israel have different options: feebleness, defeatism, submission, servility, servitude to an oppressor. And there is the opposite way: arrogance, emulation of Arab terrorism or the Nazis' systems, abuse and cruel treatment of the weak, domestic and external terrorism, wild hooliganism. These two ways should be dismissed from the Zionist perspective. A nation never dwells alone, even such a powerful nation as the English one, and ten times so a small nation like ourselves. Even when we will have a sovereign state in the borders of the historical Land of Israel, we shall have constant interaction with the world surrounding us, with the Middle Eastern countries, with Europe, and with America, and we should direct our deeds according to this historical balance.[17]

Ben-Gurion saw Zionism as a revolution, a radical alternative to the long exile. The high priority he gave to the interests of the Yishuv was one consequence of this world view, as was the stress on the new, Hebrew culture created there, based on the Bible and on the biblical heritage of the Jewish people. He saw the Jewish labor movement in Palestine and its unique social and democratic accomplishments as instruments to carry on the Zionist revolution.[18] Paradoxically, some facets of American Zionism were parallel and responsive to Ben-Gurion's ideology. Acculturated American Zionism was distinguished by its emphasis on support for practical work in Palestine. It was also noted for its detachment from the *yiddishkeyt* of the European past.[19]

Ben-Gurion could easily relate to this modern Zionism, which was one of the sources of his optimism regarding the political potential of American Zionism. He had a rapport with the main trends of the American movement. The deep personal and political friendship which developed between Ben-Gurion and Louis D. Brandeis illustrates this. Brandeis, who would later become an associate justice of the US Supreme Court, was not very interested in Jewish culture of generations past. He did not aspire to *Gegenwartsarbeit*, (which can be defined as work on behalf of Hebrew culture and Jewish rights in the Diaspora). As a modern American Zionist, he was seriously committed to the American general arena. At the same time, though, he was keenly interested in the practical accomplishments of the Yishuv.[20]

The relationship between Brandeis and Ben-Gurion developed against the background of the economic crisis of the Yishuv in the late 1920s. Brandeis began to support the Yishuv and the Histadrut. He continued to make major contributions to a variety of practical and labor projects, as well as the Haganah. This backing was a central, although not singular, link in the Ben-Gurion/Brandeis connection.[21]

Brandeis was an influential figure in American Zionism until his death in October 1941. His "representatives" in Zionist affairs were Julian Mack and later Robert Szold. Ben-Gurion developed very close working and political relations with Szold.[22]

Szold was not only instrumental in Brandeis' involvement in Palestine affairs but was also a very dynamic leader of the Z.O.A.. Other important American Zionist leaders belonged to what was loosely considered as the "Brandeis camp." Ben-Gurion's contacts were not confined to these circles, however, and they did not always agree over the issues on the agenda. Nevertheless, his ties with the center of American Zionism gave him confidence in his ability to work with and to effectively activate the American community.

The relationship between Ben-Gurion and Abba Hillel Silver, established in 1940-1941,[23] was different from that with Brandeis or Szold. As leader of the United Palestine Appeal, Silver was close to the practical, constructive work in Palestine, and this formed a significant link between the two men. Silver deliberately sharpened Ben-Gurion's understanding of the difference in America between Zionist ideology and support for the Yishuv. As a keen American Zionist, he assured Ben-Gurion, as early as 1939, that the "Eretz-Israel sentiment" of American Jewry was historically on the rise.[24] Silver's views reinforced Ben-Gurion's confidence in the tremendous political potential of the American Jewish community.

Ben-Gurion emphasized the Bible and the biblical era as the most important component in the Jewish past. For American Zionists who lived amidst their Protestant, and somewhat philo-Semitic countrymen, the Bible and its era were important elements of their Judaism and Zionism. The humanistic social laws of the Bible and its prophetic tradition played a central role in the Jewish consciousness and Zionist commitment of a large number of American Zionist personalities. The Bible was a focus where Ben-Gurion's "Hebrew revolution" and the "practical Palestinocentrism" of the acculturated American Zionists synthesized.

Ben-Gurion's conviction in the feasibility of mobilizing American Jewry behind his program was rooted in his belief in the "fluidity" and "malleability" of American Jewry, Zionists included. He reasoned that America was a country of immigrants still undergoing a formative process. His program of "establishing Eretz-Israel as a Jewish Commonwealth" was designed to be sufficiently forthright to galvanize the Jewish masses.[25]

The other dimension to sustain American Judaism and to politicize its Zionism was, according to Ben-Gurion, the social-humanistic one. During his visit in January 1939, he wrote about the weakness of American Jewishness and the vagueness of its Zionism, although he was positively impressed:

> But the young generation, the youth, the intelligentsia in America, are engaged in social-political problems ... and if Zionism does not furnish the youth with a world outlook and a living pattern that would respond to the problems emerging from this specific [American] background and intertwined with Jewish and human compassion, [then] Zionism in America will not be a cultural and educational power possessing brains and hearts.[26]

He believed that the labor movement of the Yishuv, the democracy of the Yishuv, the new social-democratic communities, and the pioneering endeavor, could all inspire and invigorate the American Zionist movement.

Ben-Gurion's relations with his party's parallel organization in America, Po'alei-

Zion, were never partisan. He consistently advised his American comrades to detach themselves from any deep partnership with the American Jewish Congress. Undoubtedly, at the bottom of this position was his fundamental objection to *Gegenwartsarbeit*. During World War II he criticized what seemed to him the unqualified support of the American Jewish Congress for Britain, indirectly reflecting his apprehension of the American Jewish Congress' Diaspora nationalism.[27]

While pressing upon Po'alei-Zion his view to weaken the party's ties with the pro-Zionist American Jewish Congress, Ben-Gurion persistently urged that it should closely cooperate with the non-Zionist Jewish Labor Committee. This strong organization subsequently increased its interest in the welfare of the Yishuv in general and in the progress of the Histadrut in particular.[28]

Ben-Gurion was quite optimistic as to the possibility of cooperating with American non-Zionists. He believed that, given the circumstances, non-Zionism locally was much less ideological and rigid than in Europe:

> American Jewry, as far as I know it, is different from any other Jewish community in the world ... this is a Jewry of transition. American Jewry is amorphous, still far from maturity.... One cannot find here the rigidity of, say, the assimilated Jew in [pre-Hitler] Germany ... and one cannot find here the distorted religious rigidity of Agudat Israel; the same is [true] regarding the anti-Zionists. This is a pliant wax. Here it is relatively easy to shape any form....[29]

Ben-Gurion's understanding of the nature of American Jewry was also reflected in his work in the Zionist arena. He especially cultivated his ties with Hadassah, the Women's Zionist Organization of America, which was the largest and most stable of all Zionist groups in the country. Once again the paradox: the radical leader of the Yishuv trusting the least ideological of all American Zionist groups. The women's movement de-emphasized Zionist ideology and concentrated instead on philanthropic work, supporting medical care in Palestine and later the rescue of Jewish youth from Nazi Germany through Youth Aliyah. During the 1930s and into the early 1940s, a belief in a binational solution to the Palestine problem was common among Hadassah's leadership and members.[30] Although binationalism was anathema to Ben-Gurion, he considered the practicality of Hadassah, as well as its deep humanistic orientation, as valid factors to bring about the politicizing of the organization. He felt that Hadassah played an active role in an otherwise moribund movement:

> When the war broke out the Zionist movement was not ready for this [political] task.... It so happened that even the constructive task of raising funds became mechanical. There is a benevolent fund in each city, and especially after the United [Palestine] Appeal merged with the Joint Appeal, there is a bureaucratic apparatus that takes care of the Appeal's affairs. In most places it is not even necessary to collect money because the fund is there. Indeed, Zionism became almost emptied of any concrete activity. This description does not include one branch, the largest of the Zionist movement—Hadassah, which has a certain enterprise [in Eretz-Israel]. Although at the beginning it was narrow, apparently philanthropic, the concrete interest in its endeavor brought it [Hadassah] closer to Eretz-Israel, especially after it began to deal with the Youth Aliyah matter, an endeavor which by itself imbued

Hadassah with a new Zionist spirit and provided the organization great satisfaction. Therefore Hadassah is, to a large measure, the key to American Zionism. And though it is not a leading force, and it cannot educate the whole movement, it is almost impossible to do anything in the Zionist movement without Hadassah or against it. [In October 1940] it seemed to me ... that the main thing to do was to ... give to the American Zionist movement political consciousness and political instincts, and to provide it with a political program and a statesmanlike course.... I began with Hadassah. I knew that this was the key. The movement is large, and it is very close to events in Eretz-Israel, and the interest in this country's affairs is greater here than in all the other circles....[31]

Ben-Gurion perceived in Hadassah a historic devotion to practical work in Palestine, a deep sense of humanism combined with a practical Zionist endeavor (Youth Aliyah), and an inherent openness to change and development. He developed a strategy for mobilizing the movement behind his political program. He instilled in Hadassah's women even greater pride in their involvement with the Yishuv's welfare and development by emphasizing the democratic and social message of the Zionist enterprise in Palestine, and depicting the establishment of a Jewish Commonwealth as a humanitarian and workable solution for the Jewish disaster.[32]

From the fall of 1940 Ben-Gurion maintained close links with the organization. He played a central role in altering the views on policy within Hadassah, which led to its adoption of a resolution for the reconstitution of Palestine as a Jewish commonwealth at its 27th National Convention (October 29-November 2, 1941) in Pittsburgh, Pennsylvania. This was, after the resolution of the United Palestine Appeal led by Silver in January 1941, the second major breakthrough toward the Biltmore Conference of May 1942.[33]

Neither the orientation of Hadassah's philanthropy nor the non-Zionism of organizations such as the Jewish Labor Committee, curbed Ben-Gurion's optimism regarding the possibilities of changing American Jewry's attitudes vis-à-vis the Yishuv. He militantly advocated his policies not out of despair but due to his belief in the ability of that community to be influenced and to share his perceptions of the political realities in Palestine. During this period and subsequently, Ben-Gurion stubbornly worked for cooperation not just with the Labor Committee but also with other non-Zionist organizations such as B'nai B'rith and the American Jewish Committee.[34] The principles that guided him were similar to those adopted by Hadassah: shelving the whole *Gegenwartsarbeit* issue; presenting statehood as a clear-cut political goal; and emphasizing the kinship of social and humanistic values of the Yishuv with those of American Jewry and the liberal American public.

Ben-Gurion's idiosyncratic Zionist outlook and the differences between him and other Zionist leaders should not be exaggerated. His concept of Zionism as a revolution and his emphasis on the development of the Yishuv were shared with other Labor Zionist leaders. Weizmann shared his willingness to cooperate with non-Zionists. However, the combination of his specific Zionist priorities and his perceptions of American Jewry and of the American political culture attuned him, more than any other Zionist leader of the period, to entrust a crucial political role to American Zionists.

Notes

1 For the background of the retreat and Britain's Palestinian policy, see Michael J. Cohen, *Palestine: Retreat from the Mandate—The Making of British Policy, 1936-45*, London, 1978; Nathaniel Katzburg, *From Partition to White Paper: British Policy in Palestine 1936-40* (Hebrew), Jerusalem, 1974; idem, *The Palestine Problem in British Policy 1940-1945* (Hebrew), Jerusalem, 1977; Yehuda Slutzky, *History of the Haganah* (Hebrew), Tel Aviv, 1972, vol. 3, pt. 1.

2 Isaiah Berlin, *Zionist Politics in Wartime Washington: A Fragment of Personal Reminiscence*, The Yaacov Herzog Memorial Lecture, Jerusalem, October 1972, pp. 25-29.

3 Cf. Yosef Gorny, *Partnership and Conflict: Chaim Weizmann and the Jewish Labor Movement* (Hebrew), Tel Aviv, 1976; Yehuda Bauer, *From Diplomacy to Resistance: A History of Jewish Palestine 1939-1945*, New York, 1973.

4 Allon Gal, *David Ben-Gurion—Preparing for a Jewish State: Political Alignment in Response to the White Paper and the Outbreak of World War II, 1938-1941* (Hebrew), Sedeh Boker Campus, 1985. (English version forthcoming.)

5 Shabtai Teveth, *David's Jealousy: The Life of David Ben-Gurion* (Hebrew), Jerusalem, 1976, vol. 1, chaps. 27-35; quotation from pp. 298-299.

6 Ibid., pp. 353-358.

7 Shlomo Grodzensky, "Thoughts about David Ben-Gurion's Personality" (Hebrew), *Davar* August 27, 1965.

8 Yehuda Erez (ed.), *The Letters of David Ben-Gurion* (Hebrew), Tel Aviv, 1972, 1974, vols. 2, 3; Alexander Manor, *The Way and Endeavor of Israel Merom (Mereminsky)* (Hebrew), Tel Aviv, 1978, chap. 6.

9 The visits until the outbreak of the war were: May-June 1935, September 1937, and January 1939; see Ben-Gurion's diary (Hebrew), Ben-Gurion Archives, Sedeh Boker Campus (hereafter B.G.A.).

10 Shlomo Avineri, *The Making of Modern Zionism: The Intellectual Origins of the Jewish State*, New York, 1981, p. 203.

11 Isaiah Berlin, *Chaim Weizmann*, New York, 1974, pp. 37-50; Leonard Stein, *Weizmann and England*, London, 1964, pp. 6-32.

12 Benjamin Akzin, "Jabotinsky's Foreign Policy," in his *Themes in Law and Statesmanship* (Hebrew), Jerusalem, 1966, pp. 83-105.

13 Ben-Gurion's address, minutes of Z.O.A. National Council, January 5, 1941, Zionist Archives & Library, New York.

14 Minutes, Jewish Agency Executive meeting, March 24, 1940, B.G.A..

15 Ben-Gurion, "Zionist Policy" (Hebrew), Rehovot, April 3-4, 1941, B.G.A..

16 Ibid.

17 Ben-Gurion, "An Address at a Friends' Meeting" (Hebrew), Tel Aviv, September 8, 1939, B.G.A..

18 Avineri, *The Making of Modern Zionism*, pp. 198-216.

19 Yonathan Shapiro, *Leadership of the American Zionist Organization, 1897-1930*, Urbana, Ill., 1971, *passim*.

20 Allon Gal, *Brandeis of Boston*, Cambridge, MA, 1980, *passim*.

21 Gal, *Ben-Gurion*, pp. 15ff.

22 Ibid., pp. 16ff.

23 Ibid., pp. 73ff.

24 Ben-Gurion's diary, entry for January 15, 1939, B.G.A..

25 Ibid., entry for January 22, 1939.

26 Ibid.

27 Interview with Ben Halpern (national secretary of Hechalutz Organization of America, 1936-1937; active in the Labor Zionist Party and contributor to its periodicals from 1937 on; editor for the Institute of Jewish Affairs of the World Jewish Congress 1941-1945; beginning in 1943 managing editor of *The Jewish Frontier*, periodical founded by the League for Labor Palestine, Brookline, MA, October 1986. Gal, *Ben-Gurion*, pp. 111-112.

28 Interview with Halpern, see note 27, above. For background, see Will Herberg, "The Jewish Labor Movement in the United States," *American Jewish Year Book* 53 (Philadelphia, 1952), pp. 3-74.

29 Ben-Gurion's, address at the Zionist Executive, Jerusalem, October 15, 1942, B.G.A..

30 Gal, *Ben-Gurion*, pp. 83ff.

31 Ben-Gurion's address at the Zionist Executive (see note 29 above).

32 See for example Ben-Gurion's remarks at National Board Meeting of Hadassah, November 26, 1940, Hadassah Archives, New York.

33 *Hadassah Newsletter* 22, no. 3 (December 1941-January 1942), esp. pp. 19-21.

34 Ben-Gurion and American Jewish leaders, Files of Minutes of Meetings, 1939-1942, B.G.A..

BEN-GURION AND AMERICAN NON-ZIONISTS, 1941-1942

MENAHEM KAUFMAN

Between November 1941 and October 1942, David Ben-Gurion, motivated in the main by political considerations, carried on intensive negotiations with representatives of American non-Zionists. Anticipating growing American involvement in the political settlement of the Palestine problem, he believed that the Zionist Organization of America (Z.O.A.) and other Zionist organizations could not, by themselves, influence the Administration to adopt a pro-Zionist policy.

Ben-Gurion posited that only under US pressure would Great Britain change the policy embodied in the White Paper of 1939 and acquiesce in the establishment of a Jewish state after World War II. Although the non-Zionist organizations were generally opposed to all shades of Zionist ideology, they supported the creation of a Jewish National Home as a refuge for those Jews who had to flee their countries of distress.

Until the mid-1930s, their support almost invariably took the form of economic and financial aid. Only once, in the aftermath of the 1929 disturbances, did the non-Zionists actually voice opposition to British policy in Palestine. The major non-Zionist groups were the American Jewish Committee (A.J.C.), the Jewish Labor Committee (J.L.C.), B'nai Brith, and organizations of Reform Jewry in America. Ben-Gurion's contacts during this period were chiefly with the A.J.C. and the J.L.C., B'nai Brith leaders watched from the sidelines, while those of the Reform movement took no part in the negotiations.

Contacts with Non-Zionists, 1930-1935

When Ben-Gurion visited the US in December 1930 in his capacity as secretary-general of the Histadrut (General Federation of Jewish Labor), it was only natural that he was almost wholly preoccupied with the Histadrut fund-raising campaign and in contacts with the Zionist socialist parties.[1] When he turned his attention to American Zionism in general, he concluded, like Chaim Arlosoroff before him, that "there is no Zionist movement in America."[2]

The effect of the economic depression on American Zionism caused him great despair. When he met with Joseph Hyman, Felix Warburg's personal secretary, they discussed the negotiations with the British Government, but not the controversies that prevailed within the enlarged Jewish Agency.

Ben-Gurion could not disregard these controversies after he became a member of the Jewish Agency Executive in 1933 and its chairman in 1935. When he visited America again in 1935, he discussed the uppermost political question of the day: whether the Jews of Palestine should participate in the proposed Legislative Council with its assured Arab majority, with Louis Brandeis and Felix Frankfurter, but not Warburg, the leading non-Zionist in the Jewish Agency.[3] At this stage, Brandeis and Frankfurter were opposed to the application of US pressure on Great Britain to adopt a more pro-Zionist policy they. They saw no need for American Zionists to petition the Administration on that score. Brandeis and Ben-Gurion were in agreement concerning the efficacy of the Z.O.A.. Brandeis termed it "useless," while his 1935 visit only strengthened Ben-Gurion's conclusion that "there is no Zionist movement here. [Morris] Rothenberg [President of the Z.O.A.] is no better than a non-Zionist and he has no political value."[4]

At that time, Ben-Gurion believed that the image of American Zionism would be enhanced if the combined fund-raising campaign with the non-Zionist American Jewish Joint Distribution Committee was disbanded and a separate Zionist campaign was conducted. Moreover, he called for union within Zionist ranks, but even his own party — Po'alei Zion — was unwilling to relinquish some of its independence.

His deliberations with non-Zionist leaders Warburg and Maurice Karpf centered round the ratio of non-Zionist to Zionist representation on the Jewish Agency Executive and ignored the burning political issues of the day. The 1929 agreement entitled the non-Zionists to one-half of the Executive. In effect they had only three members compared to ten from the Zionist camp, and were therefore unable to influence leading non-Zionists to join the Executive, a most embarrassing situation. Ben-Gurion demanded a continuation of the status quo which, he believed, fully reflected the meager contribution of the non-Zionists to the Jewish National Home. Warburg and Karpf, for their part, claimed that Ben-Gurion disparaged the important role played by non-Zionists in the enlarged Jewish Agency, threatening to disband it should the balance of power not be rectified.[5] Ben-Gurion was not impressed. When Warburg visited Palestine that year, he made it clear that political matters were outside his field of interest, which was limited to the economic development of the country. He even suggested that major personalities connected with economic affairs be co-opted onto the Executive. He specifically advocated Pinhas Rutenberg and Moshe Smilansky as representatives of manufacturing and the citrus industry respectively.[6]

Ben-Gurion rejected Warburg's proposals and voiced his strong objection to the direct aid tendered by non-Zionists to the victims of the 1929 disturbances, circumventing Jewish Agency channels. Ben-Gurion and Warburg did not deal with political questions, even those discussed by the latter with Berl Locker late in 1934 during the session of the Agency's organizational committee in New York.[7] At that time, Warburg tried to persuade the Zionists to accept the proposed Legislative

Council. Obviously, in 1935 Ben-Gurion did not consider the American non-Zionists an influential factor in the political arena.

Influence of Non-Zionists in the Late 1930s

When the Palestine Royal Commission (Peel Commission) recommended the partition of the country, in 1937 the A.J.C. leadership expressed its vigorous opposition, fearing that the existence of a Jewish state would impair the status of American Jews. British withdrawal of the partition proposal in 1938 put a temporary halt to the controversy over Jewish sovereignty. When the Mandate Government intensified its anti-Zionist policy, in effect closing the gates of Palestine to Jewish immigration, the A.J.C., J.L.C., and B'nai Brith joined other Jewish organizations in a petition to US Secretary of State Cordell Hull.[8] Nothing came of this protest, as Hull informed them that the US had no legal grounds for intervention in this matter.

Ben-Gurion's attitude toward American non-Zionists in general and the A.J.C. in particular was greatly influenced by his assessment of the Z.O.A. as a weak and powerless organization. In the critical last months before the publication of the White Paper of 1939, he characterized Stephen S. Wise as "endowed with good intentions, but naive in political matters."[9] He came to the conclusion that the World Zionist Organization could not leave the initiative for Zionist action in the US solely in the hands of the Z.O.A., but must intervene directly to mobilize American Jewry as a whole, including the non-Zionists, for the cause.

Ben-Gurion's political strategy from mid-1938 until early 1939 was to conduct an "immigration campaign" which might even compel Britain to use force against so-called "illegal immigration." He suggested that when developments reached the proper stage, a Jewish conference could be convened in the United States, with representatives from Jewish communities all over the world, to castigate British action before American public opinion and the American Government, and protest to Great Britain against the retreat from British obligations to the Jewish people. The purpose of this conference would be to express universal Jewish support for the "immigration campaign."[10]

Ben-Gurion decided to go to the United States at the end of December 1938 even though he knew that a Round Table Conference was to be convened by the British within a month (St. James Conference), at which important decisions would be made relating to future British policy in Palestine. He planned to hold negotiations with the A.J.C. as well, even though he realized that the non-Zionist organizations were not representative of American Jewry.[11] What influenced Ben-Gurion was that these organizations were considered to represent American Jewry to no small extent by those governments which might play a decisive role in establishing the future political status of Palestine. Thus, it was important to secure their support.

Two items on Ben-Gurion's US agenda in January 1939 had direct bearing upon relations with the non-Zionists: the future of the enlarged Jewish Agency, and the proposed world conference of Jews.[12]

He soon learned that the enlarged Jewish Agency was no framework for constructive political action and that it was practically useless to negotiate with the non-Zionist members of the Executive. During 1941-1942, Ben-Gurion, on the basis of his earlier experience, held direct talks with representatives of non-Zionist organizations, completely ignoring the existence of the enlarged Jewish Agency. Already in 1939, he realized that A.J.C. cooperation in the matter of a world Jewish conference could be secured only in direct negotiations with its president, Cyrus Adler. It was futile to discuss these matters with Morris Hexter, a non-Zionist member of the Jewish Agency Executive, who completely lacked authority. American Zionists—even Brandeis—had no influence over Adler and other A.J.C. leaders.

Since Ben-Gurion attached so much importance to a world Jewish conference, he asked several Zionist leaders whether it could be convened despite A.J.C. opposition. The negative replies he received from the Z.O.A. leadership convinced him that the A.J.C. was an influential organization within American Jewry despite its small membership. Ben-Gurion noted the Zionist leaders' replies in his diary:

> [Solomon] Goldman's positive reply did not convince me. The others were doubtful. Lipsky and Wise believed that they [the A.J.C.] might not be content to merely prevent the conference but may even take countermeasures. They fear anti-Semitism and seek accommodation with the Arabs.[13]

Ben-Gurion was aware that the A.J.C. leadership was apprehensive of a world Jewish conference. They always claimed that "it is a simple matter to collect a street mob, and much more difficult to disperse it."[14] In this the A.J.C. had been consistent since World War I. On the basis of their disappointing experience in the enlarged Jewish Agency, the non-Zionists planned to condition their membership in the Zionist delegation to the forthcoming St. James Conference. They would attend only if their full participation in the delegation's decision-making process would be ensured, a move intended, perhaps, to prevent the adoption of a radical policy by the Jewish Agency Executive at Ben-Gurion's bidding.

Ben-Gurion remained unconvinced that Adler was fully aware of the deteriorating status of Jews on the European continent and of the danger to the existence of the Jewish National Home in the face of British policy.[15] Since he did not hold great expectations from his meeting with the A.J.C. president, he could write home to his wife that it had a been " a good conversation."[16] Adler repeated the complaints raised since 1929 by Warburg, who died two years earlier, against the Zionist members of the Jewish Agency Executive: that they ran the Agency dictatorially. With self-satisfaction, he told Ben-Gurion of his meeting with President Roosevelt in 1937 at which he, Adler, had praised the achievements of the Jewish Yishuv. He complained that Weizmann had approached Warburg's widow "to muzzle" Judah Magnes. He rejected Ben-Gurion's suggestion that the A.J.C. participate in a conference of world Jewry, the purpose of which was to protest against British policy in Palestine, stating that "he did not want a new World Jewish Congress," an organization the A.J.C. had rejected since its establishment. As a first step, Adler suggested a meeting of the Jewish Agency Executive, in which the non-Zionists would be represented solely by the A.J.C.

Ben-Gurion saw little practical value in such a step and made it clear to Adler that other organizations, such as the J.L.C., B'nai Brith and even Agudat Israel, took an interest in the future of Jewish Palestine. He aspired to a conference attended by representatives of the entire Jewish people. Though he did not entirely abandon the conference plan after his talk with Adler, the unwillingness and inability of American Zionists to implement it without the acquiescence of the A.J.C. soon put an end to his efforts in this matter. In his diary Ben-Gurion confided: "The A.J.C. is timid and the Zionists fear the timid."[17] Realizing that no accommodation would be reached with the non-Zionists by sporadic negotiations, he concluded that only by his own intensive personal involvement could the goal of mobilizing American Jewry for the Zionist cause be achieved, for the American Zionist leaders could not be relied upon.

Zionist Policy in an Atmosphere of Pessimism and Depression, 1939-1941

During the period preceding the bombing of Pearl Harbor in 1941, anti-Semitic groups and individuals, most notably Charles Lindbergh, accused America's Jews of war-mongering. Most contemporary documentation points to a state of paralysis and apprehension that affected the establishment and upper levels of American Jewry, where the majority of the A.J.C. membership came from. Many of them continuously tried to prove their unqualified loyalty to America, sometimes at the expense of their commitment as Jews.[18]

In February 1941, while expending great efforts to transform American Jewry into a frontline ally of the Yishuv in its political struggle, Ben-Gurion described them as "five million Jews who believed that Hitler must be destroyed but were afraid to say so openly."[19] In April 1940, Ze'ev Jabotinsky wrote: "I have never seen American Jewry so scared of local anti-Semitism as they are now that the danger is really tangible and widespread."[20] Simultaneously, Moshe Shertok (Sharett) characterized the Z.O.A. as "deteriorating, rotten from within, plagued by personal and sectarian rivalries."[21] He doubted whether American Jewry would find the courage to stand up and act in the interests of Zionism. Upon his return from the US at the end of March 1940, Eliyahu Golomb doubted whether an active political ally of the Yishuv could be forged out of American Jewry under present conditions.[22]

The fall of France in 1940 completely undermined what little self-confidence still existed among American Jewry. Salo W. Baron, doyen of American Jewish historians, wrote: "Jews in this country have worked themselves into a state of panic verging on catastrophic despair."[23] Jewish Agency Treasurer Eliezer Kaplan, who was in the US when France capitulated, reported back to his party in a similar vein: "Jews in America are in a state of panic concerning their future here and even more so in relation to the condition of Jews the world over...."[24] From the deliberations of the Zionist Emergency Council, Kaplan understood that under present conditions American Jews would refrain from adopting any policy dictated by strictly Jewish interests. More than ever, they wanted to appear as "Americans First." Against this background, he foresaw growing anti-Zionist sentiment.[25] The treasurer of the

Jewish Agency, who failed to negotiate a loan for the Yishuv, went on to report that some persons were suggesting an end to all separate Jewish fundraising campaigns and that all donations be turned over to the Administration as evidence of American Jewish loyalty. To the anti-Zionists, Kaplan went on, the United Jewish Appeal was an "illicit marriage" with the Zionists.

The elderly Brandeis believed that American Zionism must prepare for Zionist action even without Palestine. He asked Kaplan to cease intervening in the internal affairs of the American Zionist movement, agreeing with him that hereafter the Jews of Palestine must be self-sufficient.

Ben-Gurion was not caught up in the general atmosphere of dejection and paralyzing pessimism concerning American Jewry's potential role, not even during the summer of 1940. On every occasion during 1940-1941, he expressed his firm belief that the Zionist movement must extend its guidance to all of American Jewry and help it overcome its present crisis.[26] He believed that a movement which simultaneously courageously opposed the British White Paper policy in Palestine and actively participated in the military effort against Nazi Germany, would have a positive effect on American Jewry's self-confidence.

During the period which followed the publication of the White Paper in 1939, Ben-Gurion, Chaim Weizmann and other Zionist leaders who visited the United States made repeated efforts to achieve a united front with all sectors of American Jewry, including the non-Zionists in the Jewish Agency. But relations within the Agency deteriorated in 1940 as a result of a rumor that additional Zionists were to be co-opted to the Executive.[27] In fact, contacts between Zionist and non-Zionist members of the Agency Executive had been severed. The non-Zionist members did not participate in the Zionist protest against the Mandatory law restricting the sale of land to Jews in Palestine. They hinted that if they had no place on the Zionist Emergency Council, they should not be expected to be actively involved in Zionist affairs.[28] Nevertheless, the A.J.C. wished to avoid a final split with the Zionists and was careful not to join ranks with the anti-Zionists, lest such an act estrange it from American Jewry.[29]

When he was in the US between October 1940 and January 1941, Ben-Gurion was guided by the premise that he enunciated before the Zionist Executive in Jerusalem upon his return: "There is no Jewish leadership in America, neither among the Zionists nor among the non-Zionists. Among the non-Zionists there is no potential of capable leaders."[30] During this visit, he tried to exert direct influence on the Zionist rank and file, for he could not envisage the movements' leaders in the fore of a militant struggle to achieve Zionist objectives. He did not even bother meeting with members of the A.J.C., sensing that after the death of Adler the organization was devoid of leaders possessing personal authority or sufficiently committed to the idea of a Jewish National Home to ensure fruitful negotiations.

Ben-Gurion arrived in the US on October 3, 1940. The establishment of a Jewish Commonwealth was a central demand in his overall policy by that time. On October 8 he met with Rabbi Abba Hillel Silver, destined in 1943 to assume leadership of the American Zionist movement which was to conduct a militant campaign for a Jewish state. He wrote in his diary: "From him I received a completely different picture of the state of the Zionist movement in America."[31] Wise, Louis Lipsky and the majority of the Zionist leadership, on the other hand, were opposed to any public protest against Great Britain even after it began implementing the policy which derived from the White Paper by deporting to the island of Mauritius Jewish illegal immigrants to Palestine.

A Zionist delegation comprised of Wise, Goldmann, and David de Sola Pool was despatched to Washington in November 1940. They consulted with Brandeis to determine whether they should present a memorandum to the British Ambassador and make their protest public. Brandeis, Felix Frankfurter, and presidential adviser Ben Cohen were opposed to the entire plan which, they believed, would embarrass the Roosevelt Administration and hamper its policy of extending aid to the British war effort. In the end, the delegation compromised. They presented the memorandum without any publicity. After the SS *Patria* sank in Haifa harbor with great loss of life amongst the refugees (and their guards), Brandeis believed that any protest action would be superfluous, but deportations were soon resumed as more refugees reached Haifa. The Zionist Emergency Council, reluctant to decide on a policy of public protest, convened the heads of all Zionist parties in the US. It took considerable pressure on Ben-Gurion's part to induce them to pass a resolution calling for a public statement denouncing the deportations.

At an annual meeting of Histadrut supporters, he appealed directly to the non-Zionist Jewish public at large as he openly protested against the cruel implementation of the White Paper policy on immigration. At a time when even the American Zionist establishment had reservations about militant action against British policy, Ben-Gurion could not have been expected to enter into detailed negotiations with A.J.C. leaders and the J.L.C. concerning the establishment of an independent Jewish state, a demand to which these leaders were traditionally opposed. Therefore, during this sojourn in the US, Ben-Gurion was content to meet with only a few non-Zionist personalities in order to explore future possibilities. Upon his return to Jerusalem, he reported to the Zionist Executive on February 16, 1941: "I decided that my objective should not be to convert non-Zionists to Zionism but to instill Zionism into the Zionists."[32]

When relations with A.J.C. members of the expanded Jewish Agency reached an almost complete rupture, the Zionist Executive made efforts to persuade other non-Zionist bodies, including B'nai Brith, the J.L.C., and various welfare organizations, to join the Agency. It is not clear whether the Zionists already considered these organizations as alternatives to the A.J.C. or as additional groups which might serve as a moderating force between the two eternally quarrelling partners.

When Weizmann returned to the United States in 1941, he made an additional effort to reach a working agreement with the non-Zionists.[33] On May 25, 1941, he invited a large number of Jewish community leaders to a meeting in New York. Not all those invited came. Among those who absented themselves were A.J.C. members Sol Stroock (president of the A.J.C. after Adler's death), his son Alan, Judge Horace Stern, James Marshall (son of Louis Marshall), and Sam Rosenman.

Leaders of other major American Jewish organizations were present at the meeting at which Weizmann stated:

> When the Jewish problem is brought before the great tribunal which will sit and carve out the new world ... only a powerful American Jewry would be able to make its influence felt in that situation.

In an attempt to disarm his audience, especially the members of the A.J.C., many of whom were wary of contributing to the establishment of a Jewish state, he added:

> That does not mean we shall have an army or run our foreign affairs. That I should leave to a "Shabbes Goy." Who will do it I do not know. It is not my business. Our business is to see that the fundamental work [immigration and settlement policy] is left to us. It cannot be left to a colonial administration.[34]

It can quite safely be assumed that Ben-Gurion would not have endorsed such a position in May 1941.

Weizmann urged the renewal of the enlarged Jewish Agency, with its non-Zionist sector to be based largely on organizations which had not previously participated in it, such as the J.L.C., B'nai Brith, and the Reform movement's Central Conference of American Rabbis. The A.J.C. was not mentioned. Henry Monsky of B'nai Brith made an attempt to implement Weizmann's suggestions, but encountered great opposition from A.J.C. supporters.[35] As a result, Weizmann's attempt failed. He concluded, somewhat bitterly, that the non-Zionists were "an amorphous mass both organizationally, intellectually, and politically."[36]

In that same month, May 1941, Ben-Gurion decided to embark on a lengthy personal mission to the United States. His main objective was to effect a change in the attitudes of Zionists and non-Zionists alike and thus transform American Jewry into an active militant ally of the Zionist movement both during and after the war. For this purpose, he spent almost a year in the US, from November 1941 to October 1942. Having learned the lesson of his failure to convene a world Jewish conference in 1939 without the agreement and support of the non-Zionists and of Weizmann's lack of success with the New York meeting, Ben-Gurion set himself the task of reaching a *modus operandi* with the non-Zionists, especially the A.J.C. and the J.L.C., by which they could support the pragmatic demands of the Zionist movement without relinquishing their ideological reservations.

On October 15, 1941, a few days before he sailed for America from England, Ben-Gurion outlined his policy in great detail.[37] He considered the establishment of Jewish military units to be the most pressing problem of the day, an objective that he believed the Zionist movement was capable of attaining. It would be a mistake to concentrate solely on the demand for a future state, for at best this could only be achieved after the war. He emphasized that a Jewish state was a means of securing the achievements of Zionism, and not an end in itself.

Ben-Gurion assumed that presenting the Jewish Commonwealth as a means for the solution of the Jewish refugee problem would enable non-Zionists to endorse it despite their reservations about Zionist ideology. This is how this tactic would apply to the United States:

> We must show them that only a large-scale territorial settlement in Palestine, by mass-immigration and colonization, making the Jewish people independent and free, the equal of all other nations, can provide a true solution. We must prove that this territorial settlement can be achieved in Palestine, and in Palestine alone. This means the establishment of Palestine as a Jewish Commonwealth immediately after the war.[38]

Unsuccessful Negotiations

Ben-Gurion arrived in the United States on November 24, 1941. Three days later he held his first discussions with the non-Zionists.[39] The key non-Zionist partner to these talks was the A.J.C., led by Maurice Wertheim, its president since Stroock's death. The Zionists tried to enlarge the scope of the discussions by approaching other non-Zionist groups. Wertheim was more sympathetic to the goals of Zionism than other members of his organization. He was supported by Morris Waldman, executive secretary of the A.J.C., who believed that the attitude of the anti-Zionists within his organization stemmed from ignorance of Palestinian affairs.[40] The November 27 meeting was attended by the A.J.C., J.L.C., and B'nai Brith. The Zionist delegation was headed by Ben-Gurion.

Waldman said that despite his inclination to cooperate with the Zionists, he did not believe in the existence of a separate Jewish nation, different from other nations only because it lacked an independent state. He held that this sort of ethnic politics, which suggested that all Jews belong to a Jewish nation whose goal is the creation of an independent state in Palestine, was a misreading of reality. In 1934 the A.J.C. opposed the establishment of the Zionist-inclined World Jewish Congress (W.J.C.) as the expression of a universal Jewish nationalism that was to be rejected, because it attacked the goals and values of emancipation. According to Waldman, the W.J.C. was a danger because it institutionalized Jewish nationalism and created a dual loyalty problem, especially for the Jews of America where religious and cultural pluralism are tolerated, but allegiance to another political entity is not. Waldman could see the possibility of cooperation between Zionists and non-Zionist in practical matters, on condition that Jewish Palestine not interfere in the life of Diaspora Jewry.

While the Jews of Eastern Europe, who had not succeeded in integrating themselves into their societies, could legitimately be considered potential immigrants to Palestine, this was not the case with regard to the Jews of North and South America, where social assimilation had succeeded or was in progress. Jewish nationalistic propaganda might well undermine the position of these Jews.

The thrust of Waldman's statement to the Zionists was that they might seek moral and financial support in America for the development of Palestine, but must not interfere with Jewish life and organization in the Diaspora. If the Zionists wished to work together with them, they must break with the American Jewish Congress and World Jewish Congress and forbid all attempts to develop any form of Jewish nationalism in the United States.

Ben-Gurion believed in the negation of the Diaspora but was reluctant to be dragged into a debate on worldwide Jewish nationalism. However, if he was to achieve a working partnership with the non-Zionists, he would find himself forced to deal with Waldman's arguments. Ben-Gurion was asked to clarify the nature of the proposed Jewish Commonwealth. Was it to be a racial entity where all inhabitants enjoy equal rights? Could an Arab be elected president? Would there be separation between Church and State? Would Arab and other non-Jewish immigration be permitted? The non-Zionists also wished to know whether the Zionists would insist on the centrality of Palestine for world Jewry after the founding of the Commonwealth and whether the Zionist movement would then dissolve or continue in existence. They were also interested in the status of the Holy Places and whether the diplomatic representatives of the Jewish state would presume to speak on behalf of Jews living elsewhere.

Ben-Gurion feared the reaction of the W.J.C. to Waldman's demands. He therefore attempted to steer the discussion away from specifics. He was convinced that Waldman's idea of creating an ideological platform that could be agreed upon by all American Jews was an exercise in futility. All that could be achieved, he felt, was a formula for unity of action.[41]

There was, however, a semantic problem that Ben-Gurion could not avoid. In American parlance, the word *nation* implied a political state, nationality, and citizenship. Thus the term *Jewish nationality* was liable to create the mistaken impression that citizenship in the Jewish state would be conferred on all the Jews in the Diaspora. The Zionists had no such ambition. Ben-Gurion merely wished for political support from the non-Zionists.

The representatives of the J.L.C. asked Ben-Gurion and Nahum Goldmann, who was also present, how the Jews could create a state in Palestine when the Arabs constituted a majority of the population, why there were no Arabs in the Histadrut, and how Palestinian Jewish socialists could oppose the employment of Arab labor in Jewish enterprises. Ben-Gurion replied, as one socialist to another, that he favored the abolition of all states. If, however, states were to be dissolved, why not start with Russia, England, or the United States? Why should the process have to begin with the Jews? He ignored the other questions.

After this session, the representatives of the A.J.C. felt that matters had gotten somewhat out of hand and hastened to apologize to Ben-Gurion. Both Wertheim and Waldman emphasized that they did not wish to abandon efforts to arrive at an understanding.

However, Wertheim also had to cope with a small but vocal anti-Zionist group within the A.J.C. Judge Joseph Proskauer and several supporters were opposed to cooperation with the Zionists in any form.[42] Proskauer held that the Zionist concept of a Jewish Commonwealth in Palestine constituted a tragedy for the Jews, and threatened to split the A.J.C. in defense of his position.[43]

B'nai Brith representatives at the meeting on November 27, 1941 took no part in the controversy between the Zionists and the non-Zionist A.J.C. and J.L.C. The election of Herbert Monsky, who held pro-Zionist sentiments, in 1938 to head B'nai

Brith signaled a more pro-Zionist orientation. B'nai Brith as such remained neutral between the Zionists and their opponents, but Monsky and his executive extended much support to the Zionists in their efforts to induce American Jewry to join in the struggle for the establishment of a Jewish state. As early as 1940, he pledged the support of B'nai Brith's 100,000 members for the United Palestine Appeal.[44] He played an important role in the organization and convening of the American Jewish Conference in September 1943, which pledged the support of American Jewry for the Biltmore Program that called for the establishment of a Jewish state in Palestine.

Ben-Gurion's strategy during November—December 1941 was to prevent the A.J.C. from becoming the sole non-Zionist spokesman and partner in Zionist—non-Zionist cooperation. As a labor leader, he was especially interested in the J.L.C., the non-Zionist Jewish labor organization. His attempts in this direction were not made easier by the Zionist labor movement Po'alei-Zion to whose leader, Hayyim Greenberg, he proposed that the party rejoin the J.L.C. to counter the influence in that organization.[45] Ben-Gurion felt that since the J.L.C. was considered the representative of Jewish labor in America by both the British Labour Party and the American government, it was incumbent on the Zionists to increase their influence in that organization in an effort to enlist its support of the Jewish Commonwealth. Since American Po'alei-Zion's affiliation with the American Jewish Congress prevented it from rejoining the J.L.C., Ben-Gurion also discussed this matter with Wise, the Congress president.[46] Both Greenberg and Wise promised to give serious consideration to his arguments, but discussion within the Po'alei-Zion Party leadership failed to effect a change in its policy. David Dubinsky, one of the J.L.C. leaders, told Ben-Gurion that he "failed to understand why, if they consider themselves to be a labor party, they joined the Jewish Congress and left the Labor Committee." Ben-Gurion found himself explaining to Dubinsky "that I myself disagree with my friends here on many things...."[47] Po'alei-Zion's refusal to rejoin the J.L.C. seriously hampered Ben-Gurion's negotiations with that organization.

J.L.C. leaders did not oppose the opening of Palestine to Jewish immigration, rather they refused to accept Ben-Gurion's program for the creation of a Jewish state or even for the formation of a Jewish army fighting under its own flag. They supported the Histadrut but opposed Jewish nationalist demands which, they felt, might endanger the position of the Jews in America. The refusal of the J.L.C. to cooperate with the Zionists, despite the support most of its members were prepared to give Jewish labor in Palestine, stemmed from internal considerations. The J.L.C. had a number of vehement anti-Zionists in its ranks, notably the Bundists.[48]

At the end of 1941, Ben-Gurion appeared before a meeting of the J.L.C. He urged that the committee develop stronger ties with Jewish labor groups in Palestine than with similar groups in other countries. This was countered on the grounds that after Hitler's defeat the Jewish labor movement in Europe would require support.[49] The J.L.C. was also unwilling to support the Jewish Agency's demand to be given responsibility for Jewish immigration to Palestine. Ben-Gurion had reached an impasse in his efforts to draw the leaders of the American Jewish labor movement into his camp. He reported to the Jewish Agency Executive in October 1942: "The

Bundists have come [to America] with a passionate hatred of Zionism. Their socialism has almost completely disappeared but their anti-Zionism has remained intact."[50]

Disturbed as he was by his lack of progress in his negotiations with J.L.C. leaders, Ben-Gurion may have overestimated their influence within American Jewry. When he had resided in the US during World War I, the Jewish labor movement represented "the masses," but extensive changes in the social stratification of American Jewish society had taken place since then. Adolph Held, Dubinsky, and their colleagues were still trade union leaders, but most of the rank-and-file membership of the unions were no longer Jewish. Since the J.L.C. did not accept Ben-Gurion's political objectives, he now concentrated on negotiations with Wertheim and his colleagues of the A.J.C., though contacts with the J.L.C. were not severed.[51]

Ben-Gurion told leaders of the A.J.C. that there was no significant differentiation between American Zionists and non-Zionists. Everyone could adhere to the idea of a Jewish state for those who would emigrate to Palestine. To allay A.J.C. fear of "the dangers of dual loyalty," he added: "Those remaining in their home countries, and not only here [in the US], must be ensured equal rights, and we shall lend them our support."[52] Ben-Gurion presented Wertheim with a draft agreement for cooperation between Zionists and non-Zionists, which Wertheim promised to discuss with the members of his Executive.

At the same time that the Zionists were attempting to enlist non-Zionist allies to their cause, the anti-Zionists were also trying to gain adherents. Arthur Hays Sulzberger, publisher of the *New York Times*, invited a group to his home on the evening of December 16, 1941. Among the thirteen guests were Wertheim, who had met with Ben-Gurion that afternoon, US Ambassador Lawrence Steinhardt, Samuel Rosenman, James Becker and Rabbi Morris Lazaron who had initiated the gathering and warned against the dangerous concept of a "worldwide Jewish nation, ... which Weizmann had broached in London."[53] Lazaron suggested that one hundred prominent American Jews sign an anti-Zionist declaration, but met with opposition by several of those present.

At a further gathering of non-Zionists a week later, it was moved that negotiations with the Zionists cease immediately in order not to give a seal of approval to the concept of worldwide Jewish nationalism.[54] However, Wertheim and Waldman prevailed at that meeting and negotiations with the Zionists continued. Even Held, the sole member of the J.L.C. present, personally agreed to continue the talks. The consensus was that while no group could claim to speak for all the Jews of the world, there were indeed common Jewish interests for the postwar period. Held emphasized the interest of the J.L.C. in the fate of the Jewish community of Palestine. Unlike his colleagues from the A.J.C., he himself did not fear Zionist nationalist domination of American Jews who would always consider themselves to be American citizens first, and would never give priority to foreign Jewish interest. He suggested that a formula be found for Jewish demands at the future peace conference, which would not force the Zionists to forego their political program.

At the close of the meeting, Wertheim was authorized to continue private discussions with Ben-Gurion, with the opponents of these talks reserving the right to demand them to cease. The meetings between Ben-Gurion and Wertheim had created an atmosphere of trust and understanding between the two. Of course, understanding and agreement were two entirely different things.[55]

Ben-Gurion attempted to reach agreement with the A.J.C., with the consent of all the parties represented on the Zionist Emergency Committee. This required a statement of the central Zionist demands, as well as recognition of non-Zionist dissent, especially regarding Diaspora nationalism and the influence of the proposed Jewish Commonwealth on Diaspora Jewry. The Zionist statement on this issue reads:

> The establishment of such a Commonwealth shall in no way be deemed to affect the political allegiance, status or position of Jews living in other countries. Only the inhabitants of Palestine, present and future, shall be considered nationals of the Jewish Commonwealth.[56]

The Zionist program also included a declaration of loyalty to the United States, urged maximum participation in the Allied war effort, and emphasized the belief that, after the war, it would be necessary to solve the problems of the Jews in their countries of residence. These included equal rights for Jews in all countries, communal rights in those countries in which minority rights were given to other nationalities, economic reconstruction of Jewish communities, and a continued campaign against anti-Semitism.

The Jewish Agency program included the establishment of a Jewish army in Palestine, abrogation of the 1939 White Paper, and aid for Jewish immigration to Palestine. In the agreement drafted by Ben-Gurion, the main political demand was the establishment of a Jewish Commonwealth and Jewish control over immigration.

Even at that point, Ben-Gurion suspected that nothing would result from the talks with the A.J.C. In a letter to Locker, the Jewish Agency representative in London, dated January 4, 1942, he wrote that the A.J.C. leaders were men "self-elected and representing only themselves," and were not spokesmen for the "masses" of non-Zionist Jews in America. After the death of men like Jacob Schiff, Warburg and Marshall, "there is no outstanding, or even influential, personality among them." However, he concluded in the same letter: "If at the next meeting, however, we succeed in having our proposals accepted, it will undoubtedly be an important step toward uniting American Jewry."[57]

Ben-Gurion negotiated with the non-Zionists while remaining in constant contact with the Zionist Emergency Committee on matters relating to American Zionism.[58] The Zionist Emergency Committee reviewed Ben-Gurion's draft agreement and made some minor changes. These included a demand for the creation of a Jewish army, supporting "the effort of the Jewish community of Palestine to serve as an ally with the United Nations through a separate Jewish military force."[59] This was in contrast to Ben-Gurion's original proposal that the Yishuv "participate as a military ally of England in this war with the same status as Czechs, Poles, and other allies of England."[60]

In a meeting between the Zionists and non-Zionists on January 7, 1942, it seemed that agreement was finally reached. Meyer Weisgal kept Weizmann, then in London, abreast of the progress of the talks.[61] A subcommittee, chaired by Wise and Wertheim, was appointed to iron out the remaining details. There were no disagreements on the demands for securing the future of European Jewry, and agreement on the issue of the Jewish Commonwealth seemed well within reach.[62]

At the next non-Zionist strategy session on January 19, Wertheim reviewed his efforts to reach an agreement with the Zionists which would be acceptable to the majority of members of the A.J.C.[63] In his opinion, the Zionists had to withdraw their demands for the establishment of a Jewish state, and for Jewish settlement rights in *all* parts of Palestine. They would also have to agree to refrain from arousing Jewish nationalist feelings outside Palestine. In return for these concessions, the A.J.C. would support Jewish settlement in Palestine and the establishment of the commonwealth. Held, of the J.L.C., whose hands were tied by the precarious consensus of his organization, argued as an individual that he did not think it proper to force the Zionists to concede their main position. He proposed rather to steer the debate away from ideology and concentrate on practical Jewish demands for the postwar era.

Despite pressures from within the A.J.C., Wertheim did not reject the Commonwealth proposal outright. He assumed that Ben-Gurion would eventually agree to establish a Jewish Commonwealth in *part* of Palestine and accede to the demand to stop W.J.C. activity in the United States. In fact, when Wertheim had to announced his candidacy for the chairmanship of the A.J.C., which he had held on a temporary basis following Stroock's death, he sought Ben-Gurion's advice and generally seems to have placed a great deal of trust in his views.[64] In a secret meeting, Ben-Gurion stated that the World Zionist Organization could neither alter the Basle program nor change the names of organizations in which the word "national" appeared. Obviously not he was authorized to propose changes in the W.J.C.'s position. In a report to the Jewish Agency Executive, Ben-Gurion summarized his conversation with Wertheim:

> He said that he wanted not only to achieve unity, but to dedicate his life to achieving a Jewish Commonwealth. After I had heard what he had to say, he wants me to tell him whether I think complete unity is possible. If I think so, he will run for the chairmanship and work for a Jewish Commonwealth.[65]

Wertheim was elected president of the A.J.C., though he lacked the support of powerful men like Proskauer and Rosenman. The fact that his support was less than unanimous forced him to approach the Zionists with caution. In his inaugural speech, he emphasized the traditional positions of the Committee and stated "our fundamental point of view" that the Jews of the United States are "Americans of the Jewish faith of American nationality and we can never permit anything that threatens to affect this status."[66] Wertheim's address indicated that his power to force the A.J.C. to accept an agreement with the Zionists was limited.

Ben-Gurion, who more than once expressed the opinion that the men and groups with whom he was negotiating did not represent American Jewry,[67] nonetheless expended great efforts to enter into negotiations with them. He recognized that, because of the personal wealth of its members, the A.J.C. enjoyed considerable political influence in the United States,[68] and he assumed that an agreement between the Zionists and the A.J.C. would likely be interpreted in government circles as the support of American Jewry as a whole for the Zionist political program. This would make it easier for the Zionists to gain the support of the President, Congress, the press, Church leaders, American labor leaders, and the liberal intelligentsia. At this point, Ben-Gurion saw no other way to organize the American Jewish public.

In addition to Ben-Gurion's intensive negotiations with the A.J.C. and his somewhat less vigorous efforts with the J.L.C., he established contact with other non-Zionist forces. He paid no attention to rabbinical, synagogue, and welfare organizations which, in 1942, the Zionists did not view as important factors in the non-Zionist camp. Although he did not overestimate the political importance of groups like B'nai Brith relative to the A.J.C., he nonetheless met with Monsky and his B'nai Brith colleagues: "They said to me: 'If unity is achieved, we will be part of it, and if there will be a fight, we will side with you'... This gave me great encouragement."[69] Ben-Gurion did not foresee that the Jewish Commonwealth concept would be the stumbling block in the way of gaining an agreement with the non-Zionists.[70] He and the leaders of the Zionist Emergency Committee could not imagine that there was any major contradiction between their preparations for the Biltmore Conference and the process of their talks with the A.J.C.

Progress in the negotiations between the Zionists and Wertheim's group in the spring and summer of 1942 was very slow. The optimism felt by some of the Zionists and their hope that, for the sake of Jewish unity, Wertheim would be willing to risk a split in the A.J.C., were baseless.[71]

A draft agreement which Wertheim presented to Ben-Gurion in April 1942, spoke of a willingness to help those Jews who wished to live in Palestine in the establishment of an entity secured by Public Law. This draft was quite similar in tone to the Basle Program, but given the realities of 1942, it was unacceptable to the Zionists.[72] Ben Gurion also rejected a non-Zionist proposal formulated by Waldman which stated that Jewish nationalism outside of Palestine reveals only a common religious and cultural heritage, which is different from the political nationalism that unites the citizens of a nation-state. Ben-Gurion countered by proposing that discussions be limited to attempts to reach agreement on a common course of action to guarantee: (1) large-scale immigration and settlement under Jewish auspices, for Jews who desire to live in Palestine; (2) colonization of Palestine by Jewish agricultural and industrial settlers; (3) re-establishment of Palestine as a Jewish Commonwealth under democratic processes, or alternatively, placing Palestine under such political, administrative and economic conditions as would secure the establishment, under democratic processes, of a self-governing Jewish Palestine.[73]

The Biltmore Conference passed an eight-point political program which included the demand to turn Palestine into a Jewish Commonwealth.[74] The Zionist Emergency Committee approved Ben-Gurion's proposal to inform Wertheim in writing that the decisions of the Biltmore Conference constituted the Zionist program.[75] The Committee also agreed not to consider the A.J.C. demand concerning Diaspora nationalism, which was interpreted as an attempt to destroy the W.J.C. or at least to make it cease its operations in the United States.[76]

On May 25, after the Biltmore Conference, Wertheim brought a new draft agreement to Weisgal, secretary of the negotiating committee. It spoke of aid "in establishing in Palestine for such Jews as choose to go and remain there, a legally secured home where, by unrestricted immigration and unrestricted purchase of land, they may expect ultimately to constitute a majority of the population and may look forward to home rule."[77] Beyond that, Wertheim proposed immediate aid in securing the rights of the Jews of Palestine under the Mandate.[78] Weizmann, then in the US, tended to accept this version but Ben-Gurion, who headed the negotiating committee for six months, influenced it to reject the Wertheim draft.[79]

On May 29, the Zionists and non-Zionists again met to discuss the Palestine problem. The former were represented by Ben-Gurion, Weizmann, Wise, Lipsky, Weisgal, and Louis Levinthal. Attending the meeting on the non-Zionist side were Wertheim, George Medalie, Sidney Wallach, and Held.[80] In order to avoid the question of a Jewish state, Wertheim proposed that the agreement be based upon Brandeis' statement in 1914 which spoke of world Jewry's aid for the settlement of Palestine and the organization of a Jewish society there. Ben-Gurion rejected this suggestion as out of tune with the times. By 1941, the Zionist movement had advanced far beyond its position of 1914. It was not for the non-Zionists to be involved with Zionist policy. They would do better to concentrate on world problems affecting all Jews, such as Jewish control over immigration to Palestine. Eventually the issue was once again referred to the Zionist Emergency Committee. As it could not reach a final decision, the Committee had no alternative but to give Ben-Gurion authority to continue negotiating with the non-Zionists.[81]

Ben-Gurion proposed that the talks be based on three assumptions — there was no need for unanimity on all issues; there was no need for the eventual agreement to include the entire Zionist program, and the agreement had to include a minimum of political demands. This minimum was to include the implementation of the Balfour Declaration, protection of Jewish rights while the Mandate continued in force, and non-Zionist agreement that a Jewish Commonwealth be established in Palestine once the Jews constituted a majority of the country's population. The phrase "Palestine as a Jewish Commonwealth," expressed in the Biltmore Program, could be interpreted by the non-Zionists as the establishment of a Jewish political entity in a portion of Palestine, without specific definition.[82]

On June 5, 1942, Ben-Gurion and Wertheim reached an accord on the Palestine question which called for united action in defense of Jewish rights under the Mandate, and the fulfillment of the terms of the Balfour Declaration through unlimited Jewish immigration and settlement. The Jews of Palestine, once they constituted a majority of the population, would create an autonomous Jewish Commonwealth in which all inhabitants, regardless of race or religion, would enjoy equal rights. The Commonwealth would not infringe on the political status of Jews who were citizens of other countries.[83]

Though Ben-Gurion was not certain that any accord with Wertheim would be ratified by the A.J.C., he believed that he was approaching the end of the negotiations with his goal in sight.[84] This was, however, prior to the release of the findings of the Kirstein Committee appointed by the A.J.C. in order to deal with the negotiations. Waldman, Wertheim's man-behind-the-scenes, sought to present the results of the committee meeting held in Wertheim's home in Cos Cob, Connecticut, as a turning point in the negotiations with the Zionists. The reality was very different. The formula hammered out was not limited to the Palestine issue which had been agreed upon by Wertheim and Ben-Gurion, but included an introduction which expressed the A.J.C.'s view that Jewish nationalism outside Palestine should be understood as a common religious and cultural heritage.[85] Obviously, this had not been agreed upon by both sides.

Eight members of the Kirstein Committee voted to accept the agreement, while three, Proskauer, Henry Ittleson, and Morris Wolf, were opposed.[86] The report also contained this statement:

> Neither Zionism nor the interests of Palestine can be accepted as the "major concern" of American Jewish life to which other communal endeavors are subordinated. On the contrary, Zionism and Palestine must be accorded their proper position functionally and financially in the total perspective of American Jewish community life.[87]

The majority then informed the Zionists that they would be unable to commit themselves fully until the documents could be seen and approved by the State Department, to ensure that the decision would not interfere with the Allied war effort.[88] The Zionists responded by pointing out that asking for the State Department's approval was tantamount to submitting the document for the approbation of the British Colonial Office. Though it was clear that the Zionists themselves were divided regarding the agreement, the dissenting minority in the Kirstein Committee declared all-out war against any agreement with the Zionists or any joint announcement.[89]

The Jewish Agency Executive in Jerusalem was equally unenthusiastic about the proposed Ben-Gurion—Wertheim agreement, although Kaplan and Shertok supported it. Shertok felt that the Jewish Agency should ratify it on condition that the A.J.C. did so first. He added, "With regard to the Jewish state, I am prepared to sign anything Ben-Gurion agrees to, sight unseen."[90]

The Zionists never formally ratified the agreement, as the A.J.C. never approved the decisions of the Kirstein Committee, which was a precondition to its consideration by the World Zionist Organization.

Ben-Gurion was not prepared to give up the ultimate political objectives of the Zionist movement as they took shape in May 1942, merely for a united American Jewry at the future peace conference. However, at the beginning of June he still believed that his efforts would win the support of Wertheim and his colleagues. He notified the Jewish Agency Executive in Jerusalem that, "I rely on him [Wertheim] fully, as I rely on the best Zionist in America."[91] Waldman, too, attempted to save the agreement, and asked Rosenman, who was responsible for amending the text, to help in this attempt.[92] He sought concessions from the Zionists, proposing deferral of the publication of the agreement until after the war. This was a point that Ben-Gurion, whose aim was to win American public opinion, could not accept.

During the summer, the battle within the ranks of the A.J.C. continued, with the Proskauer faction continually gaining strength.[93] The final decision on the agreement was deferred to the end of the summer, and then Wertheim saw himself faced with a choice between maintaining the unity of the A.J.C. or finalizing the agreement with the Zionists. He tried unsuccessfully to convince Proskauer that it would spell the end of Jewish nationalism in the Diaspora, but in the end he succumbed to the fear of a secession by Proskauer's group.[94] In a final last-ditch effort to salvage the agreement, Wertheim proposed that the A.J.C. announce it in his name alone, but Ben-Gurion could not agree to this. Wertheim finally said to him, "Listen, David, I cannot destroy the American Jewish Committee, which has existed for more than thirty years. It is an important institution ... which united the leaders of Jewry."[95]

The next time the two sides met, there was an attempt to salvage at least something of the agreement. Ben-Gurion pondered the advisability of a separate declaration by the A.J.C. in support of Jewish settlement in Palestine, while the Zionists, in return, would announce their opposition to Diaspora Jewish nationalism. However, on September 28, 1942, he rejected this idea, since the separate declarations would have signified an A.J.C. retreat from a number of pro-Zionist positions it had taken since 1918.[96]

Ben-Gurion refused to admit that the final breakdown of negotiations was a failure of his efforts to unite American Jewry behind the Jewish Commonwealth. He declared: "The importance of our political program is greater than the importance of the relations between various groups on the American communal scene."[97] He reported to the Yishuv that he had been attempting to unite American Jewry behind the Biltmore Program which was now, in October 1942, reduced to an essential minimum. The failure was due to anti-Zionist forces, and the future achievement of this objective would depend on the strength of the Zionist movement in America. There was more than a hint that the lack of success was partly due to the weakness of the American Zionists.[98]

Immediately following upon the final breakdown of negotiations between the Zionists, under Ben-Gurion's leadership, and the A.J.C., now headed by Proskauer's anti-Zionist faction, the American Zionist leaders, with the encouragement of Weizmann, initiated an American Jewish Conference. The A.J.C. and the J.L.C. at first refused to participate. They did join the Conference during the summer of 1943, but withdrew after it adopted the Biltmore Program. Only after World War II, when the full extent of the Holocaust became known and no refuge was found for its survivors, did these two organizations join in the effort to establish a Jewish state in part of Palestine.

Notes

1 Ben-Gurion's diary, entry for December 7-12, 1930, Ben-Gurion Archives, Sedeh Boker (hereafter B.G.A.).
2 Ibid., entry for December 27, 1930.
3 Ibid., entries for May 17 and 20, 1935.
4 Ibid., entry for May 25, 1935.
5 Ibid., entry for May 31, 1935.
6 David Ben-Gurion, *Memoirs* (Hebrew), Vol. 1, Tel Aviv, 1971. pp. 285-290.
7 Report by Berl Locker, May 20, 1935, Central Zionist Archives, Jerusalem (hereafter C.Z.A.), S25/1428.
8 *Contemporary Jewish Record* 1, no. 2 (1939), pp. 7ff.
9 Ben-Gurion's diary, entry for January 5, 1939, B.G.A.
10 Minutes of the Mapai Political Committee, September 20, 1938; Mapai Central Forum, December 12, 1938; Jewish Agency Executive, December 11, 1938—all quoted by Allon Gal, *David Ben-Gurion: Preparing a Jewish State* (Hebrew), Sedeh Boker, 1985, pp. 9-12.
11 Three years later he wrote this explicitly in his diary: Ben-Gurion's diary, entry for December 18, 1942, B.G.A.
12 Ben-Gurion's diary, entry made aboard the SS Franconia, January 1, 1939, B.G.A.
13 Ibid., entry for January 2, 1939.
14 Hexter in a preparatory session before Ben-Gurion's meeting with Adler, Ben-Gurion's diary, entry for January 2, 1939, B.G.A.
15 Ben-Gurion's diary, entry for January 6, 1939, B.G.A.
16 Ibid., entry for January 4, 1939; letter to Paula Ben-Gurion, January 8, 1939, B.G.A.
17 Ibid., entry for January 24, 1939, quoted by Gal, *David Ben-Gurion* p. 26.
18 M. Sklare and T. Solotaroff, *Jews in the Mind of America*, New York, London, 1966, pp. 3-28.
19 Zionist Executive Committee, February 24, 1941, C.Z.A., S25/1838.
20 Vladimir Jabotinsky to A. Abrahams, London, April 4, 1940, Jabotinsky Archives, Tel Aviv.
21 Speech at Mapai Central Forum, April 9, 1940, Israel Labor Party Archives, Beit Berl (hereafter: L.P.A.).
22 Ibid.
23 *Contemporary Jewish Record* 3 no. 4 (July-August, 1940), p. 355.
24 Report by E. Kaplan to Mapai Central Forum, August 22, 1940, L.P.A.
25 Ibid., p. 7.
26 Speech at meeting of Jewish Agency Executive, February 24, 1941, C.Z.A., S25/1838.
27 Report of G. Landauer in Jerusalem, May 16, 1940, C.Z.A., Z5/471.
28 Ibid.
29 Letter of Morris Waldman (executive director of the American Jewish Committee) to "A Correspondent," March 12, 1940, American Jewish Committee Archives.
30 Report of David Ben-Gurion to the Jewish Agency Executive, February 16, 1941, C.Z.A., Minutes of the Executive, Vol. 33/2, p. 12.
31 Ben-Gurion's diary, quoted by Allon Gal, *David Ben-Gurion*, pp. 81-82.
32 Ibid., p. 12.
33 Weizmann was relying on the report of Joseph Cohen, representative of the Chaim Weizmann Research Foundation, February 12, 1941, Weizmann Archives, Rehovot (hereafter: W.A.), 1941. Cf. "Press Release for [Weizmann's] Chicago B'nai Brith Speech," March 31, 1941, p. 6.
34 Minutes of the St. Regis Meeting, May 25, 1941, W.A., 1941.
35 Monsky had coordinated his position with Weizmann before the meeting; see Isaac Neustadt-Noy, "Toward Unity: Zionist and Non-Zionist Cooperation 1941-1942," *Herzl Yearbook* 8 (1978), pp. 149ff.
36 Telegram from Weizmann to Weisgal, June 4, 1941, W.A., 1941.
37 Outlines of Zionist Policy by D. Ben-Gurion, October 15, 1941, C.Z.A., Z4/14632.
38 Ibid., pp. 27-28.
39 Ben-Gurion's diary, entries for November 24 and 28, 1941, B.G.A.
40 Morris Waldman, *Nor by Power*, New York, 1953, pp. 212ff.
41 Ben-Gurion's summary at the October 4, 1942 session of the Jewish Agency Executive, C.Z.A., Minutes of the Executive, Vol. 36.
42 Naomi Cohen, *American Jews and the Zionist Idea*, New York, 1975, p. 60; Emanuel Neumann, *In the Arena*, New York, 1976, pp. 168-169.

43 Morris Waldman to Joseph Proskauer, April 28, 1942, American Jewish Archives, Cincinnati, Waldman Papers, Box 640.
44 *New Palestine* 30, no. 1 (January 1, 1940), p. 15.
45 Ben-Gurion's diary, entry for November 29, 1941, B.G.A.
46 Ben-Gurion's diary, entry for December 11, 1941, B.G.A.
47 Ben-Gurion to Berl Locker, February 2, 1942, C.Z.A., S25/41.
48 "Peace Demands for European Jews," Jewish Labor Committee Archives (hereafter: JLCA), pt. 3, sec. 2, no. 4.
49 Ibid.
50 Ben-Gurion's summary at the October 4, 1942 session of the Jewish Agency Executive, C.Z.A., Minutes of the Executive, Vol. 36.
51 Another meeting of Ben-Gurion with Wertheim, Ben-Gurion's diary, entry for December 16, 1941, B.G.A.
52 Ibid.
53 "Zusamentrof fun a Grupe Yiddishe Gezelshaftlikhe Toer" (Yiddish), December 16, 1941, JLCA, pt. 3, sec. 2, no. 4.
54 Report of meeting, December 23, 1941, ibid.
55 Ben-Gurion to Locker, January 4, 1942, C.Z.A., S25/41.
56 Report of the Office Committee, Zionist Emergency Committee, December 23, 1951, Zionist Archives and Library, New York City, Minutes of Meetings, American Emergency Committee for Zionist Affairs, p. 2.
57 Ben-Gurion to Locker, January 4, 1942, C.Z.A., S25/41.
58 Reports of Office Committee (note 56 above), December 23, 1941, February 6, 1942, May 20, 1942.
59 "Proposals for a Program of United American Jewry," Final Draft, JLCA, pt. 3, sec. 2, no. 4.
60 Ben-Gurion to Locker, January 4, 1942, C.Z.A., S25/41.
61 Telegram from Weisgal to Weizmann, January 9, 1942, W.A., 1942.
62 Ben-Gurion's diary, entries for November-December 1941, B.G.A. (also available in C.Z.A., S25/10237, p. 13).
63 "A Meeting at Mr. Wertheim's House" (Yiddish) January 19, 1942, JLCA, pt. 3, sec. 2, no. 4.
64 On the January 13, 1942 meeting between Ben-Gurion and Wertheim, see Ben-Gurion's summary at the October 4, 1942 session of the Jewish Agency Executive, C.Z.A., Minutes of the Executive, Vol. 36 Cf. letter from Ben-Gurion to Locker, January 26, 1942 and a report on the meeting by Ben-Gurion dated January 20, 1942, both in C.Z.A., S25/41.
65 Record of conversation at Hay-Adams Hotel, Washington D.C., January 13, 1942, Ben-Gurion's Report, (note 64 above).
66 "Address of Maurice Wertheim, January 26, 1942," *American Jewish Year Book* 44 (1942), p. 478.
67 Ben-Gurion's diary, entries for November-December 1941, C.Z.A., S25/10237.
68 Ben-Gurion to Jewish Agency Executive (note 41 above), pp. 18-19.
69 Ben-Gurion to Jewish Agency Executive (note 41 above).
70 Report by Nahum Goldmann, the Zionist Emergency Committee, January 8, 1942, C.Z.A., Z5/345.
71 A. Lourie to G. Lauterbach, March 30, 1942, W.A., 1942.
72 Ben-Gurion to Wertheim, April 17, 1942, C.Z.A., S25/41.
73 Ibid.
74 The text of the Biltmore Program may be found in *A Survey of Facts and Opinions on Problems of Post-War Jewry in Europe and Palestine*, New York, 1943, pp. 140-141.
75 Secretariat of the Zionist Emergency Committee, session of May 13, 1942, C.Z.A., Z5/345.
76 Secretariat of the Zionist Emergency Committee, Session of May 20, 1942, ibid.
77 Enclosure 1, May 29, 1942, C.Z.A., S25/1458.
78 Wertheim's plan is attached to a letter from Waldman to Held, June 9, 1942, JLCA, pt. 3, sec. 3, no. 4.
79 Telegram from Ben-Gurion to Shertok, June 17, 1942, C.Z.A., S25/1458.
80 "Dr. Weizmann Beratung" (Yiddish), May 24, 1942, JLCA, pt. 5, sec. 2, no. 5.
81 Session of the Zionist Emergency Committee, June 3, 1942, C.Z.A., Z5/345.
82 Session of the Zionist Emergency Committee, June 5, 1942, ibid.
83 "Palestine Formula Drafted by Ben-Gurion, Accepted by Wertheim, Approved by Emergency Committee," June 5, 1942, C.Z.A., S25/1458.
84 Telegram from Ben-Gurion to Shertok, June 6, 1942, C.Z.A., S25/1458; Z5/773.
85 Waldman, *Nor by Power*, pp. 224-237.

86 Naomi Cohen, *Not Free to Desist*, Philadelphia, 1976, p. 252.

87 Waldman, *Nor by Power*, pp. 226.

88 Nahum Goldmann at the Zionist Emergency Committee, Session of June 10, 1942, C.Z.A., Z5/345.

89 These positions are reflected in the publications of the American Jewish Committee's Research Institute on Peace and Post-War Problems. See Abraham G. Duker, "Political Aspects of Jewish Post-War Problems," *Jewish Social Service Quarterly* 19 (1942).

90 C.Z.A., Minutes of the sessions of the Jewish Agency Executive, session of June 14, 1942, Vol. 35, no. 41, pp. 128 ff.

91 Ben-Gurion to Shertok, June 8, 1942; Ben-Gurion to L. Levinthal, June 9, 1942; A. Lourie to L. Lauterbach, June 12, 1942, all in C.Z.A., S25/1458.

92 Summary of the conversation between Waldman and Weisgal, June 19, 1942, American Jewish Archives, Cincinnati, Waldman Papers, Box 640.

93 Waldman to Wertheim, June 29, 1942; Wertheim to Proskauer, June 29, 1942—both in American Jewish Archives, Waldman Papers, Box 640. See also Ben-Gurion's reports at the November 4, 1942 session of the Jewish Agency Executive, C.Z.A., Minutes of the Executive, Vol. 36.

94 Ben-Gurion's report of November 4, 1942, ibid.

95 Ibid. See also Ben-Gurion to Levinthal, September 2, 1942, C.Z.A., S25/1458 (Shertok's copy).

96 Ben-Gurion to Levinthal, September 2, 1942, ibid.

97 Ben-Gurion at press conference, (Hebrew) October 8, 1942, *Ha'aretz*, October 11, 1942, C.Z.A., Z5/773.

98 Jewish Agency Executive, sessions of October 6 and 11, 1942, C.Z.A., Minutes of the Executive, Vol. 36.

BEN-GURION AND THE HOLOCAUST

DINA PORAT

David Ben-Gurion's reaction to the annihilation of European Jewry and his efforts to extend aid and succor are poignant subjects which have repeatedly engaged public attention in Israel and the Jewish world during the last decades. To anyone tracing the discussion of this question in the media and in various private or public forums, it would seem that public opinion is in almost universal agreement that Ben-Gurion "did not sense [the full extent of] the Holocaust," to quote from some who were closely associated with him during the war years.[1] The feeling is that he consciously cut himself off from the Holocaust, concentrating first and foremost on the establishment of a Jewish state and on whatever was directly involved in that undertaking. In this respect, Ben-Gurion is visualized as a tenacious leader, persistently focusing on the achievement of one overriding objective, to which end he mobilized all the means at his disposal, even at the cost of disregarding unfathomable suffering. He is portrayed not only as a leader blessed with a sweeping, prophetic vision but also as a cold and calculating statesman. He is seen as a supreme manipulator, for whom European Jewry was no more than a lost instrument to be immediately replaced by another, or, at best, whose remnants could still be utilized to achieve the supreme objective.

A recent expression of this attitude toward Ben-Gurion is a poem whose author compares him to Peter the Great:

> Peter the Great paved
> The capital city, Petersburg
> In the swamps of the north over peasants' bones.
> David Ben-Gurion paved
> The way to the "Burma Road" that bypasses
> The road leading to the capital, the Jerusalem road,
> With bones of boys out of the Holocaust..
> Ben-Gurion swept together
> Human dust—to sow in the eyes of the foe.
> Over bones of boys from the Holocaust
> We paved the way that bypasses the road
> Ascending to Jerusalem.[2]

This disturbing comparison published during the Ben-Gurion centennial celebrations, when his name appeared in some context almost daily in the Israeli media, symbolizes the acme of his negative image in relation to the Holocaust. This poses the following question: Is the time ripe, some forty years after World War II, to deal with this emotionally charged subject using the tools of the historian? Will they enable reexamination of the image generally accepted by the public at large? The substantial question is whether the available historical sources lead us to the same popularly accepted conclusion or whether they paint a different, more complex picture, a construct of which not all of the components are known or have been collected or studied as a whole. Without exaggeration, one may view this as an issue of cardinal importance for Zionism, for it touches upon the attitude of the man today most closely identified with Zionism and the establishment of the State of Israel—to the most horrendous tragedy in Jewish history.

Any attempt to answer this question implies a thorough sifting of the sources at our disposal. Upon Ben-Gurion's death, his personal papers, which included diaries, correspondence and speeches—an enormous quantity of documentation produced over several decades[3]—were transferred to the Israel Defence Forces Archives, where they underwent preliminary sorting and filing. The first researchers who were afforded access to this material found little reference to the fate of European Jewry. Thus, Michael Bar-Zohar, who published a three-volume biography of Ben-Gurion in 1977 after some eight years of intensive study of these sources and much oral documentation, devoted only a few sentences to the Holocaust.[4]

In 1976, the Knesset passed the "Ben-Gurion Law" which empowered the Ben-Gurion Research Institute and Archives in Sedeh Boker, as a subsidiary of the Israel State Archives, to collect all documents in Israel and abroad having any relevance to Ben-Gurion.[5] Although the collection process is still under way, the original archives have already been doubled. The additional material includes photocopies of innumerable letters, documents, oral documents, and official stenographic records which have bearing on Ben-Gurion's response to the Holocaust. When all these are published, the accepted image of Ben-Gurion will be transformed.[6]

When Ben-Gurion chose to express his opinion on the subject of the Holocaust, the attitude of the Allies toward European Jewry, and what the Yishuv could or should do to save them, he did so briefly and succinctly, rarely elaborating. His terse statements can help us to assess his attitude to the Holocaust and especially to the various suggested plans of action, since the Yishuv's institutions—the Jewish Agency Executive, the Mapai Central Committee, the Secretariat of the Histadrut (General Federation of the Jewish Laborers in Eretz-Israel), the Executive of the Va'ad Leumi (National Council) and others—repeatedly referred to the tragic events in Europe during 1943-1944. (An evaluation of the time spent on these deliberations as compared to other Yishuv affairs is beyond the scope of this article.)

Out of all of these—the crumbs of information in Ben-Gurion's diaries and correspondence; his statements at sessions of Yishuv institutions; his speeches at public meetings and on other occasions; interviews with persons who worked closely with him; the evidence of involvement as it comes to light in reports or correspondence of other leading Yishuv personalities—the historian must try to shape a comprehensive picture of Ben-Gurion's attitude toward the tragedy of Europe's Jews and his efforts on their behalf, even if this will only constitute an intermediate summing-up until all relevant material becomes available. If Ben-Gurion expressed himself very sparingly on the Holocaust, does this necessarily mean that he ranked this subject among the least deserving of his daily attention, that he really did cut himself off from the tragic fate of the Jews of Europe? Is it justifiable to draw a direct correlation between written and oral expression on the one hand and motives and emotions on the other? Is it not possible that his silence on the Holocaust was perhaps no less significant than the grief and agony expressed by other Yishuv leaders?

These questions must be faced even if they leave the historian somewhat bewildered and hesitant, for just as written and oral statements are open to various interpretations, so is silence.

News of the Holocaust and Assessment of the Situation, 1940-1942

At a session of the Va'ad Leumi Executive, about one month after the "Kristallnacht," Ben-Gurion said:

> November 1938 is a new date, or a new chapter, unprecedented in the history of Jewish martyrology. This is not merely persecution or expulsion — this is organized extermination, physical extermination, accompanied by sadistic brutality against an entire Jewish community..but it is more than that. The Nazi pogrom of this November is an omen for the destruction of the entire Jewish people. I hope I am mistaken. Until now, even the devil himself dared not perpetrate such atrocious acts. Now the reins are slackened. It is open season on our blood, our honor, our property, and there is no limit, no limit whatsoever to the evil they plot against us.[7]

Ben-Gurion certainly did not *know* what the future held in store, just as others did not know — neither Ze'ev Jabotinsky who referred to the Diaspora that would destroy the Jewish people, nor Chaim Weizmann who even quoted the figure of a possible 6,000,000 victims as early as 1939,[8] nor other Jewish leaders who expressed themselves in similar vein. The Nazi leadership had not yet finalized its operational plans concerning the Jews; the decision to begin their mass extermination was made in spring 1941, on the eve of Germany's invasion of the Soviet Union. Certainly, no one could foretell Auschwitz or foresee the horrendous extent of the mass murders, the systematic processes and techniques which would be developed to execute them, and the planning and organization that were to be expended upon them. For to assert that someone foresaw all this a few years before it actually occurred would be equivalent to an accusation that this person's mind and heart operated similarly to those of Hitler, Himmler and their cohorts.[9] All this notwithstanding, what Ben-Gurion said after the "Kristallnacht" points to his prescient sense of the direction that events were taking, his deep understanding of Nazi objectives, of the complete lack of restraint that characterized their anti-Jewish policy, and of their unlimited evil. More than anything else, Ben-Gurion expressed a sense of foreboding as to the fate of European Jewry should a world war break out.

Destruction of the Entire Jewish People

Ben-Gurion's premonition led him to take concrete action. Events during the late thirties clearly showed that the Zionist movement could not provide a solution to the precarious condition of the Jews, which was rapidly deteriorating not in Germany alone but also in Poland and Rumania, in Austria, Hungary, and other European countries. In Palestine, Zionist relations with the Mandate Government had reached a crisis most clearly expressed in the White Paper of May 1939, the "Paper of Treachery" as Ben-Gurion termed it. These two factors—the situation of European Jewry and the White Paper—led Ben-Gurion to conclude that the Zionist movement had to seek new paths to a political breakthrough.[10]

During the first two years of World War II, he gradually developed what came to be known as the "Biltmore Program," proposing that the gates of Palestine be opened to Jewish immigration. On several occasions he spoke of the immigration of two million Jews as a first and essential stage of the program, despite the ongoing controversy over the "absorptive capacity" of Palestine. The Jewish Agency would assume responsibility for this immigration and for the economic development of the country. Ultimately, the Biltmore Program advocated a Jewish Commonwealth which would be established in Palestine as part of the postwar political settlement. Ben-Gurion sought to rally the Zionist movement around the Biltmore Program. This was not meant to be a Palestine-centered platform that placed Eretz-Israel in opposition to the Diaspora. His program conceived of Palestine as the one and only solution for the Jewish condition in the Diaspora, and of aliya as the sole precondition for the development of that country. The two were interdependent. Early in 1940 he said:

> We are faced with two possibilities. Either to be one more Diaspora, like every other Diaspora, and that is precisely what will happen if the Yishuv concerns itself only with the half-million Jews presently in Eretz-Israel and not with the millions now faced with destruction and annihilation—or to be the nucleus and the moving spirit of Zionist fulfillment.[11]

The course of Ben-Gurion's thinking must be understood against the background of events during the first war years. From our contemporary vantage point, we identify World War II as a whole with the murder of Jews, in one form or another, over the entire face of Europe. However, during 1940-1941, the Western powers believed that the situation in the ghettos of Europe had become stable and that the Jewish communities were managing to survive despite terrible conditions and the death of tens or even hundreds every month.[12]

German policy in relation to the Jews in Western Europe during these years was much more restrained than that implemented in Poland, and it was therefore difficult to perceive that what was happening all over Europe was but the first stage of a long-term policy. It was even logical to assume that the Germans were able to treat the Jews in Poland more violently and brutally because the non-Jewish populace of that country supported these measures to a greater extent than did their counterparts in the countries of Western Europe. Such an interpretation of conditions did not yet seem to necessitate the immediate physical rescue of European Jewry from the clutches of its hangmen, a need of which the Yishuv did become aware as time went on.

Moreover, traditionally European Jewry, and especially its Zionist element, had assumed responsibility for the welfare of the Yishuv, an embryonic creation in need of all the support it could muster. The Yishuv—small in numbers and poor in resources—could not be concerned with the well-being of millions of European Jews. On the contrary, it was they and especially the Zionist element, who must contribute to the upbuilding and development of the Jewish homeland.[13] Perhaps it was all these factors taken together—a belief that the condition of the Jews varied from country to country and was on the whole stable, despite its horrors, and the conception that held the Yishuv to be dependent upon Diaspora Jewry—that led Ben-Gurion to posit that the onus of extending aid and succor to European Jewry lay with the American Jewish Joint Distribution Committee (JDC), the World Jewish Congress, and the Jewish communities of the United States and the free world. "This operation cannot be conducted from here," he commented.[14] The Jewish communities of the free world, with their economic resources and access to centers of political influence, were the most suitable agents to help their brethren. He did not use the term "rescue," for total, mass murder was not yet the order of the day.

It would seem that at this time Ben-Gurion differentiated between the extension of immediate material aid to European Jewry as a whole, which he considered to be the duty of the entire Jewish people and its organizations, and the role of the Zionist movement, which he saw as the provision of a political solution to the crisis facing both European Jewry and the Yishuv. It is to the latter objective that he now devoted much of his time and energy. He made several lengthy trips abroad, to England and especially to the United States.[15] Sensing that the British Empire was in decline and that US would be most influential in shaping the postwar world, Ben-Gurion transferred the major arena of Zionist political activity from London to Washington. The fruition of Zionist aspirations lay in America, especially if its Jewish community could be mobilized to take proper action and influence democratic public opinion, which placed great emphasis on moral considerations.

This position illuminates statements made by Ben-Gurion in Palestine between his overseas visits, statements forgotten as his image of insensitivity to the Holocaust gained acceptance. "Does the fact that a war is being waged preclude us from defending our interests here in Eretz-Israel?" he asked, and replied in the negative:

> I do not give priority to the interests of the Jewish community of Eretz-Israel over those of the Jews of Germany or of any other country. The fate of three million Jews in Poland worries me more than the fate of five hundred thousand Jews in Eretz-Israel..The fact that there is a state of hostilities, that a war is being waged, is a fact of political life. Does not this fact present me with the means to further the aspirations of the Jewish people? I say: Yes.[16]

In February 1941, upon his return from a visit to the United States, shocked by the realization that people in Palestine seemed unaware of the terrible war raging somewhere in the world and were ignorant of the enormity of the Jewish catastrophe, he rebuked the Yishuv: "It is certain that we have information here about these events," he said, and that people knew about them, took an interest in them and discussed them, but "they are not a central theme in the life of the Yishuv."

His remedy for this indifference was "Zionist tension and brotherhood," by which he meant enhanced activity of the Zionist movement together with a greater sense of involvement with the fate of European Jewry. In practical terms, this called for an effort to establish a Jewish state and the immigration of millions of Jews to Palestine after the war, and "this today is the essence of Zionism and the Jewish nation."[17]

In a letter to the United States, he wrote:

> I will not conceal the sense of uneasiness which American Jewry aroused in me. I found that even the Zionists did not sufficiently realize what a tragic and desperate hour this is for the Jewish people. Does the fate of millions of their brethren in Europe affect American Jews less than the fate of Britain affects the American people? Is Eretz-Israel less dear to the five million Jews of the United States than Britain is to 130 million Americans?[18]

These statements and others in a similar vein, made both publicly and privately, show that Ben-Gurion inseparably bound together the Jewish people and the Jewish homeland. He considered the Biltmore Program to be a solution for both and a flag around which all could rally.

However, it was precisely in May 1942, as the annual convention of the Zionist Organization of America unanimously adopted the Biltmore Program, that the Western press first published news of mass murders, of the early experimentation with gas, and that the ghettos were being emptied of Jews. At the end of that month, Western news media published a detailed report originating in Poland: 700,000 Jews had already been shot and gassed to death, and the extermination process was spreading from the the Soviet Union to Poland. Upon Ben-Gurion's return to Palestine in October 1942, the Jewish Agency Executive and the Zionist Actions Committee approved the Biltmore Program, a great vote of confidence in his leadership. But it was precisely then, in November 1942, that the Yishuv learned from a reliable German source and from the first-hand testimony of a group of Palestinian citizens who arrived as part of an exchange operation, that the Germans were carrying out a scheme for the total and systematic liquidation of the Jews in extermination camps that had been specially prepared for that purpose.[19]

One may ask whether Ben-Gurion considered these reports—which in effect told of the death of millions of European Jews—as contradicting the logic of his Biltmore Program. For the strategy of that scheme was to strive for the establishment of a state whose future inhabitants were being exterminated here and now. Did Ben-Gurion's reading of the situation in 1940, which led him to shape his political program, now give way in the face of developments which he recognized to be far more ghastly than he had previously imagined, even if he was still not fully aware of all the details?

For a while—a few months—Ben-Gurion wavered between the hope that characterized his earlier interpretation of events, and terrible despair, inevitable once the implications of the news from Europe became clear. At that November meeting of the Zionist Actions Committee, he made statements that were a contradiction in terms: "...after the war, there must be—if there be such a possibility—an immediate transfer of several million Jews, at least two million, to Eretz-Israel," for if not, then

"Eretz-Israel will vacate the political arena." Settlement would be possible on the basis of the Yishuv's accumulated experience and knowledge, and "out of love and concern for these people, who will be ready to face any hardship to settle down here" after having been uprooted from their native lands. But he also said:

> Whoever does not realize what Jewry is facing today is blind, and is neither Jewish nor human..They are capable of murdering them all. I don't know if any Jews will survive Hitler.

He went on to declare that what the group of exchanged refugees had related would have been unbelievable had their evidence not been presented in person. The truth is that this group described what Ben-Gurion had prophesied as early as 1938.[20]

It seems that after these few months of fluctuation between hope and despair, Ben-Gurion, with characteristic clear thinking and sober-mindedness, understood— though perhaps not yet fully—the implications of the reports from Europe for the Jewish people and the Zionist movement. From the end of 1942, and especially after the Bermuda Conference in the spring of 1943, he kept almost complete silence on the Holocaust and rescue efforts. He did not share his thoughts, fears, and emotions with his colleagues. He absented himself from the emotional session of the Jewish Agency Executive on November 22, 1942, which was a turning point in the Yishuv's relation to and knowledge of the Holocaust. Yet one thing is certain: he did not abandon the Biltmore Program, the vision of a Jewish state, even when faced with tragedy. On the contrary:

> Tragedy is power, if channeled in a productive direction. The essence of Zionist strategy is that it knows how to transform our catastrophe not into a source of despair and paralysis, as did the Diaspora, but into a spring of creativity and spiritedness.[21]

Organizational Efforts and Rescue Plans, 1943-1944

In November 1942, having learned of the systematic extermination of European Jewry, the leadership of the Yishuv responded in two spheres—internal mobilization of the Yishuv and planning rescue operations. Simultaneously, they expressed a deep sense of guilt and remorse, and especially of disheartening despair: How had it come about that they had awakened so late, when organized liquidation was already at its height? Ben-Gurion was actively involved in both spheres of action, and in a few cases even directly influenced decisions and developments. He was almost completely silent in relation to the sense of guilt and despair.

At the end of the year, after lengthy negotiations in which Ben-Gurion played an active role, a committee of the Jewish Agency Executive in existence since the outbreak of the war was enlarged by the addition of one more member of the Executive, three representatives of the Va'ad Leumi, two from the Revisionist Party, and two from the ultra-Orthodox Agudat Israel. This "Rescue Committee" as it was called, chaired by Yitzhak Gruenbaum, began to function in January 1943. Its composition was immediately criticized by individuals, various groups, and members of other Yishuv institutions. They demanded a much more broadly-based committee which would be allocated the necessary resources and directed by the best leadership available, persons who would devote all their time and efforts to its activities. At meetings of the Executive of the Va'ad Leumi and of the Zionist Actions Committee, there was lengthy and heated debate on this subject.[22]

Ben-Gurion was steadfast in his opposition to the establishment of new organizational frameworks. By swift and determined maneuvering between the two meetings he succeeded in preventing the establishment of a new body. He was motivated by several considerations. The establishment of a new committee would entail lengthy negotiations concerning its structure, composition, financial resources, and so forth, not to mention conflicts of prestige between all the elements in the Yishuv. The Jewish Agency's Immigration, Political, and Treasury Departments were already dealing with matters bearing on any rescue operations. But his primary consideration was more practical. Ben-Gurion and the Jewish Agency Executive had already promised that, should rescue plans having any chance of success be formulated, the Jewish Agency would immediately take steps to implement them. Until then, a small Rescue Committee would be sufficient.[23]

Ben-Gurion considered the three official days of mourning declared by the national institutions at the end of November and beginning of December 1942 to be "a momentous event," a universal expression of bereavement, but "not sufficiently Zionist in nature." He intended to continue in this line of activity in coordination with the Jews in the free world. To this end he proposed to the Jewish Agency Executive that a special Zionist assembly be convened in Palestine, comprising representatives from all Jewish communities, to discuss the danger facing Europe's Jews and its result—the threat to the Zionist enterprise.[24]

Ben-Gurion's colleagues on the Mapai Central Committee and in the Jewish Agency Executive opposed this plan. In view of the strained relationship at that time between Ben-Gurion and Weizmann, such an assembly could be construed as a case of the former forcing his will upon the latter. They believed that it would be more logical for a Palestine delegation, supplied with the necessary documentation, to visit the Western countries, hold press conferences, and appeal to their political leaders. Such a delegation never left Palestine, chiefly because of disagreement over its composition. Moreover, as time passed, it became ever more clear that the Allied powers refused to consider suggestions for action to rescue Europe's doomed Jews and stop the liquidation process. Even democratic governments, generally sensitive to the pressure of public opinion, were perhaps not always willing to acquiesce to it during wartime. Consequently, it was likely that any Yishuv delegation would be a wasted effort.

Ben-Gurion came to the conclusion that while additional days of public mourning might afford an easy outlet for the sense of bereavement and frustration, they would make no actual, practical contribution toward rescue. He let the Chief Rabbinate and the Va'ad Leumi engage in these activities: he and his fellow members of the Jewish Agency Executive were obliged to find other avenues of action. Having come to this decision, he took no further part in the repeated debate over the public reaction to the Holocaust. At most, he concisely expressed his consistent opposition to the expenditure of time and energy by the Agency Executive on such efforts. This matter "is not within the province of the Jewish Agency Executive but within that of the Yishuv," he replied to Gruenbaum's suggestion that a "Hungarian Jewry Day" be declared after the invasion of that country in March 1944.[25]

A third illustration concerns the allocation of financial resources for rescue activities. As long as there were no realistic rescue plans, he declined to make available sums from the national treasury, which were actually the budget of the Jewish Agency Executive, and his refusal was reiterated time and again by Agency treasurer Eliezer Kaplan. However, he did support fund-raising for rescue operations from other sources, especially the JDC, which had millions of dollars "and nothing to spend them on." He believed that, should the Yishuv formulate a viable rescue plan and raise a certain sum for its implementation, it would be morally justified in requesting that the JDC contribute three times that amount. In other words, the JDC should supply the bulk of the necessary financial resources while the Yishuv would take responsibility for the plan and those who would carry it out, taking upon itself the execution and the risk.[26]

Despite this attitude, Ben-Gurion took no initiative to send a rescue fund-raising mission to the US, nor did he support such a step, even though his lengthy stay in America to mobilize support for the Biltmore Program taught him that with perseverance, positive results could be achieved there. His reluctance probably stemmed from two primary considerations. First, as has already been noted, in late 1942 and early 1943 he did not believe that any practical rescue plan meriting the allocation of funds had been formulated. Secondly, during 1943 it became increasingly evident that the Jewish communities and organizations of the free world, including the JDC, did not consider the Yishuv to be the body which should lead rescue operations. The very opposite was true—they suspected that the Yishuv would use its money selectively, giving preference to the rescue of Zionist elements in European Jewry. For these reasons, Ben-Gurion saw no point in sending a fund-raising delegation abroad. Commenting on the hesitation of Jewish organizations, he said:

> The rescue of European Jewry has a moral, and not only a financial aspect. Today, this is one of the major items on the agenda. This is not simply a matter of extending aid to European Jewry—it also enhances the status of Eretz-Israel. The fact that the Jews of Eretz-Israel have assumed leadership of rescue operations is an important asset for Zionism.[27]

Ben-Gurion also lectured on the plight of European Jewry before informal gatherings in private homes, together with Yishuv emissaries to Istanbul who returned home briefly to bring information and take back funds for rescue activities. He emphasized that rescue plans required financial resources (as became increasingly clear throughout 1943), he dwelt upon the Yishuv's economic recovery during 1942 and 1943 from the serious recession which had plagued it at the outset of the war, and spoke of its capability to donate funds. Thirty thousand pounds sterling were raised at one such gathering, a significant sum in those days.

Ben-Gurion, however, did not make a direct appeal for funds, largely as a means to circumvent the vigilance of the Mandate Government, which forbade the export of capital from Palestine, especially its transfer to enemy territory. He also refused to comply with the requests of his colleagues in the Histadrut that he participate in the deliberations over the allocation of funds for rescue purposes, or to support the suggestion made by the Histadrut secretary-general David Remez, that the Yishuv take a ten-year loan of 1,000,000 pounds sterling from Lloyds Bank so that, should a rescue opportunity present itself, no time would be wasted raising such funds.

Ben-Gurion wanted the Rescue Committee to be no more than an official symbol and this he achieved. The Committee did not have authority or funds, nor did it count among its members any personality fully accepted by all the Yishuv institutions. Gruenbaum had been the revered leader of Polish Jewry, but he never achieved the same status in Palestine. Moreover, his strained relations with Ben-Gurion did not contribute to the efficacy of the Rescue Committee. Ben-Gurion entrusted clandestine rescue operations, highly dangerous in themselves, to a handful of his loyal confidants: Shaul Avigur, Eliahu Golomb, Zvi Yehieli and others. They, and a few of the Yishuv emissaries in Istanbul such as Venia Pomeranz and Ehud Avriel, regularly reported to Ben-Gurion and kept him abreast of developments. Pomeranz used to spend "hours upon hours" with him each time he returned to Palestine.[28]

However, there is almost no written evidence of Ben-Gurion's conversations with those responsible for rescue activity because they generally took place *tête à tête*, no record being made in part because of the confidential nature of the subjects under discussion but also because of the mutual confidence which the participants had in each other.

Ben-Gurion did not openly associate himself with the activities in Istanbul. He never went there during the Holocaust years, unlike Moshe Shertok (Sharett), Izhak Ben-Zvi, Eliezer Kaplan, and Chief Rabbi Herzog. He agreed that some thought be given to sending a leading public figure for some time to this key center of operations—but he never really seriously considered such a step, and did not initiate its discussion by the Jewish Agency Executive or the Mapai Central Committee. The fact remains that no such emissary was despatched.[29] Nor did he bring up for discussion the possibility of carrying out more rescue operations from other neutral countries such as Switzerland, Spain, and Sweden, and the stationing of more Yishuv representatives in them.

Ben-Gurion's involvement with the Yishuv's organization for rescue activity, then, was guided by one consistent principle: since the Yishuv had roused itself to action only when the German extermination machine was already operating at full force, and since the Allied powers refused to offer any real succor, widespread rescue operations were impossible. It would therefore be a waste of time and effort to establish a broadly-based Rescue Committee, to launch an extensive fund-raising campaign, to organize demonstrations, and to send a leading personality to Istanbul.

Ben-Gurion never set out these considerations in writing, nor did he summarize them orally. The construct presented here is based on the few references he did make to the subject and whatever action he did take, all of these against the background of the prevailing situation. It may very well be that all of Ben-Gurion's considerations and his evaluation of the situation were correct in view of contemporary conditions, and that the almost cruel realism with which he weighed the prospects was justified. His decisions relating to the Yishuv's involvement with rescue activity, however, overlooked two elements. The Jewish population of Palestine, an overwhelming majority of whom had immigrated from Europe during 1933-1939, clamored for a broad framework to direct rescue action. It was willing to donate money for that purpose and wanted more public demonstrations.[30] The Jewish Agency Executive, and Ben-Gurion in particular, felt perhaps this public mood, but stood up to it and did not accede to its demands. Ben-Gurion failed to sense that he was, to a certain extent, alienating himself from the general public. Many of his colleagues criticized him, sometimes rather harshly, for supplying the opposition—especially Agudat Israel and the Revisionists—with dangerous ammunition. Either he was impervious to the public mood or he disregarded its open manifestations and did not give in to them.

Ben-Gurion's second oversight was that he did not consider what future generations would think, generations for whom the actual prospects for successful rescue operations would not be the only criterion, and which would judge the Yishuv on the basis of its expressions of involvement and willingness to take risks on behalf of European Jewry. Had Ben-Gurion acceded to the demands of his critics and agreed to ask for a loan or to send a high-ranking emissary to Istanbul, had he approached Berl Katznelson or Yitzhak Tabenkin to head a broadly-based Rescue Committee, and had he sent a fund-raising delegation to the US, the present generation of Israelis could say and feel that "we tried, but failed," that Ben-Gurion was deeply and emotionally moved and had mobilized resources, but that all conditions worked against rescue operations.

Ben-Gurion's attitude toward rescue plans and attempts to save Europe's Jews was also characterized by a very careful assessment on his part of the possibilities and prospects. Surprisingly, though, at times he did place unrealistic, even naive, hope in one plan or another. This fusion of cold realism with unrealistic optimism was most noticeable during the first weeks after the arrival of the exchanged group of refugees late in 1942, a period when he wavered between hope and despair. He signed his name to cables sent to governments, organizations, and public personalities, and joined in messages requesting governments-in-exile to influence the populace of their home countries both to help local Jews and to aid emissaries from Palestine to infiltrate into occupied territories. He believed that it was "very important to establish a framework for rescue operations," by which he meant an international body such as the Intergovernmental Committee for Refugees set up after the Evian Conference, or some similar organization under the aegis of the Allies, which would direct rescue activity, especially the saving of children.[31] In his speeches and correspondence, he expressed the hope that an extensive program of exchanging Jews for Germans could be realized. He took part in discussions and deliberations that preceded the repeated appeals to Great Britain to sanction the parachuting of hundreds of men from Palestine behind enemy lines as a contribution to the overall war effort, in return for which they would be allowed to contact, aid, and encourage the trapped Jewish communities. Ben-Gurion was certain that the US would agree without delay to the establishment of a Jewish air squadron for punitive air strikes against German targets.[32]

The plan that best exemplifies Ben-Gurion's optimism during the first weeks and months of rescue activity was the scheme to rescue 29,000 children. This was the number of unallocated immigration certificates out of the quota set in the 1939 White Paper, and the Jewish Agency Executive requested the Mandate Government to set aside the entire balance for children in Nazi-occupied Europe. The Executive, for its part, assured the Government Secretary that it would undertake to provide for the children. "There is only one matter of utmost urgency," Ben-Gurion summed up, "and that is to bring the children here."[33] Even before the British reply was received, the Mapai Secretariat devoted a lengthy session to how the children should be received and absorbed—where they would be educated and how this tremendous undertaking would be financed, especially its first stage, 5,000 children. Carried away by his exhilarating vision, Ben-Gurion expressed the hope that "these five thousand are not the end—but only the beginning..this figure can grow to ten times that number." The first five thousand had to be absorbed immediately, he said, "and then we can wage a campaign for the immediate emigration of all Europe's Jewish children." It was essential to establish a central Zionist organization to make all efforts on behalf of the children, arrange for their absorption, and present the whole enterprise as the primary responsibility of the entire Jewish people—in America, South Africa, England, and everywhere else. It was not the obligation of the Yishuv alone to adopt these children, "the Jewish people must adopt them." Their successful integration would be a model and an example, a preliminary stage for immigration from the Jewish communities of England, the United States, and the whole of world Jewry.

Furthermore, Ben-Gurion was able to visualize, beyond the immediate rescue of the children, their potential contribution to the development of the Yishuv. "Each child represents a Jewish emigrant who will settle in Eretz-Israel," which made it all the more important that they receive proper and uniform education:

> Not every Jew in Eretz-Israel is fit to take such a child into his home....We do not want these children to be brought up in the atmosphere in which children are educated in [the left-wing kibbutz] Mishnar Ha'emek...The foundations must be universal...we want to forge one nation...to make sure that these children will be educated to fill any role we shall deem necessary.

Here we already sense the concept of statehood which Ben-Gurion would strive to achieve a few years later during Israel's formative period; his vision of Palestine as a lodestone. He saw the migration of these children as symbolizing the realization of the Biltmore Program—mass immigration of those most in need of rescue and an outstretched helping hand from the Yishuv—and was carried away by his optimistic expectations. He summed up the education debate by stating that "decisions cannot be made...as long as the children are not here." For the time being, the Jewish Agency

Executive appointed five of its members—Kaplan, Gruenbaum, Eliahu Dobkin, Moshe Shapira, and Ben-Gurion himself—to form a committee which would decide on all practical aspects of the absorption of the refugee children. The composition of this committee was evidence of the importance which the Executive attached to the matter at hand.

Simultaneously with the optimism in relation to these plans, we also find the very opposite: realism and even pessimism. Ben-Gurion turned down Gruenbaum's suggestion that South African prime minister Jan Christiaan Smuts be requested to allow Jewish—and not only Polish—children to enter that country, arguing that Smuts would refuse, as was later proven to be the case. He opposed appealing to the Allies to bomb German cities or imprison German-born residents of Allied countries, claiming that the Allies could not strike at innocent civilians, nor would they allow anyone to dictate targets or the schedule of their bombing operations.[34]

Ben-Gurion took part in deliberations concerning the proposal, transmitted by circles connected with the Rumanian Government, which offered the release of 70,000 Jews from Transnistria in return for a large sum of money. He asked his colleagues—who urged action and were willing to risk the funds—to differentiate between "those Jews whom we cannot bring...and those Jews whom we are able to bring from Europe." As for the first group, this objective "is unattainable at this moment...but if we fail to aid those whom we are able to help—we will not be forgiven."[35] In other words, Ben-Gurion believed that it was feasible to rescue only as many refugees as the White Paper quota allowed, and that efforts must be concentrated on the possible, for it was useless to harbor any hopes or dreams.

He reacted in similar fashion to the "Slovakia Plan" and the "Europa Plan" broached by the leaders of Slovakian Jewry who proposed that local officials and S.S. officers be bribed to stall the deportation shipments from Slovakia and from the rest of European countries to the death camps. Ben-Gurion differentiated between the two schemes, choosing that which seemed to have more chance of success. In relation to Slovakian officials, he said "they should be bribed...the Jewish Agency is willing to play a role in such an undertaking." However, he placed no credence in reports of Himmler's willingness to put a stop to the mass deportations from other European countries—as claimed by the Slovakian Jewish leadership—for it was precisely at that time that news leaked out of Himmler's directive to speed up the extermination process.[36]

This combination of optimism and realism characterized Ben-Gurion in late 1942 and early 1943, but even then he began to doubt that the Allies would aid in rescue operations. "On the whole, our position is very bad," he said as early as the end of 1942, "for we must turn to Roosevelt to act as our intermediary, and who knows whether he will do so." He sensed bitterly "that something is wrong, but this is not a result of inactivity on our part" but because of Great Britain's indifference to rescue activity.[37] As time passed, he became increasingly realistic. By the end of February 1943 he said that even an effort to save 5,000 children (the figure earlier used to describe but the first stage) would demand a great expenditure of resources and efforts on the part of the Yishuv, the Zionist movement, and the Jewish people, and it had to be borne in mind "that there are also Jews here in Eretz-Israel," in other words that the Yishuv too was in need of resources. In March he was already convinced that "unfortunately, the chance that the use of the certificates will be authorized is very theoretical, and there is no certainty that we will be able to utilize them."[38]

It gradually became clear that the same held true for other schemes, such as effecting an exchange of population, sending parachutists behind enemy lines, the removal of Jews from Transnistria, infiltration into occupied territories, and especially the establishment of an international rescue organization. In each case the British either delayed action or openly expressed their opposition. Once this became evident, Ben-Gurion characteristically made a clean break: he devoted no more of his time to such plans, even to the scheme for the rescue of children, though the emissaries in Istanbul kept him informed of developments.

He seemed indifferent to criticism leveled against him in the Mapai Central Committee to the effect that "Ben-Gurion is not devoting maximum attention to this subject," that for at least two or three months he should devote himself solely to rescue operations, that he did not share his thoughts on this matter with his colleagues, and that "there is no possibility to communicate" with him.[39] Ben-Gurion did not budge from the path he chose to follow.

Germany invaded Hungary in March 1944. The agonizing fear sensed by the Yishuv leadership since late 1943, that the remnants of the Jewish communities in Rumania, Bulgaria, and Hungary—more than a million souls—were also doomed to fall into the Nazi clutches, was becoming a reality. This may explain why Ben-Gurion, from the moment the Jewish Agency Executive learned of Eichmann's offer—brought by Joel Brand to Istanbul—to exchange Jewish lives for equipment, expended more time and effort on this project than he had previously devoted to all other rescue plans. The main thrust of Yishuv activity was designed to secure at least a statement of Allied willingness, even if expressed theoretically and indirectly, to open negotiations on the proposal. Shertok and Ben-Gurion sat up a whole night with Pomeranz, who brought the details from Istanbul and met with the High Commissioner to report about the proposed Brand-Shertok discussions. Ben-Gurion participated in all Executive sessions dealing with this matter, chairing most of them. He termed the plan "fantastic" but was of the opinion that even a "one in a million" chance had to be seized. He agreed that Shertok should go to Istanbul—even without a visa—for "this is most urgent matter" and "no opportunity must be missed," in Istanbul as well as in London.[40]

From the outset, Ben-Gurion's handling of the Eichmann proposal clearly pointed to a policy decision: no such negotiations could be undertaken without the cognizance of the Mandate Government, otherwise "we will not be able to proceed."[41] He believed that hope of rescue lay in Germany's wish, by means of this offer, to open negotiations with the Allies. Should the Yishuv deal directly with the Germans, this would be construed as betrayal of the Allies, in whose armed forces Jewish soldiers from Palestine were serving.

All this notwithstanding, it is difficult to fathom why Ben-Gurion prevented

Menahem Bader, from Kibbutz Mizra, one of the Yishuv's leading representatives in Istanbul, and Eliahu Dobkin, a deputy director of the Jewish Agency's Immigration Department, from conducting direct negotiations with the Germans in Hungary or in Spain, as the latter proposed. We do not know today what the Nazis were willing to offer at such a confrontation.[42] Perhaps the "one in a million...opportunity" that Ben-Gurion talked about was lost because of strict faithfulness to the Allied cause and the assumption that what lay behind the German proposal was only the desire to negotiate with the Western powers.

An examination of the course of the Brand affair shows that the British were unimpressed by the Yishuv's display of loyalty, that various elements in the British administration consciously misled Yishuv representatives, and that they held regard for British interests alone, especially the fear of being "flooded" by hundreds of thousands of refugees. The Allies did not accede to the appeals of the Yishuv's leadership, even refusing to agree in principle to meet with German representatives. Meanwhile, hundreds of thousands of Hungarian Jews were being exterminated in Auschwitz. Sad at heart, the Yishuv was powerless to help.

Ben-Gurion made one last attempt. Through the offices of Nahum Goldmann he sent a cable to US President Franklin D. Roosevelt, entreating him to publicly express his readiness to appoint a representative to rescue negotiations providing that deportations be stopped immediately, and beseeching him not to miss this unique and perhaps last opportunity to save the remnants of European Jewry. Undoubtedly, Ben-Gurion well knew that this cable would bring no concrete results. This was not a proposal grounded in political considerations but an emotional appeal and protest in the face of the Allies' aggravating indifference. An answer was received from the State Department to the effect that Brand's return to Budapest would be viewed with favor. But of what use would that be if he carried no reply whatsoever to Eichmann?[43]

It is not surprising, then, that a few days before the British Foreign Office undermined the last chance that Brand's mission would prove successful by leaking it to the press, Ben-Gurion, for the first time since the news of the systematic extermination of Europe Jewry reached Palestine, publicly gave vent to the sense of anguish and anger that had been building within him in a statement almost unprecedented in the severity of its phrasing. At this moment, the Jew in Ben-Gurion gained the upper hand over the statesman and political leader, and enabled him to sound "a loud and bitter lament," to use his own words, for the Jewish people who were being destroyed before his very eyes:

> What have you done — you nations that cherish freedom and justice...to the Jewish nation, as you watch the unending, ceaseless, incessant flow of our blood without lifting a finger, without extending a helping hand, without calling out to the demon of destruction: Stop!...Would you behave thus if thousands of American, English, and Russian women and elderly people were being cremated alive every day? Would you hold your peace if every day babies and children of the Allied nations would be crushed to the pavement?...Is not our blood as red as your blood and our honor as dear as yours? Is not our humiliation as shameful as your humiliation and our self-esteem as important as yours?[44]

The Holocaust and the Establishment of the State of Israel

By the time that Ben-Gurion realized that the Nazis were systematically destroying European Jewry, the Biltmore Program had already been approved by the Zionist Organization of America and by the Actions Committee in Jerusalem. Did the reality of events in Europe change his strategy and priorities, especially in relation to the necessary steps for the establishment of a Jewish Commonwealth?

The problem of "selective immigration," as it was termed, and of the allocation of the immigration certificates, which accompanied the Zionist movement between the two world wars, posed itself with agonizing intensity as a matter of life and death during the Holocaust years. Immediately after the Bermuda Conference, Apolinary Hartglas, political secretary of the Rescue Committee, prepared a memorandum intended "for Zionists only," of which Ben-Gurion was one of the recipients. Hartglas' evaluation of the situation was that millions of European Jews faced death, and that the Allies were unwilling, while the Yishuv lacked the means, to save them. Hopefully, by the expenditure of large sums of money and great efforts, no more than several tens of thousands might be rescued. The agonizing question was, whom to save? Hartglas' reply, he admitted, was "somewhat cruel": those who could benefit Palestine and the Jewish people—children, youth who had undergone training for a pioneer life in the Yishuv, and Zionist officials toward whom the movement was under obligation.[45]

Ben-Gurion directly and openly referred to this memorandum, even though with some delay.

> The choice of rescuing all the Jews is not open to us and even if we do everything possible we cannot extricate a million Jews, at best we can bring thousands, perhaps tens of thousands. The question of whom we shall bring is a very serious one, provided that we are even afforded that alternative...Of course, we shall even bring Jews who we are positive will leave Eretz-Israel within three months, if the alternative is that they will be murdered should they remain there. But, if the alternative is either to bring a Jew who will return to Rumania immediately after the war, remaining a stranger and an outsider for the duration of his stay here, or to save a Jew who will remain here—then we must choose...Jews who will remain here.

It would be "a political disaster," he said, if at the war's end, precisely when the campaign for mass immigration would get under way, many Jews would desert the country. Therefore, priority had to be given to youth and children who would be brought up in the country to be steadfast citizens of Palestine. After the children, "Polish refugees should receive first priority...veteran Zionists—no."[46] Ben-Gurion's reply, contrary to Hartglas' proposal, gave no priority to the rescue of leading Zionist functionaries.

Ben-Gurion's policy in this matter was not acceptable to his colleagues. Several of them, such as Gruenbaum, Kaplan, Avigur, Avriel, among others, did not adhere to it when they directed actual rescue operations. The Yishuv saved Jews of all ages and political inclinations from all occupied countries, but these episodes are outside the scope of our present study. In sum, however, the Holocaust did not cause any significant modification of Ben-Gurion's policy on immigration which remained, in principle, unchanged since before World War II.

As for *political orientation*, Zionist policy until the 1939 White Paper was to rely on Great Britain. During the war, Ben-Gurion gradually shifted to an orientation based on the United States, but this still meant reliance upon the Western democracies. Did the bitter disappointment with those very democracies, which consistently ignored rescue pleas, cause a change in Ben-Gurion's political strategy? Even the hope that Churchill and Roosevelt would overcome the resistance of their cabinets and senior officials, and translate their public expressions of shock into deeds, proved unrealistic. It gradually became clear that Ben-Gurion was not mistaken when he posed the question in its sharpest terms: Could public pressure unsupported by extensive territory, by control of strategic positions, by sources of petroleum or massive resources of manpower, have any efficacy when human suffering and moral considerations were not sufficient motive for action?

Ben-Gurion did not change his outlook. At the outbreak of hostilities he posited that the Yishuv must fight the White Paper as if there were no war and help the British as if there were no White Paper.[47] Throughout the war it became increasingly evident that any open opposition to the Mandate Government would hamper whatever rescue operations the Yishuv was able to mount by itself, and would, of course, forestall any major effort should the possibility present itself. The transfer of large sums of money, mass movements of human beings, provision of refuge and shelter in Palestine or elsewhere would all depend upon the cooperation of the Mandate authorities, as the Yishuv leadership well knew.

As the war neared its end, Ben-Gurion's strategy remained unchanged. When Gruenbaum proposed that the Yishuv try to bring Holocaust survivors to Palestine without the knowledge of the British, Ben-Gurion replied sharply:

> Mr. Gruenbaum's suggestion reeks of despair of England and the United States. To whom does he suggest we turn? We will not be able, by ourselves, to determine the political future of this country after the war. Does Mr. Gruenbaum have another address to which we can direct our international political activity?[48]

An open break with Great Britain would have made the achievement of Zionist aspirations impossible. On the other hand, it was possible—as Ben-Gurion hoped—that postwar conditions, a change of government in England or public pressure, especially in the United States, would force Great Britain to change its policy toward Zionist aspirations in Palestine.

Furthermore, abandonment of the Western democracies would have meant more than just a change in political strategy. Today, with the benefit of hindsight, it seems that Ben-Gurion was somewhat naive in believing the Allies would establish an international rescue organization or agree to exchange large numbers of Germans for Jews. Ben-Gurion, however, could not abandon the framework of Zionist ideology which from the outset assumed the progress of human society in general, and that of the liberal West in particular, toward a more enlightened and tolerant world. For one who placed his faith in such a premise, it was impossible to foresee that Great Britain would openly agree to the transfer of children and then act behind the scenes to impede it. Great Britain was fighting for "freedom, justice, democracy, liberty, and equality," to use Ben-Gurion's own terms, and no one could presume that the democracies would place the Jews outside their value system. "The world's conscience will awaken, there is a human conscience in this world, events unprecedented in world history have taken place," he argued.[49]

The impact of the Holocaust on Ben-Gurion's thinking can be examined in yet another aspect of Zionist ideology: the central importance of *binyan ha'aretz*— literally "the upbuilding of the homeland." When Ben-Gurion realized that extensive rescue operations were impossible, for the Yishuv could not force the Allies—let alone the Germans—to accede to its demands, and that world Jewry did not consider the Yishuv to be the focal point of such efforts, as evinced in their refusal to transfer funds to Palestine for that purpose, he came to the conclusion that the Jewish community in the homeland was obliged to carry out by itself whatever rescue operations its limited resources and manpower allowed. His conclusion was evident in the decisions he made from time to time in connection with the several rescue proposals that were brought up for discussion. Limited rescue efforts—expedition of relief parcels, transfer of funds, help in acquiring documents and in crossing borders, as well as maintaining a link between the Diaspora and the homeland—all these could be conducted simultaneously with the continued development of the country and its Haganah para-military force, and not at their expense. The Yishuv had an "obligation of honor" not to rest for a second so that it should not have pangs of conscience about its rescue efforts. It was obligated to harness the country's economic prosperity to help in some way "to rescue the Jewish people whose very existence is in danger," for without European Jewry, who could tell what was destined for the Yishuv, and without the Yishuv, "what will be the fate of the future hopes of the Jewish people?"[50]

In the summer of 1943, when Ben-Gurion spoke of the Yishuv's "obligation of honor," he also pointed out that the Jewish Agency had not been entrusted by the Jewish world with responsibility for rescue efforts. This was "detrimental both to the Jewish Agency and to assistance for the Jews of Nazi Europe," because the Agency did not have

> all-Jewish authority over Jewish finances, over all Jewish matters—unfortunately there is no overall organization. There is the World Jewish Congress and the American Jewish Congress, there is the Joint Distribution Committee and others, but the institution called the Jewish Agency is a worldwide organization entrusted with building Eretz-Israel. I do not want to say which is more important, to build Eretz-Israel or save one more Jew from Zagreb, and it may be true that at times it is more important to rescue one child from Zagreb, but these are two different objectives and...what have we to gain...from the mix-up we are causing?...The objective of the rescue efforts, to save another Jew, to do something to stop the deportations, this is very important...but to this end there must be another organization and other financial resources.[51]

Ben-Gurion's distinction between the role of the Jewish Agency—the development of Palestine—and overall rescue efforts, which he believed were outside the scope of the Agency's responsibility, bring us full circle to the stand he took at the outbreak of the war: the JDC, the World Jewish Congress, and the American Jewish Congress were responsible for all-Jewish affairs, for lack of a better alternative. This was probably the clearest statement made by Ben-Gurion concerning the respective roles of the Jewish Agency and the rest of the Yishuv. What he seemed to be saying was that other organizations and institutions such as the Histadrut, agricultural settlements, and industrial enterprises must mobilize for rescue activity, expending funds that were not part of the Agency's budget, funds that anyway would not have been allocated to the Agency. True to this concept, Ben-Gurion himself participated in personal and clandestine fund-raising meetings to gather resources which *a priori* were earmarked for rescue efforts alone.[52] This leads to another distinction which Ben-Gurion may logically have made. Yehiel Duvdevani, then a member of the Mapai Central Committee, testifies that he understood Ben-Gurion to say that when he came to his conclusions about the Yishuv's obligation and limited capacity to rescue Jews from Europe, he set down a sort of "division of tasks": he would continue to handle the Yishuv's political affairs while Avigur, Golomb, Yehieli, and others would be directly responsible for rescue efforts, reporting to him. Should a proposal be presented which necessitated political intervention, he would handle it together with Shertok.[53] And this, in fact, is how events unfolded.

Finally, did Ben-Gurion change his attitude toward the Biltmore Program after 1942? It may very well be that he did not abandon it because he found several ways to explain its seeming inconsistency with the systematic extermination of Jews. For instance, news from Europe told of one million Jewish dead out of a total population of almost ten million Jews. There was reason to hope and assume that even should the extermination process continue for some time and not be halted immediately, enough Jews would survive the Holocaust to justify the Biltmore Program.

On many occasions Ben-Gurion, with great despair, had emphasized that "the destruction of European Jewry spells doom for Zionist aspirations, for no one will survive to build Eretz-Israel," and that it was this prognosis that kept him awake nights: "What, then, will be the fate of the future hopes of the Jewish people; what, then, will be the fate of the Yishuv in Palestine? I do not want to think about it — it is such a terrifying vision."[54] But had Ben-Gurion declared then, late in 1942 — after the approval of the Biltmore plan — that he was abandoning it in view of events in Europe, this would have been a public expression of deep and total despair. In effect this would have been tantamount to admitting that Zionism and the Jewish people had simply reached the end of the road.

Instead, he chose to follow a different course of action. He did not share his sense of despair with others, so as not to sow despondency. Secondly, he immediately sought new avenues of activity, primarily focusing on the Jewish communities in Muslim countries. In March 1943, no longer harboring any illusions about help from the Allies concerning the extrication of the children, he concluded that part of the immigration certificates should be allocated to the Jews of Yemen, Syria, and Iraq. He realized that when the Arab-Jewish conflict would erupt in Palestine after the war, these Jewish communities would be "in danger of a terrible massacre, in comparison to which the present slaughter in Europe would seem less terrible than it does today." (This statement shows that the Yishuv was not as yet aware of the full, horrendous extent of the Holocaust.) Ben-Gurion considered this matter of the utmost urgency for the Yishuv, "this small vanguard of the Jewish people," and should it choose to ignore the imminent danger, it would be held responsible "for the blood that will be spilled and the increasing degradations" of these communities.[55] Once more, it was incumbent upon Zionism to provide the solution for conditions in the Diaspora—the very essence of the Biltmore Program.

Another avenue for action were the Holocaust survivors. At the end of August 1943, when Shertok returned from Istanbul, Ben-Gurion pointed to the last large Jewish community still left in the Balkans and the need to convince it, from that moment onwards, that the Zionist solution was an absolute necessity for its survival; failure would mean a final and fatal blow to Zionism.[56] For the same reason he renewed efforts to despatch parachutists behind enemy lines in order that they be in the right place at the right time, on the eve of liberation, to convince the survivors to accept the Zionist solution, and to act as an antidote to the attraction of America, on the one hand, and of Communism, on other other. When Yoel Palgi and Chaim Chermesh, two of the parachutists, asked Ben-Gurion to define the objective of their mission, he replied: "To teach the Jews that Eretz-Israel is their country and their bastion...and that they must storm its locked gates in their multitudes in order to force them open immediately after the day of victory."[57] For similar reasons, Ben-Gurion was intensively involved with the Brand mission, as described previously.

It was precisely then, in the summer of 1943, that Avigur and Dobkin returned from Teheran to report that the majority of refugees reaching Iran were broken, hopeless human wrecks, and what was more important, they had changed. There were informers among them and deep corruption and immorality prevailed. Deeply shocked and filled with misgiving, the first emissaries from Palestine who came into contact with the remnants of European Jewry in the Displaced Persons camps a few months after the end of the war, reported home in similar vein. Whereas a few years earlier it was universally accepted that without these survivors the Yishuv would not be able to hold out, now—after that first confrontation—there was some fear that once these refugees arrived in Palestine the whole Zionist enterprise would be jeopardized. It was then that Ben-Gurion asked: "Will these Jews be an obstruction and a hindrance or an aid to Zionism?" But it soon became clear that these survivors were imbued with vigor and vitality, organizational capability, and optimism. After realizing that many who previously were not adherents of Zionism had, by virtue of their predicament, become wholehearted Zionists and were "wonderful Jews, wonderful Zionists with deep Zionist instincts," Ben-Gurion concluded that they would be the fulcrum which would determine the destiny of the movement. Therefore, all three facets of the Biltmore Program had to be achieved, for in spite of all that had passed it was still the one and only path and solution for the remnants of European Jewry, for the Jews living in Muslim countries, and for the Yishuv, "the hope of the Jewish people."[58]

The Holocaust did not effect any change in Ben-Gurion's relation to four basic precepts of Zionist policy: immigration, political orientation toward the West, *binyan ha'aretz*, and the establishment of a Jewish Commonwealth. It should be emphasized, however, that in all probability he did not decide *a priori* that the Holocaust would not deflect the Zionist movement from its chosen path. This was a process which began when he realized the true state of events in Europe toward the end of 1942, through high hopes that were soon dashed, and then an intensive analysis of the changed situation after which he arrived at the conclusion that guided his actions. However, the fact that his outlook remained consistent, as evident from his undisguised statements on the matter in question, enabled critics to point to this lack of change as overwhelming proof of complete, intentional detachment on the part of the most outstanding Zionist leader of the day from the tragedy of his people, deriving primarily from his obsession with the establishment of a Jewish state.

Ben-Gurion's Pattern of Leadership and the Holocaust

At the outset of this study, the question was raised whether the available historical sources enable us to paint an image of Ben-Gurion in relation to the Holocaust different from that widely accepted throughout the years. On the basis of the evidence presented, it seems that we have a clear-cut answer: Ben-Gurion was deeply involved with the tragic events, aware of the extermination of European Jewry, and probably distressed by it to a degree and in a manner completely at variance with the indifference and aloofness with which he has been charged. What, then, has given rise to such a negative image? The answer, in all probability, lies not in his attitude toward the Holocaust but in his character, habits, and style of political leadership.

His diary, for example, which he kept consistently over a period of several decades, does not reflect events in direct proportion to their importance, and this is true not only of the Holocaust.[59] In similar fashion, Ben-Gurion kept to himself and did not make public or share even with his closest associates many decisions, considerations, and disappointments that had bearing on other subjects, not only on the Holocaust and rescue efforts. It was characteristic of him to abstain from expressing his thoughts and doubts. His silence in relation to the Holocaust, against the background of such horrendous events which called for some reaction, was possibly more poignant than usual. To this day, individuals who were actively involved in the collection and dissemination of information about the Holocaust bitterly emphasize that "Ben-Gurion read—and was silent," or that he listened to the refugees—and was silent.[60] On one occasion he did refer to his reticence, perhaps in an effort to justify it: "I lack the words, I will not refer to the tragedy; I think that the language that can do so has not yet been created."[61] I suggest that the paucity of Ben-Gurion's oral and written reactions to the Holocaust should not be construed as indifference to the tragedy of European Jewry but rather as a penetrating and sober comprehension of the enormity of the national catastrophe, an understanding which found expression in a behavior pattern characteristic of Ben-Gurion's personality.

Furthermore, Ben-Gurion did not seek popularity, nor was he a leader who wooed the public and sought its daily approbation. He followed his own path, on the basis of his own considerations, feeling no need to keep abreast of public sentiment — or to submit to it. Had he acceded to the various proposals described earlier in this study or — even better — had he initiated them, without changing his personal conviction as to their efficacy; had he repeatedly expressed his grief in public, the Yishuv would have believed that this was a matter to which Ben-Gurion attached the highest priority, and he would have been afforded a positive image in his attitude toward the Holocaust, irrespective of the actual outcome of the rescue efforts undertaken by the Yishuv. But such were not Ben-Gurion's personality and behavior.[62]

Ben-Gurion admitted that he tended to be disputatious. During the period under examination, his relations with Gruenbaum, chairman of the Rescue Committee, were most strained. Persons who knew them both flatly assert that "Ben-Gurion could not stand Gruenbaum." This was obvious during the rescue deliberations of the Jewish Agency Executive and from the status of the Committee and its chairman. During this very period, relations between Ben-Gurion and Weizmann, which had been deteriorating since the outbreak of the war, reached a state of open rupture that endangered Zionist unity. Undoubtedly, this development obstructed coordination between Weizmann and Jerusalem in rescue affairs. "There are matters much more important than Weizmann now," Katznelson reprimanded Ben-Gurion, "the extinction of European Jewry."[63]

Ben-Gurion's relations with the Revisionist Party during these years were also marked by extreme and sharply critical statements. A detailed survey of this relationship is outside the scope of the present study. Suffice it to say that the period of Revisionist membership in the Rescue Committee, from January 1943 to June 1944, was characterized by mutual suspicion and accusations.[64]

We cannot ascertain the direct effect — if any — of these argumentative and strained relations upon the chances for actual rescue operations. There is no doubt, however, that Ben-Gurion expended much energy and thought on these acute campaigns against his adversaries and that they demanded much of his time. This is especially true in regard to his clashes with Weizmann and the Revisionists, conflicts that extend over lengthy periods of time and that took various forms, and were controversies over matters of principle between parties and ideologies.

Mapai internal affairs also demanded much of Ben-Gurion's attention at this time, especially relations with "Faction B" which culminated in its withdrawal from the party. The timing was both ironic and distressing: the crisis within Mapai first found expression at the Kfar Vitkin Convention in October 1942, just as repeated confirmation of news about the total and systematic annihilation of European Jewry reached Palestine, and the final split in the ranks occurred in March 1944, simultaneously with the Nazi invasion of Hungary.

These were difficult years for Ben-Gurion, both in his private life and public capacity. True, he did buttress his standing as the leader of the Yishuv and the World Zionist Organization, but he did not yet attain that uncontested status that he was to acquire in the late 40's and the 50's. They were also marked by a series of critical situations: the White Paper of 1939 and the resulting crisis in relations with Great Britain; the rupture between Weizmann and Ben-Gurion; strained relations with the Revisionists; friction with Tabenkin who cut himself off after "Faction B" withdrew from Mapai; the untimely deaths of Dov Hoz and Eliahu Golomb, and the greatest blow of all, the death of Berl Katznelson, his one true friend.

Ben-Gurion was a difficult, lonely, introverted individualist, who died without leaving any key to his emotions and thinking during that terrible period. True, the portrait we have drawn is based on what he said and did during the Holocaust years and is an attempt to summarize his thoughts and conclusions. But this is not a summary which Ben-Gurion himself left to posterity. Thus, even though the historian hopes that his painstaking searching, sifting, and arranging of the historical evidence will lead to a clear and correct conclusion, there is no unequivocal solution to the intricate question at hand.

Ben-Gurion did not shut his eyes to the suffering of his brethren, he did not knowingly desert them and leave them to their fate, nor did the objectives of Zionism so blind him that he was able to separate the fate of the nation from that of the homeland. The very opposite is true: time and again he emphasized that the fate of the Jewish people was the moving cause of his thoughts and actions, and that the Yishuv was not an aim in its own right, but rather "the hope of the nation."

The questions which remain unanswered are, to what extent did Ben-Gurion realize the full extent of what was happening in Europe during the Holocaust years? Could he decipher the illogical course that events took by means of his patterns of logic and political thought, patterns which originated prior to World War II? Could one be prepared for such eventualities—events unprecedented by any human or national experience? To these questions, the very basis of our discussion of Ben-Gurion and the Holocaust, there is no answer. It will remain, in the words of the poet Abba Kovner, "an unsolved human enigma."[65]

Notes

1 For example, interviews with Azriel Bigon, then secretary of the World Union of Mapai, April 30, 1982, and with Yehiel Duvdevani, then member of the Mapai Center, June 25, 1982.

2 The poem is part of a cycle which was published under the pen-name of Gabi Daniel in *Igra* 2 (1985-1986), pp. 199-200.

3 Ben-Gurion's biographer, Shabtai Teveth, wrote in *Ben-Gurion, 100* (Hebrew), a special supplement of *Yediot Aharonot*, October 3, 1986: "His complete diaries could fill 50 thick volumes; he wrote .. more than 30 .. books .. his bibliography .. up to 1959 includes about 2,500 items .. his personal archive .. contains over 750,000 documents."

4 Michael Bar-Zohar, *Ben-Gurion* (Hebrew), Tel Aviv, 1977, 3 vols. This is the first well-researched biography to appear in Hebrew. An abridged edition in English translation appeared in 1986: M. Bar-Zohar, *Ben-Gurion: A Biography*, New York, 1986. Shabtai Teveth's biography in Hebrew, *David's Jealousy: The Life of David Ben-Gurion*, has reached the events of 1942, while his English version covers the years 1886-1948. See Shabtai Teveth, *Ben-Gurion: The Burning Ground, 1886-1948*, Boston, 1986.

5 The original private archive is in the Israel Defense Forces Archives and a copy is deposited in Sedeh Boker.

6 These details have been supplied by Tuvia Friling, director of the archives at the Ben-Gurion Research Center in Sedeh Boker. He is presently completing a Ph.D. dissertation on "Ben-Gurion and the Holocaust of European Jewry, 1939-1945," which will include the relevant material collected and arranged in these archives.

7 Executive of the Va'ad Leumi, December 12, 1938, Central Zionist Archives, Jerusalem (hereafter: C.Z.A.), J1/7521.

8 Jacob Katz deals with the capability of the Jewish leadership to foresee the Holocaust. See his "Was the Holocaust Predictable?" *Commentary* 59, no. 5 (May 1975), pp. 41-48.

9 See Ernst Simon, *The Line of Demarcation* (Hebrew), Givat-Haviva, 1973, p. 29.

10 For a detailed description of Ben-Gurion's policy during these years see Allon Gal, *David Ben-Gurion—Preparing for a Jewish State: Political Alignment in Response to the White Paper and the Outbreak of World War II, 1938-1941* (Hebrew), Sedeh Boker, 1985.

11 Zionist Actions Committee, February 29, 1940, C.Z.A., S25/1828.

12 Even today Holocaust historians and survivors alike term this a period of "comparative quiet" in the ghettos.

13 For a discussion of how the news from Europe were interpreted at this time, see Yoav Gelber, "Reports on the Annihilation of European Jewry in the Hebrew Press of Palestine (1941-1942)" (Hebrew), *Studies on the Holocaust and the Resistance*, series II, vol. 1 (1970), pp. 30-58; Dina Porat, *An Entangled Leadership: The Yishuv and the Holocaust, 1942-1945* (Hebrew), Tel Aviv, 1986, ch. 1.

14 Secretariat of the World Union of Mapai, January 22, 1940, Labor Party Archives (hereafter: L.P.A.) Record Group 3, 101/40, vol. 1.

15 He left Palestine for England in March 1940, reached the US in October, and remained there until his return home in February 1941. A few months later, in June, he once more traveled to England and from there in November to the US where he remained until October 1942. After his return to Palestine he did not leave its borders for the duration of the war except for a short visit to Bulgaria late in 1944.

16 See note 11 above.

17 See his statement in the Jewish Agency Executive, March 3, 1941, and at the meeting of the Zionist Actions Committee, February 24, 1941—both in C.Z.A., S25/1838; and at the Mapai Central Committee, February 19, 1941, L.P.A. 23/41.

18 Bar-Zohar, *Ben-Gurion*, p. 163.

19 See note 13 above.

20 October 15, 1942, C.Z.A., S25/293, and at a conference of Mapai functionaries, December 12, 1942, L.P.A., Box 3/6.

21 October 15, 1942, C.Z.A., S25/293.

22 The original members of the committee, established at the outbreak of the war and known as the "Committee of Four," were Eliahu Dobkin, Moshe Shapira, Dr. Emil Schmorak and Yitzhak Gruenbaum. The additional member from the Jewish Agency Executive was Dr. Bernard Joseph (later Dov Yosef); representatives of the Va'ad Leumi were Shlomo Zalman Shragai, Yehoshua Suprasky, and Izhak Ben-Zvi; from the Revisionists, Yosef Klarman and Herman Segal; and from Agudat Israel, Rabbis Binyamin Mintz and Yitzhak Meir Levin.

23 Va'ad Leumi, January 17, 1943, C.Z.A., J1/7255; Zionist Actions Committee, January 18, 1943, C.Z.A., S25/295. For the obligation, see Porat, *An Entangled Leadership*, ch. 2-3.

24 Protocols of the Jewish Agency Executive, December 6, 1941, C.Z.A.

25 Ibid., May 21, 1944, C.Z.A.

26 Ibid., December 12, 1942, C.Z.A.

27 Ibid., September 12, 1943, and a similar statement by M. Shertok, September 5, 1943, C.Z.A. It should be noted that this was a definition by implication for Ben-Gurion did not directly mention the Jewish communities but spoke only about the Yishuv.

28 Interview with Venia Pomeranz (today Professor Ze'ev Hadari of Ben-Gurion University), April 5, 1984.

29 Protocols of the Jewish Agency Executive, July 23, 1944 and September 3, 1944, C.Z.A., and the telegram of congratulation to the emissary despatched to Istanbul, August 23, 1943, C.Z.A., S6/4587.

30 For a discussion of the public sentiment, see Porat, *An Entangled Leadership*, chs. 2 and 4.

31 See especially protocols of the Jewish Agency Executive, November 22 and 29, 1942, December 6, 20 and 27, 1942, C.Z.A., and protocols of the Mapai Central Committee, November 24 and 30, 1942, L.P.A. 23/42.

32 Protocols of the Jewish Agency Executive, November 29, 1942, December 6 and 13, 1942, and January 10, 1943, C.Z.A.; Tuvia Friling, "Ben-Gurion's Involvement in Attempts to Save Children, and the Absorption Debate, November 1942-May 1945" (Hebrew), unpublished M.A. Thesis, Hebrew University of Jerusalem, 1984, pp. 7-8.

33 Protocols of the Mapai Secretariat, December 9, 1942, L.P.A., 24/42; protocols of the Jewish Agency Executive, December 13 and 20, 1942, C.Z.A.

34 Protocols of the Jewish Agency Executive, February 28, 1943 and the continuation of the discussion on April 25, 1943 and May 2, 1943, C.Z.A. Smuts did in fact reply in the negative to a later appeal from Gruenbaum in the summer of 1943. As for the debate on bombing civilian targets, see the protocols of the Jewish Agency Executive cited in note 32 above.

35 Protocols of the Mapai Secretariat, February 10, 1943, L.P.A. 24/43.

36 Ibid., and protocols of the Mapai Central Committee, February 4, 1943, L.P.A. 23/43.

37 Protocols of the Jewish Agency Executive, December 6, 1942 and January 4, 1943, C.Z.A.

38 Ibid., March 7, 1943 and April 4, 1943, C.Z.A.

39 See note 35 above.

40 Protocols of the Jewish Agency Executive, May 25, 1944, C.Z.A.

41 Ibid.

42 A representative of the German delegation met with Bader in Istanbul in June 1944. M. Bader, *Sad Missions* (Hebrew), Tel Aviv, 1978, pp. 110-111. In June, Kasztner informed Dobkin that an S.S. representative would meet him anywhere he chose. See Dobkin's report, protocols of the Jewish Agency Executive, September 21, 1944, C.Z.A.

43 Ibid., July 2 and 16, 1944, C.Z.A.

44 See the corrected draft in Ben-Gurion's handwriting, C.Z.A., S44/201, and the final draft in his private archive at Sedeh Boker. Part of it was published in the Hebrew daily *Davar* on July 10, 1944. Interestingly enough, the entire section, three folio sheets, was deleted from his published collected speeches, *In the Struggle* (Hebrew), vol. 4, Tel Aviv, 1957, pp. 187-192. We do not know whether Ben-Gurion himself or Yehuda Erez, who collected and edited the speeches for publication, deleted it. Both Shabtai Teveth and Erez's daughter believe that Ben-Gurion gave Erez complete leeway and did not care which parts of his speeches would be included.

45 C.Z.A., S26/232.

46 Protocols of the Jewish Agency Executive, July 23, 1944, C.Z.A.

47 Protocols of the Mapai Central Committee, September 12, 1939, L.P.A., 23/39, and *In the Struggle*, vol. 3, Tel Aviv, 1950, p. 18.

48 Protocols of the Jewish Agency Executive, June 20, 1944 and July 2 and 23, 1944, C.Z.A.

49 Meeting of the Mapai Political Committee, January 26, 1944, L.P.A.

50 Quoted by Friling, "Ben-Gurion's Involvement in Attempts to Save Children," pp. 20-21; Ben-Gurion said this on September 23, 1943 at a fund-raising event during "Diaspora Month."

51 Protocols of the Mapai Central Committee, August 24, 1943, L.P.A., 23/43.

52 During February and September 1943, he participated in meetings in private homes at which he spoke, explaining the importance of rescue efforts.

53 Interview with Yehiel Duvdevani, then a member of the Mapai Central Committee, October 25, 1981.

54 Protocols of the Jewish Agency Executive. December 6, 1943, C.Z.A., and note 50 above.

55 See note 51 above.

56 See his reports that month, especially to the Mapai Central Committee, the Jewish Agency Executive, and the Zionist Actions Committee.

57 Yoel Palgi, *And Behold, a Great Wind Came* (Hebrew), Tel Aviv, 1977, p. 15.

58 Protocols of the Mapai Central Committee, May 20, 1945, September 4, 1945 and November 22, 1945, L.P.A., 23/45.

59 Bar-Zohar, *Ben-Gurion*, p. 186, and Teveth (note 4 above).

60 See note 1 above.

61 Quoted by Friling, "Ben-Gurion's Involvement in Attempts to Save Children," p. 19.

62 One characteristic example will suffice: The subjects of discussion at a gala event in honor of Stanislaw Kot, deputy prime minister of the Polish Government-in-Exile, who visited Jerusalem late in 1942, were the future status of Poland's Jewish community after the war and their rights. After the meeting, Ben-Gurion invited Kot for a night-time stroll through Jerusalem and told him privately that what was said at the meeting was not the main issue. The important subject was the mass murder of Poland's Jews, which caused him many sleepless nights. The Polish people would not be forgiven if they did not extend aid to their Jewish neighbors.

63 Meeting of the Mapai Political Committee, June 16, 1943, L.P.A.
64 Conference of the Mapai functionaries (note 20 above); protocols of the Jewish Agency Executive, April 30, 1944 and May 14, 1944, C.Z.A.
65 *On the Narrow Bridge* (Hebrew), Tel Aviv, 1981, pp. 223-224.

Statehood

THE WAR OF INDEPENDENCE

Following the end of World War II and the Holocaust, the Zionist movement resumed its struggle for independence in a mood of fierce resolution. The Jewish Agency conducted the struggle in Palestine and abroad, employing a variety of means: political campaigns and negotiations, large-scale clandestine immigration (Ha'apalah), intensified settlement activities, and guerrilla-strikes at strategic installations, intended mainly to achieve legalized mass immigration. To this end it formed the Jewish Resistance Movement (Tenu'at Hameri), in which the dissident I.Z.L. and Lehi underground movements joined the Haganah and accepted—for the time being—the authority of the Agency and its chairman, David Ben-Gurion. From Fall 1945 until the UN Assembly decision on November 29, 1947, the number of clandestine immigrants reached almost fifty thousand, eleven new settlements were set up in the Negev in a concerted overnight operation in October 1946, and during 1947 they were connected by long-distance pipelines to a regular water supply. Armed acts of resistance were stringently restricted, in order to minimize casualties and to avoid giving the British a pretext for repressive countermeasures.

Tenu'at Hameri's military operations reached their peak in 1946. On the night of June 16-17, the Palmach effectively isolated Palestine from neighboring states by destroying ten rail and road bridges along the country's borders. On the following night, Lehi attacked railway yards in Haifa. On June 18, the I.Z.L. kidnaped British hostages in order to prevent the execution of its members, convicted in military courts. On Saturday, June 29, "Black Sabbath," the British countered with the arrest of prominent Jewish leaders and countrywide searches for Palmach members and arms. On July 22, the I.Z.L. retaliated, blowing up a wing of Jerusalem's King David Hotel then occupied by Palestine government offices. As a result of internal misunderstandings following this operation, Tenu'at Hameri disintegrated. Subsequently combat activity of the Haganah was in large measure limited to naval sabotage carried out by the Palmach. The I.Z.L. and Lehi returned to their course of independent action.

At the 22nd Zionist Congress in December 1946, Chaim Weizmann was deposed as president, and, in effect, Ben-Gurion became head of the Zionist movement. Until that time, the Haganah had acted according to the guidelines laid down by the Political Department of the Jewish Agency. However, at this Congress, Ben-Gurion stressed the potentially grave security dangers posed by the Arabs of Palestine and the neighboring states, in the event of war. He proposed the establishment of a Security Department within the Agency's Executive and took personal responsibility for the portfolio. From the outset, Ben-Gurion had stood at the center of confrontations with the Mandatory authorities, and his assumption of the security portfolio thus went undisputed. His became a dual role: chairman of the Jewish Agency Executive and chief of its Security Department. Following the establishment of the Provisional Government, he was both prime minister and minister of defense.

In February 1947, the British Government abandoned its efforts to attain an agreed settlement between Arabs and Jews, and announced that it was transferring responsibility for Palestine to the United Nations. This shift in the diplomatic arena transformed Zionist policy. The anti-British struggle was de-emphasized in favor of actions designed to bring about a pro-Zionist majority decision in the UN General Assembly.

During the summer of 1947, following inspection tours of the Haganah and intensive discussions with its leaders, Ben-Gurion instructed them to prepare for a new approach:

> The confrontation between Zionism and the policy of the White Paper is basically political and not military in nature.... [The Haganah] is only one of the factors within the Jewish people, and only an overall effort, on the part of the Yishuv and the people, in immigration, the armed struggle and the diplomatic campaign in the international arena—will succeed in tilting the scales.[1]

Throughout the Yishuv's long anti-British campaign, the Arabs of Palestine had rarely acted against the Jewish community. Nevertheless, Ben-Gurion ordered that preparations be made for a war which the Arabs were likely to launch as soon as the United Nations took a stand on the Palestine problem.[2]

The United Nations Special Committee on Palestine (UNSCOP) completed its work by the end of August 1947, with the majority of its members in favor of the political partition of Palestine. Their recommendations would only be binding if at least two-thirds of the General Assembly endorsed them. During early October, a period of political uncertainty as the UN deliberated, the General Staff of the Haganah received Ben-Gurion's instructions regarding its mission in the war which was liable to erupt:

> The full capacity of the Yishuv is to be mobilized...to safeguard the entire Yishuv and the settlements (wherever they may be), to conquer the whole country or most of it, and to maintain its occupation until the attainment of an authoritative political settlement.[3]

When the General Staff asked for operational clarifications, Ben-Gurion tied his answer to the outcome of the UN debate: "If the decision [on partition] is favorable we shall defend every settlement, resist any attack, and maintain services to the Jewish Yishuv and to all the Arabs who so desire; we shall not restrict ourselves territorially."[4]

The goals outlined in this directive committed the Haganah to a twofold mission, defensive as well as offensive. Defensively, it meant protecting Jewish Jerusalem, as well as maintaining Western Galilee, the Dead Sea potash works and those Jewish settlements which could easily be cut off, such as the Etzion Bloc. The offensive significance of the mission was that Haganah forces would have to break out of the Jewish settlement zone, which extended over only about one-third of the territory alloted to the Jewish state, in order to secure the Negev, beyond Revivim and Nevatim, all the way to Eilat.

The goals were far-reaching, even pretentious, and could only be realized if the Yishuv would be able to invest considerable resources in mobilizing, equipping and training for war. The political leadership took for granted the readiness of tens of thousands of Haganah members to enlist voluntarily and assumed the willingness of Jewish settlers to stand firm in the defense of their homes against Palestinian Arab attackers and invading Arab armies.

On Saturday, November 29, 1947, Ben-Gurion was at the Kaliya Hotel. He was sixty-one years old, and, due to backaches from which he suffered, used to bathe in the Dead Sea during the weekends. After midnight he was awakened to be told that the UN General Assembly had carried the Palestine Resolution with a majority that exceeded the necessary two-thirds. Everywhere crowds gathered to dance in the streets, but after Ben-Gurion hurried back to Jerusalem he felt as a "man in mourning among the celebrators...⁴*

Since his appointment as chairman of the Jewish Agency Executive in 1935, Ben-Gurion had gained experience in leading the Zionist movement: during the crisis of the 1936-1939 Arab Revolt, the war years, and lately—the resistance. He was now keenly aware of the sufferings which the war ahead would bring, but was determined to strive for the attainment of a dual aim: statehood for the Yishuv and the successful defence of the new state.

Ben-Gurion's diary shows clearly how much of his time and energy was invested in the manifold aspects of state-building: foreign and internal affairs, the achievement of a national consensus, the forming of a provisional government and a legislative assembly, and the financing of the state of war. The success of the Jewish leadership in nation-building can be appreciated in the light of the achievements in immigration and settlement during wartime. More than 120,000 immigrants arrived during 1948 and had to be somehow absorbed, and about 40 new settlements were set up during that year in the new areas occupied and to improve security along vulnerable borders. These aspects, though mentioned only briefly here, should not be overlooked in an assessment of Ben-Gurion's role in Israel's War of Independence. His most vital and urgent task in the context of nation-building was probably the creation of an army.

The Foundation of the Israel Defense Forces

When hostilities broke out, the burden of the Yishuv's defense had to be carried by less than 4,500 men and women: Haganah members "on active service" in the skeleton staff, the Palmach, and the Jewish Settlement Police (although formally under Palestine Police command), located in rural settlements. The geographical layout of the settlements, rural and urban, determined the Yishuv's actual defensive alignment. In the relative security provided by the settlements, Jewish field-forces were able to enlist, equip and train their manpower, and organize it into companies, battalions and brigades. Thus the Israel Defense Forces (I.D.F.) came into being.

Some of Ben-Gurion's bitterest controversies with the High Command of the Haganah centered on this very process of forming the I.D.F., a process which involved transforming what had been essentially an underground militia into a regular army. This complex task was further complicated by the illness of the Haganah's Chief of Staff, Ya'akov Dori, which prevented him from functioning on a regular basis, and by the difficulty encountered in appointing a substitute who would be willing to take his place and would be accepted by his colleagues in the High Command. Yisrael Galili, who served as the "Head of the National Command," the civilian authority supervising the Haganah on behalf of the Jewish Agency, fulfilled some staff-coordination functions, and acted as a de facto deputy for Ben-Gurion. On the eve of the declaration of independence, Ben-Gurion abolished the "National Command," which was to become obsolete with the formation of a Ministry of Defense. Galili was relieved of his former position, but reconciled himself to continue in a mediating function.[5]

The Haganah became a regular army amid the campaign to contain the joint Arab invasion; this process was continued and completed during the months of the truces. At the end of the war, the I.D.F.'s composition had to be revised again in order to fit Israel's needs following the armistice, with tens of thousands of soldiers gradually being demobilized. This was a wide-ranging, complex and lengthy undertaking, accompanied by disputes over immediate military problems and organizational and doctrinal concepts, as well as by some sharp personal differences.

The establishment of the I.D.F. required the procurement of armaments from sources both in Palestine and abroad, the building and training of infantry units and their amalgamation into twelve brigades, and the formation of defensive forces able to join with civilian settlements to create a territorial defense system. This system's firm stand along the overextended front lines made it possible to concentrate and deploy field-forces in offensive missions. Residents of the defensive settlements were in effect part of the I.D.F., whether or not they had been formally mobilized; this phenomenon was part of the Haganah heritage. Air and naval forces were set up with the help of Jewish volunteers who had served in foreign armies during World War II and teamed up in Israel with veterans of the Palyam (the naval section, including the naval commando team of the Palmach) and the Palmach "air squad." An administrative echelon also had to be created to facilitate mobilization and to ensure the functioning of manpower and quartermaster units at field and base levels in conjunction with the Defense Ministry's logistical system. Supporting arms—including Artillery and Engineers, and service corps, such as the Medical and Transport Corps—were formed. Military and state intelligence services and the General Security Services were established. The I.Z.L. and Lehi, the dissident Jewish underground groups, were dispersed and their members were integrated into the I.D.F.

Nahal ("Pioneering and Fighting Youth") was set up during the second truce to absorb pre-organized groups of youth movement and "Youth Aliya" members, who were to undergo a combined military and agricultural training course. This was necessary since the Palmach was fully committed to combat and could no longer carry out this function.

Nahal was a product of prewar concepts which had developed within the unique kibbutz-based Palmach platoons. The Security Services Law of 1949 reflected Ben-Gurion's desire to combine military and agricultural training for all conscripts, and to mold the I.D.F. as "an army for defense and building."[6]

The Palmach, which had distinguished itself in combat, was dissolved; its pre-independence tasks, previously performed within the Haganah framework, were now taken up by special units and corps. Although the Palmach was formally disbanded, its values and heritage of combat leadership and command, fighting doctrine and combat morale continued to be inculcated throughout the army.

Ben-Gurion had reached the decision to dismantle the Palmach command as early as March-April 1948, but delayed implementation so as to avoid a rift within the defense establishment and a bitter public dispute, especially with the left-wing Mapam Party. Following internal and public debates during the first and second cease-fires, his goal was finally accomplished in November 1948. The Palmach itself executed the order loyally, but the public outcry took a long time to subside. In some circles the move was considered to be linked with the dissolving of the I.Z.L. and Lehi splinter groups, the common motive supposedly being the "disbanding of private armies." This was a simplistic and plainly insupportable view. Israel was forced to eliminate the dissident groups by force of arms, since they had persisted in retaining their weapons and in using them contrary to the government's directives, and in opposition to the I.D.F. The orders to disband them came as a direct response to the provocative actions which they had initiated—the "*Altalena* Affair" and the murder of Count Bernadotte. The Palmach, on the other hand, had been an integral part of the Haganah, its prewar regular force, spearheading the armed pre-independence struggle. Its units had been the first to be committed to action in the War of Independence, and had grown during the course of the war into three brigades.

In November 1948, when the order was given to dismantle the Palmach Headquarters, Yigal Allon was still nominally at its head, although his deputy, Uri Brenner, was actually in control. Allon himself now served as Commander of the Southern Front, and among the troops under his command were two Palmach brigades, "Yiftah" and "Hanegev," as well as the Eighth Armored Brigade led by Yitzhak Sadeh (who had preceded Allon as Palmach Commander). Yet the government had no need to use force to achieve its aims. In fact, the leaders of the Palmach, although hurt by the demise of their "own" cherished corps, continued to devote themselves and those under their command to the decisive operations of the war.[7]

The establishment of the I.D.F. can be seen as a creative synthesis, extensive in scale and Israeli in character. Through trial and error, disputes and clashes, the growing army absorbed the varying legacies of its components. In this process of melting and molding one can discern three main sets of experience. The first, that brought by the Haganah in general, and the Palmach in particular, derived mainly from local defense and guerrilla-type raids in Palestine. An altogether different legacy was that of the World War II volunteers, who had served in Jewish units in the British army, and thousands of whom had fought with the Jewish Brigade Group in Italy. Thirdly, volunteers and conscripts from abroad (Mahal and Gahal) offered their operational-professional expertise, vital for the establishment of the air and naval arms and the development of the Armored Corps. In the heat of the continuing controversy between adherents of the Haganah and the "British" schools over their specific contribution to I.D.F., this qualitative contribution of the Jews of the world to the war in Israel has often been overlooked. They were also important numerically: out of a total of some 100,000 conscripts in uniform at the end of 1948, about one-quarter were members of Gahal and Mahal.[8]

The army, which amounted to 15 percent of the entire population of Israel, underwent further metamorphosis following the conclusion of the armistice negotiations with the Arab states. The first armistice agreement, with Egypt, was signed at the end of February 1949, and the last, with Syria, in July. As early as the first half of 1949 rapid demobilization commenced and the evolution of a peacetime defense system began.

From the Start of Hostilities to the Arab Invasion, December 1947—May 14, 1948

The building of the I.D.F. coincided with the escalation of violence throughout the country, with which the Haganah had to contend, in accordance with the policies outlined by Ben-Gurion. Hostilities hampered inter-city traffic, Arab snipers operated in mixed towns, outlying settlements found themselves under attack, water pipelines to the Negev were sabotaged. The Arabs of Palestine were aided by an "Army of Liberation," a corps under the command of Fawzi al-Kaukji, whose battalions were deployed throughout the Galilee and Samaria. Both Arabs and the Jews were constrained in their military activities by the presence of British troops, at least until March 1948, when the latter accelerated their evacuation, thus opening up new zones to intensified fighting for control of mixed towns, roads and other vital areas.

After Operation Nahshon (March-April 1948; discussed below) changed the course of the war, Jewish forces succeeded in gaining control of Tiberias, Haifa, Safed and Jaffa, as well as strategically important neighborhoods in the Arab areas of Jerusalem. They also gained control of roads and positions necessary for the containment of the upcoming Arab invasion. However, the Etzion Bloc was overrun on the very eve of independence, and Jewish Jerusalem remained cut off from the coast.

The Jewish leadership exploited the squabble between the Mufti of Jerusalem, Haj Amin al-Husseini, and the Arab League over responsibility for the handling of the war. The intelligence service made contacts with Kaukji in order to take advantage of the personal enmity between him and the Mufti. Indeed, most of

Kaukji's battalions did not take part in the decisive battles of Operation Nahshon on the approaches to Jerusalem, but were rather entangled in their own attack on the Mishmar Ha'emek front, east of Haifa. A few days before the imminent invasion, Golda Meir went to Amman secretly to confer with King Abdallah of Transjordan in an attempt to reach an agreement along the lines of the UN partition plan and thus dissuade him from joining the pan-Arab offensive. Although the attempt failed, the meeting itself demonstrated the chance of reaching an understanding, based on mutual interests.[9]

Israel was prepared to comply with the decisions of the United Nations, since it wished to be accepted as a member-state. Much depended on whether the UN would implement its partition plan, and how it would intervene in a war launched by the Arabs of Palestine in violation of the international body's own authority. Until the departure of the British High Commissioner, they waited to see whether the organization would appoint its own commissioner for Jerusalem, so as to exert its authority in the city which, according to the partition plan, was to be internationalized. Until that time Israeli spokesmen had refrained from saying anything which might have been interpreted as an objection to internationalization. As a result, Ben-Gurion and other leaders were accused in some quarters of readiness to give up Jerusalem, despite the extensive, continuous military efforts invested in the defense of its Jewish population, in the constant dispatching of convoys to the city, and in the repeated attempts to lift the siege on it. Acting under similar constraints, Abdallah avoided any discussion of Jerusalem's future with Jewish representatives.

Israel's leaders strove to avoid opening a "second front," against the British, who had begun their military evacuation and were dismantling the civilian administration. This involved the avoidance of clashes with the army and the police force, and the exercise of restraint in cases of localized damage at the hands of hostile British personnel.

However, the Jewish authorities did everything in their power to benefit from the British withdrawal. They sought to take over civilian facilities and services in an orderly fashion, thereby preventing administrative chaos. They succeeded in negotiating the handover of considerable military facilities, including intact airfields, large camps and other vital facilities—in return for payment. This prevented the British from implementing a "scorched earth" policy of destruction and sabotage and ensured Israel's inheritance of a ready-made military infrastructure. Out of consideration for Britain's interest in the speedy completion of the evacuation, the Haganah reached a local agreement which facilitated its conquest of the Arab sections of Haifa.[10]

One of the most noteworthy operational decisions during this period was taken halfway through December—about two weeks after the outbreak of hostilities. It was decided not to "shorten lines" in the northern Negev, nor to evacuate its settlements, but rather to send reinforcements and prepare the settlements to repulse attacks, so that the region could serve as a springboard for eventual I.D.F. campaigns for the control of the Negev expanses, all the way to Sedom and Eilat.

Furthermore, a Palmach brigade was formed to secure the Negev, and the first homemade armored cars produced by the Armor Service (which preceded the Armor Corps) were sent there in order to assure adequate protection for the water pipelines. As a result of the implementation of this early decision, the Negev settlements were able to face the eventual invasion, and when the entire region was cut off, they withstood a prolonged siege.

At the end of March 1948 the road to Jerusalem was severed. Ben-Gurion decided to cull soldiers and arms from all fronts in order to muster 1,500 men for Operation Nahshon, a campaign to free the road to the city and secure its hilly "shoulders." This massing of Jewish forces was a success. Three vital supply convoys were able to reach Jerusalem before the road was closed once more on April 20 (after troops from the Jerusalem Corridor were transferred for action within the city). Ben-Gurion himself rode in the convoy of April 20, against the advice of the General Staff.[11] He spent several days in the besieged city, joining soldiers in their Passover meal. During this time he closely followed the course of Operations Harel and Yevusi, which were intended to further extend control over parts of Jerusalem and its northern outskirts.[12]

In the north, Kaukji sought to exploit the concentration of Jewish forces on the road to Jerusalem by attempting to capture Kibbutz Mishmar Ha'emek, thereby gaining approach to Haifa. However, the defenders of the settlement held fast, until the Palmach and other field-forces could be assembled under the command of Yitzhak Sadeh. These units then struck at Kaukji's flank, forcing his retreat. Having succeeded in its offensive on the road to Jerusalem and its defensive strategy on the road to Haifa, the Haganah retained the initiative. Its brigades, still in formative stages, committed their units to operations outlined in "Plan D" (which had been prepared at the beginning of March for execution following the departure of the British), and commenced a series of offensive regional campaigns, whose common objective was to prepare for strategic defense against the impending Arab invasion.[13]

Ten ministers of the thirteen member Provisional Government of Israel had yet to decide on May 12 whether to go ahead and proclaim independence. The Haganah's representatives, Galili and Yigael Yadin, estimated that the chances of successful resistance to a pan-Arab invasion were uneasily balanced, and that everything depended on the ability to check the invaders until the arrival of aircraft and artillery, procured overseas. The government was split, but narrowly avoided a draw when the decision was finally carried by a majority of 6:4. Of the four Mapai ministers, only Ben-Gurion and Moshe Shertok (Sharett) supported the motion.[14]

The members of the government accepted this fateful risk because of their faith in the resistance capabilities of almost all the settlements and the fighting performance of the defensive forces, and despite the heavy losses incurred (some 1,200 Jews were killed before the invasion). They were also mindful of what had already been achieved: the number of enlisted soldiers exceeded 36,500 and nine brigades had been formed; Jewish forces were in control of the settled regions, had even extended their position locally, and now held some 20 percent of the area of Mandatory Palestine. The government decision therefore reflected its determination, inspired by Ben-

Gurion, to adhere to the two central national policy objectives: the establishment and defense of Israel's independence.

The Invasion and Its Containment (May 15-June 11)

The Arab states intended to defeat Israel by a concerted campaign of the armies of Jordan, Iraq, Syria and Lebanon, which were to converge on Haifa, while the Egyptian army was to tie up Jewish forces in a thrust toward Tel Aviv. In fact, however, Abdallah, who was nominally the Commander-in-Chief of the expeditionary armies, deviated from the pan-Arab plan and ordered his Arab Legion to take control of Palestine's central range of hills, to come to the rescue of the remaining Arab strongholds in Jerusalem, and to cut off the city's Jewish community from the coastal plain.

The Jewish settlers and field-forces stood fast in their defensive positions, and by the end of May there were indications that the Arab armies were no longer adhering to the aim of total victory, and were turning to a more limited objective—the truncation of Israel's territory. The Egyptians turned east from the coast in order to isolate the Negev; the Syrians tried to cut off the Galilee Panhandle; Kaukji's "Army of Liberation," which had been earmarked for operations in the center of the country, was now concentrated in the Galilee; the Iraqi expeditionary force, deployed in Samaria in order to protect the Legion's flank, remained the only army still aiming for total victory in the battle for Jerusalem.

On the eve of the Arab invasion, a serious dispute over defensive strategy broke out within the Israeli High Command. Ben-Gurion thought it vital to reopen the road to Jerusalem, a move which, he believed, would decide the fate of the entire war. On the other hand, the General Staff maintained that all forces should block the Arab assaults, until the delivery of heavy arms from abroad would facilitate an Israeli counterattack strategy.

Arab achievements in the field, operational difficulties, and the insufficient preparedness of the hastily equipped and trained Jewish forces all added to the fierceness of the dispute. The counterattacks—at Emek Ayalon, Isdud,[15] and Jenin—all failed. Under pressure from Ben-Gurion, three consecutive attacks were launched to open the road to Jerusalem, and all were repelled by the forces of the Legion on the Ayalon Ridge and at the Latrun Police Fort.

But meanwhile, a substitute route to Jerusalem had been opened up south of the main road—at first only a jeep track, over which vital food supplies were transferred to the besieged city, now close to famine. During the cease-fire, the rough cross-country track was improved and widened, and became known as the "Burma Road." A parallel narrow-bore water pipeline to the city was completed at the beginning of August.

The agreement by the Arabs and the Jews to a UN truce reflected the exhaustion of both sides following the battles of the previous month. The frustrations of that month found an outlet in criticism leveled against Ben-Gurion for his interference in the Ayalon Valley battle. Beyond the operational aspects of the dispute—which force was to attack and when—this constituted a clash between Israel's political and strategic echelons.

While there was consensus regarding the indispensability of Jerusalem, disagreement arose over the assessment of its residents' ability to defend themselves, and over the preference to be given to a military decision in the struggle for the city. Unlike the military leaders, Ben-Gurion was aware of the city's political plight; the UN, with the backing of the major powers, might impose a cease-fire while Jerusalem was still cut off, and with the Arab armies—the Legion and the Egyptian expeditionary force—threatening to break into its Jewish areas. From the government's point of view, this concern was compounded by the fear that Great Britain could make the UN decision a pretext for coming to the aid of the Legion. Indeed, a truce was at first almost imposed as early as May 24, again on May 26, and on the night of June 1-2, until it was finally set to come into effect on June 11. All three of Ben-Gurion's decisions to attack were made in this context of an imminent cease-fire.[16]

At the time, the military did not recognize the political significance of the control of the main road to Jerusalem, or of the water supply to the city (the pipeline from the springs at Rosh Ha'ayin, which ran via Lod-Ramle-Latrun). Some regarded the opening of the "Burma Road" as an adequate substitute under the circumstances, and therefore objected to any additional efforts to secure the main road and occupy the pumping station near the Latrun Police Fort. However, Ben-Gurion feared that Jerusalem would be excluded from Israel in the context of an imposed settlement unless it gained indisputable control of a stable "corridor" to the city, including both the road and the water pipeline, by the start of the truce.

It appears that these political considerations were better understood during the first truce, when the government and the General Staff formulated the policy and strategy for the renewal of operations.

From the First Truce to the "Ten-Day" Offensive (July 9-18, 1948)

During the cease-fire, the UN mediator, Count Bernadotte, formulated a proposal for a political settlement which included a partition scheme of his own: the Negev would go to the Arabs while central Galilee would go to the Jews; Jerusalem would come under Arab-Jordanian rule and its Jewish inhabitants would be granted urban autonomy. This proposal highlighted the precarious political situation facing the Jews of Jerusalem, a matter which had caused Ben-Gurion much concern during the month of the invasion. But it also opened up new options, since Bernadotte, by expressing his intention to hand over the whole city to Arab rule, had in effect shelved the UN idea of internationalization. The Arab states and Israel rejected his proposals out of hand, thus making the renewal of hostilities inevitable.

With the truce in effect, the government and the General Staff attempted to learn from the fighting so far, and to prepare themselves for the continuation of the war.

However, they were distracted by a furious internal crisis which came to a head when the ship *Altalena*, bringing arms to the I.Z.L., reached the coast at Kfar Vitkin. The I.Z.L. refused to hand the armaments over to the I.D.F., and the ship slipped away at night to Tel Aviv. It was sunk by I.D.F. fire the next day, June 22.

Once this affair was settled, a different crisis broke out, now within the ranks of the High Command, as a result of the unanimous decision to form a new command echelon—the "front," and to group the twelve brigades into four such fronts. Galili, acting deputy of Ben-Gurion, Yadin and other Heads of Staff Branches, disputed the nominees proposed by Ben-Gurion and Chief of Staff Ya'akov Dori. Contributing to the general sense of dissatisfaction was Dori's illness, resulting in his frequent absences, with his functions partially carried out by Galili. The Mapam Party bitterly criticized Ben-Gurion for assuming exclusive control of the war. He was accused of slighting the heads of the Haganah and of preferring ex-British army officers. In effect, Ben-Gurion's authority as minister of defense was being challenged, as was the fact that he had merged the roles of prime minister and minister of defense. When the dispute over the nominations was reported by Ben-Gurion to the government, a committee of five ministers, led by Yitzhak Gruenbaum, was appointed to look into the dispute. Arguments were raised in Ben-Gurion's presence, with the debate spilling beyond military aspects into the sphere of public and party issues. The personal friction within the High Command came to the surface, and Ben-Gurion was strongly criticized for his interference in the battles at Sha'ar Hagai and the Ayalon Valley.

The committee's conclusions deeply hurt Ben-Gurion and he threatened to resign. The crisis was settled by a compromise proposal submitted by Yadin, Chief of Operations. It entailed curtailing Ben-Gurion's authority somewhat, and setting up a War Cabinet of five ministers under his chairmanship.[17] Galili's status was undermined, and at the beginning of September he left the Ministry of Defense. Conversely, the crisis led to a strengthening of Yadin's standing, not only due to his personality, but also thanks to developments in the field. With the I.D.F. taking the offensive, the role of the Operations Branch within the General Staff became more prominent and consolidated; at the same time the status of the General Staff vis-à-vis the Ministry of defense was reinforced.[18]

In contrast to the criticism leveled against Ben-Gurion in the appointments affair, there was unanimity regarding war policy and strategic priorities. It was decided to take the initiative on all fronts on the night the cease-fire was due to expire (July 9-10), so as to prevent the "freezing" of the lines. The main effort would be focused on the central front: to conquer Lod and Ramle—thereby relieving the pressure on Tel Aviv—and subsequently to seize Ramallah, bypassing Latrun, so as to lift the siege of Jerusalem. All remaining forces were to launch attacks—in the north against the Syrian bridgehead at Mishmar Hayarden, and against Lower Galilee from the coastal strip; and in the south—to lift the siege of the Negev.

The government and the General Staff were aware of the shortage of time, since the UN was liable to reimpose a cease-fire as soon as the I.D.F. made gains. The Egyptians resumed fighting as early as July 8. Israeli actions were renewed when the truce expired, on the night of July 9-10. They continued until July 18, under the threat of sanctions to be imposed by the Security Council which had ordered a second cease-fire on the night of July 15-16.

Although these I.D.F. operations were terminated halfway through, they achieved substantial gains. In the main campaign, on the central front, Lod and Ramle were captured. The intended drive on Ramallah was never mounted due to the need to direct reinforcements to the Egyptian front and the mounting political pressure. Instead, the Latrun positions were attacked again, unsuccessfully. However, the Jerusalem Corridor was broadened southward as far as Nahal Sorek.

In the north, the I.D.F. prevented the Syrians from breaking out of their bridgehead and cutting off the Galilee Panhandle. The pressure on Haifa was relieved in a drive which captured Nazareth and delivered Lower Galilee from Kaukji's army.

In the south, the Egyptian attackers were checked, and before the second cease-fire came into effect, the force which had been transferred from the central front managed to capture Kartia, and momentarily opened the way to the Negev. Although the Egyptians occupied hills to the south of the village after the start of the cease-fire, re-blocking the passage, the UN observers ruled that the I.D.F. was entitled to pass, a ruling which was later to prove to its advantage.

The operations of the ten-day period in effect removed the stranglehold on Jerusalem. A detour road and a wide-diameter pipeline were laid in the widened corridor, meeting the basic logistic needs of the Jewish city and of the settlements which were to consolidate the corridor. The government was now quick to give political expression to the change wrought in the situation of Jewish Jerusalem. Dov Joseph, who had led the city's residents in mobilization and in defense as the head of the "Jerusalem Committee," was appointed Military Governor of the city on August 2. This appointment in effect "annexed" the Jewish part of the city to Israel.

On the other hand, the Israeli aim of decisively defeating the Arab Legion and forcing its retreat beyond the Jordan River was not achieved; no more than a military "draw" had been attained. The political significance of this was the eventual tacit acceptance of Jordanian control over the West Bank and the partition of Jerusalem.

While the military situation in the north had improved, the situation in the Negev had worsened as a result of its continued siege. At the start of the second truce, Ben-Gurion spoke to the Security Committee of the National Assembly, appraising coming needs and defining a dual orientation — which required readiness for both the renewal of the battle and for a peace settlement process:

> Willingness to renew the war should our sovereignty or immigration be impaired, or the minimal territory we deserve; an effort to make peace not necessarily based on the possibilities our strength affords us (which in my opinion includes the whole of Palestine).[19]

The readiness for peace and for a "territorial compromise," expressed within Israeli councils, was communicated at the beginning of September to the first American ambassador, James McDonald.[20] It reflected the evaluation that a turning point had been reached in the very nature of the war: it had been transformed from a self-defense struggle into a combined political-military effort to obtain conditions for the existence of an established state. The government was united in its conviction that the war would be decided only by the defeat of the invading armies and by their forced retreat from the country, and that only then would the time come for political settlements with the Arab states. It was also conscious of the distinction between military occupation during wartime and the determination of borders in negotiations at the end of the war.

As mentioned above, as early as 1947 Ben-Gurion had defined Israel's main military goal, "to conquer the whole country or most of it, and to maintain its occupation until the attainment of an authoritative political settlement." Notwithstanding his preference for peace, even at the cost of partition, by means of an agreement with Abdallah, Ben-Gurion initiated moves to drive the Legion and the Iraqi expeditionary force out of the center of the country. Similarly, the government later decided on operations designed to force an Egyptian withdrawal from the south of the country, including the conquest of the Gaza Strip. It was aware of the possibility that the Strip might not remain in Israel's hands, especially since it had been included within the Arab state in the UN partition plan. But it felt that its conquest by Israel, necessitated by military considerations, would facilitate the attainment of a more acceptable political settlement.[21]

Breakthrough to the Negev and the Conquest of Upper Galilee (October 1948)

As the second cease-fire ensued, with the invading Arab armies deployed within the country, Israel found itself in a constant state of alert. Moshe Sharett described the cease-fire as "a war of attrition."[22]

By mid-September the Arab states were split. The Jordanians and the Iraqis—Hashemite allies—consolidated their hold on East Jerusalem, Samaria and Judea, but the other states of the Arab League challenged the legitimacy of Abdallah's annexation of the West Bank, and set up an "All-Palestine Government" of the Mufti's adherents.

Bernadotte himself proceeded on the assumption that if a political settlement could not be reached in the UN General Assembly, which was to meet in Paris on September 21, the cease-fire would collapse. In mid-September he submitted his updated proposals, taking into account Israel's military successes during the ten-day interlude between the first and second cease-fires. He now withdrew his proposal to turn the Jews of Jerusalem over to Abdallah, and returned to the original UN plan for the internationalization of the city. He again advocated giving the Galilee to Israel and the Negev to the Arabs—from the Majdal-Faluja cutoff line southward.

On September 17, before his proposal had been published, a group of Lehi members murdered Count Bernadotte in Jerusalem. In response, the government instructed the I.D.F. to break up the I.Z.L. and Lehi cells which still existed in the city. The UN General Assembly mourned the "messenger of peace," who had fallen in the line of duty; the American secretary of state and the British foreign minister heaped praise upon his plan, which now acquired the aura of a "testament."

Bernadotte's assassination and its aftermath led to the postponement of Israel's plans to renew the military campaign.[23] Ben-Gurion had still not decided whether to try to eliminate the threat to Jerusalem once and for all, or to break the siege of the Negev. An incident in the Modi'in area, on September 24, spurred him to present a plan to the government, on September 26. It called for an attack on Latrun and the conquest of the entire area occupied by the Legion, the central ridge from Ramallah to Hebron, and the slopes down to the Jordan and the Dead Sea. In fact, the plan went even further, since the defeat of the Legion would also force the Iraqis to pull out of Samaria. However, Ben-Gurion's proposal was overruled by a majority of one, with some of the ministers fearing a UN reaction against Israel now that its hands were "sullied" with Bernadotte's blood. Ben-Gurion was surprised to find Mapai ministers among the majority who had voted against him, and commented that the decision would be "lamented for generations."[24] Until then he had not been wont to conduct preliminary discussions within party institutions concerning subjects he was to present to the government. But now he concluded that he would have to "open the mind" of his party colleagues before bringing a war policy proposal before the government.

Two weeks later, on October 6, Ben-Gurion presented the government with an alternative plan which he had formulated in the meanwhile with the General Staff and the front commanders. He called for a breakthrough to the Negev, and this time he made sure that ministers from his own party would support him. The members of the government were well aware of the political danger involved in violating the cease-fire, and feared great power support for any UN response. The final decision was therefore placed in the hands of the five-member War Cabinet, which awaited the advice of the foreign minister, Moshe Sharett, who was then attending the UN General Assembly in Paris. Although the October 6 decision was only a conditional, interim one, Ben-Gurion attached such far-reaching importance to it that he wrote in his diary: "We in the government made today our gravest decision since we decided to declare the establishment of the state."[25]

Sharett telegraphed his agreement only after becoming convinced that President Truman remained firmly in support of the original UN plan (which had allocated most of the Negev to Israel), thereby indicating his rejection of Bernadotte's proposal to exclude the Negev. The government approved the operation on October 10, after Egypt had already put out feelers for a peace settlement, demanding a foothold in the south of the country for itself.[26]

In making the decision on the breakthrough to the Negev — Operation Yoav — the government hoped that, following an initial assault by an armored force in the Iraq-Manshieh sector (today Kiryat Gat), its pressure on Gaza's flank would force the Egyptian army to withdraw from the country, and that the I.D.F. would be able to exploit this success by advancing to the Dead Sea and the Red Sea. It was also decided that following a few days' wait, to see whether the battles in the south would lead to an eruption of fighting on the central front, an offensive would begin against the Egyptian positions in Judea.

Operation Yoav started on the night of October 15-16, and the attack on Judea was launched on the night of October 18-19. As early as October 19, the Security Council ordered a cease-fire, but the government of Israel procrastinated, and succeeded in delaying its implementation until October 22. By then the Negev breakthrough had been achieved, and an Egyptian brigade found itself surrounded in the "Faluja Pocket." But Israel's armor had been mauled, preventing a flanking advance toward Egyptian positions on the coastal strip. The front commander, Yigal Allon, therefore concentrated his resources on taking an alternative objective— Beersheba.

On the central front the cease-fire stopped the "Harel" brigade before it had reached its objective—the Bet Lehem-Hebron road; the Jerusalem Brigade failed in its attack on Bet-Jalah Hill (now Har Giloh). The respective commanders requested General Headquarters' approval for another joint attempt that night, although the cease-fire had come into effect in the afternoon. Opinions within the General Staff were divided; Ben-Gurion sided with the detractors. He explained the political considerations: the UN would force a withdrawal; a new threat to Bethlehem would anger the Christian world; Jordan, which had not aided the Egyptians in their hour of need, should not be provoked, for if the Legion and the Iraqis should now be dragged into the battle, the image of internal Arab divisions and of Egyptian isolation would be shattered—with Israel then finding it difficult to resist pressure to evacuate the territory it had conquered in the Negev.[27]

The Egyptians were forced to withdraw from the Isdud-Majdal wedge, and the "All-Palestine Government" quickly fled from Gaza. The Arab armies failed to react to the I.D.F.'s concerted effort against Egypt. However, on October 22, Kaukji attacked Manara, attempting to cut off the north of the Galilee Panhandle. Local counterattacks failed; the Northern Front Command awaited the return of a brigade from the south to launch Operation Hiram, an offensive on central Galilee that pushed the "Liberation Army" beyond the Lebanese border. The entire Galilee was cleared, and the panhandle was extended northward to the bend in the Litani River and westward to Wadi Duba, west of the Lebanese border-road.

In the UN, Israel was accused of violating the cease-fire in the south. The gains made in Operation Hiram increased the pressure on it, for the I.D.F. had not only broken through into the Negev, but had also taken the Galilee, which Bernadotte had intended to offer Israel as a substitute for the Negev. On November 4, the Security Council ordered Israel to withdraw north of the line which had been penetrated in Operation Yoav. The new mediator, Ralph Bunche, was forced to recognize the impracticality of this demand, but insisted on the evacuation of Beersheba (which was not within the UN borders of the Jewish state). However, on November 16 another resolution was adopted in the Security Council, calling for the sides to open negotiations on an armistice. In effect, this superseded the resolution of November 4, and shelved Bernadotte's plan, which now only the British continued to support.

Operation Horev and Anglo-American Intervention
(December 1948-January 1949)

As a consequence of Israeli gains in the south and the north, it appeared that Egypt and Jordan were prepared for direct contacts concerning political settlements. However, when no progress was made, the government of Israel resolved to complete what it had started in Operation Yoav, and to force the Egyptian army to withdraw from the country. Since October the government had feared British interference should Israel again seem to violate the truce. The General Staff estimated that it would take more than a week to complete the operation in the Negev; it was timed to coincide with the Christmas—New Year recess, in the hope that this would delay any UN response.

Operation Horev commenced on the night of December 22-23, and Auja was captured on December 27. The following afternoon, an Israeli force crossed the border into Sinai, reaching Abu Aweigila the next morning. Allon now exceeded the original plan, and ordered a deeper penetration in order to attack El-Arish and completely cut off the Egyptian expeditionary force.

This deep incursion into Sinai led to international intervention. Israel's hopes notwithstanding, the Security Council had reconvened during the Christmas recess (due to an Indonesian complaint about Dutch aggression). The Council was summoned to meet on December 22, and two days later it was presented with an Egyptian complaint concerning the I.D.F.'s activity; from December 28 onwards it began to debate the situation on the southern front. The British protested the invasion, and the Security Council ordered an early cease-fire. The British warned that they might come to Egypt's aid, under the terms of the 1936 Anglo-Egyptian Treaty; from December 30 they flew reconnaissance flights over Sinai.

In the face of these pressures, Israel now had to decide whether and how to continue the military campaign. As early as the night of December 29-30, the front commander, acting on the order of the Chief of Operations, recalled his forces from the outskirts of El-Arish to Abu Aweigila. In a discussion which Ben-Gurion held with the Chief of Staff, Chief of Operations and front commander the following morning, it was decided to refrain from any clash with British land forces. The Israeli force was to dig in at Abu Aweigila and carry out periodic raids on El-Arish, while the offensive would be switched to the Auja-Rafah axis in accordance with the General Staff's original plan. "If the English come—we'll return to our borders, to Auja. If they reach Auja—we'll fight."[28]

The following afternoon (December 31) the US ambassador demanded that the I.D.F. be withdrawn from Sinai in order to remove any pretext for British military intervention. That evening Reuven Shiloah informed the ambassador that Ben-Gurion, who was staying at Tiberias, had already ordered a pullback to Auja. Nevertheless, McDonald insisted on leaving for Tiberias to meet the Israeli leader.

Although Sinai was to be evacuated, Ben-Gurion authorized an attack on Rafah, along the road from Auja which passed partly through Egyptian territory. The attackers were blocked on their approach to Rafah and were pushed back south from the Rafah crossroads. However, during the night of January 6-7, an Israeli battalion occupied a pivotal roadblock west of the crossroads, in effect cutting off the entire Egyptian contingent. Egypt had already recognized the necessity of opening armistice talks in order to extricate its beleaguered army, and at noon on January 7 the cease-fire was due to come into effect. At the same time the Egyptians were attacking the Israeli roadblock repeatedly, only to be repulsed. However, on the same day, the British again carried out reconnaissance flights over the battle zone, but this time were intercepted by Israeli aircraft, which shot down five British planes. The air incident provided proof of the presence of I.D.F. units west of the border.

On January 9, UN mediator Bunche announced that he would not conduct the Israel-Egypt armistice negotiations unless Israel completed its withdrawal from Sinai. The United States, which had encouraged Egypt to enter talks, vigorously supported this demand. Ben-Gurion now ordered that the Israeli roadblock be evacuated by the next morning, January 10. In so doing he saved the Egyptian expeditionary force from being cut off, and left the Gaza Strip in Egyptian hands.[29] In his diary he detailed his considerations: to dissociate both the Egyptians and the Americans from the British; to open negotiations with Egypt so as to divide the Arab front and weaken the stand of the British; to prevent a rift with the United States, whose aid Israel needed for postwar rehabilitation and for the extensive development so essential to the absorption of large-scale immigration.[30]

The order to withdraw from Sinai has been the subject of historical debate, with the true extent of the British threat upon Israel again being questioned, and with a corollary issue — whether Israel deprived itself of the chance of decisively defeating the Egyptian expeditionary force — also being raised.[31] The political necessity of avoiding a clash with British forces in Sinai dictated the initial decision to withdraw to Auja. Nevertheless, the British threat — which had already been demonstrated by the reconnaissance flights — did not prevent the government from authorizing further actions inside Egyptian territory in proximity to the border. In some Israeli military circles the political leadership was accused of faintheartedness in the face of great-power pressure. Yet the I.D.F. failed to cut off the Gaza Strip in time, by January 7, in the face of a stubborn Egyptian defense and determined counterattacks. The Israeli decision of January 9 to evacuate the roadblock did not stem from any British "dictate," but rather from a desire to respond to a call for negotiations under UN auspices and with American backing. On January 13, Israeli-Egyptian armistice talks began in Rhodes.

In a long series of battles which had continued for some 15 months, from the beginning of December 1947 to the occupation of Eilat by the middle of March 1948 (with lulls during the truces), the Yishuv became a state and succeeded in attaining its defensive military goals. It defended Jewish-settled areas within the UN-mandated territory of the state. Moreover, the area of Israel was extended to include four-fifths (79%) of Mandatory Palestine, one and a half times that allocated by the UN plan (55%), and four times the area under Jewish control when independence was declared. These gains were recognized internationally, with Israel being admitted to the UN by mid-May 1949.

Ben-Gurion as War Leader

An examination of Ben-Gurion's war leadership reveals that far from domineering, he had to exert himself to rally support. Sometimes his success was limited to obtaining slim majorities at crucial moments. Indeed, on occasion, fateful issues were resolved by a single vote, as in the decision to declare independence. Ben-Gurion's decisions stemmed from a rare combination of far-sighted vision and intense preoccupation with the task at hand, meticulous inquiry, prolonged consultation and mastery of details. Of course, the intensity of his vision added to the persuasive power of his arguments. An illustration of this power of his was his cooperation with Moshe Sharett on war policy. The two were remarkably capable of listening to and persuading one another, and of making joint stands at critical moments (a fact that was obscured by the later rift between the two in the 1950s).

Ben-Gurion wanted to be personally involved in events and was not deterred by physical danger. As we have mentioned, he joined the convoy to Jerusalem despite the warnings of the General Staff and returned from the besieged city by light aircraft; his residence at the General Staff Headquarters was bombed more than once; he visited the front from time to time.

But the urgency of his efforts and the pressures of the day to day conduct of the war took their toll in terms of physical strain and exhausting mental tension. Late at night on May 23, 1948, in the hectic days of the invasion, the wait for armaments from abroad and the planning of a counterattack at Sha'ar Hagai, he wrote: "I lay down to sleep, dead [tired] after 48 hours without sleep."[32] On July 6, he fell sick for a few days after the bitter debates in Gruenbaum's committee; on July 11 his diary records: "Only today was I able to return to the office. The prolonged strain of more than six months without a day's break finally told."[33] Toward the end of the war his back pains worsened again and from December 3, 1948, he began to go to Tiberias for weekend baths. In the course of the campaign for the first elected Knesset he suffered from pains in his heart and was confined to bed for a time. However, in public and in the army he appeared to be a veritable powerhouse of energy, a man as strong in body as in spirit. This impression of an energetic and determined war leader should overshadow neither Ben-Gurion's deep sensitivity to casualties, nor his identification with the pain of bereaved families, often movingly expressed by him in person and in letters of condolence.

As busy as he was with the burdens of leadership in war, he still managed to take time off to devote himself to the formulation of long-range policies for the future. In the feverish days which preceded the impending Arab invasion, he found time to complete the text of the Declaration of Independence.[34] In the following period he publicly discussed his vision for the future of the state and the role of the army.[35] He initiated debates with intellectuals, interested himself in the revival of Hebrew (especially the adaptation of new terms for government and administration), and in the founding of the Hebrew Academy. Toward the end of the war, he used his weekend "rests" in Tiberias for writing down his reflections on policy and for formulating his political platform.[36]

Ben-Gurion appeared more than once as an uncompromising public figure. He was a merciless polemicist, who was apt to plunge into verbal battles. Paradoxically, when he lashed his adversaries, the positions he upheld so fervently were often moderate, aimed at establishing a consensus on compromises. During the course of the war he aspired to a clear military victory, but never lost sight of the goal that lay beyond, being prepared to make concessions in order to attain a "stable peace."

Notes

1 David Ben-Gurion, *Israel at War* (Hebrew), Tel Aviv, 1951, p. 15.

2 Ibid., p. 14.

3 Yehuda Slutzky, *History of the Haganah* (Hebrew), vol. 3, part 2, Tel Aviv, 1972, p. 1330.

4 David Ben-Gurion, *War Diary* (Hebrew), eds., Gershon Rivlin and Elhannan Orren, Tel Aviv, 1982, vol. 1, p. 5.

4* Ibid., p. 416.

5 See Slutzky, *History of the Haganah*, vol. 3, part 2, pp. 1587-1592; ibid., vol. 3, part 3, pp. 1960-1962; Ben-Gurion, *War Diary*, pp. 362, 373-392, 404. The abolition of the post of head of the National Command is discussed in Anita Shapira's *The Army Controversy, 1948: Ben Gurion's Struggle for Control* (Hebrew), Tel-Aviv, 1985, pp. 28-36; see also my review: "Crisis in the National Command and the Committee of Five Ministers in the First Cease-Fire, July 1948" (Hebrew), *Ma'arachot*, no. 298 (March-April 1985), p. 55, regarding the abolition of the head of the National Command.

6 An extensive study of the establishment of the I.D.F., and the contribution made by ex-British army soldiers, stressing Ben-Gurion's role, has recently been published. See Yoav Gelber, *The Emergence of a Jewish Army* (Hebrew), Jerusalem, 1986. For Ben-Gurion's views on the combination of agricultural and military training, see Ben-Gurion, *Israel at War,* pp. 304-316.

7 For the debate on the dismantling of the Palmach Command and the public controversy surrounding it, see Ben-Gurion, *War Diary* (Hebrew), introduction to the 8th chapter, pp. 715-717. Michael Bar-Zohar, *Ben-Gurion* (Hebrew), vol. 1, linked this with the "disbanding of the private armies." However, he stresses that in their degree of allegiance to national authority there were "unfathomable differences" between the Palmach on one hand, and the dissident I.Z.L. and Lehi undergrounds (pp. 845-846) on the other. For strident criticism of the disbanding of the Palmach, see Shapira, *The Army Controversy, 1948: Ben-Gurion's Struggle for Control*, pp. 50-57; and for a rebuttal, cf. Orren, "Crisis in the National Command," pp. 53(b)—55(b).

8 Ben-Gurion, *War Diary*, p. 814.

9 G. Yogev, ed., *People's Administration* [Provisional Government]—Protocols, April 18—May 13, 1948 (Hebrew), Jerusalem, May 1978, p. 42.

10 Toward the end of April the I.Z.L. attempted to conquer Jaffa—which the UN partition plan had assigned to the Arab state. A British force intervened to prevent the city's fall, inflicting heavy casualties on the I.Z.L..

11 Ben-Gurion, *War Diary*, p. 357.

12 Meir Pa'il has argued that Ben-Gurion did not want to gain permanent control of the road to Jerusalem before the declaration of independence, because the area was outside the zone allocated to the Jewish state by the UN. He was content with the passage of convoys and the consolidation of Jewish forces in the city. Meir Pa'il, "The Zionist-Israeli Strategy on the Jerusalem Question in the War of Independence" (Hebrew), in *Chapters in the History of Jerusalem in the Modern Age*, ed., E. Shaltiel, Jerusalem, 1981, pp. 358-359.

13 Yoav Lavi, "Ben-Gurion as a Decision Maker" (Hebrew), *Skira Hodshit*, October 10, 1983, pp. 4(b)—6(a).

14 Actually the government voted against a cease-fire, which would have meant the postponement of the declaration. The six who opposed the cease-fire were: David Ben-Gurion and Moshe Sharett (Mapai); B. Shitrit (Sephardim); M. Bentov and A. Zisling (Mapam); F. Bernstein (General Zionists). The four

in favor were: E. Kaplan and D. Remez (Mapai); P. Rosen (Aliya Hadasha); M. Shapira (Mizrahi). In some of the sources Shapira and Shitrit were interchanged.

15 The Arab town of Isdud, on the road to Majdal, is about 6 km southeast of Ashdod. (The town is now in ruins.)

16 For a debate on the political aspects of the battle for Jerusalem and the road to the city during the first month of the invasion, see the introduction to the fifth chapter of Ben-Gurion, *War Diary*, pp. 422-424.

17 The "War Cabinet" included, in addition to Ben-Gurion, Yitzhak Gruenbaum, Aharon Zisling, Eliezer Kaplan and Moshe Shapira.

18 Orren," Crisis in the National Command," pp. 50(a)—53(b).

19 Ben-Gurion, *War Diary*, p. 605.

20 Ibid., p. 676.

21 In Ben-Gurion, *War Diary*, and *Documents on the Foreign Policy of Israel* (Hebrew), Jerusalem, vol. 2 (ed., Yehoshua Freundlich), 1984, and vols. 3-4 (ed., Yemima Rosenthal), 1983, 1986, there is a good deal of discussion concerning the intended conquest of the Gaza Strip. These deliberations, during and after the war, reflected various possible political settlements for the Strip: a UN protectorate; an Egyptian or Jordanian-controlled zone (providing an outlet to the sea, with a corridor to the east).

22 Moshe Sharett, *At the Threshold of Nationhood* (Hebrew), Tel Aviv, 1958, p. 289.

23 For the government debate of August 1 on operational objectives, see David Ben-Gurion, *The Renewed State of Israel* (Hebrew), Tel Aviv, 1969, pp. 247-251.

24 Lavi, *Ben-Gurion as a Decision Maker*, 6(b)—8(a).

25 Ben-Gurion, *War Diary*, p. 736.

26 Ibid., pp. 739-740; and Supplement to *War Diary*, pp. 9-10.

27 Ben-Gurion, *War Diary*, p. 761.

28 Ibid., p. 913.

29 Ibid., p. 931.

30 Ibid., p. 939. According to Meir Pa'il, the government agreed to a cease-fire on January 7, and at the same time ordered the evacuation of the roadblick from the Rafah—El-Arish road (Amitzur Ilan and Meir Pa'il, "The War of Independence" (Hebrew), in *The History of the Land of Israel*, vol. 10, Jerusalem, 1983, p. 260). This was not the case. As indicated, the government already agreed to a cease-fire on January 5, before the roadblock was occupied; Ben-Gurion ordered the withdrawal on January 9, and it was completed by the next day.

31 Recently N. Lorch argued (in his article in *Ma'arachot*, nos. 294-295) that there was no real substance to the British threat. M. Gazit contested this (Ibid., no. 297) and Lorch responded. I pointed out the significance of the British reconnaissance flights in my response to the above (Ibid., nos. 302-303).

32 Ben-Gurion, *War Diary*, p. 452.

33 Ibid., p. 851.

34 Ibid., pp. 414, 416; Ze'ev Sharef, *Three Days*, London, 1962, pp. 227, 272, 277-280.

35 cf. Ben-Gurion, *Israel at War*, "In Strength and in Wisdom," January 8, 1948, pp. 23-33; "A Historic Turning Point," August 22, 1948 (ibid., pp. 213-225); "Facing the Future," September 11, 1948 (ibid., pp. 226-241).

36 Ben-Gurion, *War Diary*, pp. 901-903, 936-938.

BEN-GURION AND THE FORMATION OF THE ISRAEL DEFENSE FORCES, 1947-1948

YOAV GELBER

David Ben-Gurion, as the first secretary-general of the Histadrut (General Federation of Jewish Labor), had stood at the cradle of the Haganah, but in later years he seldom involved himself in the routine affairs of that organization. On the other hand, ever since the outbreak of the Arab Revolt in 1936, Ben-Gurion displayed a deep interest in various schemes for the establishment of a regular Jewish military force, before and during World War II. After the war he ordered the Haganah, on October 1, 1945, to commence an anti-British armed struggle; yet he did not interfere personally in the conduct of operations and preferred to devote his energy to the sustenance of the Jewish survivors of the Holocaust in Europe, their Zionist consolidation, and their "illegal" immigration to Palestine. The pressure of the survivors, rather than the armed resistance of the Yishuv, seemed to him the crucial aspect of the struggle.

Ben-Gurion's renewed involvement in defense matters began at the 22nd Zionist Congress, which convened in Basle in December 1946. At that time he foresaw that the outcome of the Zionist political campaign would probably be a British evacuation of Palestine. For many of his colleagues in the Zionist leadership, that eventual withdrawal meant Jewish independence. Ben-Gurion was the only leader to look further ahead and sense the dangers that would threaten the Yishuv after the British departure. The challenge would then stem not merely from the local Palestinian Arabs but primarily from the adjacent Arab armies, who would almost certainly invade the country.

In the face of these potential dangers, it seemed to Ben-Gurion that the traditional Zionist order of priorities should undergo a basic modification. Hitherto, diplomatic action and propaganda, immigration, and colonization had been accorded top priority; from now on, defense should become the prime issue.[1] Accordingly, he took over the defense portfolio when the Zionist Executive was reorganized at the Congress. So far, the Haganah had enjoyed a large measure of autonomy, as a result of the need for secrecy. Its submission to the authority of the national institutions was symbolic rather than actual. The creation of the defense portfolio within the Zionist Executive thus symbolized a turning point in the development of the relationship between the Haganah and the political echelon.

Ben-Gurion took upon himself the responsibility for defense matters in order to prepare the Yishuv for the imminent military confrontation with the Arab armies. When he returned to Palestine in March 1947, he began to study the situation of the

Haganah, trying to establish whether the organization was capable of countering the challenge. He consulted with the Haganah Command Council and General Staff, and held talks with the district commanders, the chiefs of the Palmach, and the intelligence service, as well as with ex-officers of the British and other armies who had fought in the world war. He also summoned persons who had previously held important positions in the organization but were now inactive. Ben-Gurion requested their appraisal of future developments and the capability of the Haganah to face them.

Ben-Gurion soon gathered that the basic problems of the organization were at its summit—both in its structure and in its personal composition. In fact, the Haganah lacked a clear chain of command. This paralyzed its further development. The Command Council consisted, with the exception of Israel Galili, mainly of second-rank party activists with insufficient status both in their parties and in the Haganah. They were sharply criticized by several field commanders, as well as by their own colleagues. In an early stage of the "seminar"—as these interviews were later called—Ben-Gurion made up his mind to introduce personal changes at the top.

The "seminar" uncovered shortcomings of the Haganah in various areas. For several years the organization had failed to extend its rank and file, despite the resumption of immigration and the increasing demobilization of soldiers from the British army. Most Haganah members—with the exception of the Palmach—were insufficiently trained, and all of them were poorly equipped and ill-organized. The organization was at best able to handle the requirements of the 1930s but not future contingencies. The commanders and staff officers were not properly educated and lacked practical experience. The company was the biggest formation, and there was no recognition of the need to organize battalions. Field intelligence and field wireless communications hardly existed at all. There were no heavy weapons and no idea how to fight against them, and there were no nuclei of logistic systems and ancillary services. Nonetheless, the main problem of the Haganah was not its unpreparedness for a war with the Arabs, but rather its position toward the British and the competition with the dissident underground organizations.[2]

Ben-Gurion looked ahead far beyond the anti-British struggle, and asked about the prospects of standing up to the Arabs. His enquiries were understood to relate to the local Arabs, and the replies were optimistic. The overconfidence of the Haganah chiefs worried Ben-Gurion, inasmuch as he felt that their optimism was ill-founded. In late May 1947 he summarized his impressions of the contemporary situation of the Haganah and the essentials for its reformation:

> Insufficient training, including the Palmach; shortage of commanders, and those who are in the ranks are not good enough. Lack of operational experience. Faulty planning. The structure of the budget is inconsistent with the purpose. The equipment is disproportionate. For many years a central idea—the role [of the organization]—has been absent. What are the principal reforms: extensive training of cadres; improving the instruction; [establishment of] an advanced school [for senior commanders] ... promotion of young talents; expansion of the organization among the youth; acquisition of scientific and technological innovations in America ... a biannual program of production and training; a force that would be able to

stand up against the military forces of the Arab states and, moreover, care for [current] security....[3]

Ben-Gurion estimated that the Yishuv had two years to prepare for the ultimate trial, not only against the Palestinian Arabs and irregular volunteers from the neighboring countries, but against the regular armies of the Arab states.

Following the series of interviews that he had held in April-May 1947, Ben-Gurion asked for proposals to transform the Haganah into an army. He received several tentative plans, prepared independently by chiefs of the Haganah and ex-officers of the British army.[4] He adopted various elements from each approach and combined all of them into a directive, delivered to the Haganah Command Council; this constituted the summary and conclusion of the "seminar."

Ben-Gurion stressed the need to differentiate between current security and preparing for a total war in the future, though he saw the Haganah to be responsible for both. He emphasized the vital need for basic reforms of its organizational structure, drilling methods, officers' training, equipment, and discipline, and indicated the urgency of utilizing the experience gained by the Yishuv volunteers in the British army during the world war, which so far had been considered irrelevant.[5]

In his general guidelines Ben-Gurion established a new order of military priorities, distinguishing between the current problems of the Haganah—the British, the dissidents, and the local Arabs—and the preparations for a war against the Arab states. However, the rate of the Haganah reorganization was too slow, and the British decision to evacuate Palestine at short notice caught the Zionist leadership, including Ben-Gurion, by surprise and disrupted the evaluation of the time they had at their disposal to mobilize the Yishuv for total war.

The reshaping of the Haganah, its recovery from the ebb in which it had been since the "Black Saturday" of June 29, 1946, and its advance toward becoming a military force capable of facing the Arab armies necessitated a solution of the Supreme Command problem. In the course of his talks with the Haganah leaders in April 1947, Ben-Gurion made up his mind to summon from the US the former chief of staff, Ya'akov Dori, and reappoint him to the post. At the same time Ben-Gurion was persuaded that Israel Galili was the natural candidate to head the Haganah Command Council. Although he had some misgivings about a leading member of a rival party occupying an office of such practical and political significance, he did finally decide to appoint him and defined the distribution of powers between the head of the Command Council and the chief of staff.[6]

The next step should have been the reorganization of the Haganah Staff according to the principles of a general staff of a regular army. Ben-Gurion wished the Staff to organize themselves in three or four branches (operations, adjutant-general, quartermaster, and perhaps a special department for arms production). This General Staff should be relieved of all concern for problems at hand in order to devote their entire energy to the preparation for war, while current matters would be dealt with by a separate body. The idea provoked fierce opposition. Intelligence warnings of an eventual outbreak of disorders were utilized by Galili to persuade Ben-Gurion of the risk of introducing basic structural changes at a time when the Haganah might be called upon to act. In the heat of the dispute Ben-Gurion expressed his poor opinion of the Haganah more clearly and sharply than ever before: "The organization, I have learnt, is not up to its functions. This is not a criticism of the past, but rather concern for the future."[7]

Pending a decision about the basic structure of the General Staff, the appointment of branch directors was also postponed.[8] The delays hindered the implementation of other reforms as well, including the recruitment of veterans to full-time service in posts of command, training, and staff work. The enlistment of new members was also slow, and in September Ben-Gurion learned that the Haganah order-of-battle had not changed significantly since April.[9] He concluded that the Haganah was not capable of organizing a general call-up, and he therefore decided to establish a separate recruitment office under Golda Myerson (Meir), to coordinate in due course the mobilization of the Yishuv's manpower.[10]

The tardy pace of the General Staff reorganization, the standstill of enlistment, and the delays in the rehabilitation of the training department all slowed down the buildup of the field force and its organization—together with the Palmach and the demobilized soldiers of the British army—as the backbone of the future regular army. Ben-Gurion's directive meant a profound change in the entire system of the Haganah, that had been based on militia principles. Hence it aroused passive opposition and sometimes active obstruction. For the time being Ben-Gurion refrained from imposing his views, while Galili and Dori considered them to be too far-reaching.

The formation of an army depended, among other things, on the Yishuv's capacity to equip it. In summer 1947, the Haganah could not provide more than half of its members with light arms. Heavier weapons were not available even for the war establishment of the 14 battalions that should have constituted the nucleus of the field force. Artillery and armor, as well as military aircraft, were not to be found at all. One of the fundamentals of Ben-Gurion's project was therefore an unprecedented increase in the procurement of arms and other military equipment through home production and outside purchase. The arms and ammunition were to be stored in temporary depots abroad and to be delivered to the country at the first possible opportunity. The chiefs of the Haganah still asked for more light arms, but Ben-Gurion ordered the acquisition of armored vehicles, field artillery, mortars, heavy machine guns, and aircraft. The funds were obtained directly from the USA, and he was freed from the tiresome job of convincing his colleagues of the necessity of the budgetary allocation. The procurement of arms seemed to Ben-Gurion the most vital component of the preparation for war. Victory might be achieved at the price of high casualties which he was determined to minimize by providing the fighters with the essential military materiel as soon as possible.

Ben-Gurion's insistence on the quick reformation of the Haganah was incomprehensible to his colleagues.[11] Although he analyzed the situation and forecast the eventual developments several times during the summer and fall of 1946, his warnings passed unnoticed by the military and political establishment of the Yishuv, and he remained isolated in his foresight.[12] While he thought in terms of total war, his colleagues considered his warnings of an Arab invasion as exaggerated and hysterical. Galili, for example, explained on September 30, 1947, that the main question was not how to prepare for war but rather how to contain Arab disturbances and prevent their escalation.[13]

Six months, from April to October 1947, had been almost completely wasted as far as the Yishuv's preparation for war was concerned. Ben-Gurion's views on the likely character of the military confrontation and the might of the enemy were for all practical purposes denied by the Haganah leadership. His only achievement during that period was in bringing them to admit reluctantly a remote possibility of invasion. The essential consequent steps—the formation of a regular army through the incorporation of demobilized officers and soldiers of the British army in the Haganah; the institution of a special department to deal with current security in order to free the rest of the General Staff for work on the preparation for war; the expansion of the Haganah to include additional circles of the unorganized Yishuv; and the mental breakthrough from militia concepts and partisan tactics to those of a regular army and systematic warfare—all these barely made any progress during that period. The only changes were the new appointments at the top, but these were not followed by the required modifications in the methods of action.[14]

The turning point came in mid-October 1947, following the concentration of the Syrian army on the Palestinian border. The Haganah was taken by surprise but reacted instantly.[15] Palmach units and other reinforcements were hurriedly dispatched to Upper Galilee, yet their deployment proved the unpreparedness of the organization for war, uncovered many of its deficiencies, and finally caused the implementation of the reforms that had been demanded by Ben-Gurion.[16]

The actual reorganization was based on a scheme that had been prepared in early September 1947 by Shalom Eshet, Ben-Gurion's military adviser, for the formation of 14 infantry battalions.[17] Ben-Gurion urged the Haganah to adopt the plan immediately, but Galili and Dori were not keen, and delayed its execution. It was not until the lessons of the October emergency were learnt that Dori commenced implementation of the reform and nominated the commanding officers of the proposed battalions.[18] Except for their commanding officers, these formations existed at that time on paper only. They were still earmarked to be militia units, and their full-time core was small. By the end of October it was decided to establish four "brigades" and appoint their commanding officers too, but for the time being those "brigades," varying in size and composition, were only administrative bodies, not military units. The changes were promulgated on November 7, 1947, in a new "Structure Order" issued by the Haganah Command Council.[19]

The organizational changes were accompanied in November by a revised appraisal of the situation, prepared by Yigael Yadin and his aides in the new G branch of the Staff.[20] The assumption of foreign Arab military intervention in the wake of the British evacuation was finally accepted, and it formed the basis for a new operational program—Plan Yehoshua—drawn up in December 1947. The scheme was actually a sketch of general principles only, but it strove to provide some answers to the problems that such intervention was likely to create, contrary to the former plans of the Haganah, which had not dealt with these issues. Nonetheless, Plan Yehoshua did not amount to a scheme against general invasion, repeatedly called for at that time by Ben-Gurion.[21]

The lessons inferred by Ben-Gurion from the emergency in October 1947 reinforced his previous conviction that the Haganah was ready to counter neither the threat of invasion nor even the likelihood of local Arab disturbances on a large scale.[22] Its recovery from the mentality and organizational routine of the underground era was hastened only by the growing intensity of the fighting.

While organizational and operational planning began to change in October 1947 under combined pressure from Ben-Gurion, the Syrian movements, and the impending resolution of the United Nations' General Assembly in regard to Palestine, Ben-Gurion failed in his attempt to reform the structural deficiencies of the Haganah high command and institute his supremacy over its General Staff through the establishment of a formal and direct chain of command.

Although the Haganah was a popular and voluntary mass-organization, many of its members also belonged to various political factions and were subject to their discipline.[23] The Supreme Command represented political and other vested interests and endeavored to conserve its autonomy and fortify it against any modifications likely to stem from the imminent change of the constitutional situation. The position of the Haganah Command Council was not only a matter of principle, concerning the status of the military within the state and its affiliation to the national institutions, but also a practical issue, closely linked to the consolidation of control over the preparation for war and later the war effort itself. Alongside the Haganah Command, various bodies dealt with specific matters relating to current security and long-term provisions. Their number increased with the outbreak of hostilities. The lack of planning and clear definition of their subordination and interrelationships soon became evident. They reflected compromises between conflicting interests, represented particularist tendencies, and displayed little capacity for action, all of which were incompatible with the seriousness of the situation. Essential actions depended on personal connections or on goodwill that was not always present. In the absence of a central and recognized authority capable of taking decisions, no means were found to overcome particularism and to integrate the various activities into an efficient war effort.

Although Ben-Gurion was chairman of the Jewish Agency Executive, his position as the individual in charge of defense matters on its behalf was still dubious, since it had had no precedent in the Yishuv's political tradition. The supremacy of the Jewish Agency as the highest executive authority in the Yishuv was indeed generally recognized, but the personal status and duties of the holder of its defense portfolio were not.

The entire issue of the reciprocal relationship between the body politic and the military during the early months of the war stood at the heart of a sharp conceptual controversy and political struggle that would be decided only toward the end of the first cease-fire in July 1948. The dispute centered around two personalities—Ben-Gurion and Galili—though it was neither a personal conflict nor mere factional strife but rather an argument stemming from profound differences of opinion about the role of the military within the state and its subjection to the government, the character of the emerging army, and the essence of the war. Various parties were also involved in the dispute, trying to preserve their position in an area that had become central to the life of the Yishuv. Ben-Gurion's conception of the army as an instrument of the state, and the state only, was a thorn in the side of all. They suspected that this was a mere cover for either a personal dictatorship or a monopoly over the army by Mapai, and some of them were determined to obstruct it.

In October 1947, Ben-Gurion revived the Yishuv's Security Committee, that had been dormant since 1946. He wanted the committee—representing a facade of public control over the Haganah—to back up the consolidation of the war effort and to rally public support for essential measures such as the mobilization of manpower and funds. Addressing the committee he called once again for reorganization of the Haganah and asserted that supreme authority was now in the hands of the chairman of the Jewish Agency Executive, since he appointed the head of the Haganah Command Council and gave him his orders. Ben-Gurion stressed the vital importance of a single chain of command, headed by one individual only, and claimed that the present political and collective Command Council was incapable of leading an army at war because of its very nature.

Moreover, the authority of the national institutions, hitherto fictitious, was about to become real, embodied by himself rather than by an emissary such as the head of the Command Council. Ben-Gurion questioned the prerogatives of that political and collective Command Council in matters of personal appointments and operational planning, and doubted its very right to exist.[24] However, his intention to abolish it stirred up opposition, including some within his own party, Mapai. Preoccupied by events, he had neglected to mobilize political support for his reforms. His comrades grasped the proposed changes in the Haganah Command only in terms of interparty relations. They did not consider the modification of the chain of command indispensable, either to the preparation for war or to its actual conduct, and were still far from comprehending the full meaning of the historical process. Zalman Aranne, Pinhas Lavon, and other leading members of Mapai argued that one should not enter into political strife with the rival socialist parties as long as relations with the right-wing parties and the dissidents had not yet been settled.[25]

In the face of the strong political opposition, Ben-Gurion was temporarily obliged to abandon his intention of dissolving the Haganah Command Council. Instead, he strove to empty it of any power and responsibility. In the fall of 1947, he also failed in a renewed attempt to reform the General Staff, this time by introducing a special department, headed by Yochanan Ratner and manned by ex-officers of the British army, for emergency planning (i.e., to design and coordinate the preparation for a total war and invasion).[26] The veteran commanders of the Haganah disregarded Ratner and his team;[27] the outbreak of disturbances in early December 1947 gave priority to immediate matters of security and discouraged the introduction of basic structural changes. The spread of hostilities necessitated the hasty buildup of an army in the midst of battle, and the idea of establishing a new General Staff to organize it in an orderly and systematic manner was set aside. Instead, the army was built by the old General Staff, but not before the latter underwent major modifications and absorbed several professional officers who completely changed its essence.

The main opposition to Ben-Gurion's reforms came from the Zionist left-wing parties, who joined together in January 1948 to found the United Workers' Party (Mapam).[28] Although the new faction was second to Mapai at the polls, it had successfully competed for ascendancy in the military forces, agricultural settlements, organization of illegal immigration, and other national tasks. Mapam struggled to ensure that no regime would be established without its participation, and in case its stipulations for joining the government would be rejected by Mapai, some of its leaders suggested "to act separately ... to appear before the UN as an independent factor and propose a government...."[29]

Mapam relied on its strong holding within the Haganah, stemming from its control of the Palmach. Hence it chose the military as the principal, though not sole, theater in which to confront Ben-Gurion. In this contest it found various allies among the leadership of the Haganah and the Yishuv politicians, including some of Ben-Gurion's comrades. They all feared the impending changes and were anxious to preserve their traditional position in the process of creating the new state.

The outbreak of hostilities diverted attention from matters of principle and long-term planning to the acute problems created by the disturbances. In the following months, the new army was gradually mobilized and trained, while the old underground militia regime and the new order resembling a regular army were in a state of symbiosis.

Tensions between the old and new schools increased as the fighting intensified.[30] Ben-Gurion himself was involved in a series of controversies with the General Staff and the Palmach Command over matters of priorities, appointments, and organization. His demand that the Negev be given first priority was obstructed after long deliberations in the national institutions.[31] A similar fate befell his aim to replace the Palmach battalion in the Negev with a regular territorial brigade. Galili and the Staff took advantage of the prolonged discussions of that issue to circumvent Ben-Gurion's original orders and establish instead a Palmach brigade in that region. The latter had missions identical to those of the other territorial formations, yet it was not controlled directly by the General Staff but through the Palmach Staff, thus preserving an autonomy that had meanwhile become an anachronism.[32] Ben-Gurion's suggestion to appoint a governor for the Negev was also blocked, and his appointment of Shlomo Shamir to command the Negev brigade was disregarded by Galili and the Staff.[33]

Another dispute concerned Ben-Gurion's decision to establish a navy and his instruction to transfer the personnel of the maritime unit of the Palmach (Palyam) to that new formation. While the Palmach had earlier given up its flight section which merged into the newly formed air force, objections were raised to the disbandment of the Palyam and its incorporation in the navy.[34] The stance of the Palmach was once again backed by Galili and the General Staff, and Ben-Gurion began to distrust

Galili, suspecting that the latter had encouraged, and perhaps initiated, several actions that undermined his orders.

The differences of opinion related also to matters of discipline in the new army. The transformation of the militia into an army, the growing number of casualties, the disintegration of the Mandatory regime, and the absence of a recognized authority brought about several cases of lack of discipline and lawlessness. Rumors of atrocities spread, and some instances were brought to Ben-Gurion's personal attention.[35] While Galili concluded that it was necessary to establish some sort of a Haganah military police force, Ben-Gurion decided that the introduction of full military discipline could no longer be postponed, though it might provoke objections within and outside the ranks.[36]

He was now convinced that the Haganah veteran Command could not adjust itself to the new circumstances. Inasmuch as it had not comprehended the need to adapt the organization's structure, equipment, and planning to the requirements of a total war, so it could not perceive that the transformation from a militia force to a regular conscript army made indispensable the adoption of strict discipline and undivided loyalty.[37]

In the early months of the war Ben-Gurion's interventions in its daily conduct were sporadic and limited to incidents of public or diplomatic importance. The British announcement that the Mandate would be terminated on May 15, 1948, was distrusted by the Jewish intelligence chiefs, who suspected a British conspiracy — with or without the concurrence of King Abdallah of Transjordan — to obstruct the UN decision on the partition of Palestine.[38] Nevertheless, Ben-Gurion was determined to avoid any confrontation with the British that might open an additional and unnecessary front, or jeopardize the prospects of British withdrawal according to the declared timetable.[39]

Although the balance of power shifted in favor of the Jewish side at the beginning of the war, the hesitations about the likely British stance, as well as the routine conceptions of the character of the conflict, prevented the General Staff from taking the initiative. The war was conducted according to principles established in 1946, assuming British hostility, which were incompatible with the conditions in the country in early 1948.[40] The Haganah forces were dispersed all over the country, passively guarding every settlement, urban quarter, and road. The Palmach was deployed in regions that had not been organized within the territorial commands: the Negev, Upper Galilee, and along the road to Jerusalem. The General Staff thus lost its central reserve and could hardly influence the fighting.[41] While the Arabs failed in their attempts to attack several Jewish settlements, the mobilization of their forces was not seriously interrupted. In spite of some local setbacks they retained the general initiative, till they could patiently discover the Jewish weak points.[42] In March 1948, they realized that the main Jewish weakness was the vulnerability of the lines of communication and supply, and therefore they began to harass systematically the roads leading to isolated settlements, and especially to Jerusalem. By the end of March, they succeeded in destroying three large Jewish convoys, and effectively placed Jewish Jerusalem under siege.[43]

Until February 1948 Ben-Gurion's attention had been focused on the Negev. He feared that in the absence of Jewish population it might be severed from the Jewish state, and he simultaneously grasped the prospects for freedom of action through the occupation of this vast uninhabited area.[44] Yet his vision of the conquest of the Negev was overruled by his colleagues, and he turned to Jerusalem, which had meanwhile emerged as the crucial point in the further conduct of the war. Once again, his priorities were incomprehensible to the military command, but on that occasion he interfered vigorously for the first time in the operational management of the war and forced the Staff to concentrate large forces by stripping other, quieter fronts, and to take the initiative to relieve Jerusalem.[45]

"Operation Nahshon," in April 1948, was a turning point both in the course of the war and in the creation of the Israel Defense Forces (I.D.F.). For the first time, the young army, still in the midst of its mobilization and transformation from a militia to a regular force, took the field openly, on its own initiative. The formations were larger than those the army had previously employed in battle, and the aim was now to secure terrain and to subdue the enemy. But the essence of that turning point was the very realization of priorities, and the comprehension that the war would be decided precisely through the concentration of forces at the crucial points and not by dispersing them to safeguard each locality. The role played by Ben-Gurion in bringing about this reorientation cannot be exaggerated. The decision was entirely his and he assumed full responsibility against the opposition and hesitations of his professional advisors, such as Yadin and Ratner.[46]

The failures sustained in the early months of the war; the operational difficulties of protecting the movement on the roads; the obstacles encountered in organizing the new recruits; the structural deficiencies; the shortcomings of the Command Staff; the multitude of authorities and the insufficient coordination; the cases of deviation from authority and the lack of discipline—all these brought Ben-Gurion to resume his exertion to restore the High Command. He strove to modify its basic principles, establish the source of authority and its delegation, as well as to formulate a proper definition of responsibilities, regardless of the risk of stimulating fierce reaction among the other parties within the Yishuv.[47]

The Haganah Command Council had already been neutralized, but meanwhile a new complication arose owing to the health of the chief of staff. An ailing Dori had gradually kept away from the daily work and in March 1948 Ben-Gurion began to search for an acting replacement, despite the objections of Yadin, who claimed that Galili was the best substitute for Dori during the latter's illness.[48] Ben-Gurion had now to deliver his instructions to the army through Galili,[49] a political personality, who deputized for the head of the professional military hierarchy.

At that time, the exclusion of politics from the army was still an unknown and unaccepted concept. The creation and growth of the army attracted the attention of all the factions, who sought to preserve influence on the army as a whole, as well as to post their own men in key positions of the new force. Mapai established a special apparatus to take care of the manning of new offices by its members. Mapam had more far-reaching ambitions. It aspired to the post of minister of defense and organized a party security committee, which functioned in the capacity of a political commissar and exercised the party's authority over its comrades in the service.[50] Various military issues were discussed by that committee in order to consolidate an agreed stance and commit the officers and soldiers belonging to the party to adhere to it. Senior officers were involved in Mapam's activities in military matters, and they were often consulted on professional and personal matters.[51]

Against this background, Galili's position at the top of the military hierarchy had a special significance. Ben-Gurion refused to comply with a state of affairs that was diametrically opposed to his own conception of the relations between the military and the political authorities. Notwithstanding Yadin's misgivings, he insisted on the appointment of a deputy chief of staff. Since there were reservations about the nomination of an outsider, such as the American colonel, David Marcus, as well as likely opposition to any of the ex-officers of the British army, he tried to persuade Ratner to take the post.[52]

Ratner was not identified with the present leadership, yet he enjoyed its confidence as well as that of the Haganah veterans. But he was apprehensive of the consequences of his appointment and probably preferred to wait until the Command's structure had been modified, rather than be involved in that painful operation. He refused Ben-Gurion's urgings to report in Tel Aviv and assume his office, though he was ready to undertake other duties. Nonetheless, Ben-Gurion was determined to implement the changes. The general atmosphere of insecurity following the convoys' crisis of late March 1948 seemed to him an appropriate background for the realization of that goal. The convening of the Zionist Actions Committee at the beginning of April presented a proper opportunity to obtain the sanction of the supreme Zionist body acting between the Congresses.[53] Ben-Gurion asked the delegates "to organize the Yishuv and the Zionist movement — not according to the Zionist constitution, not in correspondence with our habits, not as had been customary during the last fifty years, but only to satisfy the requirements of defense." Those needs necessitated, in his opinion,

> ... the establishment of a sole and supreme central authority that would control the manpower, the army, the workers, industry and agriculture, finances and the state services in the Yishuv and in the country....[54]

Ben-Gurion meant in fact a government. His opponents in Mapam did not reject his demand forthwith, but still doubted "the actuality of the Jewish state."[55] Nevertheless, they were resolved to secure their participation in the new body and demanded a role in controlling security through the institution of a small war cabinet that would restrict Ben-Gurion's personal influence.[56] On the other hand, they maintained that the proposed government might be obliged to go underground, and, hinting at the Haganah Command Council, suggested the continuous existence of a clandestine authority in defense matters.[57]

Ben-Gurion's proposals were endorsed by the Zionist Actions Committee on April 12, 1948. While he recognized a single military force to whom the Actions Committee's resolution related, Mapam asserted that another resolution accepted by that body, which concerned a suggested pact with the I.Z.L., signified a compliance with the existence of two armies, and hence Mapam pressed for the creation of a third force, loyal to the Histadrut. The issue of organizing a separate workers' militia outside the army was intensively discussed in the party's internal deliberations, as were the means to secure as many of the newly formed key positions in the army as possible for the party's comrades.[58]

Those topics, as well as the fear of a putsch by the I.Z.L., were also deliberated in meetings between representatives of Mapai and Mapam, in which the latter explained their objections to the reform of the High Command and to Ben-Gurion's alleged intention to disband the Palmach. Mapam conceived a military force equally subordinated to two sources of authority—the new government and the old Command Council.[59] The disagreements in the conception of the role of the military in the state and its affiliation to the party system would become the crux of the dispute between Ben-Gurion and Mapam, though the concrete issues on the agenda were different, such as the status of Galili, or the autonomous existence of the Palmach.

Ben-Gurion did not rush to implement the Actions Committee's resolution transferring the source of authority over the military force from the old Yishuv institutions to the new provisional government (still called "The People's Executive" until the termination of the Mandate). The increasing intensity of the fighting since April augmented the burden of building the army and conducting its actions, and demanded of him greater involvement in current operational affairs. Those were days of excitement, caused by the successes of "Operation Nahshon," the battles of Mishmar Ha'emek and Ramat Yochanan, and the conquest of Tiberias and Haifa.

However, there was growing friction between the Palmach and other formations.[60] The special status of the former, with a separate Staff of its own, seemed to Ben-Gurion increasingly anachronistic and unjustified. It is probable that already at that time he decided to cancel the Palmach's unique standing, but first of all he had to accomplish the reform of the High Command.

On April 21, Ben-Gurion informed the members of the Jewish Agency Executive in Jerusalem that:

> in view of the transfer of military matters to the "thirteen" [The People's Executive], there is no longer room for the head of the Command Council as representative of the Jewish Agency Executive in the Council, since security comes under the "thirteen." Hence the personal appointment [of Galili] and the office itself are annulled....[61]

His announcement was endorsed, but he still expected complications and meanwhile put off the formal take-over of the defense portfolio in The People's Executive, assuming only its chairmanship. On April 26, he explained that for the time being he would continue to function in defense matters on behalf of the Jewish Agency Executive.[62] It was more than a hint to his colleagues that he regarded the reform of the High Command as an essential prerequisite for accepting the office of defense minister, and that he was not prepared to be merely a formal front while someone else would direct the buildup of the army and the conduct of the war. He insisted on the institution of a clear chain of command in order to neutralize party interference.

Later that day, Ben-Gurion met with Galili and discussed with him the current state of affairs in the army. He disapproved of the special position of the Palmach, of certain personal appointments, of the lack of discipline and training, and of the absence of aggressive spirit. Finally, he told Galili that he had decided to annul his office. Galili admitted some of Ben-Gurion's points but disputed the latter's ideas in regard to the command structure and his own status. Galili proposed that he should constitute a special link in the chain of command, between Ben-Gurion and the army. Ben-Gurion rejected this suggestion forthwith, and informed Galili that he would rather resign than accept it.[63]

Galili's stance was backed up by his party, then negotiating with Mapai the stipulations for joining the government. Mapam demanded that Galili receive the defense portfolio.[64] Some of its leaders denied in principle Ben-Gurion's notion of the army as a tool of the state only, and propagated instead a workers' army.[65] Against the background of those days it was not merely a theoretical issue since, following the I.Z.L. attack on Jaffa in late April, Mapam pressed hard on Mapai to agree to the formation of a military force subordinate to the Histadrut for a possible action against the right-wing dissidents in Tel Aviv.[66]

The overt backing of Galili by Mapam, the clear presentation of the theory of a workers' army, and the growing pressures to establish such a force toward the declaration of the state strengthened Ben-Gurion's conviction, and without waiting for the conclusion of the deliberations with Mapam, he summoned Galili on May 2 to inform him that his post had been abolished.[67] A wave of protest followed, both inside and outside the army. The five branch directors of the General Staff threatened to resign, claiming that the dismissal of Galili during the absence of the chief of staff was an irresponsible act on Ben-Gurion's part.[68] Simultaneously, Mapam commenced a political campaign against Ben-Gurion's "usurpation," conducted vehemently in all the political forums in which Mapam was represented, as well as in the press. The party also initiated a campaign of discrediting Ben-Gurion among the soldiers and the general public, glorifying the Palmach's achievements, and blaming Ben-Gurion for all past setbacks while warning of the future implications of his reign.[69]

The acute crisis went on for several days. On the face of it, Ben-Gurion finally yielded and on May 9 invited Galili back to work in cooperation with him.[70] In fact, he gave up temporarily on the personal issue only but did not cancel the structural change, and he refrained from any definition of Galili's future duties. A new phase thus started, during which the General Staff was torn between Ben-Gurion's formal, yet unrecognized and unaccepted, authority as minister of defense and Galili's traditional, but now informal, personal authority as an old colleague, as well as former head of the Command Council and acting chief of staff.

Nevertheless, Ben-Gurion achieved his main objective through this crisis. The Supreme Command was transformed and the army was in effect subordinated to the political echelon. Other changes followed.

Although the state had been officially declared and The People's Executive became its provisional government, Ben-Gurion had not yet formally accepted the ministry of defense. He refused to take office, insisting on the fulfillment of his other conditions. The latter included the full and exclusive rule of the government over the army, complete equality of authority, discipline, and conditions for all people in the military service, and the restriction of their actions according to the terms of reference of their appointment only.[71] While the ministers endorsed Ben-Gurion as premier, his election as minister of defense was postponed until all the problems of the defense portfolio and his conditions for undertaking it would be resolved.

On May 26 the government approved the "Israel Defense Forces Order," that laid down the legal basis for the army's existence, ensuring its exclusiveness as the sole armed force in the state and its subordination to the government. It was an important step toward the fulfillment of Ben-Gurion's demands, and on May 30 he agreed to the official publication of the distribution of the ministerial offices, including his own portfolio of minister of defense. The same day the government approved the wording of the military oath proposed by Ben-Gurion and based on the Haganah oath of allegiance. The next day a special ministerial order was promulgated, announcing the formal establishment of the I.D.F., and simultaneously the "Israel Defense Forces Order" was published in the *Official Gazette*.[72] The swearing-in ceremonies were postponed until the cease-fire, and the Provisional State Council ratified the Order in its session of July 1, 1948. Its approval completed the creation of the formal infrastructure that defined the role and status of the I.D.F. in the State of Israel and its affiliation to the state's institutions. However, the transformation of the constitutional principles to a daily reality took several months and was associated with open as well as covert crises.

Following the dissolution of the Haganah Command Council and the consolidation of his position within the government as minister of defense, Ben-Gurion had to resolve two more issues in order to complete the reform of the High Command. Galili's status had to be defined, and Ben-Gurion's own supremacy over the army had to be asserted since some senior commanders and Staff officers found this difficult to accept. Both questions were related.[73] As long as Dori was absent and branch directors had access to Galili, there was a loophole for avoiding Ben-Gurion's orders, as well as for acting without his consent and contrary to his guidelines. Galili's ideas were closer to those of the Staff veterans and his style was known and traditional. Ben-Gurion's interventions in military matters seemed to them dangerous, either to the course of the war or to their own position.[74]

Several cases in which Ben-Gurion's authority clashed with that of Galili or encountered opposition within the General Staff occurred in May and June, 1948.[75] The most significant of them was the conflict over the formation of the 7th Brigade and its assignment of the task of taking Latrun in late May. The new brigade, commanded by Shlomo Shamir, was earmarked to be the General Staff reserve, but its creation was obstructed and delayed for several days (while each day was vital) by the Staff under Galili's influence. The intrigues stemmed from the objection to the transfer of the army's first armored battalion to the new brigade. Yigal Allon, the Palmach commanding officer, asserted that it was a Palmach unit which should not be attached to a regular formation. Furthermore, the Palmach was customarily considered as the General Staff reserve; thus the assignment of that duty to a regular formation seemed to be another infringement on the former's prerogatives and a further step in the process of its disbandment. Moreover, the charging of the 7th Brigade with the mission of attacking Latrun, considered at the time to be the main effort of the army, was grasped as an encroachment on the special status of the Palmach as shock troops designed to perform the most difficult tasks. The formation of the 7th Brigade and the battle of Latrun were hence a turning point in the process of building the army, symbolizing the termination of the Palmach's monopoly of the more important assignments, the special means of warfare, and the General Staff reserve.

The General Staff confronted Ben-Gurion both on the formation of the 7th Brigade and on its premature deployment. The attack on Latrun failed, and the defeat was utilized by Ben-Gurion's opponents to blame him for overruling the General Staff's professional advice, and to portray his favorite ex-officers of the British army as unfit to command, given the unique circumstances of warfare in Israel in which they were inexperienced. Rumors were spread that exaggerated the dimensions of the failure, and legends were disseminated about the battle fought by new immigrants who were sent from their ships directly to the battlefield, without elementary training and essential equipment, and who died of thirst or were killed with the safety catches of their rifles still engaged. Some of these stories, obviously false, were even corroborated by Yadin in front of a government commission a few weeks later.

The troops who fought in Latrun and suffered the heaviest casualties—the 32nd Battalion—were trained veterans in terms of those days. The second battalion that took part in the Battle—the 72nd—was indeed composed of new recruits, yet the percentage of new immigrants among them was small, and most of these had come from Cyprus in March 1948. The battle of Latrun was the first one the I.D.F. fought with an entire brigade, yet it was assigned to the youngest formation of the whole army, one that had existed for a week. In spite of the tactical failure, the battle—together with those of Jenin and Isdud a few days later, both of which were no more successful—played a major role in bringing about the strategic turning point of the war: it opened the phase of counterattacks, following the stoppage of the Arab invasion, and marked the taking of the initiative by the I.D.F.[76]

Simultaneous with the dispute over the formation of the 7th Brigade and its attack on Latrun, the conflict between Ben-Gurion and Mapam became exacerbated. Galili's position weakened and he was prevented by Ben-Gurion from dealing with matters of military importance. It appeared as if Ben-Gurion achieved through a gradual process the goal he had failed to accomplish by the act of dismissal.

In order to halt the deterioration of its position, Mapam resumed the political and propagandist campaign against Ben-Gurion which had somewhat abated following the Arab invasion. Now Mapam demanded completion of the transitory arrangement that had brought Galili back to the High Command, by revising the decision to abolish the Haganah Command Council and defining his status between the minister of defense and the General Staff.[77] Ben-Gurion rejected forthwith all the proposals that had been made by Mapam representatives and refused to allow an interparty discussion of military matters. He regarded Mapam's pressures as plain blackmail to which he was not prepared to succumb.[78] Moreover, it was obvious that he was not led by factional considerations since his own comrades were also rebuffed by him when they tried to interfere with the army.[79]

At that time Ben-Gurion became embroiled deeper and deeper in the routine details of operations, organization, and logistics. In addition to his daily meetings with the branch directors, he consulted with several other advisers, some of whom were foreign volunteers. Those consultations strengthened the feeling among the veterans of the General Staff that he did not trust them. Another significant cause for the growing tension in the High Command was the impression that Ben-Gurion ultimately planned to disband the Palmach, or at least to deprive it of its uniqueness.

Although he had not yet declared his aim openly, Ben-Gurion ordered the General Staff to disregard the Palmach Staff in its dealings with the Palmach brigades.[80] The orders stirred up protests on the part of Allon and Galili, and elicited an order dispatched by the former's deputy to all Palmach units to send back any instruction given to them directly by the General Staff and not through the Palmach Staff.[81] Ben-Gurion reacted instantly and forced the cancellation of that order, but soon the conflict was transferred again to the political theater.[82] In mid-June 1948 Mapam embarked on a fresh attack on Ben-Gurion, directed this time at his alleged intention to disband the Palmach. His aspiration to abolish the Palmach Staff was portrayed as a part of an attempt by Mapai to dominate the army.[83] Ben-Gurion claimed at the Mapai Council that instead of incorporating the Palmach in the army for the good of all, Mapam strove to retain it as the party's private army.[84] Galili retorted at the Mapam Council that there was no need whatsoever to disband the Palmach. He argued against other changes that were introduced by Ben-Gurion and criticized the construction of the I.D.F. on the model of the British army. The case of the I.Z.L.'s ship *Altalena* provided, in his opinion, another reason for the preservation of the Palmach, to fulfill the function of specially loyal troops for dealing with internal dangers, and finally he warned of the growth of a careerist army.[85]

The clash over the Palmach engaged Ben-Gurion and Galili in a public political debate. This argument differed from their previous controversies, which had been businesslike and restricted to the close quarters of the General Staff or to secret meetings with Mapam delegations. Now Ben-Gurion regarded Galili as a subordinate civil servant of the defense ministry apparatus, and the latter's overt criticism appeared to him to be a challenge to the minister's authority that was inconceivable under the new system of the High Command. For the time being Ben-Gurion did not react, but his suspicions of a Mapam-inspired conspiracy against him inside the army grew and soon proved to well founded.

On the eve of the cease-fire, prior to the open clash between the parties, Mapam's Security Committee resolved to revive the campaign against Ben-Gurion and escalate it to demand his removal from the office of minister of defense.[86] The scheme was frustrated by the *Altalena* affair, but Mapam soon found another opportunity to generate a crisis, the pretext now being Ben-Gurion's attempt to force on the General Staff a series of appointments to various military posts.

Ben-Gurion sought to take advantage of the cease-fire period to reorganize the army, incorporating the lessons of the recent battles. There was a vital need to build up formations larger than brigades, to relieve the latter of their territorial responsibilities, and to turn them into mobile formations.[87] This entailed, among other changes, the appointment of front commanders. In addition, Ben-Gurion planned to replace certain brigade commanders whose performance had not been impressive, and he strove to nominate some ex-officers for senior posts in the General Staff. Moreover, he wished to appoint Yadin as acting chief of staff in order to fill the vacuum at the top of the military hierarchy.[88] Yadin refused, but Ben-Gurion's manifest interest in personnel changes alarmed Mapam.[89] Toward the end of June 1948, it looked as if Ben-Gurion intended a general reshuffle that might have a considerable effect on the character and future development of the army.

On June 24, 1948, Ben-Gurion asked Yadin and Zvi Ayalon, the deputy chief of staff, to present him with an overall proposal of appointments adapted to the organizational changes that were about to be introduced. The branch directors conferred the same day with Galili to consolidate their recommendations. The sick chief of staff, Dori, was not notified of the meeting or briefed on its outcome, and the absence of the adjutant general, Moshe Zadok, was conspicuous. Since he was loyal to Ben-Gurion, his colleagues suggested to nominate him as director of training, and thus remove him from his sensitive post and replace him by Moshe Man, a previously dismissed brigade commander who incidentally happened to be a Mapam member. Taking advantage of the absence of the two most prominent officers, Mapam's Security Committee was quite active behind the scenes of that consultation. Since all three front commanders recommended were members of Mapam, the party's politicians advised the officers to suggest the creation of a fourth front and propose an ex-officer to command it, in order to satisfy Ben-Gurion.[90]

The General Staff's recommendations were rejected outright by Ben-Gurion. Galili's involvement and Zadok's absence brought him to suspect a conspiracy, and he immediately ordered that every appointment, replacement, or transfer of an officer in the army required his personal approval. The directors regarded that instruction as an expression of distrust and the tension grew.

Ben-Gurion drew up his own scheme of appointments, and when Yadin and Ayalon were informed of its contents, the crisis erupted.[91] Yadin and some other officers who were Mapam members threatened to resign their posts, in protest against the proposed appointment of Mordechai Makleff as commander of the Jerusalem road front. According to their plan, the command of that front should have been given to Allon, who had led the last abortive attack on Latrun prior to the cease-fire agreement. The real issue again concerned the fate of the Palmach: two of its three brigades were deployed along the Jerusalem road, so Mapam was determined to prevent the assignation of Makleff—an officer of the Jewish Brigade—to be in charge of that front since the party's grip on the Palmach main force would vanish if it would come under his command. Another cause for complaint was the transfer of the two members of Mapam—Ayalon and Eliyahu Ben-Hur—from their directorates in the General Staff to command posts in the field and their replacement by ex-officers of the Brigade. That would have left Mapam without any representation at the level of directors, while the party still considered the General Staff a semi-political institution that should function according to the traditional rules of factional representation and political compromises.[92]

Ben-Gurion tried in vain to satisfy Yadin and Ayalon on some points, and then promulgated his scheme of appointments in the form of a ministerial directive.[93] Some of the Staff veterans allied themselves with Mapam to check this attempt to take over the army. Rumors about a conspiracy against Ben-Gurion's domination of the army had circulated for a while and were reported to him.[94] They were corroborated by the very participation of several senior officers such as Ben-Hur, Sadeh, and Israel Ber in the party's discussions of its anti-Ben-Gurion campaign and their utterances in those deliberations.[95]

In reaction to Ben-Gurion's instructions, Galili, Yadin, Ayalon, and Ben-Hur sent him letters of resignation and requested that they be delivered to the government.[96] The other three directors (Zadok, Yosef Avidar, and Ratner) did not join their colleagues, thus making it easier for Ben-Gurion to describe the act as a political mutiny inspired by Mapam. He immediately accepted the resignation of Ben-Hur—the director of military training—and temporarily nominated his deputy to replace him. However, he refrained from acknowledging the letters of Yadin and Ayalon, and brought the matter to the government's next meeting, on July 2, 1948.

At that session, Ben-Gurion declared that Galili's direct appeal to the government behind the back of his superior minister was an act of disloyalty, and, as far as Ben-Gurion was concerned, Galili had surrendered his office in the ministry of defense. Furthermore, he asserted that the whole affair was plotted by Mapam in order to secure the nomination of party members and to check the promotion of other officers. According to Ben-Gurion, Yadin told him that he had joined his colleagues out of fear lest Mapam's agitation in response to the new appointments would undermine the army from within and destroy its capacity to resume the fighting after the cease-fire. Finally, Ben-Gurion insisted on receiving the government's backing for his action, otherwise he would have to abdicate, and he demanded the establishment of a commission of three ministers to investigate the whole affair.

The government resolved to confirm Ben-Gurion's appointments but to freeze additional changes, and instituted a commission of five instead of three ministers to investigate the High Command and recommend ways to define the delegation of authority and working procedures within it. The commission was chaired by the minister of the interior, Yitzhak Gruenbaum, who did not belong to either of the big parties.

Mapam regarded the commission's task as political arbitration rather than clarification of the facts.[97] The commission's own perception of its duty was similar. It acted hastily, in view of the imminent termination of the cease-fire. Ben-Gurion and Galili were both present and took part in its deliberations. The commission strove to reach an agreed solution without delving too deeply into the factual background. After listening to the mutual accusations of the rivals and asking several other officers for their opinion on the army's condition, it set about formulating its conclusions. These were dictated by Aharon Zisling, Mapam's representative and minister of agriculture, and supported by the chairman. They went a long way to meet Mapam's claims and contained, among other things, the institution of a war cabinet, the annulment of Ben-Gurion's recent nominations, and Galili's designation as deputy minister in charge of the army, to whom the chief of staff would be directly subordinate.

Ben-Gurion refused to comment on these recommendations, left the room in a demonstration of disapproval, and retired to his home. Later that day, July 6, he informed Gruenbaum of his resignation from the government. The commission met again that night to discuss the new crisis. It soon became clear that no one was prepared to take on Ben-Gurion's responsibilities, so the commission had to negotiate with him the conditions for his return. Its proposals were rejected by Ben-Gurion, except for the establishment of a war cabinet, an issue which he was ready to concede. Gruenbaum referred the matter back to the government plenum, together with the commission's suggestions and a report of Ben-Gurion's abdication and his conditions for resumption of his duties.[98]

The government had no other choice but to submit to Ben-Gurion's terms in spite of Mapam's protests, and on July 11 he returned to his office. Meanwhile a compromise had been found regarding the appointment of front commanders. Their nomination was postponed and it was replaced by the temporary appointment of "operation commanders" to lead the operations of the "Ten Days Campaign." That compromise, devised by Yadin, opened the way for a reconciliation between Ben-Gurion and the General Staff. The resignations were withdrawn, but for that of Ben-Hur, who remained out of office.

The crisis at the beginning of July 1948 was the climax of the conflict between Ben-Gurion and his opponents, as well as a turning point in the process of creating the I.D.F. The period of contest over the army's character, its source of authority, and the structure of its chain of command came to a close. From now on the supremacy of the minister of defense over the military was absolutely recognized by the army officers, and Ben-Gurion gained the upper hand in his struggle against the conservative elements led by Mapam. Henceforth, he would be at liberty to accomplish the essential modifications in the army's structure, organization, and discipline. The professional counsel of ex-officers of the British army and of foreign experts could now prevail.

Despite Mapam's apprehensions and warnings, the dismissal of Galili, that had become final following the July crisis, did not bring in its wake the discharge of other party members from their posts. Some of them complied with the new rules and remained in active service for many years. Others carried on until the demobilization of the war army in late 1949 and then left for their kibbutzim.

As a result of the July crisis, Ben-Gurion gave in on two points. First, he abandoned his scheme of appointments; nevertheless, he managed to attach several professional officers, such as Hayyim Laskov, to the General Staff, and to get rid of Ben-Hur. He did not nominate an acting chief of staff, apparently because he expected the early return of Dori (who indeed resumed his post at the end of July).

His second concession was the establishment of a permanent ministerial committee of five to assist him in the management of the war, though this committee did not seriously restrict his freedom of action.

The events that led to the July 1948 crisis were typical of armies that are formed in the midst of a war, comprising a veteran and ideologically consolidated nucleus emerging from the underground. The controversy over the character of the Red Army during the Russian Civil War and later in the 1920s, between its founder Trotsky and the radical Bolsheviks, was similar. Ben-Gurion managed to overcome the Yishuv's radicals in time, thanks to the support and loyalty of a group of professional officers, veterans of the British army, who concurred with his concepts of state, army, and war. These officers could replace his opponents in case of their retirement, and their very presence mitigated Mapam's threats to instruct its members to resign, contradicting the assumption that Ben-Gurion could not lead the war without Mapam's cooperation. In the later course of the war, Ben-Gurion succeeded in fusing the professional knowledge and experience that had been acquired in World War II with the enthusiasm and fighting spirit that had emerged from the underground, an amalgamation that would yield its fruits in the eventual systematic building of the I.D.F. in the 1950s.

The conflict between Ben-Gurion and Mapam would have been decided earlier, according to the political balance of power between the rival parties, but for the vacuum that had been created by the absence of the chief of staff. Galili did not antagonize Ben-Gurion because of his personality (on the contrary—Ben-Gurion appreciated his talents and sought his cooperation) or his political position (at least until the final stage of the dispute), but rather because of his aspiration to act for Dori without bearing the responsibility of the office and without clear recognition of his subordination to the minister of defense. Ben-Gurion was first and foremost opposed to the existence of two sources of authority over the army. The branch directors of the General Staff, all of whom were Haganah veterans, feared the reforms which Ben-Gurion strove to introduce; on the other hand, they were used to accepting Galili's personal leadership and therefore it took Ben-Gurion several months to enforce his authority. Meanwhile they supported Galili and balanced Mapai's political superiority over Mapam. Indirectly, they also influenced the stance of some non-Mapam government ministers, who feared a split within the High Command in the midst of the war, as well as what was termed by Gruenbaum "Ben-Gurion's aspiration for dictatorship." However, when the army High Command grasped that no one was prepared to replace Ben-Gurion as the supreme war leader, they changed their attitude and submitted to his supremacy. When the crisis was over, Ben-Gurion could continue bearing the burden of directing the war, building the I.D.F., and shaping it as a regular army.

Notes

1 Ben-Gurion's speech at the Political Committee of the Congress, December 12, 1946, in: D. Ben-Gurion, *In the Struggle* (Hebrew), vol. 5, Tel Aviv, 1949, pp. 135-136.

2 Ben-Gurion's diary, entries for March 3, 1947 till May 6, 1947, Ben-Gurion Archives, Sedeh Boker (hereafter B.G.A.).

3 Ibid., entry for May 26, 1947.

4 Ibid., entry for May 28-30, 1947; a memorandum on augmenting the capability of the Haganah, prepared by the Haganah Staff, May 21, 1947, Haganah Archives (hereafter H.A.), 73/1; a memorandum drafted by Yochanan Ratner and Ze'ev Shever, May 28, 1947, ibid.; a plan prepared by Hayyim Laskov and Shalom Eshet, May 30, 1947, H.A., 73/101. Another plan was prepared for Galili by Yehoshua Globerman, May 5, 1947, H.A., 73/102. It discussed the reform of the Haganah fighting force and the structure of its Staff.

5 Ben-Gurion's directive to the Haganah HQ, June 18, 1947, B.G.A., 1548.

6 Ben-Gurion's diary, entry for June 13, 1947, B.G.A., and his instruction, June 16, 1947, H.A., 73/107.

7 Ben-Gurion's diary, entries for June 4, 23 and 27, 1947, B.G.A.

8 Summaries of the Haganah HQ meetings, June 6 and 20, 1947, H.A., 73/72.

9 Ben-Gurion's diary, entries for June 16-23, 1947, B.G.A.

10 Protocol of the first meeting of the mobilization executive, October 5, 1947, Central Zionist Archives, Jerusalem (hereafter C.Z.A.), S25/7414.

11 See the testimonies of E. Yishay, N. Argov, and Z. Ayalon, in: M. Bar-Zohar, *Ben-Gurion* (Hebrew), vol. 2, Tel Aviv, 1977, pp. 657-658.

12 Protocol of Mapai Secretariat meeting, May 29, 1947, Labor Party Archives (hereafter L.P.A.), 24/47; protocol of the Yishuv Security Committee meeting, June 8, 1947, in: D. Ben-Gurion, *When Israel Fought* (Hebrew), Tel Aviv, 1950, pp. 16-17; protocol of the Zionist Actions Committee meeting in Zurich, August 26, 1947, B.G.A., 1549.

13 Galili's speech at the Histadrut Council, September 30, 1947, H.A., Galili files, No. 8.

14 See Ayalon's memorandum on preparation for a possible Arab action, July 5, 1947, and the Haganah Staff instructions for mobilization and alert against the Arabs, October 1947, H.A., 73/95.

15 See the Haganah Staff instructions to reinforce the Galilee, October 13-15, 1947, H.A., 73/1, 73/21, and 73/50.

16 Globerman's report on the situation in Upper Galilee, October 16, 1947, H.A., 73/50; Eshet's scheme for the defense of the Galilee, October 1947, H.A., 8/15a; and Galili's report to the Yishuv Security Committee on his visit to the units in the Galilee and its lessons, protocol of the Security Committee meeting, October 19, 1947, C.Z.A., S25/9341.

17 Eshet's scheme and the attached purchase list, H.A., 8/15a.

18 Summary of the Haganah HQ "B" Department meeting, October 21, 1947, H.A., 73/72, and the letters of appointment, October 26-November 18, 1947, I.D.F. Archives.

19 The order in H.A., 73/100.

20 "A Skeleton-Plan for a Case of Evacuation," November 1947, I.D.F. Archives; and see also Y. Avidar, "Plan D" (Hebrew), in: *Author and Warrior* (Hebrew), Tel Aviv, 1978, p. 38.

21 "Preliminary Assumptions for the Execution of Plan Yehoshua," late December 1947, I.D.F. Archives, and Avidar, "Plan D."

22 Protocols of the Security Committee's meetings, October 19 and 28, 1947, C.Z.A., S25/9342. E. Orren and G. Rivlin (eds.), *Ben-Gurion's War Diary* (Hebrew), Tel Aviv, 1982, entries for December 10, 18, 1947.

23 Y. Dori, "From a Defense Organization to an Army of Defense" (Hebrew), *Ma'arachot*, Nos. 118-119 (Tel Aviv 1959), p. 34.

24 Protocols of the Security Committee's meetings, October 19 and 23, 1947, C.Z.A., S25/9342.

25 Protocol of Mapai Secretariat meeting, October 30, 1947, L.P.A., 24/47; Ben-Gurion's diary, entry of the same day, B.G.A.; and Ben-Gurion's notes, written at the meeting of the Jewish Agency Executive, October 25, 1947, C.Z.A., S44/676.

26 Ben-Gurion's diary, entries for October 18-21, 1947, B.G.A.

27 Y. Ratner, *My Life and I* (Hebrew), Tel Aviv, 1978, pp. 351-354. See also H.A., Ratner files, No. 3 and his testimony in H.A., as well as the testimonies of Y. Sahar, Z. Ayalon, and Y. Yizraeli in H.A.

28 Speeches of Yigal Allon and Meir Yaari at Mapam's unification conference, January 23-24, 1948, according to the conference protocol, pp. 14-15, 41.

29 Protocol of Mapam Political Committee meeting, January 29, 1948, Mapam Archives (hereafter M.A.), 66.90(1), pp. 3-6.

30 See, for example, *Ben-Gurion's War Diary*, entries for December 17, 1947 and January 18, 1948, and Eshet's letter to Ben-Gurion, January 17, 1948, B.G.A., 1558.

31 Protocol of the Jewish Agency Executive meeting, January 19, 1948, and protocols of the Security Committee meetings, February 3 and 10, 1948, C.Z.A., S25/9346.

32 *Ben-Gurion's War Diary*, entries for March 5 and 10, 1948; Ben-Gurion to Galili and Dori, March 1948, H.A., Galili files, No. 25.

33 *Ben-Gurion's War Diary*, entries for January 28, 1948, February 13 and 18, 1948, March 3-4, 1948, and March 20-25, 1948; Galili to Ben-Gurion, March 1948, H.A., Galili files, No. 25.

34 *Ben-Gurion's War Diary*, entry for March 12, 1948; Ben-Gurion to Galili, March 16, 1948, H.A., Galili files, No. 25; see also E. Tal, *The Navy's Operations in the War of Independence* (Hebrew), Tel Aviv, 1964, pp. 55-57.

35 *Ben-Gurion's War Diary*, entries for January 18 and 31, 1948.

36 Protocols of the Security Committee meetings, February 3 and 10, 1948, C.Z.A., S25/9346.

37 Ben-Gurion at the meeting of Mapai Council, February 7, 1948, L.P.A., 22/35.

38 See, for example, the report of Reuben Zaslani (Shiloah) on his visit to London, March 7, 1948, C.Z.A., S25/7706, and "Tene" (Intelligence Service) summary review No. 1, "The British Obstruction of the Partition Scheme," April 6, 1948, C.Z.A., S25/9671.

39 *Ben-Gurion's War Diary*, entry for February 15, 1948, and protocol of the Security Committee meeting, February 24, 1948, C.Z.A., S25/9346.

40 Yadin to the brigade commanders, town commanders, and the Palmach commanding officer, January 18, 1948, I.D.F. Archives.

41 Galili at the meeting of the Security Committee, January 27, 1948, C.Z.A., S25/9345.

42 Yadin's memorandum on the strategic situation, February 2, 1948, I.D.F. Archives.

43 See Y. Gelber, *A Nucleus of a Jewish Regular Army* (Hebrew), Jerusalem, 1986, pp. 103-108.

44 *Ben-Gurion's War Diary*, entries for December 20, 1947 and January 2 and 9, 1948.

45 Ibid., entries for March 30-31, 1948; Yadin's testimony, B.G.A.; Avidar, "Plan D," and Ratner, *My Life and I*, pp. 361-371.

46 Ibid.; Yadin's testimony, B.G.A., and Gelber, *Nucleus of Jewish Regular Army*, pp. 113-128.

47 Protocol of Mapai Council meeting, February 7, 1948, L.P.A., 22/35, and protocols of the Security Committee meetings, February 3 and 10, 1948, C.Z.A., S25/9346.

48 *Ben-Gurion's War Diary*, entry for March 15, 1948.

49 Ben-Gurion to Galili, March 16, 1948, H.A., Galili files, No. 25.

50 Protocols of Mapam Political Committee meetings, January 29, 1948 and February 5, 1948, and protocol of Mapam Secretariat meeting, March 2, 1948, M.A., 66.90(1).

51 Lewite and Riftin to Ber, Man, Rabinov, and Sadeh, February 6, 1948, M.A., 32a.90(1); Ben-Aharon to various commanders who were members of Mapam, March 14, 1948, M.A., 90.31c(6j), and summaries of the Mapam Security Committee meetings, March 2, 9 and 31, 1948, M.A., 90.31c(6n).

52 Ben-Gurion to Ratner, March 22, 1948, B.G.A.; Ben-Gurion to Ratner and Galili, and Yadin to Ratner, March 26, 1948, H.A., Ratner files, No. 12; *Ben-Gurion's War Diary*, entries for March 31-April 1, 1948; Ratner to Ben-Gurion, April 10-11, 1948, B.G.A., and Ratner, *My Life and I*, pp. 360-371.

53 Protocols of the Security Committee meetings, March 30, 1948, C.Z.A., S25/9347, and April 1 and 4, 1948, C.Z.A., S25/9348.

54 Protocol of the Zionist Actions Committee session, April 6-7, 1948, C.Z.A., S5/322.

55 Protocol of Mapam Political Committee meeting, April 1, 1948, M.A., 90.66, pp. 3-8.

56 Protocol of the Jewish Agency Executive meeting, April 9, 1948, C.Z.A., and Mordekhai Bentov to Mapam Center, April 27, 1948, M.A., 90.32a(1).

57 Protocol of the Security Committee meeting, April 4, 1948, C.Z.A., S25/9348.

58 Protocols of Mapam Political Committee meetings, April 10 and 14, 1948, M.A.

59 Summaries of Mapam Security Committee meetings, April 13 and 20, 1948, M.A., 90.31c(6n).

60 Shealtiel to Ben-Gurion, Galili, Yadin, and Avidan, April 11, 1948, and Ben-Gurion to Yadin, April 12, 1948 both in H.A., Galili files, No. 25.

61 *Ben-Gurion's War Diary*, entry for April 21, 1948.

62 Protocol of The People's Executive meeting, April 26, 1948, pp. 20-23, Israel State Archives (hereafter I.S.A.).

63 *Ben-Gurion's War Diary*, entry for April 26, 1948.

64 Reptor's report to the Mapam Political Committee meeting, April 20, 1948, M.A., and Galili to Ben-Gurion, undated, B.G.A., 1542.

65 *Ben-Gurion's War Diary*, entry for April 27, 1948, and minutes of the meeting of that date between delegations of the two parties, M.A., 90.31c(6n).
66 Protocol of Mapam Political Committee meeting, May 3, 1948, M.A.
67 *Ben-Gurion's War Diary*, entry for May 2, 1948; Ben-Gurion to the Haganah Command Council and the General Staff, May 2, 1948, Galili to Ben-Gurion, May 3, 1948, and Galili to Dori and the branch directors, May, 1948 - all of them in H.A., Galili files, No. 24.
68 The branch directors to Ben-Gurion, May 6, 1948, *ibid.*; Yadin's testimony before the Five Ministers Commission, in A. Shapira, *The Army Controversy, 1948: Ben Gurion's Struggle for Control* (Hebrew), Tel Aviv, 1985, p. 104, and Yadin's interview in *Ma'ariv,* May 6, 1973.
69 Galili's summary of his dismissal, written in late July or early August 1948, Kibbutz Meuchad Archives (hereafter K.M.A.), Zisling files, 6/4; summary of Mapam Security Committee meeting, May 4, 1948, M.A.; protocol of Mapam Political Committee meeting, May 4, 1948, M.A.; protocols of The People's Executive meetings, May 3, 4 and 12, 1948, I.S.A.; *Ha'aretz, Davar,* and *Al Hamishmar,* May 6-9, 1948; protocol of the Histadrut Actions Committee meeting, May 10, 1948, Histadrut Archives, and letter to the Diaspora dispatched by the Diaspora Committee of Hakibbutz Hameuchad, May 10, 1948, B.G.A., 76.
70 Ben-Gurion to Galili, May 7, 1948, M.A., 90.31c(6d), and Ben-Gurion and Galili to the General Staff, May 10, 1948, H.A., Galili files, No. 24.
71 Protocol of The People's Executive meeting, May 12, 1948, I.S.A.
72 Ben-Gurion's draft of the I.D.F. Order, May 23, 1948, and its final version as promulgated in the *Official Gazette*, No. 3, May 31, 1948, B.G.A., 1497.
73 See Galili's summary of his dismissal (note 69 above).
74 *Ben-Gurion's War Diary*, entries May 28-29, 1948.
75 Ibid., entries for May 17-20, 1948.
76 On the formation of the 7th Brigade and the first battle of Latrun, see Gelber, *Nucleus of Jewish Regular Army*, pp. 242-254.
77 Ben-Aharon and Lewite to Ben-Gurion, May 24, 1948, and the latter's reply, May 25, 1948 -- both in M.A., 90.31c(6d); summary of Mapam Security Committee meeting, May 25, 1948, M.A., and *Ben-Gurion's War Diary*, entry for May 26, 1948.
78 Protocol of Mapai Secretariat meeting, May 29, 1948, L.P.A., 24/48.
79 Protocols of Mapai Bureau meeting, June 8, 1948, L.P.A., 25/48, and Mapai Secretariat meeting, June 15, 1948, L.P.A., 24/48.
80 Ben-Gurion to Avidar and to the Palmach Staff, June 8, 1948, M.A., 90.31c(6f).
81 Galili to Ben-Gurion, June 8, 1948, and Allon to Ben-Gurion, June 16, 1948 (copies at the author's disposal); Shalom Hevlin's circular letter to the Palmach units, May 24, 1948, I.D.F. Archives.
82 Ben-Gurion to Hevlin, May 26, 1948, M.A., 90.31c(6f).
83 "Is the Palmach Dispensable?" (Hebrew), *Basha'ar*, June 17, 1948; Mapam circular letter to its activists, June 30, 1948, K.M.A., 13/4.
84 Protocol of Mapai Council session, June 19, 1948, L.P.A., 22/36, pp. 51-63.
85 Galili's speech at Mapam Council session, June 25, 1948, H.A., Galili files, No. 8, p. 10.
86 Summary of Mapam Security Committee meeting, June 9, 1948, and note sent from the Committee to Y. Sadeh, June 11, 1948, M.A., 90.31c(6j).
87 *Ben-Gurion's War Diary*, entry for June 18, 1948, and Galili's minutes of the General Staff and the brigade commander's meeting the same day, H.A., Galili files, No. 25.
88 *Ben-Gurion's War Diary*, entry for June 13, 1948.
89 Protocol of Mapam Political Committee meeting, June 15, 1948, M.A.
90 Protocol of Mapam Political Committee, July 1, 1948, M.A.
91 *Ben-Gurion's War Diary*, entries for June 24-28, 1948.
92 Protocol of Mapam Political Committee meeting, July 1, 1948, M.A.; see also *Ben-Gurion's War Diary*, entry for September 7, 1948.
93 Ben-Gurion to Ayalon, June 30, 1948, B.G.A.
94 Laskov's testimony, B.G.A.; see also S. Nakdimon, *Altalena* (Hebrew), Tel Aviv, 1978, p. 432.
95 Protocols of Mapam Political Committee meetings, June 15, 1948 and July 1 and 3, 1948, M.A.
96 *Ben-Gurion's War Diary*, entry for July 1, 1948, and Nakdimon, *Altalena*, p. 421.
97 Protocol of Mapam Political Committee meeting, July 3, 1948, M.A.
98 For the full protocols of the Five Ministers Commission, see Shapira, *Disbandment of the Palmach*.

FACTS AND PACTS: BEN-GURION AND ISRAEL'S INTERNATIONAL ORIENTATION, 1948-1956

URI BIALER

> *We have both had our fill of Ben-Gurion, haven't we? Still, our world would be far more boring without a man whose enigma we are always pondering, racking our brains to understand his thinking.*
>
> [*Moshe Sharett to Zalman Aranne, 1955*[1]]

Ben-Gurion's position on the question of Israel's international orientation and its relations with the major powers in the first years after independence can only be understood in terms of several of his basic political opinions consistently held over a long period. Since the beginning of his public career in Palestine, he preferred action over the demands of diplomacy. In 1933 he wrote:

> There is ... no greater delusion than to see the Jewish people as a world political factor who can determine the path taken by great nations like England. We never were such a factor and it seems we never will be. There is, however, a group of subjects in which our strength is greater even than that of some large countries. If the subject is not a question of survival for England and is not a question of survival for another nation, but the destiny of our existence is totally dependent on this matter, then our own power in this matter is greater than that of others, and it is our will and our capability in this matter which is decisive.... Palestine ... is not a question of survival for the English people and not for the Arab people, while it represents a question of existence, a question of life and death for the whole Jewish nation ... not only from a simplified historical point of view but also from immediate, physical aspects the power of the Hebrew nation, its will and capability, are decisive. This is the foundation for Zionist policy....[2]

Ben-Gurion still referred to this passage two decades later, claiming that he would not change a word. In a letter to a friend listing the means by which Israel could extricate itself from its international difficulties, he prescribed "inner strength, inner strength, inner strength."[3] Among Israel's political leadership, he was the most prominent champion of a policy of action, disdaining external constraints. In an address to the first conference of Israel's diplomatic representatives, held in Tel Aviv in July 1950, Ben-Gurion argued:

> Foreign policy and defense policy ... both served the same purpose ... If [verbal] explanations do not persuade, use is made of force.... Force is not only an army but also the creation of the fact. The dispute between the two methods preceded the state.... There are things which cannot be explained to the opposite side.... When the state was established it faced three problems: borders, refugees, and Jerusalem. None of them was solved or will be resolved by the force of explanation—but on the

strength of facts. In the summer of 1948 we foiled the Bernadotte plan by means of the southern campaign. We captured Beersheba in defiance of the UN and the Security Council. The same applies to Jaffa, Lydda, [Lod] and Ramle. The same applies to Western Galilee. The refugee problem will also be resolved by the force of facts — our refusal to allow them to return. Here most of all it is hard to explain the justice of our stand.... The creation of a fact in the solution of the three problems takes precedence over explanations, and there must be no holding back from an act [just] because it involves an unfriendly reaction and arouses anger against us. No matter, there is of course a limit to this indifference, we are dependent on the whole world like every country and more so than every other country. However, a change in relative strength in practice comes before friendly relations. Our foreign policy is nothing but an auxiliary tool of secondary importance, not as in an established, stable country.[4]

Ben-Gurion's perception of Israel's special character as a Jewish state, committed to defend its spiritual independence, was an additional factor influencing his position on the problem of Israel's international orientation. As he explained to his colleagues at the Mapai (Labor Party) Central Committee at the end of July 1948:

We must remember ... our special position in the world where over a period of two thousand years we appear as rebels: we all revolt against the world, the whole world accepts Christianity and we refuse, a part of the world accepts Islam and we refuse.[5]

The refusal to accept principles and deeds, automatically and *a priori*, was, according to Ben-Gurion, above all of important normative political significance. Independence is not only a political matter. Independence is an intellectual and moral matter. We are free men and we think for ourselves, judge for ourselves, and regard matters as we see them and not as we are commanded to see them.[6]

The third principle underlying Ben-Gurion's approach to the problem of Israel's political orientation was a fundamental lack of trust in the outside world, its goodwill and morality. At the end of 1947, in private writings, he quoted the saying "a wise Jew says two Gentiles are worse than one, and it is better without Gentiles altogether."[7] In a more analytical and gloomier tone eight years later, before the General Staff of the Israel Defense Forces, he detailed his view of the Gentile world and its relationship to the Jewish people:

There is one world bloc which wants to destroy us — and that is the Arab bloc. There is a second bloc which is not prepared to destroy us but is willing to help the Arab nations in their war against us — and that is most of the Islamic nations. Then there is a third bloc which has nothing against us but for a variety of reasons does not want to acknowledge our existence ... like India.... There is also a fourth bloc which recognizes the state of Israel but does not acknowledge the existence of the Jewish people — and that is the Communist bloc. Then there is a fifth bloc which recognizes the state of Israel, and does not reject the existence of the Jewish people though it does not care whether it will continue to exist or not — and that is all the rest. For the Gentiles are under no obligation to take care of the Jews.[8]

This pessimism led to the fourth ideological component in Ben-Gurion's approach to Israel's international orientation, the principle of reliance on Jewish aid as a central axis of the country's foreign policy. A short time after Britain had turned the Palestine issue over to the UN, Ben-Gurion stated that "the Jewish people will be able to rely mainly on itself and only to a very small extent on a little understanding, perhaps a little sympathy from someone in the world, but able to depend only on itself, trusting definitely only itself."[9] He explained to the Israeli diplomatic community in mid-1950:

> The strength of this country lies not in the Jews who live within it, its importance is not only the influence of the one million Jews in Israel. If we do not learn how to add the influence of all the Jews throughout the world to our strength we sabotage our [own] diplomacy; world Jewry is a great political, economic, and moral factor.[10]

The corollary was Israel's responsibility for the fate of world Jewry and the need to maintain communications with, and to ensure the integrity and survival of Jewish communities throughout the world—admittedly in part for utilitarian reasons, but also as a moral precept.

Ben-Gurion was among the first to relate the sharpening conflict between the powers to the danger of global war on the one hand, and the implications in the Middle East, and the enhancement of Israel's strategic worth, on the other. Contrary to his conviction that the political value of the Arabs to the Great Powers in time of international stability was far greater than that of Israel, he understood that the situation would be completely reversed in a military conflict on a global scale.

> I cannot imagine that in a world war, America, England or anyone else would be able to send here a quarter of a million soldiers and maintain them with all the equipment they need. They would therefore be in need of our industrial, scientific, and technical capability. Thus we would not exist on charity in a case like that.[11]

Ben-Gurion's general relationships toward Britain and the USSR in the 1950s must be added to these basic concepts as factors shaping his approach to the question of Israel's international policies. Each of these countries represented different sides in the local and international conflict between the powers in the Middle East, and Ben-Gurion's attitude set concrete parameters for Israel's global orientation.

In the wake of a favorable turn in late 1946 in the stand taken by the USSR toward the national aspirations of the Zionist movement, the Russian Section of the Jewish Agency (a body which until then had been largely moribund) acquired great momentum. In a survey it conducted of the verbal references to the USSR by Ben-Gurion, the Section concluded that "no exaggerated affection for the USSR could be detected...."[12] This was a resounding understatement. The basic hostility which Ben-Gurion developed in the course of his political career toward Communist ideology, and the Soviet regime and leadership, was well known within the Yishuv. Prior to 1948, his disputes with Hashomer Hatzair and the Palestine Communist Party gave him a reputation as one of the more outspoken anti-Communist members of the Zionist Executive.[13] His negation of the ideological and political totalitarianism inside the Soviet Union, as well as his recognition of the hostility of Communism to the Zionist movement, was absolute.

Nevertheless, it was hard for Ben-Gurion to ignore the support that the Soviet Union gave to the establishment of Israel before and for a long time after May 1948. This backing was exceptional, given the relations between Zionism and Communism. In June 1948, Moshe Sharett described the Soviet Union's new policy as "the most revolutionary change which took place in the political standing of

Zionism and that of the Jewish people in the world since the Balfour Declaration."[14]

Between 1948 and 1950, Ben-Gurion believed that in view of the Soviet Union's new policy a certain political *modus vivendi* could exist in the relations between the two countries, in spite of ideological differences. However, he would not abandon the struggle against Soviet Communism as an idea, as he told his colleagues in the Mapai Secretariat in July 1949: "Moral liberty which is not complete is not liberty. There are matters which cannot be taken apart; truth cannot be divided."[15] Beyond the practical problem of dealing with the USSR, Ben-Gurion faced an uncompromising ideological and political contest over foreign policy with Israel's extreme left, particularly Mapam, which Ben-Gurion made a political target of major importance ever since its establishment in 1948.[16]

Recognition of the danger from the left was due not only to its electoral strength, but also to its being a serious ideological opponent. At a conference of Mapai in September 1951, the prime minister derided the challenge presented by most of the other political parties in the country. However, he did not underestimate the challenge of Mapam, which he saw as a Communist fifth column within Israel.[17] These domestic political concerns must have made far more difficult the complexities of relating pragmatically to the Soviet Union while opposing Communism. The extensive sources available concerning his resolute stand in the confrontation with Mapam reveal an enmity to the Soviet Union which is hard to mistake. The freedom of expression which Ben-Gurion allowed himself in the contest with Mapam and its pro-Soviet orientation, was instrumental in resolving the difficulties of state he faced in publicly presenting his views. Throughout this period he remained consistent, regarding the Soviet Union as a dangerous ideological foe with which a political-strategic tie was inconceivable, but which might be utilized in particular sets of international circumstances. In either case, he believed care should be taken to avoid direct confrontation with Russia.

Ben-Gurion did not have the same adverse reaction toward Britain—the country which for decades dominated the international politics of the Middle East. His views were influenced by the severe struggle during which, in the critical period of the political fight for the establishment of the state, from the last years of World War II to the middle of 1948, he opposed the British as the leader of the Yishuv. During the War of Independence he firmly believed that Britain was the "unseen" enemy of Israel in the course of that political and military conflict.[18] Britain's recognition of Israel in 1949 and the subsequent establishment of full diplomatic relations between the two countries were not sufficient to obliterate for Ben-Gurion his bitter memories of the British Government as continuing the anti-Israel line of foreign secretary Ernest Bevin, and he considered its policies hostile to Israel.

This conception of the British persisted. Thus, for example, at the beginning of January 1950 he explained to one of the leading friends of Israel in the US that he did not know whether Britain was capable of being pro-Israel, whether "following her own calculations she would not pursue a hostile policy as she does and encourage the Arabs, and thus would not let them make peace with us."[19] The following year, before the heads of Israel's Foreign and Defense Ministries, he argued that "neither

Cripps, nor Morrison or Bevan was directing [British] foreign policy, but rather Bevin, and that policy was one of hostility."[20] According to Ben-Gurion, changes in the British leadership did not lead to changes in the anti-Israel conception, and two years later, before the Political Committee of his party he stated that "Eden is continuing the policies of Bevin."[21] His belief in the continuity of British policy vis-à-vis Israel was reflected in a letter to Sharett, his successor as prime minister, where Ben-Gurion stated that "the mentality of the [St. James] London Conferences of 1939 was still current, with no change whatsoever. This is how Malcolm [MacDonald] and [Lord] Halifax spoke. Without a doubt they are reflecting Anthony [Eden]'s position."[22] At the beginning of 1956, Ben-Gurion told an envoy of US President Dwight D. Eisenhower that in the governments of the US, France, and Scandinavia there was goodwill toward Israel, "which cannot be said for Britain."[23]

One of his principal biographers described Ben-Gurion's fear of a strategic partnership with Britain as very deep rooted.[24] The political developments of the second half of 1956 were not enough to alter this entrenched perception. When the joint Israeli-Anglo-French incursion into Egypt was being planned, Ben-Gurion demanded of the British as a fundamental precondition that "not only should they undertake, but also explicitly promise nonintervention against us."[25]

The caution which characterized Ben-Gurion's relations with Britain was also a feature of his views of the world community in general. As a pragmatic politician, he understood Israel's dependence on foreign ties, especially in critical fields such as economic aid, immigration, and arms acquisition. This dependence might have led to a readiness to rely on outside powers and concurrently to make major political concessions to the demands of the international community. Ben-Gurion, however, mapped a careful course among the powers during the first years of Israel's independence.

Israeli foreign policy in the early years of statehood has been generally categorized as one of "non-alignment." In reality, however, it was not guided by principled non-alignment but by a desire to exploit all opportunities without foreclosing any as a result of a close identification with one bloc or another. The aid extended by the Eastern bloc toward the establishment of the state in the UN, in the sphere of military aid and, most important, in the field of immigration, made an anti-Soviet policy in the first years after independence completely irrational. A clear anti-Western line would also have been senseless given the economic and political aid which this bloc extended to the state, and in view of the presence of large Jewish communities, free and influential, in the non-Communist world. The pragmatic approach of seeking aid wherever it might be found, while refraining from crossing the international Rubicon of alignment, was therefore natural.

Ben-Gurion's contribution to this policy was undeniable, finding expression in a number of its central elements. Perhaps the most important of these was his early recognition that the era of traditional Zionist policy of leaning on one or more large outside force, ended at a certain stage of history. Conceptually and practically, forms of international thought and action which had been characteristic of the Zionist enterprise needed to be radically changed. In a letter to the members of the Jewish Agency Executive in October 1946, he determinedly cited the "independence of the Zionist movement in its relations with world rulers" as a point of principle. "No longer absolute dependence on and one-sided attachment to English policy, and no subjection to the policies of some other power. In our foreign policy the chapter of Anglo-centric policy has ended and a policy of Jewish independence must begin, to the full extent and meaning of this term."[26] Ben-Gurion did not seek a substitute for Britain. Instead, he recommended that the political leadership of the Yishuv adopt innovative thinking. As early as April 1947, not long after Britain passed the problem of the Mandate in Palestine to the UN, he presented an analysis of the events to his party.[27] He argued that the debate over international orientation, as a foundation for the political existence of the state-in-the-making, above all expressed antiquated ways of thinking which accepted external control and influence. In his opinion, such thinking derived from the special circumstances in which "one country assumed sovereignty in order to enable a foreign nation, another nation, to come into a country and there to turn into a majority and its ruler." This situation, which was characteristic of the Zionist presence in Palestine, created an attitude

> which no longer draws on reality, but ... on inertia. We have become so accustomed to [this] that we do not understand why it should not continue to be done, why England should not go on doing this, or England and America, or England, America, and Russia, why they should not undertake the "pleasant" chore of being policeman in the country and suppress whoever needs to be suppressed, and the Jews would be free of the burden of rule...

Although Ben-Gurion was referring to possible solutions to the problem of Palestine within the framework of the debates at the UN, he was also apparently attempting to implant a new principle in the field of Zionist foreign policy—"orientation upon ourselves." Beyond the political upheaval in the status of the Yishuv, which in Ben-Gurion's opinion demanded changes in international thinking in the direction he indicated, there were also a number of pragmatic reasons which gave concrete content to the categorical rejection of the approaches which were then current. He defined the supreme objective in the sphere of foreign policy as taking "all steps insofar as this is possible in order to find understanding if not friendship everywhere in the world. First of all, after England and America, in Russia and in the countries under its influence." Ben-Gurion supported this statement by refuting three specific trends then current among different streams in the political elite of the Yishuv: the traditional British orientation which set its hopes in aid from England; the anti-British school which saw the antithesis to England in the US; and those who wanted to turn to Russia. Ben-Gurion believed that although England and America were not two equal powers as they had been at the beginning of the twentieth century, there exists between them a profound community of interests which they both accept. An outspokenly anti-British policy is therefore to a large degree an anti-American policy; as no Zionist policy was conceivable without the Jewish people having a part in it, this eliminates the possibility of an anti-American policy, since one-half of the Jewish people was in America. The second fundamental reason for rejecting a specific approach in foreign policy arises out the concept that Zionism did in fact have to seek understanding in Russia for this is a great and growing world power, because it controls a number of countries which from a Zionist point of view are not hostile to us, and [within the USSR] and in countries under its rule and influence there is the other part of Jewry. Ben-Gurion realized that alliances and sympathies in international affairs were fleeting phenomena, subject to change. At the same meeting he argued that it was feasible that the Cold War between the US and the Soviet Union would not last:

> It is not out of the question that in view of the internal situation in Russia, the destruction and needs of reconstruction will lead to a situation where there is a great affection between Russia and America, where all the Communists in the world sing love songs for Truman or [Senator] Vandenberg if he becomes President, and the opposition to America will at some time become a crime with the Communists, just as there was a well-known time when it was forbidden to show anything that censured Nazism. We shall earn ourselves the contempt and hatred of the Anglo-Saxon world but will also get nothing at all from the Soviet world....

This largely anti-alignment stand was expressed in the basic principles of the government plan formulated after the first elections at the beginning of 1949, which stated that Israel's foreign policy would be based on "loyalty to the principles forming the basis of the UN Charter and friendship with all peace-seeking nations and particularly with the US and the USSR."[28] In the course of extensive negotiations on the possibility of Mapam's participation in the government coalition, Ben-Gurion did not conceal from its leaders that the policies he set for Israel were utilitarian rather than reflecting any ideological neutrality. He informed them "that he would not surrender his soul, but was prepared to give his pants for the absorption of immigrants."[29] At another meeting a few months later, he clarified his categorical rejection of international neutrality, at least in the formulations of Mapam, since "this was a trick, a Communist political dodge, the term neutrality in its international interpretation is only valid in time of war."[30] Yet it was to the leaders of this particular party that Ben-Gurion disclosed:

> I am not prepared to be neutral. [I] see the Soviet Union as Enemy No. 1 of Zionism and the whole world. [I] am prepared for only one thing, that there should be no anti-neutral expressions. [I] am ready to continue with actions and to stop declarations. That is the limit.

Before foreign personalities, Ben-Gurion was at times less blunt, but equally unequivocal. For example, in a conversation with a representative of the US State Department, who had been sent to the country at the end of 1948 to discover whether Israel would be a "red" state, he argued:

> The nature of the Jews of Palestine—even before the establishment of the state—was no dependence (economic, intellectual, or political). We do not imitate anyone—but rather go our own way. We are not like Labour in England, Communism in Russia or the Social Democrats in Germany ... we will not bow down, not to America and not to Russia. We will go our own way.[31]

To Bishop Thomas McMahon, envoy of the American Catholic Church, the prime minister explained at the beginning of August 1949 that "the essence of our special national heritage could never accommodate itself to a system which denied essential human liberties.... The Jewish character must necessarily brand Communism as a mortal peril to human values."[32] Several months later he promised the US ambassador in Tel Aviv that "Rome would become Communist before Jerusalem."[33]

On a number of occasions in the course of 1949, Ben-Gurion also clearly stated why Israel could not deviate in the other direction. At the beginning of 1950 he explained to a visiting American Jewish leader, why, in spite of the anti-Communist atmosphere in Washington and notwithstanding a certain unease there with Israel's global policy (which caused a degree of embarrassment for American Jews), there remained three sets of considerations against a radical change of policy.[34] The first which worried the Israeli leader at that time, was the uncertainty concerning US military plans in the Middle East. Would America go to war over the Middle East? In any case, the US would not despatch a large military force just to protect Israel. From the Israeli perspective, a strategic alliance with the West was seen to conceal many hazards. The second argument, which continued for a long time afterwards, concerned Jewish immigration:

> I do not know if war will break out or when. Meanwhile, what will happen in the next few years is important to us. Immigration is our only hope. Rumania is closed but we cannot easily give up hundreds of thousands of Jews. There is still immigration from Poland, Czechoslovakia, and Bulgaria. If there is any chance whatever to bring Jews from the East and especially Rumania—we must not abandon them.

In conclusion, Ben-Gurion told the American Jewish leader that a serious restraint inhibiting Israel from turning "to the West" and forming a strategic tie with that bloc was the fact that in the interim, it was still Britain and not the US which played a decisive role in shaping international policy in the Middle East. Ben-Gurion's reluctance to link the fate of the state of Israel to that Britain was unambiguous.

During the first two years of statehood, no tangible challenge to Israel's basic global policy at home or abroad had been suggested. This reality began to change in early 1950, however. In Washington there was a change in attitude toward countries which did not explicitly identify with the US in its political conflict with the Soviet Union. The Israeli embassy in Washington already gave an indication of this toward the end of 1949, and the messages reaching Jerusalem became more ominous as time went by.[35] The basic danger was that in such an atmosphere, even in the absence of open official censure, Israel could not expect vital economic aid.

The same message also reached Ben-Gurion from prominent American Jews. Israel was not asked for a radical change in its global policy, because Washington showed no interest whatever in a military or diplomatic pact. Israel, however, was pressured to publicly clarify its stand—to declare that in spite of being neutral it objected to the "Communist outlook on life."[36] This message was also conveyed directly to Ben-Gurion's personal envoy, Eliezer Livneh, who went to the US toward the end of 1949. In meetings which Livneh held in Washington with a coordinating committee composed of representatives of the State Department, the Department of Defense, and members of the intelligence community, he was told that only if Israel announced that it "would defend the country against a [Soviet] attack from outside, would there be a fundamental change in the reaction to our arms requirements."[37]

Initially, these developments did not modify Ben-Gurion's basic approach. In the course of April and May 1950, Israel made two decisions related to the subject, to which Ben-Gurion was a partner: one was on the party level—to recommend that the Histadrut (General Workers' Federation) should leave the Communist International Trade (Union) Federation; and the other was political - to sign an agreement of friendship with the US which was limited to technical and commercial matters. But the agreement included nothing to indicate a deviation from Israel's policy of non-alignment.[38] However, the first signs of change in Israel's basic policy appeared two months later. In the absence of archival sources, it is not clear what impact the Korean War, which had broken out several weeks previously and brought the accompanying threat of a world war, had on Ben-Gurion. The fact that at the beginning of July the government of Israel decided to support the American anti-Soviet stand on the subject in the UN, suggests a possible connection between the two events.[39] However, at a general meeting of Israeli ambassadors abroad which was held in Tel Aviv at the beginning of that month, Ben-Gurion did not mention the Korean War or its broad implications for Israeli policy.[40]

Concurrently with the convention of envoys, a series of consultations was held in which a planning objective was set for the absorption of between 600,000 to one million new immigrants within a period of some three years, at a total cost of $1.5 billion. Two-thirds of this amount was expected to come from the US.[41] Whether it was this factor or some other, or a combination of the two, the US ambassador was called to the prime minister at the beginning of the fourth week of July and informed of Israel's intention "with American arms to build an effective Israeli army of 250,000 men, capable and anxious [to] aid the United States, United Kingdom and Turkey to resist Russian aggression."[42] When questioned about the opinion of the Israeli left on the subject, Ben-Gurion answered confidently that

> the Israeli people would support crushing any form [of] Communist collaboration in the event of world conflict ... a pre-equipped and enlarged Israeli army would guarantee Israeli unity in support of [the] West.... If Russia attacked Israel's strategic airfields, Israel's new army could and would hold until the United States' and United Kingdom's forces could arrive.

In his report, the American ambassador pointed out that "the Prime Minister could not have been more explicit in [his] willingness [to] commit Israel unreservedly to [the] West."

There is no doubt that at this meeting Ben-Gurion signaled a radical change in his thinking, which had an effect on the development of Israel's future international orientation. It is hard to overestimate the importance of this new outlook. From then on, Ben-Gurion was ready in practice to identify Israel strategically and militarily with the West, against the Soviet Union. He reached this position alone, a fact which was important enough to him to bring it to the knowledge of the US administration several weeks later. It is not clear whether at the end of July and the beginning of August he tried to persuade the government to pass a decision in principle and failed, or whether he was afraid to do so. It is, however, quite evident that the fear of a serious rift in the Histadrut, which most severely troubled several of the heads of his party in connection with pro-Western orientational decisions, did not at that time have a significant influence on Ben-Gurion. In any event, the position which he conveyed to the US at the end of July 1950, that "though in peace we try [to] maintain political independence, in [the] event of war we [will] stand [one] hundred percent with [the] West,"[43] became the theme of Israel's quiet diplomacy during the second half of 1950.

The climax of the Israeli effort to implant the message formulated by Ben-Gurion came in a visit Sharett made to Washington in December 1950. He presented the American Defense Secretary with a series of requests, while stressing that "Israel is anxious to be in a position to contribute as effectively as possible to the security of the [Middle Eastern] region."[44]

Messages sent to the US at the end of 1950, on the authority and initiative of Ben-Gurion (as the US ambassador in Tel Aviv reported to the Secretary of State) showed what was "little short of [a revolution] in Israeli thinking."[45] However, Ben-Gurion's new explicitly pro-Western approach was not unqualified. The Israeli proposals were mainly intended to obtain the greatest possible economic and military advantages in relations with the US, while stressing a readiness to be integrated into the economic framework of American strategic plans in the Middle East. At the end of 1950, Ben-Gurion sought to obtain 150,000 American rifles to replace those used by the Israel Defense Forces (IDF), as a first step toward the standardization of Israeli light weapons with those of America. He also tried to interest Washington in the peacetime stockpiling of strategic materials and food in Israel, and to gain the approval of the US administration for the development of the Israeli small arms industry. This new industry would sell its products to NATO countries.[46]

These requirements were premised on a clear anti-Soviet perspective and an equally clear pro-Western line. Nevertheless, the Israeli policy contained a number of latent reservations which reflected Ben-Gurion's thinking. The general signal to Washington was not intended to be publicized, and Israel's official stand on the conflict between the powers remained the preservation of friendship with both the Soviet Union and the US. Furthermore, Ben-Gurion refused to commit himself to the obligations of a global political link with the US in peacetime. Among the Israeli plans transmitted to Washington there was no proposal for setting up American military bases in Israel nor any joint anti-Soviet strategic planning with the IDF. The Israeli signal was not an offer of help as much as a request for aid.

Another important reason for Israeli caution in this field was pointed out to the prime minister by his confidant Teddy Kollek, at the end of December 1950: "If anything should happen [a military conflict] only the English would be in the Middle East."[47] Thus, in spite of the global weight of the US, on the regional strategic level, the Israelis would be obliged to make practical arrangements for cooperation with the British. This was very problematic for Ben-Gurion and when, at the beginning of January 1951, Britain suggested that Israel should give favorable consideration to the establishment of British bases in the Gaza Strip as well as in Israel, the prime minister spurned the proposal categorically.[48] Ben-Gurion's rejection of the most

far-reaching offer up to the Sinai Campaign of a strategic tie with Britain was based
on his fear that behind it lay "the wish to return to the country."[49] He was also
reluctant to give an Israeli undertaking that would adversely affect immigration from
Eastern Europe but whose benefits were uncertain. As Ben-Gurion told the Chief of
Staff:

> We must not jump in prematurely and give undertakings on a future that is not
> clear—and who will give us undertakings? We can commit ourselves on only one
> thing—not saying how we will behave in some misty future but what we do from day
> to day, become strong, increase our power, and take help from those who are
> prepared to offer it. And our helpers are Jews and the Jews are in the land of
> freedom, [to obtain that goal] we must win confidence—not by deceit and not by
> cunning but by what we are.[50]

The evidence presented here refutes the claims of Michael Bar-Zohar, one of Ben-
Gurion's biographers, that during the visit of General Robertson in early 1951, when
the British proposals were communicated to Ben-Gurion, the latter wanted to
arrange "different relations" between Israel and Britain and indicated his intentions
of joining the British Commonwealth of Nations.[51] During Robertson's stay, the
prime minister referred to the model of New Zealand's relations with the United
Kingdom, based on an equality of status, instead of the contractual bond which the
British proposed.[52] It is also clear that as he conceived them, Ben-Gurion preferred
strategic ties with the Americans to links with the British. To a senior American
diplomat who visited Israel at the end of March 1951, the prime minister explained
his reluctance to rely on contractual undertakings with the British and the West as a
whole, by arguing:

> A nation must be self-reliant. We cannot foresee what the shape of the world will be
> after the next war—what the relations between the great powers will be, even if the
> Western powers win the war. The US perhaps will no longer take an interest in the
> Middle East, will leave this region, but we will remain and the Arabs will remain.[53]

By the end of 1951, Ben-Gurion was confronted for the first time with the problem of
Israel's global orientation in a new context, which persisted for the next five years.
Until that time the West had not clarified for itself how security was to be maintained
in the region. Though the Tripartite Declaration of 1950 was, to a large extent, an
expression of the protection of this bloc in the regional strategic sphere, it was still
far removed from an operational apparatus and was not viewed favorably by Israel's
prime minister.[54] This situation was radically changed on completion of the Anglo-
American plans for the establishment of the Supreme Allied Command Middle East
(SACME), inviting Egypt to join as a founding partner while Israel was specifically
excluded.

An additional, related development presented the problem of Israel's global
orientation in its full severity. In September 1951 for the first time, an American plan
gave the US administration the ability to allocate sums of money for free military aid
to the countries of the Middle East. The grant was intended for the protection of the
whole region from an outside threat.[55] Although the real threat involved in the
inclusion of Egypt in the regional defense organization was imminent for only a very
short time, until that country had rejected the invitation, Israel was obliged to react.

This seemed to be the first time that the British monopoly on security in the region was about to replaced by a balanced Anglo-American arrangement. Furthermore, it appeared that Israel's relationship to the proposed organization was liable to affect American readiness to continue extending economic aid.

In consultations at the beginning of November, Ben-Gurion set a line which to a large extent was an extension and refinement of the concept he had already favored for about a year—that Israel needed to create an atmosphere of trust regarding its overall foreign policy position, while eschewing any public undertakings on questions involving the conflict between the superpowers. The proposal for setting up a regional defense pact under the patronage of the West was particularly problematic. The possible inclusion of Israel in a common military organization with Arab countries was a security risk which Ben-Gurion, as minister of defense, could not accept. Meanwhile the problems of immigration and contacts with the Jews of the Eastern bloc remained.

Ultimately, it was resolved not to press for Israel's inclusion in the proposed Western defense pact, while at the same time discretely advocating the proposal to strengthen the IDF, to develop Israel's military industries, and to offer facilities for the storage of raw materials. Clear priority was given to direct arrangements between the US and Israel. Thus, at the beginning of November, Ben-Gurion informed the American ambassador that "the main thing is not the Middle East Command itself but to keep the purpose of the Middle East Command before our eyes. That is, to look to the defense of the Middle East and keep the Russians out."[56]

The Western plan for the organization of Middle East defense by a regional pact, in preparation for a military conflict with the USSR, was in complete contradiction to Israel's orientational conception as formulated by Ben-Gurion, although its open and categorical rejection was not politically feasible. In accordance with policy concerning SACME, he determined the government's stand on the subject of the plan for American military aid in the Middle East. During the last weeks of 1951, the only hesitation Ben-Gurion had concerning the decision itself was the unavoidable need to accept American supervision as an essential condition for the receipt of free military aid. His stand, which was adopted contrary to Sharett's advice, was to approach the US for aid within the framework of the Mutual Security Act for the purpose of financing building projects related to defense, and not for the supply of free arms. The request which Israel submitted to the US at the beginning of February, in accordance with Ben-Gurion's position, was acknowledged by someone close to him as "retreat from stuttering on neutrality,"[57] but the prime minister's reluctance to engage in what involved foreign supervision also influenced the outcome.

Not surprisingly, Israel's position on the establishment of a Western defense organization in the region became a matter of great interest to the USSR. At the beginning of November 1951, the latter sent Israel a message, the first of its kind, explicitly warning Jerusalem of the implications of involvement in the program. The reply, formulated after consultations headed by Ben-Gurion, stressed that Israel "did not and would not agree to operations or the preparation of aggression against the Soviet Union."[58] There is no doubt that the Soviet approach *ex post factum* heightened Ben-Gurion's caution regarding security aid from the West.

In the course of 1951-1952, there was another significant development in Israeli decision-making on the subject of the Western alignment. Following the Israeli rejection of the British proposal to establish bases on both sides of the Israeli-Egyptian border at Gaza, Ben-Gurion wrote to the British prime minister proposing the examination of possibilities of cooperation in strategic matters.[59] Formally, this letter was only part of a longer correspondence between the two countries, which began after General Robertson's visit and which, up to that time, had produced no results. After receiving confirmation of the forthcoming arrival of a British parliamentary delegation, Ben-Gurion's suspicions found expression in his insistence on Britain's prior formal written agreement that both countries would have an equal standing in negotiations. This demand, and the British desire to form ties with Israel on a regional rather than a bilateral basis, delayed the talks until October 1952.

Ben-Gurion prepared a policy paper in anticipation of the talks, instructing the Israeli delegation to make inquiries about the defense plans of the Western powers in the Middle East, the types and quantities of weapons they would be prepared to supply to Israel, and whether Britain would be willing to aid Israel in the development of transportation and fuel supplies. At the same time, he instructed the Israeli delegation to offer only very general information on Israel's economic and military strength in times of emergency. Sharett severely criticized this approach, arguing:

> I fear this kind of negotiation, where we invite the other side to tell us [everything] and even commit themselves on all that is of importance and necessary to us, while we keep our mouths closed ... it will be fruitless, and we will only lose by it, since the other side will form the impression that we are barricaded against them with extensive reservations which keep them from reaching any sort of mutual understanding with us.

The foreign minister favored providing the British with more information, and expressing Israel's readiness to protect "the whole region even beyond the country's borders." This was to be dependent "on the readiness of the Western powers to protect us," and to offer, insofar as all Israel's requirements were met, "participation in regional defense in accordance with agreed plans on the distribution of forces and tasks." Sharett also favored conducting the negotiations on the clear understanding that "the US was a principal partner in the whole matter."

The British and Israeli delegations met secretly in Ramat Gan at the beginning of October 1952. It is not clear whether the adoption of Sharett's program would have led to a different outcome. However, the basically reserved British stand played a major role in the developments which came in the wake of the meetings. Nevertheless, it is hard to deny that Ben-Gurion was not ready to make concessions in the field of strategic cooperation with Britain, and it is not surprising that these talks had no sequel till the eve of the Sinai Campaign.

This anti-British stand on Ben-Gurion's part was accepted by most of his colleagues in the Mapai Central Committee. Sharett was prepared to be more forthcoming, but, as long as Ben-Gurion was prime minister, he could not give substantive expression to his own approach. A year later, during a discussion on the possible evacuation of British bases in Egypt, Ben-Gurion blocked a proposal to offer Britain strategic cooperation as a possible substitute for the lost Egyptian bases. He justified his position by asserting that "for me only America exists." His antipathy acquired an economic dimension of great importance in early 1952, when Her Majesty's Government turned down a request from Israel for a loan of £5 million. This Israeli failure was seen by even the Anglophiles in the Israel Foreign Ministry as proof that Britain remained fundamentally pro-Arab.

October 1952 marked the end of a period, albeit brief, when the question of strategic military cooperation between Israel and Britain was at least formally current in Israeli politics. Several years later, it was the special background of the Sinai Campaign which brought Ben-Gurion to military cooperation with a British Government, and even then this was undertaken with deep reservations on the Israeli side.

In the course of 1953, Ben-Gurion continued to try to implement his strategic policy of fostering ties with Washington. At the end of February, after Eisenhower's inauguration, the US ambassador to Israel was summoned to the prime minister's office, and the familiar scene was repeated:

> There are three possibilities. a) True peace in the region and cooperation of all countries in its defense. b) Since this does not seem realistic at the moment, the second possibility is to make separate arrangements with all the Arab states who are ready to defend the region, as well as a separate agreement with Israel. c) But the second alternative is also not feasible, that is, if no Arab state is ready to cooperate in defending the region, the US must defend the region together with those countries who are ready to participate. It is essential to make all preparations for any trouble that might ensue. We [Israel] could also be of help. Everything possible must be done by the two of us together.[60]

The following month he explained to the political conference of Mapai that his aim then, as it had been in 1950, was to strengthen Israel while avoiding contractual obligations.[61] This message was also conveyed to the US Secretary of State, who visited the country in May 1953.[62]

The anti-Jewish trials in Prague at the end of 1952, the "doctors' trials" in Moscow at the beginning of 1953, and the break in diplomatic relations between Moscow and Jerusalem in February 1953, all had a bearing on Ben-Gurion's attitude toward alignment. His comments on these developments illustrate unequivocally his bleak view of all that concerned the Soviet regime and ideology. He began to fear that a catastrophe was threatening the Jews of that country.[63] His concerns were expressed in an unprecedented political and polemical struggle with Mapam and the Israel Communist Party. For the first time in the relations between the two countries, he was prepared to go to the world with the call "let my people go." As he told members of the government at the end of January 1953, "We must in any case be on the side of the West. We have no choice just as we had no choice in the days of Hitler."

This extreme hostility did not survive long. When Russian policy toward the Jews and Zionism softened not long after the publication of the details of the doctors' trial, Ben-Gurion, contrary to the opinion of his foreign minister, considerably lowered the antagonistic profile on the subject of Soviet Jews, on which the Israeli Government had previously agreed. By mid-1953, he consented, as a condition for the renewal of relations between the two countries, to give the Soviet Union an undertaking not to join "any alliance which had aggressive aims against" it.

Ben-Gurion's involvement in the conduct of Israel's foreign policy during 1954 was limited. During his brief retirement from politics, his few comments on foreign affairs demonstrate great concern for a hardening of American policy on the subject of the settlement of the Israel-Arab conflict, in particular in the sphere of the plan for regulating the sources of the Jordan River. From Sde Boker he frequently sent messages on the need to protect Israel's sovereignty and independence of decision-making, despite American pressure. As he explained at an unofficial meeting attended by a number of government ministers at the beginning of August that year:

> My first fear is [of American] guardianship ... a thing like that begins with small matters.... [Although] one must not always learn from history, the Romans also did not come in all at once. There were concessions here and there, and they came in little by little.[64]

In an interview he gave to the daily newspaper *Hador* in mid-January 1954, he even expressed a willingness to give up the American grants, in order to maintain friendly relations with the US.[65]

In the course of the next two years, Ben-Gurion was mainly concerned with domestic and security problems, although developments in the Middle East gravely affected Israel's position. The Western attempt to establish regional defense pacts led to the Baghdad Pact in 1955, and resulted in the unprecedented American decision to supply arms to Iraq. At the same time, the Czech arms deal with Egypt became known, and presented Israel with the most serious threat to its existence since 1948. As is known from Sharett's published diaries, Ben-Gurion supported Israel's use of force to preempt the dangers on its borders during this period. However, force was not the only remedy which he pursued. He also considered a security pact with the US and, paradoxically, the possibility of going to the Soviet Union to obtain arms.

The prospects of a defense treaty with the US arose as the result of an American initiative in the middle of 1954, which was intended to compensate Israel and to allay its fears following the arms agreement with Iraq and the Anglo-Egyptian Agreement on evacuation of the British bases in the Suez Canal area.[66] Ben-Gurion was a partner to the deliberations which led Israel to consider such a treaty desirable, although secondary in its importance to the demand for the preservation of the arms balance in the Middle East. His hesitations and those of the government were connected with the form which such an agreement would assume, the cost in terms of Israeli concessions to the Arabs which it would probably require, and Israeli acquiescence to American arms supplies to the Arabs which it would imply.

Nevertheless, Ben-Gurion saw the potential of the international situation prevailing in the region in the middle of 1954, and in the possibility that the US would guarantee Israel's borders and security in the framework of an agreement that would not by its nature be anti-Soviet. At a meeting with the American ambassador several months after returning to the government, Ben-Gurion argued:

> Though I am not dealing with foreign policy, there are three things closer to my heart than anything: Israel's security, peace in the [Middle] East, and friendship between Israel and the US. The US government has the ability to achieve all three with one stroke—by a mutual defense treaty with Israel. [Even] if America could force the Arabs to make peace, I would not advise it to do so. A strong power does not need to impose its will on a country weaker than it. But the moment the US makes such a pact with us—the Arabs will know that their dream of wiping us out has evaporated....[67]

Two months later he disclosed to the IDF General Staff that the fear of Soviet censure should not undermine the pursuit of a mutual defense treaty with America.[68]

The question of the political and military price Israel would have to pay for such a treaty was an important point of contention between Ben-Gurion and Sharett. The foreign minister considered a treaty to be of prime importance, both in its own right and also as a means of dispelling Israel's feeling of insecurity. This, in turn, would reduce Ben-Gurion's pressure in support of the use of force against the Arab countries. Sharett stressed the value of a defense pact while at the same time pointing out that it would not materialize if Israel undertook the military action advocated by Ben-Gurion right after his return to the government at the beginning of 1955.[69]

Israel's official request for a treaty with America was presented after one of the most serious Israel reprisal operations in Gaza. A few weeks later, Sharett made extensive use of the pending request to discourage the adoption by the Israeli Government of Ben-Gurion's proposal to occupy the Gaza Strip.

While Ben-Gurion saw an American guarantee of the security of Israel as an important objective for the country's foreign policy, he was not willing to pay for its advancement with serious restrictions on Israel's freedom of military action. Neither did he agree with his foreign minister on another important issue related to the desired security pact with the US. Sharett hoped for a real American undertaking to despatch soldiers to defend the country if needed. Ben-Gurion, however, absolutely refused to accept the idea that American soldiers would defend Israel. He saw such a pact primarily as a political deterrent to the Arabs and a means of ensuring American arms so that Israel could defend itself. But even for these important objectives, Ben-Gurion refused to restrict Israel's military freedom of action. (His differences with Sharett became apparent during the Kinneret Operation at the beginning of 1956).

Another field of diplomatic activity was connected with Israel's extremely serious arms predicament in the nine months after the Czech arms deal became known. The Anglo-American refusal to arm Israel in response, strengthened the temptation to launch a preemptive war, and eventually caused one. It also encouraged unorthodox thoughts of a diplomatic military approach for aid to the Soviet Union. The historic fact that such a break in Israeli policy in the mid-1950s did not materialize should not disguise the fact that this subject did engage Israel's policy-makers during this period. The revolutionary proposals considered inside the Foreign Ministry and elsewhere suggested the involvement of the Soviet Union as a partner, with rights equal to those of the Western powers in the international politics of the region. The purpose of the proposals was to limit the injury to Israel expected from competition for the affection of the Arabs, in which Israel would find itself isolated. It was also a moot point whether Israel should approach the Soviet Union with a request for the purchase arms.[70]

These two lines of action were eventually rejected, in part because of the expected response of the US but mainly because of the fear of falling into a sophisticated Russian diplomatic trap. Surprisingly, Ben-Gurion stood at the head of those who demanded a request for arms from the Soviet Union in the context of the Israel-Arab conflict in the region, and on at least one occasion agreed to granting it a diplomatic status equivalent to that of the Western powers. His reasoning was based on his unwillingness to give up the slightest chance of obtaining arms, and relied on information reaching Israel in late 1955 and early 1956 that the Soviet Union would probably respond favorably to such an Israeli overture.

In April 1956, Ben-Gurion was prepared to go even further. As a result of America's final refusal to supply arms, Israel contemplated seeking closer ties with the French. One of the points of latent disagreement between France and Israel was the question of making the Soviet Union a partner to matters concerning the Middle East. Ben-Gurion was prepared to support the French desire to involve the USSR, on the condition that Russian arms be made available to Israel. Fulfillment of this condition was in his opinion likely to meet two other Israeli objectives: first to make it easier for the French themselves to open their arsenals to Israel, and second to make Israel's stand acceptable in the eyes of American Jewry. "The American Jew knew we were in danger, and America and [US Secretary of State John Foster] Dulles were refusing to give us arms, and Russia is [willing to] — so they will accept this."[71]

Ultimately, nothing came of this episode. But Ben-Gurion's willingness to adopt very unorthodox measures in the context of accepted Israeli thinking during that period is significant in the broader context of his approach to questions of diplomatic alignment. Perhaps no less so, this is also indicative of the unusual readiness of Israel's prime minister at the end of 1957 to offer the Russians the division of spheres of influence in the Middle East together with the granting of international guarantees by the two major powers to all the countries there.[72]

Finally, to what extent did Ben-Gurion see the tie with France as a basic change of orientation and a genuine long-term strategic alternative to the American connection?[73] A few sources suggest that neither was true. Ben-Gurion was too firmly convinced of the unchallenged strength of the US in the Western camp. He was very aware of the importance and value of the existence in the US of the largest Jewish community in the world, much larger than that of France. Finally, he was acutely conscious of the constant fluidity of international alliances. Regardless of the diplomatic and military benefits which Israel received from the exceptional relations with France, Ben-Gurion still considered the United States as the prime focus of power and the most important objective of Israel's diplomatic efforts.[74]

In the first eight years of Israel's statehood, four main themes underlay Ben-

Gurion's global outlook in the context of the conflict between the superpowers: the centralization of the control of foreign policy; considerable caution in accepting outside strategic and diplomatic undertakings; accompanying wariness of direct confrontations with the Soviet Union; and recognition of the special significance of winning the basic trust of America. For a long time afterwards, even following Ben-Gurion's retirement from politics, these themes remained the corner stones of Israeli diplomacy.

Notes

* This research focuses on the continuity of Israel's foreign policy in the 1950s rather than on dramatic incidents such as the Reparations Agreement with Germany, the events which led to the Sinai Campaign, and reprisal actions. I have attempted to fill an obvious gap in the historiography of the field. However, the sources for such research are problematic. Although, in principle, Israel Foreign Office documents for this period have been opened to research, their release has been only partial. There are significant gaps due to administrative difficulties in the transfer of the papers to the State Archives. More importantly, the records of the Cabinet, the Knesset Foreign Affairs and Defense Committee, the Ministry of Defense, and the military establishment have not been made available. Ben-Gurion's diaries contain important material, but on many topics they leave open questions concerning his opinions and attitudes, and foreign policy was not his prime concern during this period. Consequently, the conclusions presented here must be viewed as tentative, as is all research on this topic until additional sources are opened. The writer wishes to thank the Leonard Davis Institute for International Relations of the Hebrew University for help in the preparation of this article.

1 Moshe Sharett, *Personal Diary* (Hebrew), vol. 3, Tel Aviv 1978, p. 678.
2 Ben-Gurion to Editor of *Davar*, April 3, 1954, Ben-Gurion Archives, Sedeh Boker (hereafter B.G.A.).
3 From his letter to Ari Ankorion, October 30, 1954, B.G.A..
4 Ben-Gurion's diary, entry for July 22, 1950, B.G.A..
5 Meeting of Mapai Center, July 24, 1948, Labor Party Archives, Beth Berl (hereafter L.P.A.).
6 November 7, 1948, Eliezer Kaplan papers, Israel State Archives (hereafter I.S.A.).
7 Draft for a speech, undated, apparently from the end of 1947, Central Zionist Archives, Jerusalem (hereafter C.Z.A.), S44/57. On this theme, see also U. Bialer, *David Ben-Gurion and Moshe Sharett: Images and Decisions on the Eve of the Establishment of the State* (Hebrew) M.A. thesis, Hebrew University, Jerusalem, 1971.
8 July 5, 1955, I.S.A., Prime Minister's Office, 5565/7/g.
9 Meeting of Mapai Center, April 26, 1947, L.P.A..
10 July 17, 1950, I.S.A., Foreign Ministry, 2384/15.
11 March 28, 1953, I.S.A., 26/53.
12 Bialer, *Ben-Gurion and Sharett*, p. 50.
13 See S. Sandler, "Ben-Gurion's Attitude towards the Soviet Union," *Jewish Journal of Sociology* 21 (1979), pp. 145-160.
14 Mapai Council, June 18, 1948, L.P.A..
15 July 7, 1949, L.P.A.. This is the source for the following quotations till indicated otherwise.
16 See U. Bialer, *Our Place in the World: Mapai and Israel's Foreign Policy Orientation, 1947-1952 (Jerusalem Papers on Peace Problems* 33), Jerusalem, 1981.
17 See interview of E. Shaltiel with Y. Ben-Aharon, 1976, B.G.A..
18 M. Bar-Zohar, *Ben-Gurion* (Hebrew), Tel Aviv, 1975, vol. 2, p. 859.
19 Ben-Gurion's diary, entry for January 20, 1950, B.G.A..
20 Ibid., entry for January 27, 1951, B.G.A..
21 March 28, 1953, I.S.A., 26/53.
22 Sharett, *Personal Diary*, vol. 2, p. 600, entry for November 9, 1954.
23 See D. Ben-Gurion, *My Talks with Arab Leaders*, Jerusalem, 1972, p. 319.

24 Bar-Zohar, *Ben-Gurion*, vol. 3, p. 1216.

25 Moshe Dayan, *Milestones* (Hebrew), Tel Aviv, 1976, p. 231.

26 October 13, 1946, B.G.A..

27 April 26, 1947, L.P.A.. This is the source of the following quotations till otherwise indicated.

28 See letter from Ben-Gurion to Zalman Aranne, March 4, 1949, I.S.A., Prime Minister's Office, 5373/1184.

29 Protocol of Mapam's Political Committee, November 10, 1949, HaKibbutz HaMeuchad Archives (hereafter K.M.A.).

30 Protocol of Mapam's Political Committee, February 9, 1950, K.M.A..

31 Ben-Gurion's diary, entry for November 25, 1948, B.G.A..

32 See U. Bialer, "The Road to the Capital: The Establishment of Jerusalem as the Official Seat of the Israeli Government in 1949," *Studies in Zionism* 5, no. 2 (Autumn 1984), p. 285.

33 See report on this meeting in *Foreign Relations of the United States* (hereafter *FRUS*), vol. VI (1949), pp. 1521-1522.

34 Ben-Gurion's diary, entry for January 20, 1950, B.G.A. This is the source of the following quotations till otherwise indicated.

35 See correspondence in I.S.A., Foreign Ministry, 2308/16 and 2479/8.

36 See Ibid., 2479/9.

37 See letter from Livneh to Ben-Gurion, May 1, 1950, Ibid., 376/4.

38 On this see correspondence in Ibid., 2479/8 and 64/5.

39 On this subject see M. Brecher, *Decisions in Israel's Foreign Policy*, London, 1974, pp. 111-173; idem, *Israel, the Korean War and China*, Jerusalem, 1974.

40 See protocol of negotiations in I.S.A., Foreign Office, 2384/15.

41 See correspondence in Ibid., 2460/9.

42 See *FRUS*, vol. V (1950), pp. 960-961,986, which is the source of the following quotations till otherwise indicated.

43 Cable to Elath, October 9, 1950, B.G.A..

44 December 23, 1950, I.S.A., Foreign Office, 2456/6.

45 See *FRUS*, vol. V (1951), pp. 561-562.

46 See note 44.

47 Letter from Kollek to Ben-Gurion, December 22, 1950, I.S.A., Foreign Ministry, 342/19.

48 See correspondence in Ibid., 37/10.

49 Ben-Gurion's diary, entry for January 29, 1951, B.G.A..

50 Ibid.

51 Bar-Zohar, *Ben-Gurion*, vol. 3, p. 904.

52 See letter from M. Comay to Elath, June 24, 1951, I.S.A., Foreign Ministry, 30/16.

53 See protocol of meeting held on March 27, 1951, Ibid., 2479/9.

54 See Ben-Gurion's diary, entry for May 30, 1950, B.G.A..

55 The following analysis and quotations until indicated otherwise are based on Ben-Gurion's diary, entries for October 9, 1951, October 14, 1951, November 3, 1951, November 5, 1951, November 10, 1951, B.G.A., and also correspondence in I.S.A., Foreign Ministry, 2475/15.

56 See I.S.A., Foreign Ministry, 2475/15.

57 Livneh in Foreign Affairs and Defense Committee, as quoted by Ben-Aharon at meeting of Kibbutz Meuchad Secretariat on September 3, 1952, K.M.A..

58 See late November 1951 correspondence in I.S.A., Foreign Ministry, 2512/27, 2492/17, 2445/12.

59 The following analysis and quotations until indicated otherwise are based on correspondence in Ibid., 2582/6, 2408/9, 2457/5; Ben-Gurion's diary, entry for January 30, 1952, his letter to Chief of Staff, October 1, 1952, B.G.A., and Bar-Zohar, *Ben-Gurion*, vol. 2, pp. 909-911.

60 Meeting on February 22, 1953, I.S.A., Foreign Ministry, 3063/13.

61 See note 11.

62 See correspondence in I.S.A., Foreign Ministry, 40/19 and 3063/13.

63 The following analysis and quotations are based on the protocol of meetings of the Political Committee of Mapai, November 23, 1952 and January 16, 1953, L.P.A.; letters from Ben-Gurion to government ministers on January 14 and 20, 1953, I.S.A., Foreign Ministry, 4211/21 and 2457/14; correspondence in ibid. 2458/12, 1511/9 and 2404/12.

64 See letter from Kollek to Avner, August 12, 1954, I.S.A., Foreign Ministry, 41/7, and also Ben-Gurion's diary, entry for June 26, 1954, B.G.A. At the end of 1953 Ben-Gurion declared before an

American journalist: "I believe in the US and in her mission in spite of [a] McCarthy in the world, but if the US should demand of us anything against our conscience—we would tell you to go to the devil with all your monetary aid. We will not take orders from anyone, that would be a distortion of the whole of Jewish history. We are not a Balkan state. We are the heirs of the Jewish nation" (Ben-Gurion's diary, entry for August 18, 1953, B.G.A.).

65 See *Hador*, January 15, 1954.
66 The following analysis is based on correspondence in I.S.A., Foreign Ministry, 2384/14 and 2414/28; Dayan, *Milestones*, p. 122; Ben-Gurion's diary, entry for August 20, 1954, B.G.A..
67 Ben-Gurion's diary, entry for May 12, 1955, B.G.A., and also cable to Israel embassy in Washington, May 15, 1955, I.S.A., Foreign Ministry, 47/3.
68 See note 8.
69 The following analysis and quotations are based on Sharett, *Personal Diary*, vol. 3, pp. 894, 898-899; vol. 4, p. 1018; vol. 5, p. 1355, till indicated otherwise.
70 The following analysis is based on correspondence in I.S.A., Foreign Ministry, 2410/18, 2410/20, 2457/15, 2403/19, 2507/3; Sharett, *Personal Diary*, vol. 5, pp. 1348-1359; and meetings of the Mapai Foreign Affairs Committee, December 28, 1955, L.P.A..
71 See protocol of meeting on April 10, 1956, I.S.A., Foreign Ministry, 2539/16.
72 See Joseph Govrin, *Israel-Soviet Union Relations, 1953-1967* (Hebrew), Ph.D. thesis, Hebrew University, Jerusalem, 1983, p. 261.
73 See arguments of Bar-Zohar, *Ben-Gurion*, vol. 3, p. 1179.
74 See ibid., pp. 1316-1332. Significant treatment of the subject is presented in the biography of Reuven Shiloah, one of the architects of this "peripheral pact," Haggai Eshed, *One Man "Mossad": Reuven Shiloah—Father of Israeli Intelligence* (Hebrew), Tel Aviv, 1988.

IMAGES OF IMMIGRANTS—
STEREOTYPES AND STIGMATA

MOSHE LISSAK

With the renewal of immigration to Palestine in the last quarter of the nineteenth century, a folkloristic culture of the images and stereotypes of immigrants developed both in the eyes of the veteran community and vice versa, as in other countries with mass immigration. The positive or negative quality of the stereotype was a product of the sense of kinship or estrangement felt between the established community and the new arrivals, as well as the tensions that developed between them on an ideological, political or cultural basis. Such metaphors as "barefoot boys," "speculators," "Frankim" (used to denote Oriental Jews), and "Yekkes" (denoting German Jews) were presumably intended to provide a precis of the entire range of characteristics possessed by certain social groups as they appeared in the eyes of others. As the years passed, these images became part of a system of communication between the various groups who, in the majority of cases, did not view these nicknames as fundamentally pejorative, despite their stinging and provocative nature.

The immigrants of the 1950s did not escape these patterns of negative tagging. Together with the genuine enthusiasm over the phenomenon of mass immigration to Israel and intoxication with the frequently published statistical data, reservations were voiced, as soon as free immigration became possible, regarding the quality of the human material reaching Israel.[1] These tendencies found their expression in an open and public debate on the dangers threatening the veteran settlement tradition following the waves of immigration.

Negative tagging, although originating many years before the establishment of the state, reached marked proportions both within the staff of the absorption bureaucracy and in the established population at large. Already with the beginning of the encounter with mass aliya, talk of the "backwardness," "primitiveness," and Levantine character of the immigrants began. The power of this tagging, both in personal encounters and in its public expressions, such as in newspaper reports,[2] dismayed those responsible for absorption. They viewed it as a danger to the personal and collective morale of those engaged in this difficult task. The biographer of Giora Josephthal, head of the Jewish Agency's Absorption Department in the period under discussion, writes in this regard:

> The feeling that the immigrants are of an inferior moral and cultural level, and with impoverished intellectual baggage, could plunge the young state into the murky depths of a Levantine society, to a cultural nadir, equal to the nations of the region.

Such a feeling, if one provides it with scope, and encourages it, if one adds the oil of "objective" impressions to the conflagration ... can easily uproot the will of the most active persons. The *esprit de corps* is thereby endangered, and hence Giora was deeply alarmed.[3]

A debate which Josephthal conducted with one of the heads of his medical staff attested to the currency which these opinions had gained not only among the public, but also among the senior officials dealing with immigrant absorption. The latter not only adopted the accepted tagging of "primitiveness and backwardness" but even attempted to ascribe a hereditary genetic basis to the traits of immigrants from the Islamic countries. The doctor asked: "How can one build a people's future on such ruins of human souls?... If we fill the houses which we are building and the lands which we maintain with them, we will become an indolent people, and one vast public welfare office."[4] "Backwardness," "primitiveness" and "Oriental" culture[5] were general appellations. There were also specific tags, such as the inherent lack of productivity, presumably latent in the character of most of the Oriental Jews. Josephthal, who personally combated this negative label, ascribed this characteristic to immigrants from Europe also.[6]

Stereotypes of this sort found expression in the press:

> The transporting of tens of thousands, if not hundreds of thousands of people unsuitable to the country, has not provided an increment of strength to the state, or any benefit to the established community, and does not proffer a better hope for the future. It does not even benefit the people themselves, who in many cases are miserable here and feel much more disconsolate than they ever were amongst their neighbors.[7]

An editorial in *Ha'aretz* expressed a similar opinion:

> Is Israel ready and capable to continue to absorb immigrants who are welfare cases and are not suitable for any effort at building? In reality, Israel will never be capable of this. It just will not do to inflame the Messianic fervor; "earthly Jerusalem" can only be constructed by working hands.[8]

The stereotypes also reflected popular attitudes concerning the absence of aesthetic characteristics, diligence, and pleasantness, as well as fatalism and even a lack of combat motivation.[9] Negative social stereotypes tend toward generalization, lumping groups which are similar to each other under one broad umbrella. This occurred in the 1950s as well. The negative stereotypes extended to all the Oriental communities, until country or continent of origin became almost the sole criteria for personal status in interpersonal relationships.

Some communities acquired a plethora of negative labels while others avoided them or even received a positive tagging, albeit one of an ambivalent nature. The principal target of the negative tagging was the Moroccan community, as the veterans comprehended it in their encounter with Moroccan immigrants in the years 1948-1951. The gallery of stereotypes included such concepts as "Morocco-knife," "unstable," "temperamental," "impulsive," "untrustworthy," "Arak-guzzlers," etc. The most extreme and bitterly slanted expression of the feelings prevalent in at least part of the population was provided by the journalist Aryeh Gelblum, in a series of articles which surveyed what was happening in the immigrant camps.

This is an immigration of a race we have as yet not experienced in Israel. It appears that there may be some differences between those who emigrated from Tripolitania, Morocco, Tunis and Algeria, but I cannot say I was able to grasp the essence of these differences if there are any. They say for example that the Tripolitanians and the Tunisians "are somewhat better"; the Algerians, Moroccans and the Mughrabim are "a bit worse," but in general the problem is one and the same. (Incidentally, none of these immigrants will be happy to admit that he is an African "Je suis francais," they are all French, they are all from Paris and almost all of them were captains in the Maquis). We have before us a people who have reached the pinnacle of primitiveness. Their level of education borders on total ignorance. Even more appalling is their lack of talent to absorb anything spiritual. In general, they surpass the general level of the Arab, Negro and barbarian in their countries of origin by only the slightest degree. In any case this is a level inferior to what we have experienced among the Israeli Arabs in the past. As opposed to the Yemenites, they lack also roots in Judaism. Conversely, they are totally subject to the play of primitiveness and wild instincts.[10]

This unusually harsh depiction was widely condemned.[11] But a large degree of ambivalence and paternalistic arrogance was discernible even among those who defended the new immigrants. Thus, for example, one critic of Gelblum adduced a long list of Moroccan Jews who belonged to the cultural, economic and political elite of both Morocco and Israel, although he could not ignore the absence of this stratum among the Moroccan immigrants of the 1950s. Ultimately, even this commentator concluded that the Moroccans are

primeval material, a sort of dough that can be kneaded to the best ability and will of the baker, good-natured children who are awaiting a hand that would mold them.... We are suffering from a surfeit of intelligence, from workers of the brain, and brainwork. The psychic background of Zionism and the distinguishing trait of labor Zionism was the desire to flee the exaggerated burden of intelligent nitpicking, to more simple, more natural and better lives. We need these bountiful infusions of naturalness, simplicity, ignorance and corporealness as air to breathe. These childlike Jews with their simplicity ... are a tonic against our intellectual nitpicking, which was the source of many misfortunes....[12]

The Yemenite community was one of the most popular. It is no coincidence that David Ben-Gurion, who rarely revealed his emotions, departed from his usual custom in the context of the immigration of Jews from Yemen. This was especially true concerning the difficulties which faced the children of these immigrants. In a debate on immigration in December 1949, Ben-Gurion informed the Knesset that he had been advised that it was necessary to slow down the pace of immigration from Yemen because of lack of facilities to receive them. In response, he said:

I immediately sent a person to Aden to investigate the situation and I received a full and detailed report on what was occurring throughout the Yemen. I heard of the messianic exodus from Yemen; the departure of Jews from all corners of the Yemen, on foot, by vehicle, young and old, relinquishing their property, their health, their lives, and they were all headed for Aden, because from there it was possible to reach Israel.... I ... dispatched a telegram to our friends in America that they should for Heaven's sake send us additional planes to Aden to speed up the transfer of Jews from Yemen to Israel. We knew that there is still no place ready for them, there is no housing, no health services, but there was not the slightest doubt, not for a single minute, that we had, first of all, to do everything, the possible and the impossible, to enable them to reach us in the State of Israel, rather than allowing them to be vagabonds in the camps in Aden or on the roads in the Yemen. Even if some of them are destined to die, it is better that they should die here, in this country, among their brethren and not in that alien land. There were cases of immigrants dying as soon as they reached the airport in Lod, and children arrived bearing the marks of famine. I saw them in the military hospital of Tel Hashomer. This was one of the most shocking scenes that I have ever witnessed in my life. In the ward allotted by the army to the Yemenite children, children and babies resembled skeletons more than living persons. They had no strength to cry. Many did not even have the strength to absorb food. The light of life showed only in their eyes, and the eyes were the eyes of Jewish children, dear children. And Jewish doctors and Jewish nurses were treating them diligently and with love. I understood, at that moment, what rejoicing amidst trembling meant. I began quaking and was strongly moved by this terrible yet wondrous scene. Yes—these were truly the birth-pangs of the Messiah.[13]

However, negative images were mixed with the positive ones. Gelblum wrote:

The principal difficulty regarding this [Yemenite] immigration stems precisely from a tendency toward excessive frugality, which borders on the paralysis of all personal initiative. They are grateful and content with what people do for them, and they don't really care how long they will sit in the immigrant camps.... But on the other hand, the Yemenites are a community, suffused with a Hebrew religious and cultural tradition, and are of a gentle and nonaggressive personal nature—this is a community that loves work and contents itself with little.[14]

Despite the great affection which Ben-Gurion had for the Yemenite community, he was severely critical of them in private. In a letter to Chief of Staff Yigael Yadin, he wrote:

[The Yemenite community] is in some ways more easily absorbed, both culturally and economically, than any other. It is hardworking, it is not attracted by city life, it has—or at least, the male part has—a good grounding in Hebrew and the Jewish heritage. Yet in other ways it may be the most problematic of all. It is two thousand years behind us, perhaps even more. It lacks the most basic and primary concepts of civilization (as distinct from culture). Its attitude toward women and children is primitive. Its physical condition poor. Its bodily strength is depleted and it does not have the minimal notions of hygiene. For thousands of years it lived in one of the most benighted and impoverished lands, under a rule even more backward than an ordinary feudal and theocratic regime.[15]

Although it is difficult to judge how common such opinions were among the veteran population, it appears that they provided a widespread expression of forebodings and even dread regarding the far-reaching influence of the immigrants of the 1950s upon the sociocultural tradition which had crystallized in the Yishuv in the pre-state era.

Concern about Harming the Social and Cultural Heritage

The encounter with the immigrants from the Islamic countries in general, and with specific groups such as those from North Africa in particular, was undoubtedly traumatic for both sides. Its impact was felt already at the very early stages, even though its ramifications were long-range. The public expressions of this frustrating confrontation between veterans and newcomers were varied. On the part of the former, it was reflected principally in the press and in unpleasant confrontation with officials and employers. The immigrants responded occasionally with outbursts of anger and violence. The more sophisticated literary expressions by "graduates of the camps and shanty towns" appeared much later.

The confrontation with the immigrants of the 1950s posed a difficult dilemma to the Yishuv. On the one hand, everyone accepted the fact that the state required a great amount of manpower to quickly populate the new territories that were added in the wake of the War of Independence and to strengthen traditional areas of settlement from before 1948. Additional manpower was also required for the army and for rapid economic development.

These considerations were particularly emphasized by Ben-Gurion, and he opposed any restrictions on immigration, even when it appeared that the absorption apparatus was facing total collapse.[16] He reiterated on innumerable occasions that immigration and absorption could not be judged by economic criteria:

> As far as I know, there were no available houses and employment for the 600,000 who left Egypt. Nonetheless, Moses did not hesitate for an instant and took them out of there.... One cannot adjust immigration to our economic ability. On the contrary, we have to step up our economic efforts, in order to meet the needs of the departure from the Diaspora. And even should we prove unable, and even if we in our economic efforts should fall behind the waves of immigration, which are cresting and bursting upon us, immigration takes precedence, even if it involves suffering.[17]

Nevertheless, reservations regarding the quality of the manpower multiplied. Although they were not publicized by those engaged in the actual absorption process, direct and indirect echoes of these sentiments were discernible among public figures, journalists, and politicians. Ben-Gurion shared these concerns, although his position was often contradictory. In moments of pessimism, he gave way to serious doubts about the quality of the Oriental immigration. Evidence of this is plentiful. In one characteristic passage he wrote:

> The diasporas which are being liquidated and are gathering in Israel do not yet constitute a people, but a motley crew and the dust of man, without language, without education, without roots, and without links to the tradition and vision of the nation. It is no simple task to transform this human dust into a cultured independent nation possessed of vision, and the difficulties are no less than those involved in the economic absorption. A prodigious ethical and educational effort is required—an effort that must be accompanied by a deep and pure love to unite these outcasts and inculcate them with the values and principles of the nation. We must plant these distant and oppressed diasporas in our society, culture, language and creativity, not as alms givers but as those who have shared a similar fate.[18]

The characterization "dust of man" does not refer exclusively to immigrants from the Islamic countries but also to those from Eastern Europe. Conversely, Ben-Gurion was also given to optimism concerning the human potential of the immigrants and their ability to contribute to the construction of the state and society. Thus he commented:

> There is no basis to the assumptions that the Jews of North Africa, Turkey, Egypt, Persia or Aden are different in their essence and nature from the Jews of Lithuania, Galicia or America. They too have their latent and rich fonts of pioneering ability,

and wellsprings of heroism and creativity. If we were only to invest here part of the same efforts that we invested in Jewish youth in the European countries, we could also obtain fruitful results here.[19]

In another article, Ben-Gurion argued that "the history of our people in the Diaspora has proven that no tribe—if we use this term to define a specific Jewish geographic center—in its essence is inferior to another or surpasses another in its cultural ability or its basic characteristics."[20]

No one shared this optimism. One of the most prominent public figures of that time, MK Eliezer Livneh, attacked the preference given to the principle of quantity over quality in immigration: "Freedom of immigration has at times been interpreted as the right of parasitism, and the anti-Zionist concept that the quantity of immigration alone establishes its worth, without any connection to activation and its obligations, has taken root." Livneh supported a policy of strict selection:

> One cannot agree ... that precisely the retarded and dubious portion from an ethical or health standard should be brought to Israel, especially when the root and strong Jewish strata remain in the Diaspora. It is not a question of the physical means required to maintain these immigrants. Even if the Joint [Distribution Committee], Malben, or other charitable organizations would guarantee the expenses of the handicapped, or educational problem cases, we will not solve the problem in this manner at all, because the problem is not in the main a fiscal one but a social and spiritual one. Israel cannot be a refuge to the backward and unproductive circles of the Diaspora, it can only be a center for their pioneers and their best sons. Even if outside bodies will guarantee the support of all the "social cases" with a lavish hand, we cannot accept this gift on the grounds of principle. A state where the "social cases" exceed a certain limit has its social basis undermined. One cannot compare modern support for victims of the Diaspora to the old "Haluka" subsidy. The elders of the old Yishuv came here out of powerful yearnings, experienced bold adventures and faced uncertainty regarding their future. Can we say the same about the bulk of those who are supported today?[21]

Elsewhere, Livneh wrote:

> In no way could one permit a reverse selection namely that the healthy and the young, the professionals and people of means should remain in their diasporas whereas the laggards and the most backward should be brought to Israel. This would be tantamount to a total corruption of Zionism.[22]

In his controversial articles of April 1949, Gelblum argued that Israel was at risk of being transformed into a Levantine state. He concluded that "up to now we attempted to avoid the question. Indeed, the truth is a bitter problem, but a reality which one avoids exacts a still more bitter revenge."[23]

The common denominator in all these expressions was public concern in the face of the Orientalization and Levantinization of the established community, and the diluting of the pioneering fervor which had motivated the earliest settlers from Europe. Thus, journalist and author Jacob Zerubavel wrote, for example:

> The mass immigration which is streaming to us from the backward and primitive countries can inundate all our activities in its wake. We must impart the experience and will of the founders. How can we impart to them [this] experience so that they too can consider themselves founders in practice?[24]

Some polemicists defended the Oriental immigration, and accused its critics of being

primarily concerned with the eventual impact of that immigration on the
demographic balance and the ballot box. The press frequently aired exchanges of
opinion, which were often very acrimonious. However, in general, the highest
echelon of the Israeli political leadership did not take a public stand. The polemicists
were chiefly veteran Israelis from the Oriental communities themselves.

If one can judge by an opinion poll conducted at the end of 1949, the public
supported unrestricted immigration—about 75 percent of the respondents rejected
the imposition of restrictions. A tendency toward greater reservation was marked
among the more educated. However, more than half of those questioned (2,211
persons) did not have even an approximate knowledge of how many immigrants
were arriving in Israel. Furthermore, at the time of the poll, at least half of the
newcomers originated from Europe. The encounter with the immigrants in general
and with the Oriental communities in particular was still quite limited at the end of
1949. All these factors influenced the results of the poll.[25]

From Guardianship to Pluralism

The attitudes of the political leadership and of the heads of the absorption
bureaucracy found clear expression in their approach to dealing with the
immigrants. The approach was paternalistic and can best be described as
"guardianship." Shlomo Gross, journalist of the prestigious daily newspaper
Ha'aretz , formulated the contemporary thinking clearly:

> The veteran Jewish community must concern itself with the "Westernization" of the
> new immigrants.... However, we must be careful not to exaggerate the pace and force
> the issue. If the transition from the Oriental way of life to an Occidental one will be
> sudden and immediate, then all the manifestations of a precipitous assimilation
> which turned the first generation of assimilated Jews in Europe into such unstable
> persons, as occurred, are liable to be created.... The new immigration will not find its
> place in our society unless it continues to be guided for a much longer time by the
> veteran Jewish community.... Israeli society will continue to be built on inequality
> and not egalitarianism.[26]

However, the principle of "guardianship" was not clearly enunciated, and it was
inconsistently implemented. Furthermore, the very nature of Israeli society dictated
that the debate regarding the content of the directing guardianship would soon
become intertwined with and an inseparable part of the political conflicts and power
struggles between the central ideological and social currents of Israeli society.

A plan to establish work battalions, although stillborn, was a typical expression of
feelings of disappointment and even despair among the leadership circles regarding
their ability to control the flow of new manpower. The concept of work battalions
can be attributed to a number of policymakers.[27] Ben-Gurion aggressively adopted
the idea and established a special committee to implement it. The central guideline
was to "ascertain the possibilities and methods of implementation of employing
immigrants (from the ages of 18 to 45) in public and construction works which were
to be performed for public benefit and not for individual profit, in the form of work
battalions and groups, under military or quasi-military discipline."[28]

This plan was intended only for immigrants who had no means of supporting themselves. The committee began its deliberations at the end of January 1950, and encountered many difficulties in the operative formulation of the proposal. In the course of discussions, it recommended constricting the scope of the target population, and sought to content itself with immigrants of draft-age only.

The committee pondered this issue for two months, but its final recommendations were received unenthusiastically by the political leadership and by opposition figures. Golda Meir, the minister of labor, was concerned that the concentration of immigrants in work battalions would cause bitter disputes with unemployed immigrants who would not be attached to a battalion. Even if this idea was not realized, it reflected the anxieties, the disappointment and above all the skepticism regarding the quality of manpower that had arrived in the mass immigration.[29]

Commentators repeatedly demanded strict adherence to the principles of selection of immigrants. Some argued that each newcomer should undertake to work a number of years in agriculture, and advocated that those who refused would risk far-reaching sanctions of deprivation of civil rights.

> An immigrant who does not meet his obligation, or does things half-heartedly, forfeits his privilege to all benefits from the services of the state ... his right to vote lapses, for there are no privileges without obligations. A person who betrayed his principal obligation toward the nation will have his privileges vis-à-vis that same nation voided.[30]

Despite the great heterogeneity of the social and cultural system of the veteran community, it seems that at least in the initial period the immigrants felt that they were being directed by an altogether monolithic system which possessed a solid base and a very broad common denominator. The patterns of tagging in regard to the immigrants soon yielded a more or less uniformly negative image of the bulk of those who had arrived from the Islamic countries and part of the European immigrants. This unvariegated image also produced a uniform policy toward the various groups of immigrants despite the great differences between them.

The disparities in the normative cultural realm between the two parts of the population found their expression in various areas: the dialect of Hebrew which was spoken by the immigrants from the various Islamic countries (in addition to various non-Hebrew languages), the versions of prayer, religious dietary customs, and what was even more important, the very essence of religiosity. Religiosity within the Oriental communities was grasped by the Ashkenazi community as less rational, devoid of consistency, and even of a reformist nature. Another sphere of dissimilarity was the system of intra-family relations which found its expression in the division of labor between the sexes and between generations, and the diverse approaches toward family planning. Further, there were differences in recreational patterns, the use of spare time, clothing style, external appearance, and the attitude toward the physical environment.[31] In the ideological-political sphere, basic concepts such as "political Zionism," "socialism," "modernity," "collectivism," and "pioneering" were completely alien to a significant portion of the immigrants.

In the sphere of socio-political thinking, the feeling of guardianship and the monopoly of the veteran community was total. There was no place for intellectual confrontation, especially since the demands for ideological identification upon the immigrants were restricted to a bare minimum, and the instrumental organizational linkage appeared in its stead. The acquiescence of the immigrants in this sphere, even though it was of a passive nature, was hence clear and unambiguous. This did not apply to such areas as folklore, clothing style, lifestyle, etc.[32] But even in such cases, the absorbing community apparently embraced with great seriousness the idea of the intermingling of the exiles, or in its more poetic wording, the idea of the "melting pot."

In its simplest meaning, the "melting pot" implied severance from all the particularistic elements of communal tradition and the creation of a cultural system which, while possessing components of various cultures, is in the main governed by a dominant component in the form of the Western European Ashkenazi culture (whatever that meant). During the first stages of the mass immigration, the responsible agencies adopted a series of measures to implement the principle of the "melting pot." However, the absorbing community and the immigrants were too different to realize the "melting pot" in its simplistic version. In a very short while, far-reaching changes were discerned among the leadership elites, public figures, and in public opinion. These changes also found their expressions in the conclusions of academic researchers who studied the subject of absorbing immigration.

Enforced integration began with an intense, and at times crushing, involvement in the lives of the immigrants. They were directed toward settlement frameworks and modes of employment, instructed in personal hygiene and family planning, and had forms of schooling imposed upon them.[33] The formal and normative imprimatur for this involvement was expressed by Ben-Gurion. During a debate on the education of children from Yemen, he stated:

> It is not the intention of the government to freeze the Yemenite way of life.... On the contrary, we want to accustom the Yemenite immigration to the Israeli being, to Israeli freedom, to Israeli equality, to Israeli bravery, to Israeli culture and society. We want army commanders to emerge from Yemenite youth, just as they emerge from the Ashkenazi youth. We want the founders of farms, the builders of settlements, and scientists to emerge from them. We want to erase any superfluous difference between them and other Jews. We don't want the attitude toward the woman, the child, the boy and the girl to remain what it was in the Yemen. The Yemenite Jew is not a Yemenite for us—he is a Jew. He is a man like all of us. A Yemenite Jew is first and foremost a Jew, and we want to transform him as speedily as possible from a Yemenite to a Jew who has forgotten where he came from, just as I have forgotten that I am a Pole.[34]

It is no coincidence that this opinion was expressed during a debate on the subject of education for the children of immigrants. All currents in Israeli society, and especially the religious public, have always been highly sensitive to questions of school syllabus and the employment of teaching staff close to their ideological position. If in other spheres the ideological demands upon the immigrants were restricted to a bare minimum, this was not the case in the educational sphere. The contest over their education was to become the most dramatic one in the history of the absorption of immigration during the 1950s. The source of the debate concerned the essence of the socio-cultural tradition that had to be imparted to the immigrants during the process of assimilation. The struggle faithfully reflected the nature of the Israeli political culture, which was shared by nearly all the socio-ideological currents.

The religious camp, with its various wings, protested against the "child hunt" conducted by the secular camp and against "anti-religious indoctrination" and coercion.[35] It accused the ministry of education of conducting an "inquisition against the Jewish religion," of committing "cultural and religious murder,"[36] and using material benefits such as living quarters and employment as inducements for secularization.[37]

The background to these grave charges was the competition between educational systems, especially between those of the religious and the labor school networks. The confrontations generally occurred in the settlements, as formally at least the Ministry of Education and the political leadership adhered to the principle of free choice of the parents in all that concerned the education of their children.[38] The dispute which was at first local and latent, developed into a general and public conflict from the second half of 1949, as the influx from the Islamic countries grew. The religious camp viewed the immigrants from traditional societies as a significant demographic reinforcement, and they attached great importance to the struggle on this front.[39]

This view was unacceptable to the labor movement, because it had no wish to waive critical electoral support, and on ideological grounds, since it was also not prepared to give up the possibility of influencing the new immigrant children.[40]

The dispute over education in the immigrant camps ended with a compromise. Such a solution was inevitable given the coalition government in which the religious parties held the balance of power. The (temporary) solution determined that in camps populated by immigrants from Yemen, education would be religious, while in the other camps the nonreligious education that had prevailed up to then would be replaced by two frameworks, one of them religious.[41] Different arrangements emerged in the camps controlled by the Jewish Agency, and in the *ma'abarot* (shanty towns).[42]

An additional perspective of the problems encountered in inculcating the socio-cultural legacy of the established community was evident in the cultural and information activities among adult immigrants. The government and public institutions, and especially the Histadrut (General Federation of Labor), viewed their principal task as trying to interest the new immigrants in popular Israeli culture and in more sophisticated, individual artistic creativity. However, transferring sophisticated cultural contents, which were almost entirely the product of Western influence, was practically an impossible mission during the 1950s. Attempts to draw the immigrants closer to Israeli popular culture proved difficult, as the cultural life they brought with them was a very effective competitor with Israeli creativity.[43]

It is difficult to establish when the first serious doubts arose concerning the success of the absorption policy, which was intended to guarantee social integration while providing optimal safeguards for the sociocultural makeup of the established community. Field experience, public opinion, and the original social research on the absorption of immigrants,[44] all led to criticism of the existing policy. Both theoretically and in terms of implementation and realization, new principles of social and cultural absorption began to crystallize. Alongside the principle of the "melting pot" and the slogan of "intermingling of the exiles," a lessened involvement in the life of the immigrants, and social and cultural pluralism were advocated. Pluralism was defined as recognizing the cultural autonomy of immigrant groups and respect for their particularity, despite their being to a large extent alien to the dominant Israeli culture. This conception still stressed preserving the cultural values of the veteran community, but also provided legitimation for a certain degree of cultural self-determination by the immigrants. It even viewed the encouragement of this self-determination as a lever for the gradual change of the immigrants.[45]

Behind this limited legitimation of cultural self-determination and autonomy was the assumption that the majority of the immigrant cultures were not completely enclosed and autarchic. Most of them, with the exception of the Yemenite community, had been exposed, even before arrival in Israel, to external influences that facilitated their penetration by alien and heterogeneous components. Furthermore, many of the immigrants viewed this exposure as an unavoidable and desirable process which attested to their unwillingness to return to their traditional-cultural point of origin.[46] But even within this framework of limited legitimation, everyone accepted the principle that it was necessary to provide a more differentiated treatment of the various immigrant groups in all that concerned guiding the rate and direction of the change which the immigrants as individuals and as groups would undergo. In other words, even the pluralistic model expressed a large measure of paternalism and self-identification of the veterans as the reference group, even if this was now stated in a more concealed fashion and with less self-confidence.

In retrospect, the new educational-cultural policy which crystallized in the mid-1950s was based on a central assumption regarding the expected connections between groups of various origins in Israeli society. This assumption, never publicly expressed, accepted the existence of social groups in Israel as a fact and that hidden normative and cultural limitations were placed upon the contact and reciprocal relations between them, especially in the informal sphere (such as close friendships, marriage, etc.). These limitations, it should be stressed, were not the result of legislation but a product of the free determination of the potential partners to a reciprocal relationship. In comparison, contacts in the formal-instrumental sphere (such as in the job market, economic relationships, utilization of services, etc.) would be many and varied, and would increase as the economic and political system expanded and became more complex. This social strategy undoubtedly greatly diminished the tension that was created in the encounter between veterans and newcomers. It freed the former from the need to act with complete resolution and without delay in order to mold the immigrant in the image of the absorbing society, whereas it allowed the latter a certain degree of freedom of action according to the practices which were acceptable to them.

The changes that ensued in the strategy of absorption, hesitant and limited though they were, quickly toppled the policy of "the melting pot and pressure cooker." The previous policies could only have been effectively implemented by a determined elite which was politically, culturally and socially homogeneous, and which possessed an almost total monopoly on the power centers of society. Israeli society, even during the 1950s, was very far from this model. The coalition nature of government, and the power foci of the secondary centers that acted with a great deal of administrative and ideological autonomy, did not permit the presentation of a uniform cultural and social model before the immigrants.[47] Furthermore, Mapai itself, which stood at the center of Israel's political and economic power system, experienced significant internal differences of opinion.[48]

The attempt by Mapai, led by Ben-Gurion, to give a uniform hue to the demands of the integrative system on the new immigrants was doomed to failure. It was impossible to conceal from the immigrants the internal disputes, both within the labor movement and between it and other parties and movements. These disputes reflected basic processes of change in the veteran Israeli society itself. They took place in the course of absorbing the immigrants and to a large extent resulted from it. These changes include growth in the economic sphere, employment differentiation, an increase in the power of the bureaucracy, and the collapse of the voluntary movement frameworks and hence the speedy eclipse of movement and party ideology.

The immigrants, soon began to perceive the absence of a uniform profile within the Israeli society. The criticism by public figures, social scientists and professionals that handled various aspects of the absorption process, and criticisms by the immigrants themselves regarding the ethnocentric character of absorption policy, began to be assimilated by the decision makers. The self-confidence of this group regarding the socio-cultural legacy that they were supposed to impart to the immigrants began to erode as a result of processes of change. Above all, it was weakened due to the disappointments which the personnel of the absorption apparatus sustained in their encounters with the residents of the immigrant camps, the *ma'abarot*, and the moshavim. Exaggerated expectations of speedy and voluntary processes of change among the immigrants quickly disappeared. In their place, the stereotypes of stubbornness, backwardness, and the immigrants' lack of motivation to escape from their depressing and degrading circumstances began to emerge. Indeed, these absorption frameworks were far from being constructive socializing ones. In practice, they played a destructive role whose bitter fruits are still evident today.

Notes

1 Stereotypes typical of this period can be found in the belles lettres written subsequently. Cf. for example, A. Stahl, *Intercommunal Tensions among the Jewish People* (Hebrew), Tel Aviv, 1978, p. 44. Cf. also D. Almagor, "The Kazablans Who Preceded Kazablan" (Hebrew), *Shiva Yamim* (*Yediot Aharonot*), July 13, 1979, pp. 20-21.

2 Cf., for example, A. Gelblum's series of articles, "I was a New Immigrant for a Month" (Hebrew), *Ha'aretz* April 22 and 24, 1949. A. Elon establishes that the term "primitives" became one of the most common soubriquets. See A. Elon, "The Prime Minister Departs" (Hebrew), *Ha'aretz*, December 23, 1955.

3 C. Laufbahn, *A Man Goes out to His Brothers* (Hebrew), Tel Aviv, 1967, pp. 102-103.

4 Ibid., pp. 103-104. For a study that examines stereotypes and prejudices among doctors toward Moroccan Jews, see J. Shuval, "Ethnic Stereotyping in Israeli Medical Bureaucracies," *Sociology and Social Research* 46 (July 1962), pp. 455-465.

5 For explicit testimony regarding the ascription of Orientalism or Levantism to immigrants, see S. Smooha, *Israel: Pluralism and Conflict*, London, 1978, pp. 86-88. See also Y. Zerubavel, "The Central Problem" (Hebrew), *Yalkut Hamizrah Hatihon*, August-September 1951, p. 2.

6 Mifleget Po'alei Eretz Israel, *Giora Josephthal, His Life and Work* (Hebrew), Tel Aviv, 1963, pp. 157, 163, 166.

7 S. Ussishkin, "On the Problems of Aliya" (Hebrew), *Haboker*, November 16, 1951.

8 *Ha'aretz*, June 23, 1953.

9 Smooha, *Israel: Pluralism and Conflict*, pp. 190-119, 195.

10 A. Gelblum, "I Was a New Immigrant for a Month: The Immigration from Yemen and the African Problem," *Ha'aretz*, April 22, 1949. Regarding the image of the Moroccans in post-War independence literature, see Almagor, "The Kazablans Who Preceded Kazablan."

11 K. Shabbetai, "Those for Whose Children There is No Hope" (Hebrew), *Davar*, March 3, 1950. Cf. also A. Friedman, "Regarding Immigration from North Africa — A Reply to Mr. Gelblum" (Hebrew), *Ha'aretz*, May 8, 1949.

12 Shabbetai, "Those Who Have no Hope for Their Children." For additional testimony on the negative attitude to Moroccan Jews, see J. Shuval, *Social Problems in a Development Town: A Study in Preparation for the Planning of an Experimental Neighborhood in Kiryat Gat* (Hebrew), Jerusalem, 1959, pp. 5-8, 12-15, 31-71. In subsequent years, attempts were made to rehabilitate the Moroccan image.

13 *Divrei Haknesset*, November 21, 1949, p. 128.

14 Gelbum, *Ha'aretz*, April 22, 1949. Regarding the negative images of the Yemenite community that diverged from accepted opinions, see P. Cohen, *Community and Stability in an Immigrant City* (Hebrew), Jerusalem, 195, p. 10. For a mention of the favorable image of the Yemenite community, see Y. Ben-David, "Ethnic Differences or Social Change" (Hebrew), *Megammot* 3, no. 2 (January 1952), pp. 174-176; and J.J. Berreby, "De l'intégration des Juifs Yeménites en Israel", *L'Année Sociologique* 3 (1953-1954), pp. 112-114, 120-121, 128-141.

15 Cited by T. Segev, *1949: The First Israelis*, New York, 1986, pp. 186-187.

16 On the opposition to imposing limitations on immigration, see D. Hacohen, *The Policy of Mass Immigration Absorption in Israel during the Years 1948-1953* (Hebrew), unpublished doctoral dissertation, Bar-Ilan University, 1984, p. 27; Segev, *The First Israelis*, p. 139.

17 *Divrei Haknesset*, January 21, 1949, pp. 128-129.

18 D. Ben-Gurion, "Distinctiveness and Mission" (Hebrew), *Government Year Book*, 1951, p. 25.

19 Ibid., p. 26.

20 D. Ben-Gurion, "The Eternity of Israel" (Hebrew), *Government Year Book*, 1954, p. 17.

21 E. Livneh, "There is No Immigration without Pioneering" (Hebrew), *Davar*, November 9, 1951.

22 E. Livneh, "A Decisive Turn in Immigration — A Decisive Turn in the Economy" (Hebrew), *Beterem* 6 (May 15, 1952), p. 5.

23 Gelblum, *Ha'aretz*, April 22, 1949.

24 Y. Zerubavel, "The Central Problem," p. 2.

25 *Dapei Aliya* (Hebrew), January 1950, p. 27.

26 Sh. Gross, "From Poverty and Equality to Property and Social Stratification" (Hebrew), *Ha'aretz*, April 14, 1958.

27 Yehuda Almog and Yosef Almogi, *inter alia*, are mentioned. Cf. Hacohen, *Mass Immigration Absorption*, p. 108; Y. Almogi, *In the Crux of the Problem* (Hebrew), Tel Aviv, 1980, pp. 80-82; Segev, *The First Israelis*, pp. 152-153.

28 Hacohen, *Mass Immigration Absorption*, p. 108; Laufbahn, *A Man Goes out to His Brothers*, p. 106.

29 Hacohen, *Mass Immigration Absorption*, p. 110.

30 See note 21.

31 Smooha, *Israel: Pluralism and Conflict*, pp. 111-116; R. Patai, *Israel Between East and West*, Philadelphia, 1953, pp. 298-305.

32 R. Bar Yosef, "On the Intermingling of Cultures in Israel" (Hebrew), in *Studies in Social, Educational and Cultural Problems*, ed., N. Tamir, Tel Aviv, 1968, pp. 136-137.

33 On the degree of active involvement on the part of the absorbers, see for example P. Cohen, "Ethnic Group Difference in Israel," *Race* 9, no. 3 (1968) p. 306; and Patai, *Israel Between East and West*, pp. 308-313. On attempts to enforce Israeli culture on youth who studied in the framework of Youth Aliyah, cf. *The Jewish Agency: Office of Children's and Youth Aliyah, A History of the Project* (Hebrew), Jerusalem 1968, pp. 38-40, 48-50, 70-73.

34 *Divrei Haknesset*, February 14, 1951. p. 1102.

35 See, for example, the accusations of the representative of the Yemenite List in the Knesset, Zechariah Gluska, *Divrei Haknesset*, October 17, 1950, p. 25.

36 This was how MK Pincus, in a query to the minister of education, defined it. Cf. E. Don-Yehiya, *Cooperation and Conflict Between Political Camps—The Religious Camp and the Labor Camp, The Crisis of Education in Israel* (Hebrew), unpublished Ph.D. dissertation, Hebrew University, Jerusalem 1978, p. 626.

37 Remarks by Pincus, *Divrei Haknesset*, December 18, 1950, p. 482. For a wide-ranging discussion on the ethical and educational problems of educating children of immigrants from the Islamic countries from the standpoint of a religious educator, see U. Simon, "Problems of Fathers and Sons among Children of Immigrants from the Islamic Countries" (Hebrew), *Megammot* 8, no. 1 (January 1957), pp. 41-55.

38 *Ibid.*, for a description of the struggle regarding the principle of self-determination. Cf. also Yisrael Yeshayahu, *Divrei Haknesset*, pp. 1064-1065 and the speech of Izhak Ben-Zvi, *Divrei Haknesset*, pp. 1088-1089—both dated February 13, 1951.

39 Don-Yehiya cites Yitzhak Raphael, who stated at a meeting of the joint forum of the Mizrahi faction in the Knesset, and the World Center of Mizrahi: "If we are, God forbid, to lose this battle, then we are all doomed, unless a miracle takes place" (*Cooperation and Conflict* p. 635).

40 Ibid., pp. 567-571, 667.

41 Ibid., pp. 606-614, 669. Cf. also *Divrei Haknesset*, February 13, 1951, p. 1065.

42 Don-Yehiya, *Cooperation and Conflict*, pp. 676-677. On arrangements in the *ma'abarot*, see ibid., pp. 679-690. See also *Divrei Haknesset*, February 14, 1951, p. 1105.

43 Bezalel Shachar, *Culture and Society* (Hebrew), Tel Aviv, 1963, pp. 189-190. On the inconsistencies between the motivation of the adults to accept cultural activity and the ideological conceptions of the initiators of the activity, see ibid., pp. 144-146, 152-154.

44 The initial social studies that warned about this were primarily carried out by those who were engaged in absorbing immigrants in the moshavim. These opinions found expression chiefly in reports to the Settlement Department of the Jewish Agency. These views were reflected by the majority of the participants in a symposium on the absorption of immigrants that took place in the Hebrew University in October 1966. See *The Integration of Immigrants* (Hebrew), Jerusalem, 1969.

45 S. N. Eisenstadt, "Absorption of Immigration, Integration of Immigrants and Problems of the Transformation of Israeli Society" (Hebrew), ibid., pp. 7-8.

46 N. Rotenstreich, "Conclusion" (Hebrew), ibid., p. 139. On the nature of pluralism in Israeli society, see also J. Shuval, ibid., pp. 181-182.

47 The term "secondary centers" refers to centers such as the Histadrut, the kibbutz movement, and economic and political organizations of the parties of the center and the right as well as the religious sector, including its educational network and its financial and economic organs. See D. Horowitz and M. Lissak, *The Origins of the Israeli Polity* (Hebrew), Tel Aviv, 1977, pp. 91-94.

48 Ibid., pp. 278-279.

BEN-GURION AND PUBLIC EDUCATION

SHIMON RESHEF

Although Ben-Gurion considered state-run education as one of the cardinal revolutions of his time, few of the biographical works about him have touched on his approach to national education either before or after the establishment of the state. On the surface it might seem that in questions of education his position differed from his stand on other enterprises created by the labor movement, but he himself insisted that his approach to education was fully consistent with his own line and the one generally followed by the movement. He maintained that it was the movement's institutions that erroneously decided to deal with questions of education differently from the way they dealt with other vital questions, and he considered this one of his party's historical errors.

Even if he did not actively intercede in the Histadrut's educational policy, his approach, as expressed in debates on related issues, consistently reflects his views on the fundamental questions of national rebirth and the place of the labor movement in that rebirth. Ben-Gurion's approach is informed by his overall conception of the labor movement in Palestine as not only participating in but spearheading the movement of national rebirth: in full cooperation with all other shades of Zionism it formulated the objectives which had to be realized. This was the case with settlement and defense, and education was no exception. It was the manifest destiny of the labor movement to expand narrow class interests into a broad framework that would encompass the interests and objectives of all the people; it would thus become the nation as a whole. Jewish statehood had to be crystallized in the spirit of this movement's values—values it bequeathed to the entire nation. The creation of special, exclusive systems to be run, as it were, by the people and in response to their needs, conflicted with Ben-Gurion's way of thinking. In crucial spheres such as aliya, settlement, and security, the labor movement indeed acted according to Ben-Gurion's conception. In regard to national education, which he considered the foundation of the state-to-be, it acted like a party with narrow class interests. The movement thus missed a historic opportunity to influence all the children of Israel through the Hebrew school system, and even forfeited its influence on the children of workers, as prior to independence most of them attended general schools, and not those of the labor or religious movements.

The unavoidable question is why Ben-Gurion, who acted so forcefully to transform enterprises created by his movement into enterprises of the Zionist movement as a whole, did not consider it essential to fight for this in connection with education. Until the early 1950s he permitted his movement to maintain its autonomous educational framework. In fact, until 1939 it had been autonomous from the administrative and financial standpoints as well—even though he saw this as the root of all evil for both the nation and the movement. An examination of his involvement in this issue both before and after the state was established reveals the pragmatic fashion in which Ben-Gurion formulated his positions and chose the time for active intervention. It was not until three years after the creation of the state that he found it necessary to participate actively in the question of education or, more precisely, to abolish the separate educational trends and establish state-run education. Study of his dynamic intervention at this stage shows that he was not satisfied with merely convincing antagonists in his own movement that the time had come for labor's values to dominate the education of the children. Characteristically, he gave much thought to the nature and content of education and delineated the factors which became the foundations of state education, although they were construed differently by various bodies. As far back as the 1930s, Ben-Gurion had already declared that the decisive factor in the education of children would be the parents. This approach was revived after the establishment of the state, but was interpreted as meaning that parents had the right to introduce diversity in state-run education, in accordance with their own world view. It was Ben-Gurion who formulated the relationship between the authority of the state and the rights of the parents, just as it was he who often reiterated the fundamentals of statehood and the movement that should become the property of all of Israel's children.

Ben-Gurion bore matters of education in mind even while dealing with other issues that demanded his immediate decision as secretary-general of the Histadrut, chairman of the Zionist Executive or prime minister. His approach to Hebrew education was consistent from the end of the 1920s until the enactment of the State Education Law in 1953. Although he probably based his arguments more adamantly than any other leader on a visionary view of his movement's mission in the changing situation, essentially his struggle for state-run education was furthered by social, political, and above all demographic conditions.

The State Education Law was the result of a protracted national debate that began at the end of the 1920s. It centered on whether there should be uniform Hebrew education under a single organizational and financial authority for all children in the country, or if social and political groups organized under the aegis of the national institutions had the right to create educational frameworks—known as "trends"—that would offer a particular type of schooling to children of different groups. This debate resulted in the creation of an educational network consisting of three subsystems or trends, each of which was affiliated with a political framework: the general trend, at first considering itself the "national education system," refused to admit political affinity but later acknowledged its connection with the General Zionists; the religious trend, initiated and supervised by Mizrahi; and the labor trend that was under the influence of the Histadrut. Each of these trends had its own supervisory apparatus, teachers' training seminaries, and curriculum. Unlike Mizrahi, which sought no more than pedagogical autonomy, the labor trend insisted upon administrative and financial autonomy as well until the end of the 1930s.

As stated, Ben-Gurion became involved in questions of Hebrew education both under pressure of events and because of his leading position in the Zionist movement. During the 1920s and early 1930s the national agenda included the question of whether responsibility for Hebrew education in Palestine should lie with the world Zionist institutions or with the institutions of the Yishuv. This debate reflected the differing views as to the place of Palestine in the realization of Zionism and the degree of each movement's attachment to the country. The representatives of the labor movement were the only ones who fought for transferring responsibility for education from the Zionist Organization to Knesset Yisrael and the Va'ad Leumi (representing the Yishuv). But when this transfer was agreed upon, the leaders of the labor movement—and Mapai in particular—could not bring themselves to agree to abolish the financial-administrative autonomy of the workers' educational trend and fully integrate it into a national educational network. This gave rise to an absurd situation: the Va'ad Leumi, which was to be responsible for education, was led primarily by representatives of the labor movement. The bitter debate over the right of independent education for workers' children continued from 1933 until the end of 1938—a period of great social tension in the Yishuv—when the administrative autonomy of the workers' trend was finally abolished. The struggle was waged not only between the labor movement and external elements, but within the movement itself.

Ben-Gurion took part in the debate, expressing the general principles he believed should guide Palestine's labor movement and apply particularly to education. Until the enactment of the State Education Law, he remained true to the concepts he articulated at that time. When the workers' trend eventually did enter the general system, the controversy over education subsided: it was not renewed until the establishment of the state. The drastic demographic changes that then took place in the Yishuv found expression in the educational setup. In only two years—from 1949 to 1951—the number of schoolchildren was doubled, causing changes that involved much more than merely statistics. The school became the arena—the melting-pot—where young people of highly dissimilar cultural and ethnic backgrounds met. The attempt made by the educational system to blend these heterogeneous elements was essentially little more than an effort to mold the newly-arrived children in the image of the minority born and raised in the country, who lived in accordance with patterns that had evolved during pre-state days. For all intents and purposes education was still organized in accordance with the system of trends which fought for hegemony over children and their parents. This ugly conflict was an expression of the deep chasm between the idea of statehood and the existing social and political polarity—a polarity that was alien to most of the new immigrants.

It was against this background that the First Knesset was dissolved, and the question of state education became one of the central topics in the interparty struggle on the eve of elections to the Second Knesset. Ben-Gurion considered conditions ripe for "transforming class into nation" in the sphere of education, by which he meant inculcating the educational and social concepts of the workers' trend and thus making the labor movement the soul of the educational system for all children in Israel. By virtue of his leading role in the realization of national rebirth, he now actively intervened in educational problems. He dealt with questions of content, form, quality, and structure, and frequently claimed—although primarily in discussion with people of his own movement and party whom he wanted to convince—that the time had come to effect a major revolution in the life of the young state.

From Class to Nation

Early in the 1920s a number of schools and kindergartens were established for workers' children in settlements where, as Ben-Gurion put it, community and territory, both belonging to the workers, were identical—"socialist republican territory."[1] Indeed, the agenda of the founding convention of the Histadrut in 1920 already included questions of culture and education as falling within the province of the Histadrut. The two major workers' parties agreed that the Histadrut should be a unified framework representing the workers in all spheres of life, but they disagreed about whether to include culture. Ben-Gurion's party, Ahdut Ha'avoda—as opposed to Hapoel Hatzair—considered culture an inseparable part of the life of the worker. A compromise was eventually reached that declared the Histadrut "also" responsible for culture.[2] In the report which Ben-Gurion, as secretary-general of the Histadrut, submitted to the second convention, he wrote that it was not easy to overcome the psychology of "also" in connection with cultural questions. A Central Cultural Committee was duly chosen and the education of workers' children was included as one of its responsibilities. When the Histadrut Council met in May 1922, the following decision was taken:

> The Cultural Committee is to devote special attention to the education of the children of workers: it must clarify the foundations on which their schools will function and the teaching methods to be employed. The Committee is to initiate discussions with the Education Department of the Jewish Agency with a view to ensuring the maintenance of these schools.[3]

In other words, public responsibility for the budgets of the schools coupled with pedagogical and educational autonomy.

Ben-Gurion, as the outstanding spokesman for the philosophical outlook of Ahdut Ha'avoda in the early 1920s, contended that identity of class and national interest existed only in the working class of the Yishuv. The moral force behind the demand for labor hegemony derived from this identification of class and nation, which meant that the Jewish worker in Palestine was fulfilling a national mission.[4] Ben-Gurion maintained that this implied national unity and inter-class cooperation, whereas those in the left wing of his party sought to negate the connection between the Jewish proletariat and Jewish bourgeoisie, believing that the former had to remain institutionally independent of bourgeois Zionism. Ben-Gurion's approach was based on class creativity rather than class struggle, and had its source in the indivisibility of the socialist-nationalist idea. He believed this bond between the labor movement and the Jewish people rested on the past, because the roots of the movement were nurtured by the two thousand years of Jewish hope and suffering; on the present, in that the movement was a practical expression of the striving for liberation of the masses of the people; and on the future, as it was the movement that would realize the nation's messianic longings for redemption.[5]

It was Ben-Gurion's belief that the bourgeoisie were weak because they lacked statesmanlike concepts of sovereignty and historic national consciousness. As the workers' concept of class involved sovereignty, the building of the country would be in their hands.[6] He thus expressed the identification between Socialism and Zionism, seeing the class-consciousness of the Jewish workers in Palestine as inspired by visions of redemption. The worker did not negate either values or possessions, nor did he isolate himself from the people. On the contrary, he was at the forefront of the nation and aspired to be transformed from a member of the working class to one of the working nation.[7]

When the third convention of the Histadrut was convened in 1927, the Central Cultural Committee was responsible for 12 schools—one of them in Tel Aviv—and 26 kindergartens. A year before, by decision of the Zionist Congress, a committee of representatives of the Zionist movement, the Yishuv, and the Teachers' Union had been formed to discuss the question of control of education and autonomy for religious and labor schools. Most of its members were in favor of giving these schools some autonomy, but objected to the demand for administrative and financial autonomy made by the Histadrut representatives.[8] Pursuant to these discussions, the Zionist Organization adopted an education policy which established an ambiguous status for the labor trend. It was included within the scope of national education but a special provision enabled it, should it so desire, to retain its independence and sever its administration from the general educational network.[9]

The labor movement then initiated an internal debate about the pedagogical, financial, and administrative independence of the labor schools. The first stage of these discussions ended in 1933 when responsibility for Hebrew education was transferred from the Jewish Agency to the organized Yishuv. The labor schools experienced severe financial problems and the Histadrut could give only minimal support. On October 8, 1928, a discussion about these difficulties was held with representatives of the teachers.[10] Shmuel Yavne'eli, who was close to Ben-Gurion and a leader of the Cultural Committee, advocated maintaining the administrative independence of the workers' trend despite the trying situation. He believed such independence was essential for molding the positive character of workers' children. Furthermore, the teachers in these schools were paid Histadrut wages, which kept them within the workers' fold. This equality with other workers would no longer prevail if they were employed by the Jewish Agency.[11]

In other words, the assumption was that autonomy covering payment of wages as well as hiring and firing of teachers and principals would act as a guarantee of the staff's ideological loyalty to the workers' movement and its institutions.[12]

At that stage Ben-Gurion still exercised restraint, but he nevertheless pointed out that the Histadrut was the only body paying for the education of children, thereby diverting funds needed for activities among adults; the schools should be the responsibility of the Jewish Agency.[13] Here he introduced a matter of principle that would continue to be a bone of contention even after the establishment of the state. There was no disagreement about the importance of extending the influence of the labor movement's schooling to encompass all children receiving Hebrew education. But whereas Ben-Gurion and others maintained that such an influence would be most effective if the framework were opened to as large a teaching and student body as possible, their opponents fought for perpetuation of special workers' schools organized autonomously within the Histadrut. They felt this would attract both parents and children, increase the movement's influence, and guarantee the future.[14] At that time, however, and actually until the establishment of the state, Ben-Gurion's viewpoint was more realistic: the number of pupils in the labor schools was very small—only a minority even of workers' children attended them. When the Cultural Committee's financial situation deteriorated, Ben-Gurion suggested transferring the financial management of the schools to the Zionist Executive.[15] The Histadrut Executive tended more and more to agree with him, and in the early 1930s it was decided to expedite the transfer of the administration of these schools to the Education Department of the Jewish Agency.[16]

There had been a previous decision, however, to transfer all Histadrut educational institutions, while safeguarding the rights of their staffs.[17] This decision became a severe stumbling block. Because of the financial situation, the national institutions were ready to accept responsibility for primary schools only, not for kindergartens or secondary schools. The kindergartens had become the cornerstones of the labor movement's educational system, and regional secondary schools had also begun to make their appearance in the course of the 1930s. Those who objected to abolishing the administrative independence of the labor trend made such a move conditional on the transfer of all the institutions, thereby delaying the entire process for several years. As a result, the debate within the labor movement became sharper, with the leadership taking an active part. Although the argument focused on administrative and financial autonomy, seemingly presupposing agreement with respect to the need for educational autonomy, from Ben-Gurion's words it nevertheless becomes apparent that his own stand was based on a principle deriving from his overall views of the place of the labor movement in the realization of Zionism.

Meir Yaari and Yitzhak Tabenkin disagreed with Ben-Gurion. Yaari, one of the leaders of Hashomer Hatzair, considered administrative autonomy a "barrier to liquidation."[18] He maintained that there were also religious teachers in the labor schools, who posed no danger as long as they worked within a defined class framework. Autonomy, then, was the instrument of the class struggle. With respect to the influence of the labor movement on education in general, he believed, as did other members of Ben-Gurion's party, that only by way of self-participation—of actually doing—could a position of influence be achieved. Tabenkin, one of the leaders of Hakibbutz Hameuchad, considered autonomy as part of the concept of personal participation: "self-building." The entire private economy in Palestine was built by workers and the movement had no intention of relinquishing its influence therein—but that did not mean giving up its own independent enterprises.

> We do not say that we will give up *Davar* [newspaper published by the Histadrut], because we want to see changes in the press as a whole, or that we will give up Kupat Holim [the Histadrut Health Fund] because there are other hospitals, or that because there are private factories we will give up the cooperatives.... Obviously, it is not good that there are only 2,000 children in our institutions, but does that mean that we should give those children up as well?[19]

Like Yaari, he believed that financial autonomy gave a measure of control. "Education depends upon the teacher and the teacher depends upon administrative direction."[20] Others added their voices to those of Tabenkin and Yaari, among them Ben-Gurion's close associates Yavne'eli and David Remez.

Ben-Gurion's tone became more belligerent and he maintained that everything the labor movement in the country had achieved was through the instrumentality of children who were not from labor circles. He did not believe that there was a difference between a worker's child and other children—a viewpoint he would reiterate after the establishment of the state. This differentiation among children, he felt, kept the Histadrut out of the general schools that so many workers' children attended. This was detrimental to both the children and the educational system. He also regretted that the teachers in the labor trend had not become members of the Teachers' Federation that was established in 1903. A schism had thus been created between them and the country's organized working population.[21]

At the end of 1932, primarily because of its financial difficulties, the Jewish Agency was prepared to transfer responsibility for education to the Yishuv, meaning the Va'ad Leumi. The latter's influence was growing steadily and it was ready to accept such responsibility. The agreement worked out provided for a management committee to deal with education in the country. As there were relatively more general schools, three out of the five committee members were to be representatives of the center parties.[22] Thus, at the end of 1932, Hebrew education became the province of the organized institutions of the Yishuv. The workers' schools, however, despite the fact that throughout the years they had fought to bring about such a situation, retained administrative and financial independence, because the national institutions did not agree to take over the kindergartens and secondary schools as well as primary schools.[23] Important individuals in Mapai did not hide their anger. Eliezer Kaplan's reaction was typical. He stated: "We are the ones who fought to transfer the administration of education to Knesset Yisrael. Have we been fighting for the sake of others, while we ourselves have been excluded?"[24] Yosef Sprinzak added:

> This decision is against the line followed by the party [Mapai] throughout this year. It was the party that fought constantly to bring the schools under the auspices of Knesset Yisrael, and suddenly we are left with our own network.[25]

The social and political tension that was rife in the Yishuv during the 1930s brought about the establishment of labor schools in villages and cities. At the same time, non-labor circles, afraid that they might have to finance the founding and maintenance of these schools, increasingly opposed their inclusion in the general system. The demand heard during the 1920s to abolish administrative autonomy but permit educational autonomy, now gave way to the demand to establish single, unified schools for all children in villages and cities. This was the inception of the struggle for state-run schools that would incorporate the characteristics of the three trends.[26]

Ben-Gurion began to participate less frequently in the discussions on education held by the labor movement as most of his energy was now directed to national institutions and political questions. Nevertheless, his contribution to several decisive deliberations indicates the line he would follow after the establishment of the State of Israel. Historically, Ben-Gurion viewed the development of trends in Hebrew education as the result of non-national considerations. The organization of education for workers' children in the *kvutzot* (collective settlements) had evolved naturally from the identity between the workers and their land. The labor movement then would tolerate no interference and the national institutions acquiesced. In the meantime a working community had developed in heterogeneous settlements such as towns and villages, creating a new situation which made autonomous schools anachronistic. The labor movement, however, found an ally—the religious public—which also sought autonomy. Thus, in matters of education, a covenant was created between the workers and Mizrahi, which Ben-Gurion described as opportunistic and unprincipled. The vacuum existing between the two autonomous bodies was filled by the "general trend": the situation was such that many workers' children did not attend the workers' schools.

Ben-Gurion felt that the heads of the workers' trend and leaders of the labor movement were disloyal to the movement's organizational objectives in that they advocated abandoning workers' children to the enemy. He himself, being a class-conscious man, laid claim to all children and was not prepared to give any of them into the hands of politicians of the middle class or the right wing,[27] whose ideologies he wanted to eradicate. Knowing the situation and the system of trends as he did, for the first time Ben-Gurion suggested that the sovereign element in education be the parents, so that, as he expressed it, the children of urban workers would receive "our" education. He proposed general educational and pedagogical autonomy, the maintenance of which would be the responsibility of the parents.[28] He repeated this formulation so frequently that it was included in the State Education Law enacted by the Knesset in 1953.[29] Parental freedom of choice as a factor in determining the nature of the school was Ben-Gurion's answer to people like Aharon Zisling and Remez who claimed that abolishing administrative autonomy would prevent expansion of the labor trend.

In the mid-thirties the leaders of Hashomer Hatzair took up the cudgels, emphasizing the growing differences within the labor movement. The workers' school, Yaari claimed, was for those parents who wanted to "save their children's souls," particularly in a situation where the labor movement had controlling power in the Va'ad Leumi but did not exercise it. Autonomy at least guaranteed the *status quo*, which was all that could be asked as long as the movement lacked a clear perception of what it wanted in the area of education. "We are now under siege. During a siege one strengthens the walls and reinforces the guardhouses."[30]

Ya'acov Hazan agreed with him that nothing would be accomplished by abolishing autonomy: what would suffer would be the real achievements of the labor movement. "I do not believe in spiritual autonomy,"[31] he added, representing as he did a movement that tended to polarize issues and drew its strength from rigid organizational and ideological unity. The spirit of the times was such that there was ever less faith in the ability to influence the general schools. Berl Repetur said: "Just now, when hatred of the worker has infiltrated all spheres of life, we will be unable to exert any real influence on the general schools and will only be giving up our own enterprise."[32]

However, precisely because the foregoing was a true description of the situation, and circles of the political center and right-of-center were opposed to accepting the workers' schools, there was growing pressure in Mapai to put the Va'ad Leumi to the test by incorporating the labor schools into the general administration. On June 4, 1935, after protracted negotiations, a memorandum was signed by the Va'ad Leumi and the Histadrut Actions Committee regarding the inclusion of the workers' schools in the central educational network of Knesset Yisrael.[33] Paragraph three of the agreement stipulated that after the transfer the labor trend would continue to enjoy educational autonomy which would include its right to interpret current events for the pupils in the spirit of the Zionist labor movement. It also provided for celebrating labor holidays as organized by the Histadrut, with the schoolchildren participating in the preparations.

These proposals evoked a storm of protests in the Yishuv, the workers' trend was accused of politicizing education, and dissension flared anew within the labor movement itself. Some groups threatened to leave the Va'ad Leumi[34] if the agreement were signed, and the Histadrut representatives refrained from submitting it to the Va'ad Leumi plenum for approval. The entire issue of integrating the labor schools into the general network was brought to the Histadrut Council for decision. Before the Council met, the journal Hashomer Hatzair severely criticized the "opportunism" of Mapai, accusing it of being intimidated by the power and determination of a small non-labor minority. "They are leaving the walls of our own schools without a flag, without security, without ammunition—they are placing themselves in the hands of the bitterest enemy of our education."[35] Berl Katznelson, a leading Labor politician, called for imposing the will of the majority within the party to prevent Mapai members from supporting the stand taken by Hashomer Hatzair.[36]

The 34th Histadrut Council, held on March 19, 1936, finally brought the debate within the labor movement to a head. Thereafter, until the establishment of the state, Ben-Gurion would be concerned with other questions, but his words on this occasion merit being reported in full.

Ben-Gurion's central thesis was that in questions of education the Histadrut had to follow the general line taken by the labor movement in Palestine. With respect to the administration of education, this line had been "warped" and the direction taken was that of the "Left Po'alei Zion" which believed in class struggle, in creating separate working class tools, and in the power of the workers alone. But "class" education of children worked against itself, Ben-Gurion suggested, applying three criteria by which to determine the quality of class education: (a) did it educate the children of workers?; (b) was it under the control of labor?; and (c) was it conducted in a socialist-labor spirit? His conclusions were unequivocal: the workers' trend was following an anti-class line. Out of 39,000 schoolchildren, only 6,000 were in the labor schools. In Tel Aviv, out of 11,000 children, only 600 attended such schools.

> It is a sign of abject failure if in a country where [the workers] have acquired important political and organizational strength their education reaches only 4% of the children. This is certainly not commensurate with our achievements in other fields.[37]

The labor movement was influential in the Yishuv, in Zionism, and even in the Tel Aviv Municipality, but it was not felt in education because in this field it had sealed itself off hermetically. Since only a small minority was exposed to the Histadrut's education, it had become irrelevant for the working class. The crucial question Ben-Gurion posed was whether national education would be unified or not. Anyone desiring unified education wanted national control whereas whoever did not, preferred anarchy. He stated clearly that as a class the workers aspired more than any other elements in the Yishuv to national control, including control of education. Such control, which the labor movement had to strive for and realize—and which other classes were fighting against—was the guarantee of the victory of Zionism.

Against those who criticized him and his comrades for speaking in the name of all the people, he said: "Because we have grown and encompass almost all the people, we obviously speak in their name—they have entrusted us with their affairs."[38] He contrasted this inclusiveness on the part of the labor movement with the approach of General Zionism which had been emptied of its national content and had become Zionism with a specific class interest. He accused the General Zionists of evading responsibility for any Zionist enterprise that did not serve their self-interest.[39] This anti-national approach was expressed in four spheres: Jewish labor, national settlement, pioneering aliya, and overall national organization. But the workers' interests were identical with the national interest. "Unity of the nation—yes, built on equality and common interest—this is the worker's social aspiration and the objective of his historic struggle."[40]

Ben-Gurion took the left-wing parties—particularly Mapai's partners—severely to task for their approach. He declared that he did not have a fatalistic belief in eternity, in inevitable victory or inevitable defeat—the important thing was how to live under given historic circumstances. Ben-Gurion stated that the line followed by Mapai in the present circumstances had won out in all fields because his party was not afraid to embrace general principles supported by the nation, while the left was afraid of being strangled by a reactionary majority at the Zionist Congress.

> Understanding what Zionism is, what its historic content is, we have not been afraid, knowing that we were the ones who were realizing Zionism. If it succeeds, we will rise. For us the only failure will be if Zionism is vanquished by outside forces.[41]

Identifying class aspirations with the objectives of Zionism called for a non-separatist, overall national approach. Hence, as the labor movement became more inclusive, in other words, became the nation, it became the instrument for realizing

Zionism. Its actions carried the rest of the nation, including non-socialist elements, along with it. The same must apply to education as applied to other spheres of life. It must be indigenous-Hebrew labor education which in its content and vital essentials expressed the full essence of Zionism. In Palestine, Ben-Gurion declared, victory would come not by way of Hashomer Hatzair's unremitting class struggle, but by way of "from class to nation."[42]

Unlike Hashomer Hatzair, Ben-Gurion believed that the worker could represent all the people, even without a socialist revolution. To him this question was completely irrelevant. By its deeds, the labor movement was bound to Knesset Yisrael, to the Yishuv, and to the Jewish people.

> We do not have class aspirations. I object to class distinction. Stemming from the nature of the labor movement, we must constantly struggle against discrimination, against class privilege, against the very existence of classes. Our education is not based on class. We want to educate all the children of Israel, not only our own, to labor.[43]

He was convinced that were he to declare that a certain school truly educated to concepts of the oneness of the nation, equality, labor, and abolition of classes, he would find understanding among parents who were neither Marxists nor Socialists. Unless they were rabidly opposed, they would support the labor movement's educational direction. This approach called for a strategy consonant with "historic circumstances," which had nothing in common with the partisan jargon and empty speech-making that he believed isolated Hashomer Hatzair.

Ben-Gurion's strategy called for a national educational network run by society as a whole, which would therefore ensure the labor movement's influence over the children. He returned to his suggestion that a distinction be made between aspects of education that would be identical for all and those aspects that would be autonomous. By identical he meant a minimum that would be taught nationally, including hygiene, certain theoretical subjects, and the Hebrew language. Beyond that minimum, parents would control the education of their children. Such parental autonomy would guarantee that, unlike the prevailing situation, the majority of children would receive a Zionist education as conceived by the labor movement. Education guided by the parents would provide the autonomy that would ensure the realization of the evolution "from class to nation."[44] At the end of 1938 it was agreed to transfer the primary school network of the labor trend to the general administration. The next stage of development started some two years after the establishment of the state, when Ben-Gurion brought about the realization of the educational aspect of "from class to nation" through sovereign, legislative means.

Statehood and Education

In 1936, in the midst of the debate about the agreement between the Va'ad Leumi Executive and the Histadrut Actions Committee concerning the educational autonomy of the workers' trend after it gave up administrative independence, Dr. M.

Glickson, editor of the daily newspaper *Ha'aretz*, published a series of articles about education in Palestine.[45] In them he attacked the separatist approach of the workers' schools as political education par excellence. He proposed a unified Hebrew school that would combine the characteristics of the three existing trends which he described as the nation's spiritual creation, its contributions to human progress and education of the people in their homeland to labor—training both mind and hands. He assigned this task of integration to the general schools which did not profess a specific ideology. They would have to synthesize a central idea, maintain what was positive in the concepts of the right and the left, and add a national-humanist dimension of their own. He formulated his proposal optimistically:

> Recognition of the need to encourage and strengthen the integrative element in Zionism will in the future conquer hearts. Everyday there are more signs that this recognition is waning. Indeed, much time will elapse from the onset of twilight until the sun rises again in full force.[46]

This "sunrise" occurred in 1953 when the Knesset enacted State Education Law, and Ben-Gurion, more than any other political figure in the country, brought it about. The educational objectives as formulated in the Law express the synthesis of the characteristics of existing educational trends that Glickson advocated. Ben-Gurion became actively involved in matters of education in the years 1951-1954, as he considered state education one of the revolutions that had to accompany the independence of Israel. Although he believed that questions of education must first of all be debated within the movement, he engaged in discussions with various other groups—among them teachers and students as well as the religious parties that were the main partners in the governmental coalition.[47] The demographic change that affected primarily the spheres of education and politics, gave added impetus to Ben-Gurion's insistence on establishing state-run education. As already noted, from 1949 to 1951 the number of schoolchildren had doubled. Due to their disparate cultural origins and patterns of life, the schools reflected Israel's new society.

Many recently-arrived children came from countries that offered fewer years of schooling than was the norm in Israel: many had attended schools where only Jewish subjects were taught, while others had never been exposed to coeducation. The conspicuous difference at school between the immigrant children and "Israeli" children not only reflected the cultural and social gap in adult society, but helped create it. As a result of the new influx of pupils, there was a painful lack of good, qualified teachers, the demand in the early 1950s being twice as great as the supply. Unqualified teachers were used, most of whom were sent to transit camps and new immigrants' settlements, where educational progress was further hampered by difficult economic and social conditions.

Even after the Education Ministry was established, the educational trends continued to exist. The Compulsory Education Law of 1949 established the parents' right to choose the trend in which their children would study.[48] The inter-party struggle to influence the parental decision was fierce, although on the whole the parents knew very little about the ideological and political currents around them. A political crisis ensued that led to the resignation of the government and dissolution of the First Knesset.

This situation helped Ben-Gurion, as it lessened his own party's objection to abolishing the trends and establishing a state-run educational system. These were the "historical circumstances" Ben-Gurion had referred to, and they convinced him that the time had come to transform class education into national education. He could now repeat his earlier arguments, strengthened by the fact of Jewish statehood. His priorities, as well as his consistent reiteration of key concepts, distinguished Ben-Gurion from other leaders and prompted him to act decisively in order to exploit the opportunities that emerged from historic circumstances. With the establishment of the state, education took its place alongside aliya, settlement, and security as an essential building block. He concentrated on clarifying the significance of state education and the paradox inherent in maintaining the labor trend now that statehood was a fact. He tirelessly tried to convince his comrades that state education was the instrument through which to realize the concept of "from class to nation."

The Significance of State-Run Education

The first Mapai debate about education in the state took place at the beginning of 1948, before Israel formally declared its independence. A committee was appointed to discuss the question of whether the separate trends should be maintained. Opinions differed among the educators and public figures serving on the committee. Some of them advocated centralized education, the teachers being civil servants paid by the local authorities. Others were in favor of combining the general and labor schools in order to increase the labor influence on workers' children who attended general schools.[49] Opposing them was a group led by Yisrael Gurfinkel (Gury) who objected to even mentioning the possibility of eliminating trends—and this was the view that prevailed.[50] This meant postponing the decision, but rather than concluding the matter, discussion was now intensified. Definitive clarification by Mapai's institutions became essential.

Early in 1951, when Ben-Gurion was vacationing in Tiberias, the Mapai Executive placed education on its agenda. Ben-Gurion sent a letter in which he said that the perpetuation of trends—originally intended to distribute the educational influence among three parties—had become an anachronism now that there was a state, and was destined to cause endless schisms. A divided educational system would work counter to the need to forge one nation out of the heterogeneous immigrant communities and was already "a divisive element that endangers the wholeness of the state.[51]

Some time before, he had written a description in his diary of the situation in transit camps caused by registration according to trends:

> There is not enough strength for education. Schools are not being opened, the neighboring communities [kibbutzim] do not help, there is no budget for the transit camps. The existence of trends introduces terrible demoralization—there are threats and bribes, signatures on registration lists are forged.[52]

Ben-Gurion distinguished between allowing self-determination and party control of education. Even parents did not have absolute freedom of self-determination because the young generation belonged first of all to the nation and it was the nation that would establish the educational principles. After that the parents, and they alone, had the right to express a view, on condition that it did not conflict with principles of sovereignty. For this reason Ben-Gurion preferred state-run schools to unified schools. State education must not be totalitarian. In a free, democratic country, different pedagogical and intellectual objectives are taken into consideration, but the state maintains supreme responsibility and prevents the disintegration that would be caused by partisan control of schools.[53] The state must establish the administrative and educational fundamentals that are mandatory for all schools, and official bodies must determine qualifications for teachers and be responsible for their appointment. A basic compulsory and officially supervised curriculum must be followed in every school.

Ben-Gurion formulated a series of elementary principles for state-run education that were presented to his party's forums for discussion and approval: (a) abolition of party control over education and elimination of trends; (b) state control of all schools; (c) only the Education Ministry was authorized to qualify and appoint teachers; (d) the state would establish a compulsory basic curriculum including Hebrew, Bible studies, Israeli literature, physical training, sciences, history, geography, education to pioneering labor, love of the homeland, values of Judaism, loyalty to the state (appropriate adjustments to be made for Arab children); (e) teachers and parents would be free to add to the governmental program without removing any general fundamentals; (f) for children of religious parents religious schools would be available including the minimal compulsory curriculum as well as studies and activities that would invest the school with a religious character.[54]

Ben-Gurion at first refused to consider the possibility of a separate framework for religious schools, but his position became more flexible as enactment of the Education Law became imminent and the religious groups remained adamant. Thus two-and-a-half years before the Law was passed, Ben-Gurion had formulated its most important principles, but this did not satisfy him. He continued to present his views on the contents and targets of state-run education, based on his concept that the state, which had formally been established on May 14, 1948, "had to be reestablished every day, and reforming education was, as it were, reestablishing the State of Israel."[55]

As the time approached to make final decisions about the Education Law, Ben-Gurion engaged in controversial debate with the diehards of his own movement and of parties further to the left. He now also dealt with the values that state-run education must inculcate. The first value he enumerated was labor—the source of his own movement, the root of Zionism and Socialism. "A nation that does not live by labor is not free, and obviously there can be no Socialism without workers."[56] Ben-Gurion considered his movement's great victory as the transformation of the value of class to that of nation—the central value of the Zionist movement. Agricultural or other work would be compulsory in every school, "for if its citizens do not work, do not support themselves by the fruits of their labors, this state will not last long."

The second educational value Ben-Gurion listed was the "bond between homeland and nation." He feared that the very return to the homeland would cause a rupture with the two-thousand-year-old Jewish tradition, signs of which he noted in the Canaanism and nihilism apparent among some of the youth. Acclimatizing schoolchildren to "the air of this country" essentially meant recognizing that Jewish history started long before the establishment of the state. When Ben-Gurion spoke of the bond between homeland and nation, he was referring to universal and Jewish moral-humanist content. He called for redeeming the Bible which had been expelled to foreign lands, bringing it back to the homeland, and rooting the youth in it. He expounded on the need to give the child tangible contact with his country through acquaintance with its landscape and resources. "The teachers too must recognize this and not spend their entire lifetime without leaving the limits of Tel Aviv, Hadera or Jerusalem."[57]

The third value Ben-Gurion described as "education to heroism":

> We need the spirit more than ever before, for the spirit is the main thing, but spirit accompanied by [military] power and strength.... Thus every school, from kindergarten on, must be a school for heroism ... we must plant this concept in our children and bring them the message of Jewish heroism throughout the ages—particularly in those generations when it was not passive but active.[58]

And finally he preached the value of pioneering, of *halutziut*. The youth must be educated to fulfill the pioneering tasks demanded of them, otherwise they implicitly disavowed the existence of the state and of Zionist aspirations, to say nothing of class values. It was the labor movement that invested the state and its educational system with the value of pioneering. Consistent with his way of thinking, Ben-Gurion negated the theory that the primary school can create a class or supraclass society. The most one could hope for was that it would imbue every child in Israel with the fundamental values he needed. The Socialist revolution would be accomplished by the adults:[59]

> We have a conception of the nation we want to form and one of the tools for this is the primary school based on the culture of Israel, elements of science, agriculture or craftsmanship, love of homeland, pioneering training, Jewish and human fraternity.[60]

By adding scientific achievements and Jewish and human brotherhood to all the elements he had enumerated some two months before, Ben-Gurion in effect completed the synthesis of characteristics of the three trends, although he and his comrades believed that this was the legacy of the labor movement.

Ben-Gurion made it clear that the state wanted the primary school to bring the young generation closer to "the destination we desire," which was a regime without exploitation, discrimination, deprivation, or enslavement. "Our greatest desire is to create a society based on liberty and equality, without competition or exploitation, bound together by love of humanity and mutual aid."[61] About a year after the Law was enacted, Ben-Gurion spoke at a teachers' forum. Discussing his concept of the

Law and of conditions prevailing in the young state, he declared unequivocally that the State of Israel would not exist without the Jewish people, just as the Jewish people would not exist without the State of Israel. This mutual dependency dictated the foundations of education which were loyalty to the state and the people of Israel,[62] and the value of labor and pioneering embodied in the unique Jewish state. These elements encapsulated the two central tasks of Israel: ingathering of the exiles and creating an exemplary state.[63] He felt that for the teachers it was particularly necessary to define the essence of pioneering as recognition of a historic mission and

> placing oneself unconditionally and unflinchingly at the service of that mission, despite all difficulties or dangers. Pioneering is the moral ability and the spiritual imperative to live day after day obeying the command of one's conscience and fulfilling the demands of the objective. Pioneering is what one demands of oneself. It is individual realization of the tasks and values that a person believes in. Pioneering is the ability to bring something into being—it is "genesis."[64]

He expressed doubt as to whether they would indeed be capable of fulfilling the pioneering task that rested upon their shoulders. His concern was not whether the teachers were adequately informed, but whether they had the intellectual and moral qualities and the spiritual strength and loyalty necessary to inculcate the kind of education required by the new law.[65]

The Controversy: On the Verge of Decision

On May 17, 1953, Ben-Gurion addressed the Mapai Central Committee:

> ...In matters of education one does not engage in coalitional give-and-take because this is one of the most important bases for the present and the future. Nor is this an argument between our members in the party and our members in the government. It is an argument among comrades, and nothing is fixed, frozen or forced. The movement is free to decide as it wishes.[66]

Despite a changed atmosphere in his party brought about by the establishment of the state and the demographic transformation of Israeli society, Ben-Gurion was again forced to argue about state education with the party leadership. He reiterated his old arguments, adapting them to the new situation. It will be recalled that a few months before the state was founded, a Mapai committee discussed the future of education. Its stand had been that the existing structure was so deeply ingrained that, at a time when the party was discussing the burning problems involved in establishing the state, it would not be possible to do anything other than continue the *status quo*.[67] But for thirty years Ben-Gurion had already considered the system of trends in education as the root of all evil, and he now expressed his amazement that the largest party had not examined this question in the light of the tremendous change wrought by statehood and the ingathering of the exiles.[68]

Indeed, at the beginning of 1951, the Mapai Central Committee debated the question of "unified state education,"[69] and conflicting views were presented by Ben-Gurion and Gury. Ben-Gurion was out of town and enumerated a number of principles in a letter to the Central Committee. In his concern for the fundamentals of state education he differed from his colleagues, most of whom concentrated on the question of how to ensure the influence of the movement or fortify its positions. Ben-Gurion made it absolutely clear that he objected to uniformity because of the danger of educational totalitarianism. This point, and the proposal that parents should have a say in matters of education, won over people who had been hesitant about joining the advocates of state education. Gury, speaking for those who opposed Ben-Gurion's views, objected that neutral education such as would be provided by unified state schools did not fulfill its purpose. He denied that the system of trends endangered the unity of the nation, maintaining that the problem really threatening to split the nation was the disparate living standards prevailing for old-timers and new immigrants. Faithful to his position of 1948, he stated that the time had not yet come for the legislative branch to deal with education. If, nevertheless, the proposed change elicited a majority among the parties, it had to be made contingent on the schools being run in the spirit and with the content of the workers' schools.[70]

Gury's position gained some support, but more and more voices were heard calling for a reexamination of the existing structure. Zalman Shazar and Moshe Sharett merit special mention. Shazar objected to the term "unified school." Although it was not desirable that every parent choose the way he wanted to educate his child, "...this is better than intolerance, oppression, and refusal to give each of us [the opportunity] to function as we wish in our cultural life."[71] Unified education was obviously inconceivable as long as the religious parties insisted on a separate and independent framework. Shazar suggested maintaining the four types of schools that existed previously, but under the auspices of the government.[72] David Remez, who for years had opposed Ben-Gurion and advocated the independence of the workers' trend, admitted that conditions had changed and there was no point in continuing to object to abolishing the trends which might even be detrimental now that there was a state.[73] He proposed removing education from the political frameworks and ensuring a compulsory program in the name of the state, with added features in response to local desires. He believed the labor movement would have the strength to influence education by virtue of the fact that children absorb anything that rings true. They would be influenced because the movement's people were in actual fact the builders of the country, and almost all the teachers belonged to the Histadrut.[74]

Sharett said that the public was uncomfortable with the existing situation. It was inconceivable, he claimed, that the educational system remain unchanged at a time when so many revolutionary changes were taking place. He implied that the maintenance of the workers' trend was a cover-up for a deep breach with respect to fundamental educational concepts such as the nature of Zionism or of a democratic society, the meaning of loyalty to the State of Israel. He stressed the need to examine concepts used by the labor movement and adapt them to the new situation.[75] As a result of these discussions, the Central Committee decided to appoint a committee that would bring recommendations on questions of education to the Party Council where the issue would be resolved.

The lack of clarity concerning state-run education was also expressed in discussions held in Mapai's Committee on Education and Culture. Yaakov Niv

(Halprin), one of the heads of the workers' trend, articulated the problem when he demanded a decision:

> I myself am in favor of trends, but I am awaiting instructions from the party and they are not forthcoming.... Ben-Gurion favors unified education and I agree with him, but there are different interpretations of the concept "unified" and the question is which of them is correct.[76]

The Mapai Council had to come to a decision when the governmental committee was formed to work out the State Education Law. The party was given no choice other than to crystallize its stand.[77] Mapai's platform for the elections to the Second Knesset, as well as the basic principles approved by the Knesset, spoke of "state", not "unified", education, and safeguarded the parents' right to introduce diversity.[78] It was clear that the State Education Law would not recognize a trend or diversification that meant association with political parties, but the question of just how parents would influence education remained unclear.[79] In preparation for the Mapai Council's session, it became apparent that there were some who believed there was no need at all for diversifying education, because they hoped to make the values of the labor movement the main part of the curriculum.[80] There were others who sought to have the labor schools recognized as a diversification,[81] and still others insisted that diversification had pedagogical and not social significance.[82]

Ben-Gurion appeared before both the Mapai Council and the Central Committee and presented a comprehensive review of the historical record for the purpose of bringing about a final decision to abolish the trends and establish state education. He knew that he was repeating what he had said previously, but the importance of the issue gave him no choice. In cogent terms he returned to his basic approach according to which the labor movement's undertakings in the country were neither fortuitous nor transitory, but the result of an inevitable historical partnership between the Jewish worker and the nation, "and it does not depend upon any temporary configuration but is ordained by force of our historic mission ... as Jewish workers."[83] The Socialist movement in Israel was not a combination of two separate movements—Zionist and Socialist. It was one movement, had one outlook and objective, and was an indivisible entity. This movement's task was to concentrate the people in their homeland as a free nation that had to be transformed into a working nation with equal rights in the worldwide family of free nations of workers.

Just as building settlements was the fruit of the historic partnership between the pioneering workers and the nation as a whole, which meant that settlement could be attributed to the entire nation of Israel, so the ingathering and absorption of the exiles would be accomplished only through such a partnership. Leftist theories were built on the conflict between the bourgeoisie and the proletariat, but most of the workers in the country had followed a path that emanated from needs, from faith in the strength of the labor movement, from an understanding of the situation of the Jewish nation and the utopian enterprise it sought to build in Palestine. Obviously, this required the partnership of the nation and in no way conflicted with the historic mission of the labor movement. Now that a state existed, the need for partnership was much greater, as evinced by the coalition government, "...the bonds tying us inseparably to redemption—to the State—remain clear."[84] This applied to education as well, and the change that was about to take place in education "is a factor in renewing the establishment of the State of Israel."[85] Ben-Gurion concluded by saying:

> Let us move toward the state school armed with the values of labor, love of nation and homeland, and pioneering heroism. Let us advance wholeheartedly, out of loyalty to the state, out of faith in the mission of our movement, which is not only the mission of a class, but of the nation as a whole.[86]

Ben-Gurion devoted serious attention to the different directions taken by the labor movement and the left. He described the profound feelings that characterized his movement, extolling its boundless loyalty to its self-assumed historic objective, despite the most difficult obstacles. The path was not clearly marked but the objective was clear and so was the perception of what would or would not lead to that objective. Nothing that conflicted with the objective could play a role in the labor movement.[87] It had adopted three major principles: a geographic change in the situation of the Jewish nation by concentrating it in its homeland; guiding the entire nation to social and economic change through revamping its way of life in its homeland; and the ultimate goal—to transform class into nation in the image of the class, i.e., to create a workers' society.[88] Ben-Gurion added that they had not always known that the function of the laboring class was to guide the nation, for that was the meaning of Socialism. In order to guide the nation, the most inclusive approach must be used. The way to all hearts must be found. The Israel labor movement followed the direction taken by the left only when it came to education. Before the establishment of the state, this could be explained by the lack of an obligatory framework. But in 1948 conditions changed, as did the lives of the hundreds of thousands of people who had arrived. The framework, Ben-Gurion declared, was the nation as a whole and the content was Socialist. Here he added a thought that he hoped would convince all who still favored retaining labor schools. "We want it to be the state that will imbue all the children in the country with our educational content."[89]

Ben-Gurion warned that there was no guarantee that even the third generation of Degania's children would live by labor unless they were educated in that direction. He considered labor an educational value for all children in the country—"one as important as the establishment of the state."[90] In this context the class served as a historic objective and force, and the nation as a goal. "Everything that can possibly be done by the people now for the people now, in the framework of the nation now, shall be done now." As an example of such sovereign action Ben-Gurion cited the Haganah which for a long time had been made up only of workers, "but we had the historic sense to put it into the general inclusive framework of all the people, even though those who bore the burden were all from the labor movement."[91] What a catastrophe it would have been if he and his comrades had agreed to Mapam's idea of maintaining a separate class army alongside the general army. The Arabs would have been entirely superfluous—Israel would have destroyed itself. The same held true for education bestowed on the state by the labor movement. The epitome of the labor movement's aspirations would thus be realized, as Israel became a working nation, a labor society.

Using the Israel Defense Forces for comparison, Ben-Gurion explained that in those years he was obliged to look upon the army as more important and effective than the school. But woe to Israel if the state had to depend on the army—even if it had become the largest school in the country. Nothing could be equated with education as the test of the spiritual image of the nation and the measure of its cultural level.

Ben-Gurion envisioned the primary school, in conjunction with Nahal and Gadna, as exerting the most significant influence. He assumed that no more than 20% of primary school graduates would go on to secondary schools. The youth movements appealed almost exclusively to youngsters at educational institutions, "because affluent youth is more desirable for the kibbutzim than immigrant children."

He had his final say in the argument about the labor movement and state education after the Knesset passed the Law. The Mapai Council convened ostensibly to discuss implementation of the new law, but in actual fact its debate centered on whether it was permissible to raise the red flag and sing the workers' anthem in schools.[92] (This was after Ben-Gurion had announced his desire to resign from the government.) Gury suggested that the red flag and the "International" be permitted in homogeneous labor communities where all residents belonged to the Histadrut, and class and nation were two sides of the same coin. Ben-Gurion felt that those who wanted to retain the workers' flag and anthem were finding it hard to digest the change from state-in-the-making to statehood. He declared: "Things have changed, Comrade Gury. We now have national sovereignty, the schools belong to the sovereign state, and every school is open to every child in Israel...."[93] In this debate, as in others that dealt with the question of the red flag, Ben-Gurion often compared the state-run school with Nahal which he defined as an educational framework within the army. Nahal, too, functioned in homogeneous labor communities but anyone visiting its units in kibbutzim on the First of May or Histadrut Day would find only the Zionist flag. This was unquestioned because everyone, including the kibbutz members, understood that Nahal was a state institution "and an official institution created by the state flies only the national flag."[94]

It is worth noting the stand taken in the ensuing discussion by Zalman Aranne. He felt that in all government schools it was permissible, in addition to the obligatory national flag and anthem, to raise the red flag and sing the workers' anthem—if most of the parents agreed. This did not conflict with the governmental nature of the school or with Israeli sovereignty, nor could it be compared with the Haganah, Nahal or the army, "as we are speaking of something called education, and by its very nature education is open to diversity. This is true even in a state-run school."[95] (Later, as minister of education and culture during the 1960s, Aranne was unswerving in his sovereign approach.) Yavne'eli, whom Ben-Gurion called "the man who created the workers' trend ... and for many years was its very embodiment,"[96] expressed his support of state-run education, agreeing that the values of the labor trend would now become the property of the entire nation.[97]

Thus Ben-Gurion overrode the historic differences and won out in the struggle for what he described as "the law that has profound revolutionary significance, both from the general national standpoint and from the standpoint of the educational and moral contents of the workers' movement and the pioneering movement in the country."[98] By the time he became prime minister for the second time, this struggle had become part of history. It is doubtful, however, if it can be proven that the values of the labor movement became the dominant values of the state-run school system.

Conclusions

The effective implementation, as Ben-Gurion envisioned it, of the law providing state-run education was obstructed by certain of the conditions that induced his colleagues to agree to abolish the separate trends. There is no doubt that the drastic demographic changes that occurred in Israel's society and schools during the early days of statehood engendered conflict between the needs of the government and the obsolete structure of the educational system. Just as having separate schools divided in accordance with ideological or political trends was alien to most of the new immigrant population, so that population—struggling to be absorbed socially and to find an economic foothold—was hardly receptive material for education to labor and pioneering. To many of the new immigrants, labor symbolized the more humiliating aspect of their realization of Zionism. At the same time the national educational network was deeply involved in the melting-pot process, which meant unremitting efforts to absorb tens of thousands of schoolchildren and mold them to fit new and unfamiliar life patterns. Very soon it also became clear that the parents were not prepared to take advantage of the right to introduce diversity into the school curriculum, nor did they wish to do so. In actual fact, the curriculum that in 1954 officially replaced the programs of study previously followed by the various trends, left no room for diversification in accordance with world outlook. It became both the minimum and maximum curriculum for the primary schools and even restricted the initiative of individual teachers.

This curriculum, based on Paragraph 2 of the Education Law, reflected a synthesis of the attributes of the three trends: attachment to the nation and its spiritual heritage, striving for scientific achievement, and education to labor and pioneering. The overall human values such as tolerance, liberty, mutual aid, equality, and fraternal love were included as well. In 1954 veteran teachers and some of the better-known individuals of the labor movement organized for the purpose of establishing a movement of educators who could introduce what they called major principles of the workers' trend into the government's educational aims. Although this was not parental initiative, it certainly seemed commensurate with the spirit of the Law. But the group's first meetings incurred the wrath of the Mapai leadership. The party institutions, therefore, thwarted the initiative. Consequently, the educational network, engaged in current problems of absorbing immigrant children and trying to raise their level of achievement, was divided into state-secular and state-religious schools.

Under a Mapai minister, the structure became conformist, centralized, and tended to uniformity. Until the end of the 1970s the concept of diversity to be introduced by parents was an archaic formula that had fallen into disuse. Even those educational values which Ben-Gurion had visualized as the *sine qua non* of the Jewish state, became marginal and essentially unimportant over the years. The "synthesized" state school became the general school as understood by Glickson in the 1930s.

In recent years the system has been called into question and ideas have been mooted — primarily by parents — with a view to adapting the school to contemporary life. Cognizance of the essential connection between the school and its social environs, the resurrection of principles enunciated by Ben-Gurion, is not the result of nostalgia, but is due to social processes and conditions prevailing in Israeli society and its educational system.

Notes

1 Ben-Gurion, minutes of Histadrut Actions Committee meeting, July 25, 1934, Labor Movement Archives (hereafter L.M.A.).
2 Decision of Histadrut Founding Convention, minutes of founding convention, December 1920, L.M.A.
3 *Histadrut Council Journal*, vol. 1, no. 5 (May-June 1921).
4 See Y. Gorny, *Ahdut Ha'avoda, 1919-1930* (Hebrew), Tel Aviv, 1973, ch. 3, p. 44.
5 Ibid., ch. 3.
6 Ibid.
7 D. Ben-Gurion, "Changing of the Guard," lecture at 21st Histadrut Council, January 7-10, 1929, publication of the Histadrut Actions Committee, Tel Aviv, 1929, pp. 61-62; L.M.A.
8 Minutes of the Committee of Twenty, Central Zionist Archives (hereafter C.Z.A.), 22835.
9 See Appendix 3 to the Education Policy of the Zionist Organization, 1929.
10 Minutes of Histadrut Actions Committee meeting, October 8, 1928, L.M.A.
11 S. Yavne'eli, ibid.
12 M.A. Beigel, ibid.
13 Ben-Gurion, ibid.
14 M.A. Beigel, ibid.
15 Minutes of Histadrut Actions Committee meeting, December 17, 1928, L.M.A.
16 Minutes of Histadrut Actions Committee meeting, September 14, 1931, L.M.A. From the time of Jewish Agency's establishment onward, many sources refer to the Education Department of the Agency while they mean the Education Department of the Zionist Executive.
17 Minutes of Histadrut Actions Committee meeting, August 17, 1931, L.M.A.
18 M. Yaari, minutes of 26th Histadrut Council, October 4-8, 1931, L.M.A.
19 Y. Tabenkin, ibid.
20 Ibid.
21 D. Ben-Gurion, ibid.
22 In 1933, 55% of the schools were general, 20% belonged to the Workers' Trend, and 25% to the Mizrahi. Ben-Gurion angrily attacked the proposed composition of the management committee. See Ben-Gurion, minutes of Histadrut Actions Committee, October 3, 1932, L.M.A.
23 See minutes of 28th Histadrut Council, November 6, 1932, L.M.A.
24 E. Kaplan, minutes of Histadrut Actions Committee meeting, October 18, 1932, L.M.A.
25 Y. Sprinzak, minutes of Mapai Central Committee meeting, November 7, 1932, Labor Party Archives (hereafter L.P.A.)
26 See, for example, the series of articles by Dr. M. Glickson, editor of *Ha'aretz*: "Between Educational

and Political Trends in Education" (Hebrew), *Ha'aretz*, March 25-27 and 29, 1936.

27 Ben-Gurion, minutes of Histadrut Actions Committee meeting, July 25, 1934, L.M.A.

28 Ibid.

29 Paragraph 6, State Education Law.

30 M. Ya'ari, minutes of Histadrut Actions Committee meeting, July 25, 1934, L.M.A.

31 Y. Hazan, ibid.

32 B. Repetur, minutes of Mapai Central Committee meeting with its representatives in the Va'ad Leumi and the Education Center, August 13, 1934, L.P.A., 24/34.

33 Appended to minutes of Va'ad Leumi meeting, July 3, 1935, C.Z.A., J/7237.

34 Avraham Katznelson, minutes of Mapai Central Committee meeting, July 7, 1935, L.P.A., 23/35.

35 "In the Conflict" (Hebrew), *Hashomer Hatzair*, March 15, 1936.

36 B. Katznelson, minutes of Mapai Central Committee meeting, March 18, 1936, L.P.A., 23/36.

37 D. Ben-Gurion, minutes of 34th Histadrut Council, March 19, 1936, L.M.A.

38 Ibid.

39 D. Ben-Gurion, "The Crisis in Zionism and the Workers' Movement" (Hebrew), *Hapoel Hatzair* XXV, July 11, 1932.

40 Ibid.

41 D. Ben-Gurion, minutes of 34th Histadrut Council, March 19, 1936, L.M.A.

42 Ibid.

43 Ibid.

44 Ibid.

45 M. Glickson, "Between Educational and Political Trends in Education" (Hebrew), *Ha'aretz*, March 25-27 and 29, 1936.

46 Ibid., March 29, 1936.

47 This study does not deal with the negotiations about state education conducted with the religious parties. It should be noted that Ben-Gurion objected throughout to creating an independent framework for state-religious education, although the results indicate that he had to resign himself to the establishment of such a framework.

48 Compulsory Education Act, 1949, Law Registry, V. 26, Ch. 4, Paragraph 10.

49 Y. Laufbahn, E. Lulu et al., minutes of Problems in Education Committee meeting, January 19, 1948, L.P.A., 7/1/48.

50 Ibid., summaries.

51 D. Ben-Gurion, letter sent from Tiberias to Mapai Central Committee, March 10, 1951, L.P.A., 23/51.

52 Ben-Gurion's diary, entry for December 29, 1950, Ben-Gurion Archives, Sedeh Boker (hereafter: B.G.A.). In his diary he blames the Mizrahi for its members not understanding that this was no educational crisis, but rather a crisis in Israeli sovereignty, owing to excessive party fragmentation, aggravation of cultural, class and political conflicts, and the press and party leaders' misunderstanding of state issues, all against the background of the ingathering of exiles. Ben-Gurion's diary, entry for February 12, 1951, B.G.A.

53 See note 51.

54 Ibid.

55 D. Ben-Gurion, 44th Mapai Council, March 13, 1953, L.P.A., 22/44, Section 2.

56 Ibid.

57 Ibid.

58 Ibid.

59 D. Ben-Gurion, "The State School, a Lever for Unifying the Nation and Building the Land" (Hebrew), *Dapim Lehasbara*, no. 14; The Debate on State Education, May 1953.

60 Ibid.

61 D. Ben-Gurion, "Trends in State Education" (Hebrew), lecture at 19th National Pedagogical Conference of the Teachers' Union, October 17, 1954, *Hahinukh*, 27 (1954), pp. 3-8.

62 Ibid.

63 Ibid.

64 Ibid.

65 Ibid.

66 D. Ben-Gurion, minutes of Mapai Central Committee meeting, May 17, 1953, L.P.A.

67 Y. Halprin, minutes of Problems in Education Committee meeting, February 2, 1948, Jewish Education Archives, Tel Aviv University, Gurevitch Collection, 5/2338.

68 D. Ben-Gurion, *Vision and Way* (Hebrew), vol. 3, Tel Aviv, 1951, pp. 66-67.
69 See note 51.
70 Y. Gury, minutes of Mapai Central Committee meeting, March 11, 1951, L.P.A. 23/51.
71 Z. Shazar, ibid.
72 Ibid., to which Pinhas Lavon interjected: "That's exactly Ben-Gurion's suggestion." In referring to four trends, Shazar was including Agudat Israel, which had been recognized as a trend by the Compulsory Education Law of 1949, while Shazar was minister of education and culture.
73 D. Remez, ibid.
74 Ibid.
75 M. Sharett, ibid.
76 Y. Niv, minutes of Knesset Education and Culture Committee meeting, May 28, 1952, Israel State Archives.
77 The Committee, which included 18 members, eight of whom belonged to Mapai, was headed by the minister of education and culture.
78 Mapai's Electoral Platform for the Second Knesset of the State of Israel (Hebrew), ch. 19, p. 12.
79 The General Zionists interpreted the right to diversity as being bestowed by the state at its prerogative, with parents choosing from among the options offered. Mapai's members demanded the right to diversity as a parental prerogative, ensuring pedagogic and social pluralism. Y. Sarid, minutes of Problems in Education Committee meeting, January 19, 1948, L.P.A., 7/1/48.
80 P. Lavon, minutes of Mapai Secretariat meeting, January 20, 1935, L.P.A., 24/53.
81 Y. Sarid, ibid.
82 Benzion Dinur, ibid.
83 D. Ben-Gurion, minutes of 44th Mapai Council, March 15, 1953, L.P.A., 22/44.
84 Ibid.
85 Ibid.
86 Ibid.
87 D. Ben-Gurion, minutes of Mapai Central Committee meeting, May 17, 1953, L.P.A., 23/53.
88 Ibid.
89 Ibid.
90 Ibid.
91 Ibid.
92 Minutes of Mapai Council meeting, November 27-28, 1953, L.P.A.
93 D. Ben-Gurion, ibid.
94 Ibid. See also D. Ben-Gurion in meeting with Mapai Students Section, June 21, 1953, B.G.A., Meetings. Characteristically, Ben-Gurion claimed that the flag in and of itself was no more than a rag, whether blue and white or red or any other color. It was what the flag symbolized that was of value and importance.
95 Z. Aranne, press release about the Mapai National Council, November 27-28, 1953, L.P.A., 22/45.
96 D. Ben-Gurion, minutes of 45th Mapai Council meeting, November 27, 1953, L.P.A.
97 S. Yavne'eli, press release about the Mapai National Council, November 27-28, 1953, L.P.A., 22/45.
98 D. Ben-Gurion, minutes of 45th Mapai Council meeting, November 27, 1953, L.P.A.

BEN-GURION AND REPARATIONS FROM GERMANY

YEHUDIT AUERBACH

Political realism is one of the qualities for which David Ben-Gurion is famous. His attitude toward postwar Germany in general, and reparations in particular, is an instructive example of this realism.

On January 9, 1952, the Knesset adopted a resolution stating that "after hearing the Government's announcement concerning a demand for reparations from Germany for plundered Jewish property, [the Knesset] empowers the Foreign Affairs and Defense Committee to make the final decision as to the form of action to be taken, in accordance with circumstances and conditions."[1] Sixty-one members of the Knesset voted in favor of the resolution, fifty voted against it, and five abstained. The deliberations preceding the resolution lasted for three tense tempestuous days. An agitated and angry public demonstrated outside the Knesset building, resulting in violence which was unprecedented in Israeli history. Stones hurled by the demonstrators, and the tear gas used by the police to disperse them, intermittently entered the plenary hall, further enflaming the passions of the speakers.

This marked the dramatic climax of a long and complicated process of debate which pitted mind against heart, logic against emotion, and realism against morality. Ultimately realism won out.

1949-1950: Ambivalence and Absence of Policy

Initial attempts at claiming compensation from Germany for Holocaust-era damages had been made before the State of Israel was established. The most important of these early initiatives was Chaim Weizmann's appeal to the Allied Powers in September 1945. Weizmann spelled out the claims of the Jewish people against Germany, and laid the foundations for the reparations claim.[2] The Powers recognized the legitimacy of the Jewish people's claim for compensation,[3] but took no concrete step toward dealing with it—if for no other reason than because there was no official Jewish body with which they could negotiate.[4] East Germany, which was under Soviet control, could not adopt a position of its own. The leaders of West Germany, however, were willing to meet the Jewish claims to some extent. Their reasons included their desire to atone for the past, as well as their ambition to rejoin the world community. In the latter context, they were aware that the willingness of other countries—especially the United States, Great Britain, and France—to readmit postwar Germany to the international community would have much to do with Germany's attitude toward the Jewish people and the State of Israel.

Konrad Adenauer, in his first interview after being elected Chancellor of Germany, recognized the obligation of the German people to compensate the Jews for the terrible crimes perpetrated against them, and suggested, as a gesture of goodwill, that "goods worth DM 10m. be placed at the State of Israel's disposal for rehabilitation purposes."[5] The proposal was greeted in Israel with outrage. In talks on the matter held in Ben-Gurion's home, someone suggested initiating a parliamentary question in the Knesset, thereby giving the prime minister an opportunity to present the Israel Government's stand to the Israeli public and to the world. Replying to the question, Ben-Gurion could reject the German Government's offer of "gifts as compensation for the Jewish blood the Germans spilled," and would nevertheless insist on the right "to demand compensation from the German people for the evil and the damage done to the Jewish people." However, Ben-Gurion never delivered the forceful speech prepared for him.[6]

Instead he chose a low-key approach based on two important precepts in the *realpolitik* which guided his attitude toward Germany in 1949 and 1950. First, he did not want to be embroiled in a superpower controversy concerning Germany, in view of the limitations of Israel's strength and influence. Second, he understood that Germany would not remain beyond the pale indefinitely. As a result, although he acceded to Israel's boycott of Germany, he did not want to burn his bridges with pointless rhetoric.[7] In internal, off-the-record consultations, Ben-Gurion supported direct contacts with the German Government, but he did not throw his full weight behind this policy with intent to further it.[8]

Ben-Gurion's attitude toward Germany in 1949 and 1950 was ambivalent: giving the boycott his support, while actually favoring direct contacts in a period when no one dared to speak openly of even indirect contacts.

The major reason for his low profile concerning Germany during these two years can be found in his belief that statesmanship, before anything else, is a matter of setting priorities among many objectives competing for limited resources. In 1949 and 1950, Germany was not a high-priority concern for the young state. The first item on Ben-Gurion's agenda was immigration. This was clearly a monumental task, calling on Israel to stretch its meager resources to provide food, housing, health services, education, and livelihood for hundreds of thousands of Jews—mostly destitute. Another important challenge involved strengthening the fragile armistice between Israel and its neighbors. Ben-Gurion saw an initial opportunity to widen the cracks in the wall of Arab enmity by exploiting King Abdallah's willingness to enter into dialogue with Israeli representatives, thereby eventually converting the armistice agreements into stable peace accords. The failure of this attempt in the wake of Abdallah's hesitancy and then his assassination, accompanied by serious border incidents, elevated defense to top priority. It also placed in focus the need to establish friendly relations, including treaties when possible, with the important countries, principally the United States and the United Kingdom.

Ben-Gurion devoted all his attention to achieving these ends. He did not consider defeated, occupied Germany important or strong enough to help Israel meet its most immediate needs. He left the economic aspects of relations with Germany, centering on problems of personal indemnification and restitution of property, and not reparations on a serious scale, to the Government ministries in charge of economic affairs. He entrusted the diplomatic aspect of Israeli policy—boycotting Germany, excoriating the country in international forums, etc.—to the Foreign Ministry.

1950-1951: Strategy of Indirect Contact

Toward the end of 1950, developments in both the domestic and the international arenas indicated the need for a reappraisal of Israel's relations with Germany, both economically and politically.

The domestic scene was dominated by a catastrophic deterioration in the country's economic situation. The major problem was how to attract foreign currency to cover the Government's mounting deficit. Ben-Gurion invoked a regime of austerity and controls, and approached the US Government for loans and grants. In addition, he launched a fund-raising drive aimed at World Jewry by floating bonds worth close to $1 billion. All these efforts, however, were not sufficient. He rejected the advice of experts, including finance minister Eliezer Kaplan and Finance Ministry director-general David Horowitz, both of whom encouraged him to take unpopular measures such as currency devaluation, reduction of incomes, and imposition of heavy indirect taxes. He felt his hands were tied with regard to adopting a daring policy which might stop the economic decline, fearing public opposition which would cause irreparable harm to the young state.

The offer of reparations—essentially a sizable injection of capital grant which would aid the economy without increasing the debt burden—was a virtual *deus ex machina*. Horowitz, the originator of the proposal, considered it the only chance of averting economic disaster.[9] He tried to persuade policy-makers to adopt his view, and received an attentive if doubtful reaction on the part of Moshe Sharett. Only after talking with Ben-Gurion did he draft a memorandum which detailed the State of Israel's claims against Germany. This memorandum was submitted to the foreign ministers of the four occupying Powers in March 1951. To his credit, it should be noted that Ben-Gurion swiftly grasped the economic significance of the idea of reparations, and was even more aware of its political ramifications, which became increasingly important in light of international developments.

Germany's amazing recovery and rapid reintegration into postwar frameworks became the most important development in the international arena in 1950-1951. As the Cold War intensified, Germany became more important to both superpowers. The United States viewed West Germany as a strategic asset which should be fortified in order to contain Soviet expansion in Europe. As a result, Germany received massive assistance through the US Marshall Plan. Great Britain and France followed America's lead.

In August 1950, the three Western Powers, convening to redefine Germany's status, decided to end the state of war. On October 24, 1950, they sent Israel a communique expressing their wish that Israel do the same. This request "stunned the Israel Government,"[10] which had believed that Germany could not be readmitted to the family of nations until it had restored its relations with the Jews. In effect, this decision recognized Germany as having been rehabilitated without any atonement for its crimes against the Jewish people, and without agreement from either the Jewish people or the Israel Government. The rebuff of the boycott policy pursued thus far by the Israel Government, which was meant *inter alia* to intensify pressure on Germany and increase the cost of Israel's "seal of approval," seemed irrelevant in the wake of these fast-moving developments.[11]

The Foreign Ministry insisted that the Government adjust its policy to these events, and make new decisions with regard to Germany. However, the Government, led and largely inspired by Ben-Gurion, rejected the pressure. Totally contrary to the Foreign Ministry's recommendations, the Government adopted a resolution on October 30, 1950, instructing that Ministry to reject the three Powers' appeal.[12] At the Foreign Ministry's request the Government met once again at the end of December to reconsider the proposal for direct contact with Germany in order to expedite treatment of the reparations problem.[13]

The ministers' views were divided. Dov Joseph, the minister of supply and rationing, vigorously opposed contact of any kind, "even if it means giving up IL100,000." Moshe Shapira, the minister of immigration, the interior, and health, expressed the opinion that "we should not defile ourselves by having contact with Germany for a small sum; but if the sum is large—it's worth it." The two ends of the political spectrum seemed to converge in a proposal raised by agriculture minister Pinhas Lubianiker (subsequently Lavon): to send a delegation to the occupation authorities, not directly to the Germans. This would skirt the moral and emotional issues involved while leaving open the chance of obtaining reparations. Ben-Gurion stunned everyone by suggesting "that Israel declare that a state of war has existed between the State of Israel and West and East Germany since May 14, 1948, and that this announcement be made with Knesset approval and be given legal status."

Walter Eytan, the Foreign Ministry director-general, vehemently resisted Ben-Gurion's proposal, suggesting that a legal opinion be obtained before any decision was made.[14] When the Foreign Ministry's legal adviser also took a dim view of Ben-Gurion's proposal,[15] it was defeated as was the Foreign Ministry's position favoring direct contact with Germany. On January 3, 1951, the Government met and adopted a resolution for Israeli representatives "to apply to the central governments of the occupying powers concerning Germany's promise of reparations and restitution of Jewish property."[16] Thus the strategy of indirect contact with Germany received formal backing.

This resolution, led to the formulation and presentation in writing of two types of claims to the Four Powers. The first relied on precedents and existing laws concerning the restoration of stolen property to individuals. The second claim was presented in a letter dated March 12: the two Germanys were asked to pay the Jewish people $1.5 billion in reparations.[17] The sum was computed on the basis of estimates of the expenses incurred by the Israel Government in absorbing approximately half a million refugees from the Nazis.[18] Addressing the Knesset the following day, the foreign minister read the letter which concluded: "There is a day of reckoning, and that day has arrived."[19]

The Allied Powers, however, were in no hurry to enforce Israel's claims. The Soviet Union did not reply at all. The Western Powers responded by citing legal and other reasons for their refusal to force Germany to make reparations payments to the State of Israel, and recommended that Israel "enter into direct and free negotiations with the Government of Germany on this matter."[20] The strategy of indirect contact with Germany thus finally came to a dead-end, as the Israeli Foreign Ministry had predicted. The pursuit of a strategy of indirect contact raises serious questions. It could be suggested, for instance, that Ben-Gurion was unaware of developments around him. In fact, he was a realist who had no interest in forcing the issue of normalization of relations with Germany, but wanted to move in this direction slowly. Not only was Ben-Gurion alert to the growth in Germany's status, but he harbored no illusions as to the chances of the indirect strategy. He predicted there would be no way to avoid direct contact with Germany,[21] and even took a favorable attitude toward closer relations between Israel and Germany. His constant concern about Israel's political isolation, combined with his sober regard for Germany's increased importance, laid the foundations for Israel's "German policy." The State of Israel should make use of Germany, engaging German guilt to the fullest, in order to strengthen itself.

Precisely because his was a long-term view, Ben-Gurion understood the importance of obtaining the support of public opinion. His fear of the public's reaction to a policy of immediate reconciliation with Germany was partly political, and this aspect grew stronger against the background of the crises which ultimately resulted in early elections.[22] Further, he dreaded the development of a state of alienation between the people and their government. Ben-Gurion did not want to pursue a policy without public support, which he tried to obtain in small increments. The indirect contact strategy was an essential step on the way to securing public support for direct negotiations with Germany.

1951-1952: Direct Contacts with Germany

The Israel Government now faced an acute dilemma: entering into direct negotiations with Germany in order to sue for reparations, or forgoing reparations altogether, which would result in a further deterioration in the country's already desperate economic condition.

For Ben-Gurion, the fateful decision boiled down to a choice between a do-nothing attitude which observes events with neither the desire nor the ability to intervene, and an active approach which exploits circumstances for the promotion of the national interest of a sovereign state. Ben-Gurion had no doubt about the correct choice. A state could not afford to handle its concerns with the fastidiousness and impotence of ghetto dwellers. International circumstances, and direct negotiations with Germany had to begin.[23] Since the Israeli public was still not mature enough for an attitude as sweepingly realistic as this, a moralistic "coating" was required. A public declaration by the Government of Germany, including recognition of its responsibility for crimes against the Jewish people and willingness to make recompense, would serve as proof of Germany's sincere desire to rid itself of its Nazi past. The main difficulty centered around extracting such a declaration without meeting the Germans directly. Israel's representative in Paris, Maurice Fischer, proposed a solution. A non-Israeli Jewish figure would organize an informal, secret meeting between senior-echelon Israeli and German participants. Fischer suggested that the meeting be held in a neutral country, and stressed that the initiative for the rendezvous had to come from the Germans.[24]

The German invitation indeed arrived, though in an indirect manner which confirmed preconceptions of the German Chancellor's ambivalence. On the one hand, he wanted a direct encounter with the Israelis and a settlement with the Jewish people in order to put Germany's conscience to rest, and to confirm Germany's international rehabilitation. On the other hand, he sought to minimize the price Germany would have to pay. Eschewing a direct approach to the Israel Government, which might be turned down flat, thereby offending Germany's pride and dignity, he opted for the use of indirect channels to bring Israel to the negotiating table.

Adenauer's contacts included Karl Marx, editor of a German-Jewish newspaper, and Jakob Altmaier, a Jewish Social-Democrat and member of the Bundestag who was known for his connections with Eliyahu Livneh, Israel's consul in Munich. Both men were involved in preliminary contacts between the two countries.

Israel's hopes to extract a direct appeal and official request for negotiations from the German Government were disappointed. However, the desire to meet with Adenauer to promote the reparations issue proved stronger than the disappointment and frustration. In early April, the Israel Government decided "to accept Germany's approach" for a meeting between official representatives of the two states for deliberation of the reparations claim. Maurice Fischer was appointed to represent Israel in the first meeting.[25]

This was the first decision concerning direct negotiations between Israel and Germany. The Government of Israel, aware of the significance of the proposal, and apprehensive of public reactions, shrouded it in a thick mantle of secrecy.[26] Following the Government's decision, the Foreign Ministry sent Fischer a detailed communique with Ben-Gurion's instructions concerning the technical and formal aspects of the historic meeting.[27] "Fischer must behave with a reserved coldness, and refrain from any external expressions of anger about anything related to the past." The main purpose of the meeting was to make it clear to Adenauer that, before any negotiations began, the Government of Germany would have to issue a public declaration including the following points:

> Expression of shock and regret concerning the crimes committed against the Jewish people during the period of Nazi rule.

Recognition of the German people's obligation to ensure that no German government repeat similar crimes against humanity.

Acknowledgement that although the crime could be neither forgiven nor expunged, Germany had an elementary obligation to correct the damage it wrought.

Furthermore, Germany must promise to do everything it could to expedite the claims for restitution, indemnification for damage to life and property, and collective reparations to the Jewish people.

In his talks with Adenauer, Fischer was to stress that a public declaration along these lines was Israel's *sine qua non* for future contacts between the two countries. Adenauer must be told that the opening of negotiations without such a declaration would meet with the fierce opposition of Jewish public opinion in Israel and around the world.

Concern for Israeli public opinion was a principal motif in this communique. Ben-Gurion wanted to go before the Israeli public with an airtight defense. The public declaration he demanded of Germany was to be the very heart of this defense.

For Adenauer, in contrast, an admission of German national responsibility for crimes committed under the Nazis was more than he, as a proud German, was prepared to give. It was also more than he thought Germany had to provide in view of its improving status. In the meeting on April 19 in Paris with Fischer and Horowitz (who was sent to the meetings at Sharett's insistence), Adenauer tried to circumvent the declaration issue by discussing other topics, primarily the timing, site, and nature of the upcoming open meeting between representatives of Israel and Germany. Direct, formal talks between representatives of the two peoples was Adenauer's major objective. He viewed such talks as an obvious seal of approval which would remove the last obstacle on Germany's road to full rehabilitation. In contrast, Horowitz, who became the senior Israeli representative at the talks, made it clear to Adenauer that Israel's demand was an ultimatum, and refused to let him avoid a commitment to provide the sought-after declaration. Nevertheless, Horowitz failed to extract from Adenauer an acknowledgment of the legitimacy of Israel's demand for collective reparations; nor did Adenauer accede to the sum specified in the Israel Government's suit—$1.5 billion—as a basis for the negotiations.[28]

A further measure called for by the Israel Government at this stage was a study of Germany's economic situation, meant to verify that Germany actually could assume the financial burden required of it. Horowitz wrote a memorandum providing clear proof that Germany's situation was improving with amazing speed. As long as Germany's standard of living and balance of payments were much better than those of Israel, he added, there was no reason to excuse Germany from paying reparations. On the contrary, he suggested, it was a moral imperative.[29]

Jerusalem waited impatiently for Adenauer's announcement. Initial reports about the German Government's intention to issue an official declaration "shortly" appeared in early August 1951. The intent, however, was not carried out until about two months later. During this interval, numerous exhausting contacts were held between the German representatives on the one hand, and representatives of the Israel Government and the World Jewish Congress on the other, as to the phrasing of the declaration.

The difficulty stemmed from the two sides' conflicting interests. Adenauer was interested in arriving at a phrasing that the Israel Government would approve in advance, thus insuring that the declaration would not be rejected on the spot. At the same time, he wanted to insure minimum damage to Germany's dignity and maneuverability. On the other hand, Ben-Gurion feared the rage which would greet a lukewarm declaration, and sought one that would make explicit mention of the points raised in Paris: admission of responsibility, willingness to pay reparations, and agreement to the sum Israel specified.

A draft of a declaration including these three points was forwarded to Ben-Gurion and Sharett for study, and received their approval. The final phrasing, however, did not resemble that approved by Ben-Gurion and Sharett, and none of the aforementioned points appeared in it.[30]

On September 27, Adenauer addressed a standing room only audience in the West German Bundestag and delivered his historic declaration. The Chancellor acknowledged that "in the name of the German people, terrible crimes were committed which require the provision of moral and material recompense for the damages suffered by individual Jews, and for Jewish property for which no claimants remain." He tempered his admission: "The decisive majority of the German people related with disgust to the crimes committed against the Jews, and did not take part in them," he added. Adenauer then insured himself against exaggerated claims: "Thought should be given to the limits placed on Germany's ability to pay, because [Germany must face] the distressing necessity of taking care of the innumerable victims of the war, and providing for the refugees, and the expelled persons."[31]

Since Adenauer's declaration did not resemble the approved phrasing, Ben-Gurion and Sharett chose to ignore his restrictions. Jerusalem cited Adenauer's remarks as indicating that "the Federal German Government admits *without reservation* that crimes indescribable by man were committed in the name of the German people, and this implies an obligation to provide moral and material reparations to both the individual and the aggregate."[32] With this statement, the Government of Israel recognized Germany's right to join in direct negotiations with Israel on reparations. Representatives of the world Jewish community were also asked to add their legitimization.

The Conference of Jewish Material Claims Against Germany—an umbrella organization of 22 Jewish groups—was established in order to represent world Jewry in negotiations with Germany. Meeting in New York on October 25-26, the "Claims Conference" provided the Israel Government with the moral backing of world Jewry by adopting a resolution which supported the claim presented by Israel to Germany through the Allied Powers, and insisted that all practical and legal steps be taken to honor all the Jews' claims against Germany.[33]

It was still necessary for Germany to invite Israel to negotiate its claim. On December 6, at Nahum Goldmann's request and with Ben-Gurion's agreement, a meeting was arranged between Goldmann and Adenauer.[34] At the end of the meeting, Goldmann dictated to Adenauer's secretary a letter which was addressed to Goldmann and signed by Adenauer.[35] This letter contained an explicit invitation to the Israel Government to enter into dialogue with representatives of the German Goverment concerning reparations, based on Israel's letters of March 12, 1951. As such, it marked the birth of the formal process toward a reparations decision.

Toward a Decision on Reparations

The debate on direct negotiations with Germany was conducted at two distinct levels: within Mapai and in the Government during December 13-30, 1951; and among the other parties and in the Knesset during January 1-February 1, 1952.

The Mapai Central Committee convened on December 13, 1951, to discuss a proposal presented by the prime minister concerning direct negotiations with Germany for the purpose of obtaining reparations. The deliberations began after Ben-Gurion reviewed the chain of events leading to the necessity of deciding on direct negotiations with the Germans.

The discussion reflected the controversy which enflamed all levels of the public on the reparations question.[36] To reach a decision for or against direct reparations talks with the Germans, two issues had to be addressed: Should Israel demand and accept money from Germany, and should Israel negotiate directly with the Germans?

The most extreme negative reaction to both questions was expressed by Mordechai Dvorjhetsky, a Holocaust survivor, who vigorously protested any contact with Germany. "We should maintain a perpetual hatred of the German people," he said. "We should spit in their faces with all the payments that could help us."

A different, still negative attitude was articulated by Yosef Sprinzak: "I can sit with Adenauer; I do not shun him, and I am capable of believing that the German people will be good one day." On the other hand, he categorically rejected the idea of accepting money from the Germans: "I do not want to receive money for a cause called six million." Yet another negative position objected to sitting with the Germans in an attempt to reach an agreement which, it was felt, the Germans would not honor in any case. Most of the other speakers at the Mapai meeting supported direct negotiations on reparations—some hesitatingly, others without ambivalence.

The emotion-versus-logic conflict faced by many in and out of Mapai was substantiated by remarks of Golda Meyerson (later Meir). "My attitude is definitely racist. To me, every German is retroactively a Nazi." Calling upon her party colleagues to respect the necessity for irrationality in this case, she argued that "we haven't done enough to keep the German matter fresh in everyone's mind." Although the anti-German emotions which surfaced in her comments were no less powerful than those of the opposition, Meyerson supported Ben-Gurion's proposal for direct negotiations, because "I have only one standard of measurement. The cause of Jewish dignity without the State of Israel does not exist. For me, this is the prime consideration." She buttressed her position with ethical arguments: "Anything that might harm the state is immoral, undignified, sinful." Meyerson called for collecting "this repugnant debt" in a "fearful" frame of mind, and for conducting the negotiations with "these defiled people [while preserving our] purity and dignity."

A less emotional approach was expressed by Eliahu Dobkin, Haim Yahil, Pinhas Lavon, and others. "We'll buy artillery with the Germans' money," said Mapai secretary-general Meir Argov, substantiating the practical significance of the reparations and the importance of supporting the idea of obtaining them.

Ben-Gurion hardly mentioned the reparation funds themselves in his remarks. He even doubted the possibility that the negotiations would produce the desired financial gains. "I make no promises of my own for Adenauer. It could be that he may cheat." Ben-Gurion did not present the talks with the Germans as a means, perhaps illegitimate but essential, toward obtaining reparations, as argued by almost everyone who considered reparations essential. Rather, he perceived and depicted the reparations as means toward entering into direct bilateral talks. He felt that irrational reluctance to have contact with the Germans was a remnant of the "do-nothing" period of exile:

> We are not living in a ghetto, but in our state. We will not cloister ourselves apart from this world, and in this world there is the German people, with its Nazis and its murderers and its executioners.... We cannot flee the world. We will not shun them.

Ben-Gurion's assertions constitute a powerful expression of sober realism. Its thrust was that fortifying and strengthening the state was an end of supreme importance, to which every other consideration was subordinate. This pragmatism was vastly different from the moralistic approach he offered the public from the Knesset rostrum one month later (see below), and it undoubtedly helped Ben-Gurion secure an impressive majority (42:5) for his proposal to open direct negotiations with Germany on reparations.

The Mapai Central Committee's decision had far-reaching significance. It determined how the party would behave in every forum where the decision would be discussed—including the Government, the Knesset plenary, and the Knesset Foreign Affairs and Defense Committee—and it created a significant constraint on the other parties.

The Government convened on December 30 and by voice vote reached a decision in principle to open negotiations with Germany on the topic of reparations. At this meeting, the Government decided upon operative measures including an assembly of all members of the coalition, deliberations in the Knesset Foreign Affairs and Defense Committee, and decisive debate in the Knesset plenary.[37]

To strengthen the commitment of the coalition partners to the Government's position, the coalition was convened on January 1, 1952. The parties had to decide for or against the Government decision asking the Knesset to empower it to open direct negotiations with the West German Government, and whether to impose coalition discipline on coalition members.

The first question was resolved with relative ease. Mapai members, who constituted an absolute majority in the coalition, spoke unanimously in favor of the Government proposal. Representatives of the Orthodox and ultra-Orthodox parties were divided. By majority vote, the coalition affirmed the Government's position. In contrast, the dispute concerning freedom of conscience was not resolved. Those who were opposed in principle were permitted to abstain. Rabbi Nurock was allowed to vote against. All other coalition members were required to vote in favor of the Government proposal. This arrangement was subject to changes which might occur in the wake of parties' deliberations up to the day of the Knesset vote. The coalition executive was supposed to convene once again on January 7, the day the announcement was to be made in the Knesset, to finalize voting and coalition discipline procedures.[38]

Deliberations within the parties ended just before the Knesset debate began. On the morning of January 7, 1952, the tension mounted. An advance poll indicated a small majority for the coalition, but this was not certain.

The debate was opened by Ben-Gurion[39] who reviewed the Government's efforts to sue for and obtain recompense from Germany. In view of the occupation powers' refusal to serve as the Israel Government's agents vis-à-vis Germany, he said:

> The Israel Government considers itself obliged to act together with representatives of world Jewry, without delay, in making all appropriate efforts to restore with all possible speed as much stolen property as possible to individual Jews and the Jewish people...."[40]

Ben-Gurion had two ready arguments to justify accepting reparations from Germany. The first was based on recovering as much Jewish property as possible, thereby extricating the "Jewish legacy from the murderers' hands ... so that the murderers do not become the heirs as well...."[41] The second argument was based on using the reparations to finance the absorption and rehabilitation of the Holocaust survivors in Israel.

In the course of his speech, Ben-Gurion developed these two themes, without even hinting at the circumstances which instigated the reparations claim (Israel's desperate economic situation, the rapid improvement in Germany's status, or the matter of direct contact with Germany).

In his Knesset address, Ben-Gurion shed his statesman-realist role and became more of a prophet. He was careful not to create a gulf between himself and the public, and even uncharacteristically refrained from quarrelling with rivals. He stressed the factors unifying the Jews, rather than belittling the feelings of hostility and rage toward Germany: "The Government of Israel and the entire Jewish people regard the entire German people as being responsible for the horrible acts committed during World War II against European Jewry." He concluded his carefully balanced remarks with an appeal: "May the murderers of our people not be their heirs."[42]

Ben-Gurion knew how to select the most efficient tools of persuasion in order to gain public support for the most daring, far-reaching measures. While he did not succeed in changing the outcome of the vote significantly, his address was directed beyond the Knesset chambers to the Jewish people in Israel and around the world.

His major goal was to align popular support behind a process which would begin with reparations and end with full normalization of relations with Germany.

After the prime minister finished his speech, the debate among the Knesset members began. The discourse was tempestuous and often violent, reflecting the attitudes of the public. After two days of tense, exhausting debate, the Knesset voted in favor of affirming the Government's announcement (61:50 with five abstentions),[43] and transferred the final decision concerning the reparations claim against Germany to the Foreign Affairs and Defense Committee.

On January 15, 1952, this Committee met and adopted a resolution which, for the first time, makes mention of direct negotiations with Germany:

> ...the Foreign Affairs and Defense Committee has resolved to empower the Government to act on the question of reparations from Germany, including the possibility of direct negotiations as the matter and the occasion require....[44]

Thus empowered to act, on February 18 the Government adopted a resolution accepting Bonn's offer of reparations and asked Goldmann to inform the German Government accordingly.[45]

The Wassenaar Negotiations

The tripartite negotiations between the representatives of the Israel Government, the Conference on Jewish Material Claims Against Germany (representing the leading Diaspora organizations), and the West German Government opened on March 21, 1952 in Wassenaar, a small town near the Dutch capital, The Hague.[46] The Israel Government did not consider the timing of the talks fortuitous. Germany was also participating in negotiations in London to settle all outstanding claims; the outcome of the London Debt Conference would affect its ability to pay significant reparations to Israel. The Israelis wanted to advance their own talks by two months, but the Germans' delay in approving the agreement made this impossible.[47]

The opening session took place in a cold, formal atmosphere. Gershon Avner, the head of the Foreign Ministry's Western European Department, who was the spokesman of the Israeli delegation, read the opening declaration and reviewed Israel's main demands as drafted in the letter of March 12, which Adenauer had recognized in his letter to Goldmann of December 6. In the Germans' initial statement, their delegation leader Franz Böhm pointed out Germany's legal and financial limitations, and stressed the connection between Israeli and Jewish claims and other German reparation obligations that were being discussed in London.[48]

This declaration marked the beginning of a protracted and obstinate struggle between the Israeli and Diaspora delegation and the Germans concerning the extent, form, and conditions of payment. The main bone of contention between the two delegations was the relationship between the reparations talks and the London negotiations. The German delegation, pressured by German representatives in London and financial circles in Bonn, claimed that this relationship, and its implications as to Germany's ability to make reparations, must be taken into account. The Israelis argued for a differentiation between the talks in Wassenaar and in London, and rejected the distinction made by the Germans between what they owed and what they could afford. On April 8, the talks ground to a halt.

On May 6, 1952, the Knesset convened a plenary session to discuss the breakdown of the Wassenaar talks. The Foreign Affairs and Defense Committee recommended a suspension of the talks "until such time as the Bonn Government submits a clear and binding proposal...."[49] Despite opposition proposals to cease the talks immediately, the Committee's recommendation was adopted by the house.

At the same time, Israeli representatives, through British and American intermediaries, were exerting pressure on Adenauer to resist his domestic political and financial circles that opposed the Israeli claims. Additional pressure came from within the Social Democratic Party in Germany and was strengthened when Kuster resigned as leader of the German delegation and Böhm threatened to do so.[50]

The breakthrough came on May 23. In a meeting attended by Böhm, Goldmann, Giora Josephthal, and Shinnar, the German representative issued a "private" proposal whose major provision was the payment to Israel of $714 million over 12 years. Neither the Israeli representatives nor Goldmann rejected the recommendation outright.[51] On June 10, a decisive meeting was held between Goldmann and Shinnar on the one hand, and Adenauer, assisted by his financial adviser Herman Abs, as well as Secretary of State Hallstein, Böhm, and Assistant Secretary Blankenhorn, on the other. A framework agreement was signed, resolving most of the differences between the two sides.[52]

The reparations agreement was then concluded on September 10, 1952, at a modest ceremony conspicuous for its lack of formal statements.[53] Adenauer signed for the Government of West Germany, and Sharett for the Government of Israel. The main points of the agreement were payment of DM 3 billion (about $715 million) "to pay for the purchase ... of the goods and services required to settle and rehabilitate Jewish refugees in Israel;" and payment of DM 450 million (about $107 million) to the State of Israel on behalf of the Claims Conference.

In the name of the Claims Conference, Dr. Goldmann signed two protocols relating to personal indemnification and the separate payment to the Conference. Another agreement, concerning German property in Israel, was signed by Shinnar, Josephthal, and Böhm.[54]

On March 18, 1953, the Bundestag approved the reparations agreement by a two-thirds majority. Two days later, representatives of the "Lander" in the Bundestag unanimously voted in favor. On March 22, 1953, the Government of Israel approved the agreement against a background of sharp protest demonstrations. Despite the gloomy predictions, the accord was carried out, with implementation completed in 1965. During this period (1952-1965), an Israeli Purchasing Mission was established in Cologne, directed by Shinnar. Officially charged with implementing the agreement, this delegation also performed quasi-diplomatic functions.

Conclusion

The significance of the reparations resolution with respect to continued ties with West Germany cannot be overemphasized. This agreement broke the moral taboo and hurdled the psychological barriers that had prevented relations with Germany. The "normalization" process began penetrating the consciousness of the two peoples, and received concrete expression in the establishment and expansion of ties between the two countries in a variety of fields.[55]

To a certain extent, normalization was an almost inevitable consequence of a psychological process that worked on the subconscious of both nations. It was Golda Meir who expressed the significance of this process when, during the reparations debate in the Mapai Central Committee, she said: "We shall not be able to educate or impress [Israelis] that we are accepting reparations from a murderer." This assertion reflects a prophecy fulfilled. The acceptance of reparations was envisioned as setting in motion a process among the Jewish people which included repression of hatred, gradually forgetting the Holocaust, and emotional preparation for full, normal ties with Germany.

To no lesser degree, normalization can be seen as a deliberate policy encouraged by Ben-Gurion, and one that he tried to realize even in the preparatory stages of the decision-making process concerning reparations. For Ben-Gurion, reparations were neither an end in themselves nor a means of rehabilitating the Israeli economy. The reparations—and, to an even greater extent, direct negotiations between the representatives of the Israel and the West German governments—served as a point of departure for an obstacle course called "normalization."

As a far-sighted statesman, Ben-Gurion considered the first signs of Germany's recovery as an indication that the process of renewed German growth had begun, and would gain speed as superpower rivalry intensified. He understood that the Germany of the early 1950s, courted by the American, British and French governments, still required a Jewish-Israeli sanction in order to win the support of public opinion in these countries and to be reaccepted into the international community. Ben-Gurion sought to take advantage of Germany's relative weakness in this regard in demanding "special relations" with it, even if this implied the repression of hatred toward Germany and the overcoming of memories that were still fresh in the nation's heart.

However, the gap between Ben-Gurion's rational viewpoint and the emotional approach pursued by the majority of the Israeli public fanned by the opposition parties, was vast. To bridge it, Ben-Gurion was able to present the reparations as an act of historic justice: the return of stolen goods by the murderers in order to rehabilitate the survivors.

Out of the thin web of the reparations agreements Ben-Gurion wove an extensive network of ties with West Germany. Even as he tried to keep the existence of these ties secret,[56] he took action to prepare public opinion to accept his "German orientation."

In the intensive information campaign he launched to justify his policy, Ben-Gurion relied in the main on *realpolitik* rationales:

> The well-being of the State of Israel ... requires the existence of stable relations with Germany, since we are dealing not with the world of yesterday but with the world of tomorrow; not with memories of the past but with the ways of future; we are dealing not with a reality that has vanished but with a concrete reality that changes and renews itself ... [one in which] today's Germany plays a significant part....[57]

Realpolitik, however, was not a sufficiently strong foundation to bear the weighty structure of normalization between victims and murderers. Ben-Gurion also wanted to justify his policy in moral terms. In order to prove to himself, to the public, and to history that ethical considerations were central to his German orientation, he developed the thesis of "a different Germany." This thesis implied that the Germany of the 1950s was not the same Germany that had massacred the Jewish people: "The young generation is now a different generation ... the German people no longer espouses the Nazi philosophy ... [and] Adenauer is not a Nazi." He added the verdict of the Torah and the Prophets: "A man shall die [only] for his own sins." On these bases Ben-Gurion ruled that "the sin of the Nazis should not be visited on the German people." Thus he inverted the moral grounds on which his policy had been attacked. Normalization with Germany was depicted as the realization of the vision of the Prophets, and boycotting Germany became racist.[58]

Logically and demographically, of course, the "different Germany" thesis was totally absurd. A nation — its character, philosophy, and essence — does not change in a decade.[59] Ben-Gurion's assertion signified the severance of the heritage that links different generations of a nation, and the denial of the national tie among the members of a nation at a specific historical moment. The Hebrew poet Nathan Alterman expressed the distortion in this thesis caustically by noting that:

> This [application of the verse 'each man shall die for his own sins' to the field of Israel-German relations] contains a denial of the stubborn and concrete existence of entities such as society and nation, and of the the existence of feelings and thoughts that exist within these general categories.[60]

If there is no "nation of murderers," Alterman claimed, then there is equally no "nation of poets and philosophers." As an extension of the same reasoning, even the nation of Prophets ceases to exist, and any tie between the Jewish people of today and the law and land of the Prophets is null and void. The price of the "different Germany" thesis was too high. In the field of education in Germany, it served to encourage attempts on the part of Germans to detach themselves from their past and to forget it. In debates among Germans and among German political parties on extending the Statute of Limitations for Nazi crimes, and on the educational and political benefit of bringing Nazi criminals to trial, Ben-Gurion's message could serve as support for those who promoted a clean break with the past. There is no way of estimating with any precision the contribution the "different Germany" thesis made to the process of forgetting the past in Germany, but its influence should not be underestimated in view of Ben-Gurion's status and the Germans' sensitivity to world opinion in general and world Jewish opinion in particular.

On the level of German-Israeli relations, this thesis had paradoxical results. The argument that "Germany is different," invoked in order to justify normalization, actually delayed the process. The "new" Germany, bearing its seal of approval from the greatest Jewish leader of that generation, had no further need to atone for the "old" Germany's crimes. The omission of an ethical basis underlying Israel's requests for special relations with Germany allowed Germany to avoid fulfilling these requests in the name of a *realpolitik* that preferred the wealthy Arab world to Israel.[61]

In Israel itself, the "different Germany" thesis helped blur the distinction between what was and was not permissible in future relations with Germany. Ben-Gurion expressed opposition to personal ties with Germany, and refrained from visiting it. But he was forced to admit "that there is something of a contradiction here."[62]

This contradiction between a general feeling of repulsion and reluctance to make even private visits to Germany on the one hand, and the need for normalization of relations between the Jewish people and Germany on the other hand, is part of the relations between the two nations even today. Ben-Gurion's desire to solve this problem by portraying postwar Germany as "different" was doomed to failure and was in fact superfluous. His greatness was that he faced the contradiction, could distinguish between emotion and logic, and chose logic.

Notes

* I wish to thank Yehoshua Freundlich and other employees in the Israel State Archives (hereafter I.S.A.) for making their knowledge and the requisite documents available to me.

1 *Divrei Haknesset*, 10[2], p. 961.

2 Israel, Foreign Ministry 1953, documents relating to the agreement between the Israel Government and the German Federal Republic, Jerusalem, Government Press (hereafter: FM Documents), pp. 9-10.

3 Under the Paris Treaty of 1946, a special agency was set up to deal with the problem of reparations by Germany for its activities during World War II. Paragraph 8 of that treaty recognized the Jewish people's right to compensation from Germany.

4 In an opinion on Israel-German relations drawn up by Dr. Yaakov Robinson of the Foreign Ministry in August 1950, the situation with regard to Jewish claims for German reparations was described as "chaos." The list of Jewish claimants included individuals, groups, attorneys with individual or collective powers of attorney, various Jewish organizations, the Jewish Agency, etc. The author of the opinion went on to assert that "I have no advice about putting an end to this confusion but to concentrate all Jewish and Israeli claims ... in the State of Israel alone." I.S.A., no file number.

5 The interview with Adenauer was published in the German-Jewish newspaper *Allgemeine Wochenzeitung der Juden in Deutschland*, and is quoted in R. Vogel, *The German Path to Israel*, Chester Springs, PA., 1969, pp. 17-18.

6 The speech was prepared by Leo Kohn, Foreign Ministry adviser, and was sent to the Government Secretary on November 30, 1949, to be forwarded to Ben-Gurion. I.S.A., no file number.

7 Foreign Ministry correspondence in the I.S.A. mentions several Government decisions from 1949 onward recommending a total boycott of Germany. One of them forbids "any [diplomatic] contact with Germans" (from a telegram sent by the foreign minister to Israel's ambassador in Moscow on September 7, 1949, quoted in a memorandum by the Director of the East Europe Department to the Director of the Consular Department, Ref: 41473/4321. Another Government decision quoted is "to forbid the import of German goods," in a letter by the finance minister to the directors of the import departments in the Government ministries, dated November 18, 1949 (no file number). Foreign Ministry department directors suggested such measures as issuing Israeli passports prohibiting travel

to Germany, opposing the admission of Germany into international organizations, and refraining from "all direct governmental negotiations with German institutions." I.S.A., protocol of meeting on December 15, 1949, no file number.

8 In his letter to Eliezer Kaplan of March 21, 1950, Sharett mentions a consulation held in Ben-Gurion's house to discuss various recommendations concerning indemnification and restitution. "The outcome of the consultation was clear," wrote Sharett. "The Government must initiate direct action." He added, "I don't recall hearing any opposition to this line from members of the Jewish Agency Executive." His comment included Ben-Gurion. I.S.A., 32/553.

9 An authentic description of the atmosphere of depression and helplessness that characterized the leaders of Israel's economy in 1949-1950, and which formed a natural backdrop to the decision for reparations, can be found in Horowitz's autobiography: David Horowitz, *In the Heart of Events* (Hebrew), Ramat Gan, 1975. pp. 11-79.

10 From a letter by the Foreign Ministry's legal advisor to the foreign minister, February 23, 1951. I.S.A., 5531.

11 An interesting account of how the boycott was used to increase pressure on Germany to pay compensation is found in a secret communique sent from the Western Europe Department to the United States and Latin America Departments on June 15, 1950. In this communique, Gershon Avner asked the Embassy in Washington to ask the Jewish Chamber of Commerce in Mexico "not to relax the boycott [on German goods], and, if possible, to tighten it." Avner continues: "The more Germany realizes that substantial markets will remain closed as long as she refuses to pay suitable reparations, the more willing she will be to speed up payment of these reparations." I.S.A., 32/5531.

12 The Government's decision is quoted in a letter by government secretary Yael Ouzai to Walter Eytan, director general of the Foreign Ministry, on January 4, 1951. I.S.A., 804/32/4403.

13 The Foreign Ministry's request was sent by the director general to the government secretary in a letter dated December 17, 1950. In this letter, Eytan specifies the points on which the Foreign Ministry requires a decision: a response to the letter of the Allied Powers; a letter concerning the State of Israel's claims; ways of approaching East Germany; and, in particular, a decision in principle concerning contact with German authorities. Eytan stressed that "All parties ... are unanimous in their belief that real progress concerning the claims is possible only through Israel's initiating direct negotiations with the German authorities in Germany." I.S.A., 32/1434.

14 A detailed report on the Government session of December 27, 1950, can be found in a letter sent to Sharett at Eytan's request, December 29, 1950. I.S.A., 23/553.

15 Shabtai Rosenne's opinion was presented to Sharett on February 23, 1951. I.S.A., 32/5531.

16 The resolution was quoted in writing in a letter by the government secretary to the director general of the Foreign Ministry, dated January 4, 1951. I.S.A., 804/32/4403.

17 The full text of all letters mentioned above are recorded in FM Documents, pp. 13-28.

18 The idea of basing the claim on an estimate of $3,000 per refugee absorbed in Israel was Horowitz's. See Horowitz, ibid., p. 81. A similar account appears in P. Shinnar, *Israel-German Relations, 1951-1965* (Hebrew), Jerusalem, Tel Aviv, 1967, p. 17.

19 Stated by Sharett in the Knesset, March 13, 1951. *Divrei Haknesset* 8, p. 1323.

20 The full replies of the three Western Powers appear in FM Documents, pp. 28-41.

21 In a session of the Mapai Central Committee in which he reported on the chain of events leading to the decision to enter into direct negotiations with Germany for reparations, Ben-Gurion said: "When we presented this claim, our intention was *to approach the Germans* with our request, once we knew that such a request was practical." Mapai Central Committee, December 13, 1951. Labor Party Archives (henceforth L.P.A.) Emphasis added.

22 A recurring motif in Foreign Ministry correspondence is the Government's concern for public opinion as elections approached. A typical example appears in Gershon Avner's letter to Sharett, dated February 26, 1951. Avner prods Sharett to bring about a resolution in favor of direct negotiations with Germany. "During the election campaign, no party can risk taking up a matter such as this, which could be dynamite." I.S.A., 32/5531.

23 Stated by Ben-Gurion to colleagues in the Mapai Central Committee, on December 13, 1951. L.P.A.

24 This recommendation is included in Maurice Fischer's letter to Avner, head of the Foreign Ministry's Western Europe Department, dated February 15, 1951. I.S.A., 32/5531.

25 The Government's decision, as well as a review of the chain of events that led up to it, can be found in a letter dated April 6, 1951, sent by Avner to Fischer, Israel's representative in Paris. I.S.A., 32/5434.

26 Only on August 15, 1951, four months after the resolution was adopted, did Avner report to the Israel

Embassy in Washington about the Government's decision to agree in principle to direct negotiations with Germany. The Embassy was taken by surprise. In a reply by the adviser to the Israel Embassy dated July 7, 1951, Keren describes the decision as "new and explosive." I.S.A., 32/5434.

27 Avner apologized to Fischer for its length, which was due to Ben-Gurion's insistence on accurate transmission of every detail of the sensitive meeting. Letter by Avner to Fischer, April 6, 1951. I.S.A., 32/5434.

28 On May 3, 1951, Fischer sent the Foreign Ministry a detailed report on the meeting, including his impression of Adenauer's cold personality and rigid position. I.S.A., 32/5531.

29 A copy of Horowitz's memorandum appears in I.S.A., 32/5331.

30 Documents relating to the drafting of this declaration make it apparent that there were two drafts. The first, apparently prepared by Adenauer's aide, Blankenhorn, was delivered by N. Barou to Goldmann, who proposed some amendments and presented it to Israel. This version was returned, after approval by Sharett and Ben-Gurion, for inspection by Adenauer, with the expectation that with the amendments incorporated, the text would serve as the basis for Adenauer's public declaration. Adenauer, however, apparently considered the first version with the amendments a far-reaching concession to Israeli demands, and prepared a second version. This version was sent by Jakob Altmaier to Fischer in Paris. After consultations between Fischer, Barou, and Goldmann on September 21, 1951, the draft was sent to Israel. It met with harsh reactions in the Foreign Ministry. "The last version Fischer sent is much worse than the previous one," Avner wrote to Sharett on September 25, 1951. I.S.A., 32/5531.

31 The full text appears both in the original and in Hebrew translation—from which the quotations in the original Hebrew version of this study were taken—in FM Documents, pp. 41-43.

32 The complete reaction of the Israeli Government appears in F.M. Documents, p. 44. Emphasis added.

33 A detailed report on the discussions and resolutions of the Claims Conference was sent on November 1, 1951, by the Israel Embassy in Washington to the Foreign Ministry in Jerusalem. I.S.A., 137/31/7.

34 Goldmann provides details of this meeting in his autobiography: Nahum Goldmann, *Autobiography*, New York, 1969. pp. 260-261.

35 The letter appears in FM Documents, pp. 56-57.

36 All quotations from this debate are taken from the minutes of the Mapai Central Committee on December 13, 1951. L.P.A.

37 There are press reports on the Government meeting. *Haboker*, in its edition of December 17, 1951, recounts another Government session on the subject of reparations on December 16. According to its December 31, 1951 issue, it was only during the second session—on December 30—that the formal decision was adopted.

38 *Ma'ariv*, January 2, 1952.

39 Coverage of the entire debate appears in *Divrei Haknesset* 10[2], pp. 895-964.

40 Ibid., p. 897.

41 Ibid., p. 896.

42 Ibid., p. 897.

43 Those voting in favor of the resolution were all Mapai members (including Sprinzak and Livneh who had opposed it during the intra-party debate); Mizrahi members, excluding Rabbi Nurock, who voted against; Hapoel Hamizrahi members, excluding Warhaftig and Genihowski, who abstained; the three Progressives; MK Deutsch of Agudat Israel; MKs belonging to the Arab list affiliated with Mapai. Those voting against the resolution were: all members of Herut, Mapam, General Zionists, MK Harari of the Progressives, and R. Nurock of Mizrahi. Those abstaining, apart from Warhaftig and Genihowski, were Kalman Kahane and B. Mintz of Po'alei Agudat Israel, and M. Levine of Agudat Israel. *Divrei Haknesset*, 10[2], pp. 962-964.

44 The resolution was published in FM Documents, p. 61.

45 M. Brecher, *Decisions in Israel's Foreign Policy*, London, 1974, p. 90.

46 Israel Government representatives were Giora Josephthal, head of the Jewish Agency Finance Department and a senior member of the Mapai leadership, and P. Shinnar, director of the Reparations Claims Department in the Foreign Ministry, both of whom served as joint and equal heads of the delegation. Also participating were Gershon Avner, who was appointed spokesman of the delegation, Eli Nathan, and the jurist Dr. Yaakov Robinson. Y. Bazner, who was appointed to the delegation, died in a plane crash en route to Wassenaar. Representing world Jewry as members of the Claims Association Board were Nahum Goldmann (Conference chairman), Noah Barou (Conference vice-

chairman), Moses Leavitt (acting head of the Delegation), and Dr. Georg Landauer, who, it was decided, was to serve in both delegations. Leading the German delegation was Franz Böhm; his deputy was A. Koster. The Foreign Ministry, the Finance Ministry, and the Ministry of Economic Affairs sent another four participants, as well as a translator. Shinnar (n. 18 above, ibid.), p. 28.

47 A detailed report on the preparations for the opening of the talks, and on the difficulties that arose during them, was forwarded by Sharett to the members of the Mapai Political Committee on May 5, 1952. L.P.A.

48 The atmosphere that prevailed during the opening meeting is described by Vogel, *The German Path to Israel*, p. 42. The full text of both countries' opening declarations appears in FM Documents, pp. 69-81.

49 *Divrei Haknesset*, 11[2], p. 1944.

50 Sharett, the Mapai Political Committee, May 5, 1952. L.P.A.

51 As reported by I. Deutschkron, *Bonn and Jerusalem*, Philadelphia, 1970, pp. 56-66.

52 As described by Shinnar (n. 18 above), pp. 38-39.

53 Sharett was about to deliver a speech that consisted, in his words, of "a mixture of extremes": on the one hand, "denunciation of the Holocaust and emphasis on the unforgivable nature of such a crime," and, on the other, "praise of the agreement ... and emphasis on the positive fact that it was undertaken not under duress but rather in recognition of moral responsibility." The main points of the speech were presented to the Mapai Political Committee on September 5, 1952. The speech was never delivered. Adenauer, who read the speech before the Luxembourg gathering, replied: "I am ready to hear it. Germany is not." By Adenauer's recommendation, no speeches were made. As reported by Sharett to the Mapai Political Committee, March 28, 1953. L.P.A.

54 For details of documents, protocols, and accompanying letters, see FM Documents, pp. 95-168.

55 Comprehensive reviews on the development of security, economic, and cultural ties between Israel and Germany after the reparations agreement appear particularly in Deutschkron, *Bonn and Jerusalem*; L. Gardner-Feldman, *The Special Relationship Between West Germany and Israel*, Boston and London, 1984; Vogel, *The German Path to Israel*; and Shinnar (see n. 18 above).

56 The topic most carefully hidden from knowledge of the public (and, in practical terms, from the Government) was the network of security ties and bilateral arms deals that began to develop through contacts between the Defense Ministries of both countries in 1954. See Vogel, *The German Path to Israel*; Deutschkron, *Bonn and Jerusalem*; Shinnar (n. 18 above); Shimon Peres, *The Next Stage* (Hebrew), Tel Aviv, 1965; and idem, *David's Sling*, London, 1970.

57 *Divrei Haknesset* 23, pp. 482-483. Stated by Ben-Gurion on December 24, 1957, in response to a call to order presented by Chaim Landau (Herut) concerning the dispatch of a high-level delegation to Germany. Ben-Gurion spoke in this vein on other occasions, both inside and outside the Knesset. (Cf., for example, July 15, 1957, in response to a call to order presented by Herut MK E. Raziel-Noar. *Divrei Haknesset* 22, p. 2391; July 1, 1959, with respect to the arms deal with Germany. *Divrei Haknesset* 27, pp. 2408-2410; January 20, 1960, in response to calls to order presented by Shmuel Mikunis of the Israel Communist Party, and Shoffman of Herut. *Divrei Haknesset* 28, pp. 418-421; interview of Ben-Gurion by *Ha'aretz*, October 2, 1959; interview of Ben-Gurion by the *Time* correspondent on June 27, 1959; *Davar*, June 28, 1959; interview of Ben-Gurion by *Ma'ariv*, June 21, 1960.)

58 Quoted from interviews of Ben-Gurion in *Ha'aretz*, October 2, 1959, and in *Ma'ariv*, September 21, 1960.

59 The logical contradiction surfaced clearly in Ben-Gurion's answers to questions by editors of *Ha'aretz*: "*Ha'aretz*: As far as Germany is concerned, wouldn't you say it's the same generation? *Ben-Gurion*: No. It's not the same generation. Not at all. It's a different generation. *Ha'aretz*: Would you say that we in Israel are now a different generation as opposed to what we were in 1942-1945? *Ben-Gurion*: We are not a different generation. But there, it is a different generation."

60 *Between Poet and Statesman* (Hebrew): *Nathan Alterman—Twelve columns and a Letter; David Ben-Gurion—2 letters*. Hakibbutz Hameuchad, 1972, pp. 42-43.

61 On the vain efforts of the Israel Government to urge the West German Government to establish diplomatic relations between the two countries, see Y. Auerbach, *Foreign Policy Decisions and Changing Attitudes: Israel-Germany, 1950-1965* (Hebrew), Ph.D. dissertation, Hebrew University of Jerusalem, 1980.

62 From an interview with *Ha'aretz*, October 2, 1959. Ben-Gurion travelled to Germany for the first time in April 1967, to take part in Adenauer's funeral.

DAVID BEN-GURION AND THE SINAI CAMPAIGN, 1956

NETANEL LORCH

On February 2, 1955, Pinhas Lavon, who had been selected by Ben-Gurion as his successor in the Ministry of Defense, presented his resignation to Prime Minister Moshe Sharett. Ben-Gurion agreed to serve as minister of defense under Sharett, until the elections scheduled to be held in July of that year. Ben-Gurion reluctantly resumed public office on February 20, serving under a man who for many years had been his lieutenant. The partnership was an uneasy one: Sharett and Ben-Gurion did not agree on a number of issues. Several of Ben-Gurion's initiatives (to capture the Gaza Strip, in order to put an end to the increasing *fedayeen* attacks from across the border; and to prepare for the forceful breach of the blockade of the Straits of Tiran) were either not brought to a vote, or defeated. No doubt there was also a personal element in their relations. Ben-Gurion was ill-equipped to play a subordinate role, whereas Sharett would not forego his position as prime minister or surrender any authority.

When the general elections were held in July 1955, Ben-Gurion's party, Mapai, lost a number of seats, but it still remained the largest party. Negotiations to form a new coalition continued for eighty days, and it was only on November 2, 1955 that Ben-Gurion, now as prime minister designate, was able to present a new government to the Knesset.

In September 1955, during the course of the coalition negotiations, the first Egyptian-Czech arms deal was announced. The Soviet Union, which opposed the Baghdad Pact then being strongly advocated by the United States, had changed its attitude towards the Free Officers' regime in Egypt (which opposed the pact for its own reasons), and engaged, by proxy, to supply Egypt with significant quantities of modern offensive and defensive weapons. According to information obtained by Israel at the time, the deal involved "300 medium and heavy tanks ... 200 armored personnel carriers ... 200 MIG-15 jet fighters, 50 Ilyushin bombers, in addition to transport planes, radar systems, two destroyers, four minesweepers, 12 torpedo boats, ammunition [and] spare parts...."[1] At the same time, Great Britain was about to complete the evacuation of its forces from the Canal Zone. These forces, which might have served as a buffer between Egypt and Israel, would now be removed. Possibly urged on by Israel's increasingly massive retaliatory raids, Nasser stepped up the *fedayeen* raids. At the same time, Egyptian public statements concerning the inevitability of a "second round" became increasingly vehement and ominous.

When Ben-Gurion presented his government to the Knesset, a major part of his speech was devoted to security matters. He announced:

> In order to avoid the dangers of the existing situation, I am prepared to meet with the prime minister of Egypt and with any Arab leader at the earliest possible opportunity, in order to reach a mutual agreement, without any prior conditions. The government of Israel is prepared to make peace and to embark on political, economic, and cultural cooperation with its neighbors, on a long-term basis. If the other side is not yet ready for this, we are prepared to make a more limited agreement: guaranteeing adherence to the armistice agreements, preventing mutual attacks, ceasing all hostilities, boycott and siege, and maintaining freedom of navigation.[2]

Just prior to the presentation of the new government (which he joined as foreign minister), Sharett returned from an unsuccessful mission designed to convince the foreign ministers of the four Great Powers, then assembled in Geneva, of Israel's need for defensive arms. Soviet Foreign Minister Molotov attributed the deterioration in the Middle East to Israel's aggressive policy; the US saw no clear indication that the arms balance had been or was about to be upset, and subsequently urged Israel to rely on the collective security of the UN; Great Britain refused even to forego its own arms sales to Egypt.[3]

However, whereas at the public and diplomatic level France supported the position of its Western partners, an increasingly intimate relationship was developing between the defense establishments of both countries. Maurice Bourgès-Maunoury, French minister of defense, considered that the 1,000,000 Frenchmen in Algeria and the 1,000,000 Jews of Israel were each suffering from Gamal Abdel Nasser's policies. Beginning in the fall of 1955, France agreed in strict secrecy to sell considerable quantities of arms to Israel, including planes, tanks, artillery, and destroyers. The main difficulty related to the supply schedule. There was a danger that Egypt would receive its MIGs before Israel would possess even a single jet plane.

The personal sympathy of Prime Minister Guy Mollet for Israel was an important factor in the development of these relations, which were concealed even from the foreign ministers of both countries.

Previously, Ben-Gurion had contemplated a determined military response if the Egyptians continued to violate the 1949 Armistice Agreement, particularly by denying Israel freedom of passage in the Suez Canal and the Gulf of Eilat, and by encouraging *fedayeen* raids. The scenario he envisaged was the passage of an Israeli ship through the Straits of Tiran. If, as expected, it was blocked by the Egyptians, the Israel Defense Forces (I.D.F.) would capture the western shore of the Gulf, which might involve full-scale war with Egypt. In the meantime, he gave instructions for necessary preparations to turn Eilat into an operating port.

In December, however, he and the entire cabinet had unanimously rejected the option, advocated by Chief of Staff Moshe Dayan, of an attack before Egypt became too strong as a result of the continuous influx of Czech arms. As he explained to Dayan: "On the morrow of victory we shall be facing the same problems, under more difficult circumstances, because we shall have been branded as aggressors in the eyes of the world."[4]

This rare unanimity on a subject of fundamental importance should have augured well for smooth cooperation between Ben-Gurion and Sharett. In fact, however, the tension between them grew. There were clashes on concrete issues, including whether to break the blockade in the Straits of Tiran, and over the establishment of a settlement in Beerotayim near Nitzana. These tensions were also the result of a clash of personalities. Ben-Gurion believed Sharett had changed since 1953. "His arrogance has increased and he takes responsibility for matters for which he does not possess sufficient moral authority."[5]

The showdown came over a party matter—Sharett's refusal to become secretary-general of Mapai, after having presented himself as a candidate. Ben-Gurion was about to inform his colleagues that he could no longer continue in the existing framework, and would therefore step down.[6] However, a few hours earlier, on June 18, 1956, Sharett presented his resignation and Golda Meir took his place as foreign minister.

In the subsequent Knesset debate, both Ben-Gurion and Sharett refrained from giving a detailed explanation of the resignation, maintaining a semblance of cordiality and consent. However, when replying to the debate, Ben-Gurion gave certain clues:

> After the last elections I insisted that Moshe Sharett join the government because of our differing viewpoints, not despite them.... I am unable to work with "yes-men." I do not believe that I am unable to err and I wish to test my opinions against those of others.... That was not the only reason I begged Sharett to join the government, and I was very grateful to him for giving in to me on that matter.... But of late, when both defense and foreign policy matters have become exceedingly grave ... I reached the conclusion that ... we need the fullest possible coordination between the Ministries of Defense and Foreign Affairs, and that the Foreign Ministry needs a different leadership now.[7]

In June 1956, the last British troops evacuated the Canal Zone. On July 26, six days after American secretary of state John Foster Dulles announced the decision of the US Government not to finance the construction of the Aswan Dam, Nasser nationalized the Suez Canal.

All the military and organizational measures necessary for a smooth Egyptian takeover of the Canal installations had been taken; all possible repercussions had been contemplated. Nasser had even considered the possibility of Anglo-French military intervention. He ruled out the contingency of Israeli participation in such an operation, arguing that "[British prime minister] Eden will not accept it. Israel might try but Eden will refuse. He will prefer to leave this as a European issue."[8]

Israel did not take a position for or against the nationalization. It merely served a reminder that ever since 1951, long before nationalization, Israeli ships had been barred from passing through the Suez Canal, in spite of a Security Council decision of that year, itself based on the provisions of the Constantinople Convention of 1888.

During August and September, parallel to strenuous efforts to find a political solution to the problems arising from nationalization, Great Britain and France concentrated considerable military forces in the Eastern Mediterranean, in preparation for a possible joint operation against Egypt and as a means of applying pressure. On September 9, the mission of Australian prime minister Robert Menzies—who came to Nasser as the representative of the Canal Users Association—failed. The gap between the positions of both sides seemed unbridgeable.

The US, aware of the preparations for military operations, strove to dissuade Great Britain from such a venture. Similar efforts were made by the Soviet Union. In a note, dated September 11, to the British prime minister, Soviet president Nicolai Bulganin pointed out that under the UN charter the use of force was permissible only in self-defense, and warned of the dire consequences that would ensue, should Great Britain fall into "the French trap"—destruction of the Canal; destruction of oil installations in the Middle East; an Arab *jihad*; interruptions of oil supplies from the Middle East; instigation of hatred in Asia and Africa; a vague threat of reaction by the Soviet Union itself.[9]

Great Britain joined France, on the following day, in notifying the president of the Security Council that Egypt's refusal to discuss the establishment of an international Canal Authority constitued "a clear threat to peace and security"; but there were indications that Great Britain had second thoughts, and began dragging its feet. At this stage the possibility of military cooperation with Israel, if necessary in lieu of the British, became the subject for serious deliberations in Paris.

Israel's possible attitude had already been sounded out much earlier. In a conversation with the French minister of defense concerning the acquisition of French planes, which took place a few days after the nationalization of the Canal, Shimon Peres, director general of Israel's Ministry of Defense, was asked how long it would take the I.D.F. to cross the Sinai Peninsula and reach the Suez Canal. Peres replied that the I.D.F. estimate was between five and seven days. One of the participants in the conversation posed a direct question: "If France should go to war against Egypt, would Israel be prepared to join us?" Peres replied affirmatively.[10]

Immediately after the nationalization, Ben-Gurion held the view that this move might provide an opportunity to bring about the fall of Nasser. He decided, first, to sound out the US attitude, but obtained a noncommittal reply from the CIA. An entry in his diary, of July 29, indicates Ben-Gurion's mood: "The Western powers are furious ... but I am afraid that they will not do anything. France will not dare to act alone; Eden is not a man of action; Washington will avoid any reaction." The only effective solution, he argued, would be to turn the Canal into a genuinely international waterway, with only one bank held by Egypt. "But the West will not dare to take such a step; Israel does not have sufficient manpower ... to hold such a vast and empty desert. Also, there is no doubt that Russia stands behind Nasser."[11]

When Dayan proposed three different options for military operations (capture of Sinai, of the Gaza Strip or of the Straits of Tiran), Ben-Gurion refused to consider them. "At this stage we have to ensure the receipt of the equipment with maximum speed, and the training of our men. When the equipment has arrived we shall decide what to do. Meanwhile we have to sit still, if there is no serious provocation from Egypt."[12]

At the same time, Ben-Gurion did not hesitate to accede to French requests for information concerning not only Egypt's military strength and capabilities, but also Israel's ports and airfields: "We have to treat them as brothers, all along the line." He also gave instructions to investigate the possibility of using the Port of Djibouti for an eventual operation against the Straits. At the end of August he agreed to let France use Israeli airfields in the case of war. Early in September he approved a meeting between the I.D.F. director of operations, General Meir Amit, and the French deputy commander of the Anglo-French task force.

Ben-Gurion considered this crisis as the first opportunity to establish an alliance with a Western power. However, he remained skeptical of the possibility of a joint operation by Great Britain and France. He did not believe that Eden would act without American support, and "there is no hope of the devious Dulles supporting any daring action against the Arabs and the Russians."[13]

Ben-Gurion's suspicions vis-à-vis the British were confirmed when he was informed that they had insisted, in their conversations with their French partners, that Israel should not be associated in any way, whether in action or in information.[14] At a meeting of the Baghdad Pact, Great Britain had declared that it would not permit Israel to exploit the Canal issue for its own purpose. It was not their unwillingness to act in concert with Israel, but rather their willingness to act at all which Ben-Gurion doubted.

By the middle of September, the French themselves entertained similar doubts concerning their potential British allies, who now favored a postponement of the operation by two months, during which time further diplomatic efforts would be made. When Peres came to Paris on September 18, ostensibly to deal with the acquisition of arms, and with the newly conceived project of the supply of a nuclear reactor to Israel—the most recent and potentially most important outcome of the budding alliance—he came at an opportune moment from the French point of view. The French were in need of a new ally, who due to his proximity to the Canal would be able to provide them with bases in case the British opted out and Cyprus would no longer be available. Having consulted with Dayan, prior to his departure, and accurately reading Ben-Gurion's approach, Peres proposed that France officially invite Israel to talks about cooperation. He also proposed that Israel be assured that it would not be involved in a military confrontation with Great Britain, in the event Jordan (linked with Great Britain by a defense treaty) intervened; and that following the war Israel's borders should include Sharm el-Sheikh and Rafah. Israel's possession of Sharm (at the Gates of Tiran) would guarantee freedom of navigation.

Bourgès-Maunoury told Peres that there were three possible timings: that preferred by the French, who advocated immediate action against Nasser—because of the political situation in France and for military reasons (winter would make operations in the eastern Mediterranean difficult); the British timetable, which left two more months for political action; and the American one, allowing for a prolonged campaign of subversion and undermining, designed to bring about Nasser's fall.[15] Ben-Gurion, when informed of the possibilities, supported the schedule proposed by France: "If they act at a time convenient for them, we shall assist them to the utmost."[16]

Peres' report about his meeting with Bourgès-Maunoury was characterized by Ben-Gurion as "possibly of historical importance." He noted in his diary that the French had decided to act, without the British but with their knowledge and consent. With British acquiescence they wished to act in concert with Israel, stipulating only that Israel not attack Jordan. And they invited Israel to send a delegation to Paris, including at least one cabinet minister, to "hold discussions ... for cooperation on a basis of parity." [17]

Ben-Gurion now informed the cabinet ministers of his own party and of the traditionally activist Ahdut Ha'avoda party, but swore them to secrecy for the moment. He knew that if the negotiations with France resulted in an agreement, he would have to obtain the approval of the entire cabinet, but for the time being the matter was not to be discussed even with cabinet colleagues. [18]

The delegation dispatched to Paris for the conference at St. Germain consisted of the foreign minister, Golda Meir, Moshe Carmel (minister of transportation, representing Ahdut Ha'avoda), Dayan and Peres. Prior to the group's departure, Ben-Gurion outlined for them the basic conditions for a partnership with France:

> 1) Israel would not launch a war on its own. If our friends started we would join. If we were asked to make a parallel start, we would consider it sympathetically. 2) The US should be apprised of the impending war and offer no objection (or at least express no specific opposition). We should be ensured that the US would not impose sanctions or an embargo against Israel. 3) Britain should be informed, should agree, and should not undertake to go to the assistance of the Arab states if they should join Egypt.

On the other hand, the delegation was authorized to make a commitment that Israel would not attack other Arab countries so long as they did not intervene on behalf of Egypt. The delegation should ensure that the US be informed of the joint initiative and give its tacit blessing. They should see to it that the US will not impose sanctions on Israel, primarily in the economic and financial fields.

> 4) It was our aim to gain control of the western shore of the Gulf of Eilat so as to guarantee freedom of Israeli shipping through that waterway. Consideration might perhaps be given to the demilitarization of the Sinai Peninsula, even under the supervision of an international force. [19]

The delegation was not authorized to make a definitive commitment, but could say that whatever it supports will most likely be approved by the cabinet. "Ben-Gurion was apprehensive about the US and suspicious of Britain," Dayan wrote in his diary. [20]

The St. Germain Conference was inconclusive. It became clear that without Great Britain, France was unlikely to act. Moreover, Israel was expected to act alone against Egypt, with French logistical, but not direct military support.

In a concluding conversation with Guy Mollet, who had not participated in the conference, Golda Meir emphasized that the government of Israel had not yet decided on any action. Nevertheless, Dayan and his French counterpart tentatively set October 20 as the date for an operation. The Security Council was scheduled to end its deliberations by October 12, and the I.D.F. would mobilize its reserves thereafter.[21] The delegation returned from Paris on the night of October 1-2, accompanied by a French military team dispatched to assess Israel's needs and capabilities.

Ben-Gurion was not enthusiastic about the outcome of the conference. He did not believe that the British would permit the French to use their bases on Cyprus if Britain itself would not participate. Nasser might not fall as a result of the initial attack, and might continue fighting. Ben-Gurion did not believe that the French alone would be able to hold on to the Suez Canal for long. However, Dayan, with some vehemence, prevailed on Ben-Gurion to refrain from expressing his doubts to the French delegation:

> It would be easy now to extinguish this tiny flame of [French] readiness to go to war against Nasser, but it will be impossible to rekindle [it].... Three months ago, we would have regarded a situation in which France was prepared to join us in taking military action against Egypt as a dream; and now, when this is happening in reality, we are liable to draw back.[22]

Although Ben-Gurion accepted Dayan's advice and authorized the continuation of preparations for joint action, he was increasingly skeptical.

During the following days attention was focused on the Jordanian front. After a particularly vicious incident of murder and mutilation of corpses by Arab infiltrators, the I.D.F. undertook its largest retaliatory operation to date, against the police station of Qalqilia. Great Britain chose this moment to reiterate support for territorial compromise between the partition boundaries and the armistice lines, a position it knew perfectly well to be unacceptable to Israel.

The Security Council wound up its deliberations on the Suez question on October 13, with the expected Soviet veto of an Anglo-French resolution calling for internationalization of the Canal. On the following day, General Maurice Challe flew to Great Britain, and proposed the "Israel pretext" formula. Israel would initiate military operations against Egypt and the two powers would subsequently intervene to separate the belligerents and halt the hostilities. This formula, which cast Israel in the role of the aggressor, had not been discussed at St. Germain. Evidently, the French believed (possibly having consulted some Israelis) that once they had swayed the British by means of the "Israel pretext" formula, they would not find it difficult to overcome Israel's misgivings.

Eden accepted the formula enthusiastically, and flew to Paris to discuss its implementation with the French. After five hours of deliberations, they agreed on a document which the French would be authorized to transmit to Israel. On the assumption that Israel would initiate operations against Egypt, the two powers undertook to "request both sides to withdraw their forces from the Canal, and should one of them or both refuse — Anglo-French forces will intervene to ensure the smooth operation of the Canal." In order to mollify Israel, Great Britain undertook not to assist Egypt in case of war with the former; the same did not apply, however, to Jordan with whom Great Britain had an effective Mutual Defense Treaty. Eden did not object to the French conferring with Israel, and after lengthy hesitation also agreed to dispatch a high-level representative for such talks in Paris.

On October 15, while Eden was still contemplating the "Israel pretext" formula proposed by General Challe, Ben-Gurion delivered a wide-ranging address to the Knesset, surveying the current political situation:

> We must preserve peace—even this unstable peace of ours—as long as we can, while at the same time ... increasing our military strength.... The Egyptian ruler has stated quite openly that his object is to destroy Israel, and that his quarrel is not only with us but with "international Jewry and Jewish capital," formulae which we remember from Hitler.... The Opposition has advocated that we initiate a war with the fascist tyrant in Cairo before the Egyptian army manages to absorb the large quantities of weapons it has received from the Soviet Bloc. My colleagues in the government and myself disagree with that approach. We are in favor of self-defense, and if we are attacked we will fight with all our strength until the end, that is, until we are victorious. But we know how terrible war is.... In view of the growing Egyptian threat, we regard it is our duty to make a concerted effort to reinforce the I.D.F. and increase its deterrent power. And also to preserve peace—inasmuch as this depends on us....[23]

In an uncharacteristic ploy, in order to meet the need for secrecy while informing the Knesset of recent arms supplies, he quoted verbatim a lengthy poem by Natan Alterman describing the arrival and unloading of arms.

On October 17 a cable was received with the summary of the discussions between Eden and Mollet, inviting Ben-Gurion to come to France for further discussions. Ben-Gurion did not consider the Anglo-French document as a basis for discussions. As Dayan noted at the time, the prime minister

> insisted that we should not be the ones to launch the campaign and fill the role of aggressor, while the British and French appeared as angels of peace to bring tranquility to the area. He was not prepared to accept a division of functions whereby, as he put it, Israel volunteered to mount the rostrum of shame so that Britain and France can lave their hands in the waters of purity.[24]

Dayan tried to convince him that ultimately Great Britain and France did not need Israel for its military prowess. Providing them with a pretext was the only thing only Israel could do:

> ...if we refused the British proposal ... we would lose a historic opportunity which would never recur. In our clash with Nasser, we would have to continue alone, without the forces of Britain and France and without the aid in equipment we would get from France within the framework of the joint campaign. In such circumstances and from the political point of view, could we on our own make war to capture Sharm-el-Sheikh, so as to secure freedom of shipping to Eilat?[25]

Ben-Gurion was not convinced. He considered the "British plan" (in fact, it was originated by the French) as a classical example of British perfidy. He suspected that Eden, whom he regarded as an archenemy of Israel, was trying to involve Israel in a war with Egypt, and meanwhile to let Jordan (where pro-Nasserite elements had shortly before won an election) be overrun by a pro-British Iraq.[26] According to Peres, he also suspected Eden of trying to undermine the Israel-French alliance.[27]

At this point, Ben-Gurion, for all practical purposes, abandoned the idea of war with Egypt, and turned his attention to the option of counteracting the entry of Iraqi forces into Jordan. His objections were conveyed to the French.[28] Nevertheless, Mollet repeated his invitation. Ben-Gurion reluctantly accepted the opportunity to initiate a dialogue, but with the firm intention of replying negatively to the "British plan." When he was informed, on the way to the airport, by Dayan and Peres, on the basis of their conversations with the French emissaries then in Israel, that the Anglo-French position had not changed, he was furious and wanted to stop the car and return to Tel Aviv. "In that case, what is the trip for," he growled. "I am afraid that it can only spoil our relations with France." Peres and Dayan prevailed upon him to go to Paris anyway. Meeting the French emissaries—who were about to return to Paris on the same plane—at the airport, he remarked, "If you intend to present the British proposal to us, the only benefit of my journey to France [will be] that I will make the acquaintance of your prime minister."[29]

The conference was attended on the Israeli side by Ben-Gurion, Dayan, Peres, and Nehemia Argov, Ben-Gurion's aide, and on the French side by Mollet, Christian Pineau (the foreign minister), Bourgès-Maunoury and their aides.

In his opening remarks, Ben-Gurion firmly rejected the "British plan," and outlined one of his own for settling the problems of the Middle East, which was to follow detailed talks with the US and Great Britain. He admitted that the plan might sound fantastic, but given "goodwill and good faith" on the part of the British (which he doubted), he considered it feasible. His scheme entailed the defeat and removal of Nasser, and the partition of Jordan, with the West Bank going to Israel (with autonomy or some other arrangement for its inhabitants). The East Bank would be ceded to Iraq when that country signed a peace agreement with Israel and consented to settle the Palestinian Arab refugees in its territory. Lebanon should be truncated—a part of it going to Syria, a part, south of the Litani River, to Israel. The remainder should be constituted as a Christian state. The enlarged Syria would be ruled by a pro-Western leader. The Suez Canal would be given international status, and the Straits of Tiran would come under Israeli control. Ben-Gurion emphasized the advantages the Western Powers would derive from such an arrangement—France would be able to count on two allies (Lebanon and Israel) and possibly three (including Syria).[30] Great Britain would be assured an uninterrupted flow of oil. Nasser would be ousted with the help of the US.

Mollet doubted whether the Americans, "who usually understand reality after a delay of two years," or the British would be willing to consider a plan which would considerably increase the territory under Israeli control. Although he did not refer to this, it was obvious to all present. Politely and firmly he steered the discussion to the immediate issue—Nasser and the Canal.[31]

Ben-Gurion's plan was not discussed any further—then or afterwards. It is significant not only for its substance, but also because he presented it at that time. Ben-Gurion was willing to entertain the idea of a joint military operation as a means of achieving a long-term strategic alliance with a Western Power. France and Great Britain were willing to consider a temporary alliance with Israel for the sake of a coordinated military operation. Ben-Gurion spoke in terms of long-range solutions; the French insisted on concentrating on the coming hours and days.

Concerning the plan for joint military operations, Ben-Gurion had many misgivings. Among them was the risk of Soviet volunteers coming to the Middle

East, a risk which was not allayed by Pineau's assertion that the Soviets were fully occupied with the internal problems of the Eastern Bloc which had surfaced in Poland and Hungary. However, his main concerns were a lack of confidence in Britain's willingness to cooperate with Israel, or even to refrain from acting against Israel by the side of Jordan and Iraq; and the danger—enhanced by his own experience during the Battle of Britain—of Israeli civilian centers being bombed by Soviet Ilyushin bombers, some dozens of which had already been delivered to Egypt.[32] He was also apprehensive about the reaction of the US and about worldwide repurcussions from Israel's actions, since Israel was expected to initiate military operations on its own. He was concerned that he might not be able to convince his cabinet colleagues, or public opinion in Israel, of the necessity and justification of war under existing cirumstances—"and that is the biggest question."[33] Ultimately, he was not sure of the military outcome of the proposed operation.

The French were insistent. They could not indefinitely keep their ships and reserve units mobilized. An operation in three months' time would find France a passive bystander. The beginning of November was the latest date. They offered, however, to provide French ships and planes to protect Israel's skies and shores.

Ben-Gurion retreated. He proposed unleashing the I.D.F. during the coming week, provided that immediately after the night-time start of Israel's operation Egypt's airports would be bombed on the following morning, and a full partnership established between Britain, France, and Israel. At this point, British foreign minister Selwyn Lloyd joined the discussion. The mutual disdain of Ben-Gurion and Lloyd was immediately evident. Ben-Gurion later recalled that Lloyd "tried to treat him as a subordinate."[34]

The conference broke up, without an agreement. Great Britain and France insisted on a major military operation by Israel, to provide a pretext for their "ultimatum," and a lapse of 48 hours, at least, between the onset of hostilities and the beginning of Anglo-French intervention with the bombing of Egyptian airfields. Ben-Gurion insisted on a maximum of 12 hours between the two. He was offended by the British refusal, not opposed by the French, to consider Israel as an equal partner, and by the British concern for their image and moral standing, as opposed to their indifference to the standing of Israel.

Lloyd returned to London empty-handed. At this point, Dayan proposed the plan which was eventually implemented: Israel would undertake a parachute drop at the Mitla Pass, about 30 miles from the Canal, and its forces would subsequently link up overland with the paratroopers. This would provide the British and French with the pretext they required. From the Israeli point of view it had the advantage of being reversible—if things went wrong, the operation could be described as a large-scale retaliatory raid and the troops withdrawn. Ben-Gurion authorized Dayan to present the plan in his own name, and, in order to emphasize the tentative nature of the proposal, did not participate in the meeting at which it was conveyed to Pineau and Bourgès-Maunoury. The two were impressed. Pineau flew to London to present it to Eden. After a few hours he returned with a positive reply.

It was now up to Ben-Gurion. He deliberated by himself for a whole night. Of his original conditions—simultaneous initiation of hostilities; tacit US acquiescence; safeguards for Israel's civilian population—only the last one was met, and only partially, by the promise to transfer French planes to Israel, and to station French ships near its coast. However, it was clear to him that it was either this plan or no plan at all.

Several Israeli participants in the conference have described the lonely struggle of Ben-Gurion, during the sleepless night of October 24-25, 1956. Peres has dramatically described it as a night he will never forget:

> The man sitting under the tree had ... almost certainly made up his mind, having grappled through the night with intangibles, with unknown and unknowable factors. Perhaps he was still grappling with them, for he had yet to announce his decision. But there was not much time left, only a few hours, and the clock was a harsh and immutable master. He was a very lonely man.[35]

Dayan merely stated: "Ben-Gurion remained in his room, Peres and I returned to our Paris hotel and decided to take the evening off. For the 'evening off,' we went to a Montmartre nightclub."[36] But Dayan admits feeling relieved when they met Ben-Gurion on the following morning, and he presented them with a series of twenty questions. "It was clear that Ben-Gurion had decided in the affirmative concerning our joining the campaign. The questions were not related to 'whether,' but to 'how.'"

In fact, once Dayan's proposal had been adopted by the French, and subsequently by the British, Ben-Gurion was left little choice. It would appear that he gave in not to the British and the French, but to Peres and above all to Dayan, who emerged as the real initiators of policy.[37] That afternoon the three parties signed the Protocol of Sèvres. The French and the Israelis also agreed on the timing and dimensions of French air and naval support for Israel. Ben-Gurion himself never referred to the Protocol in public.

On his return to Israel, Ben-Gurion devoted the remaining few days to "zero hour" (1700 hours on October 29) to obtaining the support of his cabinet colleagues and the Opposition.

Meanwhile, Guy Mollet had informed Ben-Gurion of the French government's approval of the "results of the Sèvres discussions and the terms of the final protocol." He also attached—"for your information"—a copy of Anthony Eden's letter confirming that His Majesty's Government "in the situation there [at Sèvres] envisaged, will take the action described." Ben-Gurion characterized the text as "a typical British Foreign office letter open to various interpretations," in contradistinction to the French, who had enunciated their obligations clearly. He was referring in particular to a letter he had received that same day from Bourgés-Manoury, in which the French government had undertaken to station in Israel, from October 29 through October 31, one squadron of Mystère 40's and one of Chasseur bombers, and to dispatch two warships to Israeli ports.[38]

As he had undertaken at Sèvres to keep the tripartite agreement secret, he presented the plan to his colleagues as a "raid" intended to destroy the *fedayeen* bases in the Gaza Strip and Sinai, and to seize strongholds along the coast from Eilat to Sharm el-Sheikh. The decisive cabinet meeting took place on October 28. Ben-Gurion referred to prior consultations, but said that "only the decision taken here will be binding." All cabinet members, except for the representatives of Mapam, voted in favor.

As had happened several times before in Ben-Gurion's career, at moments of supreme tension and awareness of the great burden of responsibility, he fell ill with a bout of high temperature.[39] He continued his work from his sickbed. It was there he met with the leaders of the Opposition, including his arch-rival Menachem Begin — but excluding the Communist Party. Those consulted gave their blessing to the operation. He only rose to meet the US ambassador, who brought a note from President Eisenhower, warning against warlike action. Eisenhower suspected that the large-scale mobilization of the last few days was in preparation for an offensive against Jordan. Ben-Gurion, in line with his undertaking at Sèvres, could not reveal the truth. His reply to Eisenhower, drafted by his newly appointed political advisor Ya'acov Herzog, was a masterpiece of ambivalence.[40]

Apart from Herzog, senior officials were not made privy to the secret. Israel's ambassadors to major capitals, assembled in Jerusalem for routine consultations, were not informed; nor was Abba Eban, the ambassador to Washington and the UN, who learned of the operation from the State Department after it had started. Sharett gained knowledge of the operation from an Indian newspaper on his way to a meeting with Nehru.[41]

The Sinai Campaign of 1956 began as scheduled. A paratroop battalion was dropped near the Mitla Pass and two remaining battalions of the brigade rushed overland to link up with it. The Anglo-French ultimatum was delivered. As agreed, Israel accepted; as anticipated, Egypt rejected its demands. Ben-Gurion's apprehensions concerning massive Ilyushin bombings did not materialize, and the French planes stationed in Israel remained unemployed, beyond taking part in some strafing attacks on Egyptian columns.

However, Paris reported that the bombing of Egyptian airfields had been postponed by twelve hours because of unexpected groundfire. Ben-Gurion was furious and demanded immediate action. When no reply was received from Paris, he demanded that Dayan bring the paratroops back to Israel in the course of the night. This was the only moment in which Ben-Gurion lost his composure. The fate of the entire operation hung in the balance. It was only with great difficulty that Dayan was able to prevail on Ben-Gurion to desist, and to convince him that even if the Anglo-French operation ("Musketeer") were called off, the I.D.F. would be able to continue on its own.[42]

The landing of Anglo-French forces was still three days away. In order to avoid any semblance of collusion, the British had ordered the invasion fleet to be held up in Malta until the expiration of the ultimatum, so that landing operations could be initiated only on November 6.

The French contemplated an operation on their own, on November 4, and asked Israel to capture Qantara, on the east bank of the Canal, to facilitate their entry into

Port Said. Although Ben-Gurion had strenuously opposed an I.D.F. presence on the Canal itself—he did not want to be a party to the international complications involved ("our Suez is Eilat," he stated over and over again)—he now agreed without hesitation. The French had lived up to their commitments, and he felt that they deserved full cooperation and confidence.

Ben-Gurion had meanwhile recovered his health; his mood was buoyant. When Foreign Ministry officials came with bad news from the UN, he said: "So long as they are sitting in New York, and we are in Sinai, the situation is not bad!" At the same time he refrained from promising Dayan that Israel would hold on to Sinai at any cost, arguing that Sinai was not Jerusalem.[43]

On November 4, the General Assembly, which convened under the "United for Peace" resolution in order to circumvent the British and French veto in the Security Council, called for a cease-fire, and Eban declared that in fact the fighting had come to an end. The British and French protested to Israel; by agreeing to a cease-fire the pretext for their landings would be dissipated. Ben-Gurion angrily pointed out that the two powers had had six days at their disposal, and now that the General Assembly had decided on a cease-fire, Israel was asked to refuse in order "to suit the political convenience of the British." All the same, he instructed Eban to explain that Israel's initial willingness to accept a cease-fire had been misunderstood and it in fact depended on Egypt's replies to several questions, related to the boycott, blockade, *fedayeen*, and the willingness to enter into peace negotiations. The "pretext" had been revived.

By the next day, November 5, the I.D.F. completed its occupation of the Sinai Peninsula, with the capture of Sharm el-Sheikh. At same time the Anglo-French landings—put forward by twenty-four hours—began with the landing of paratroops near Port Said. On the same day the Soviet Union, following the suppression of the Hungarian Revolt, decided to intervene by addressing threatening notes to the heads of the three governments. The notes were published even before they reached their destination. Those to Great Britain and France evoked the possibility of Soviet missile attacks on their territory. The one to Israel did not include a specific threat, but was far more brutal in language. "The government of Israel," it states, "is playing with the fate of the world, the fate of its people." Unlike the notes to Great Britain and France, the one to Israel announced the recall of the Soviet ambassador. When the French ambassador to Washington approached President Eisenhower to ascertain the US attitude in case of a Soviet attack, he found him adamant in his insistence that before anything else the aggressors should desist. In what has become a famous dictum, Eisenhower asserted that he wished to come before his Creator with clean hands.[44]

Dayan noted that "the emotional effect of the Soviet ultimatum was to spur him [B-G] to struggle."[45] Yosef Avidar, Israel's ambassador to Moscow, believed that the Kremlin was bluffing, but Ben-Gurion did not feel reassured. It was decided to dispatch Golda Meir and Peres to Paris, to obtain France's assessment of the new situation, and if possible an assurance of assistance. Pineau took the Soviet threat seriously, and, although sympathetic, declared that France was incapable of assisting

Israel in case of a Soviet attack. Bourgès-Maunoury, who had been present at the meeting, later phoned to express his view that the Soviet note was only a psychological threat, but emphasized that this was just a "private opinion."[46]

In spite of his misgivings, with the Bulganin note in his hands and with Meir and Peres en route to Paris, Ben-Gurion addressed a "victory speech" to the Knesset, on November 7. In it, he outlined his government's policy for the near future. He asserted that Sinai had never constituted an integral part of Egypt, and referred to medieval texts in which Sanapir and Tiran, the twin islands at the mouth of the Gulf of Eilat, are described as belonging to an ancient Jewish kingdom.[47]

These declarations were widely interpreted as indicating refusal to withdraw from territories captured in the course of the operation. Years later, Ben-Gurion was to confess that for once he had allowed himself to get carried away.[48] The events of the previous week, the abrupt transition from extreme anxiety to supreme relief, had overwhelmed even his ingrained natural skepticism.

In the course of the same day, information was received from several quarters indicating Soviet preparations for military intervention: unidentified planes over Turkey; 100 Soviet MIGs in Syria; a British Canberra brought down over Syria from an altitude of 45,000 feet, possibly by Soviet MIGs; Soviet "volunteers" on route to Egypt; the Soviet request for permission to sail five warships through the Dardanelles; Soviet submarines at Alexandria. It is not clear whether these reports were the result of deliberate disinformation or of self-deception caused by panic. But the Soviet threat was taken at face value in many quarters. Herbert Hoover, the undersecretary of state, warned Reuven Shiloah, minister at Israel's embassy in Washington, that "Israel will be the first one to be devoured. Israel's refusal to comply with the UN demand for withdrawal ... lays it open to charges of endangering the peace of the world." He also added a specific warning of the US "concerning the cessation of governmental and private aid, sanctions, expulsion from the UN."

Renewed on the previous day, following a bout of illness, Ben-Gurion's diary entries for November 8 mention contact made by Eban—a phone call "full of fears," and cables "which sow terror and fear." They note, as well, a warning from Walter Eytan, director general of the Foreign Ministry, that the "whole world is uniting against us," due to Israel's remaining in Sinai.[49]

Ben-Gurion's doubts were evident. At a meeting on November 6, he had reminded his colleagues that Budapest had been "wiped off the face of the earth," while warning against "undue panic."[50] The text of Ben-Gurion's reply to the Bulganin note was approved at the end of that consultation. It was stern and unyielding, outlining Israel's grievances against Egypt, and insisting that Israel's policy was determined solely by its own vital interests and its aspirations for peace, and not by any external factor.

In the reply there is no mention of a possible withdrawal. However, the need to agree to a withdrawal became apparent during the next few hours. Another note from President Eisenhower (delayed by several hours because of a technical breakdown in communications) was received, demanding, first and foremost, the withdrawal of foreign forces—with the exception of United Nations forces—from Egyptian territory. Abba Eban reported from Washington that the CIA warned that if Israel refused to evacuate, Soviet fighter planes and bombers would arrive in Syria within a few days. He added: "There is no need to point out the significance to Jewish history if we appear as the root cause of the danger of a world war."[51]

Ben-Gurion described this day as "nightmarish":

> From Rome, Paris, and Washington there is a succession of reports on a stream of Soviet planes and "volunteers" to Syria, on a promise to bomb Israel—airfields, cities and so on—if the Syrians and Jordanians go to war against us.... There may be a great deal of exaggeration in these reports, but Bulganin's note to me ... and the Soviet tanks' rampage in Hungary testify what these Communist Nazis are capable of doing.[52]

Dayan describes the mood in Ben-Gurion's office as "chaotic." "Mapai ministers, Foreign Ministry officials hustle about. Ben-Gurion is pale; rages like a wounded lion, refuses to discuss memos and cables brought to him, refuses to discuss details."[53]

It was in this mood that the ministers reconvened in the afternoon of November 8. They had the above information before them, and a draft reply to Eisenhower, based on Eban's proposal that the I.D.F. would retreat once satisfactory arrangements were made to replace them with United Nations, not Egyptian, forces. Israel would not return to the armistice lines, but would remain in Gaza and the Straits. And the withdrawal would be conditional upon a US promise to make a sincere effort to bring abut a final peaceful solution in the Middle East. In addition to discussing this conditional withdrawal formula, the ministers also debated a proposal for an unconditional retreat. The need to agree to some form of withdrawal was not called into question.[54]

Once more, Ben-Gurion's doubts and hesitations became evident. He reiterated that "we cannot stand against Russia," but questioned whether the danger of Russian intervention really existed. "I am not prepared to panic out of fear that they will bomb us.... If they are determined to do so, they will bomb us even if we go down on our knees and lie prostrate on the ground." In the end, Eban's conditional formula was adopted. But he was authorized to delete the conditional provision of the withdrawal if the Americans were not prepared to commit themselves to a serious effort toward an overall peaceful solution to the Middle East problem.[55]

At midnight, between November 8-9, Ben-Gurion, tired and disappointed, announced his decision in a broadcast to the nation. The agreement to withdraw had been made conditional and restored to Israel some room for maneuvering, and this was fully utilized. The Anglo-French forces completed their evacuation by December 18. Israel attempted to hang on, evacuating step by step—at first in order to salvage some gains in the Gaza Strip and the Straits. But in the end, it became clear that the US would not acquiesce to anything but total withdrawal, and Israel could be comforted only by the fact that at least some "understandings" had been reached with the US concerning freedom of navigation in the Straits, and the non-return of Egyptian military forces to Gaza. It was on the basis of these understandings that

Ben-Gurion announced to the Knesset the completion of the last phase of retreat.

There can be no greater contrast than that between the Knesset's victory session on November 7, 1956 and its final withdrawal session on March 5, 1957. From the very first moment, Ben-Gurion was heckled and taunted by the members of Herut. A few days earlier, Golda Meir had announced to the UN Israel's consent to complete the evacuation, fully expecting, as had been agreed beforehand, that Cabot Lodge, the US ambassador, would confirm Israel's "assumptions." However, Lodge's speech had been changed at the last moment, and the promised confirmation deleted.

Dayan had not been consulted about the decision to withdraw. From his diary it emerges that he opposed it.[56] He was not invited to subsequent discussions of a political nature, but when he asked Ben-Gurion to be relieved of his post, the prime minister refused.

*   *   *

In his autobiography, Dayan describes Ben-Gurion's style with the terms "determination, activism, leadership, concentrating on the main issue, and proceeding fearlessly, even if many risks and difficulties were involved".[57] Bar-Zohar characterizes Ben-Gurion's deliberations as pessimistic, but his decisions as optimistic.[58] Peres juxtaposed Ben-Gurion's deeds with his words, the former hardly ever being misconceived or erroneous, and always characterized by an underlying sense of realism, combined with a strong, almost daring, personal willingness to undertake responsibility. The latter were inherently distinguished by their tumultuous, stormy, thought-provoking nature.

It is doubtful whether any of these definitions of Ben-Gurion's behavior, particularly that given by Dayan, could be deduced empirically from his conduct before, during, and after the Sinai Campaign. Setting aside his previous record, above all the course of the war of 1948, and the image which had been created, one is faced with an old man—his seventieth birthday coincided with the preparations for the campaign—at war with himself, consumed by doubts and fears concerning dangers from abroad, and possible reactions at home of a civilian population subjected to Egyptian bombing attacks.

He willingly consented to everything the French requested, in return for their support. An alliance with a major power had been his longtime dream, just as a confrontation with a major power had been his perennial nightmare. To him the alliance was an objective worth sacrifice. It was partially for the sake of such an alliance that he reluctantly, hesitantly agreed to go to battle, whereas for the French, and certainly for the British, the three-day alliance (as Pineau called it, referring to the days during which French planes would be stationed in Israel) was the means for the successful waging of war. Armed conflict was anathema to Ben-Gurion; he was fully conscious of the fact that even a successful war involved casualties. He had advocated war against Nasser in 1955 when he was convinced that it was inevitable, and the only choice lay between hostilities then, or later on, under infinitely worse conditions. In the fall of 1956, however, with the arms balance largely restored owing to the influx of French arms, he sought every possibility to avert it.

Israel's moral standing in the eyes of the world was a decisive consideration, much more than Ben-Gurion's much-publicized derisive reference to the UN ("Um-Sh'mum") suggested. When he learned that the Israel-pretext scenario (the "British plan") was the only one to be discussed at the Sèvres Conference, he was willing to call off the entire enterprise. A scenario by which Israel would be branded as the aggressor, with the implication that its moral standing was somehow less valuable than that of Great Britain and France, irked him beyond measure. His intuitions concerning the conduct of major powers, based, as they were, to a large extent on his assessments of the character of their leaders, were on several occasions simplistic. He trusted the French, but it was they who hatched the "British" plan. He suspected the British and was about to order a withdrawal of the paratroopers when he learned of the postponement of the British bombing attacks—yet ultimately they lived up to their commitment.

He feared the Russians much more than was warranted. The Soviets, at the time, lacked the capability for effective military intervention, particularly in the face of a massive Anglo-French naval and air presence in the eastern Mediterranean. However, Ben-Gurion was not alone in misjudging the seriousness of the Soviet threat. His error was shared, indeed, largely induced, by others: President Eisenhower, Dag Hammarskjöld, even his trusted French allies. Ben-Gurion respected and feared the US. He did not trust the "devious" Dulles, but did have great respect for Eisenhower, in view of his role during World War II and particularly his assistance to Jewish DPs after the war. He was overly optimistic concerning the US, believing, together with other Israeli decision-makers, that Lodge would indeed confirm the "understandings," and that Egyptian troops would not be permitted to return to the Gaza Strip in the wake of Israel's withdrawal.

Ben-Gurion hesitated at every decisive turn, and had it not been for the proddings of his younger colleagues, particularly Dayan, it is doubtful whether he would have carried on. He was anxious to hear the opinions of others during the events of fall 1956, to receive their advice, and to share with them the burden of responsibility. But that was granted to him only partially. Dayan and Peres offered their suggestions but, as Dayan correctly points out, they were assistants, not colleagues.[59] At the time they possessed no political weight of their own; their standing derived from that of Ben-Gurion himself.

His colleagues in the cabinet, particularly those from his own party, accepted Ben-Gurion as the ultimate authority. On one memorable occasion, just prior to the decision on withdrawal, he asked his colleagues for their opinion, before expressing his own, but they insisted that he should speak first, and it was his proposal which was ultimately adopted.[60]

This description of Ben-Gurion's behavior would indicate that the difference between him and Sharett was not as great as one is led to believe. However, this is only one side of the coin. Ben-Gurion had appointed Dayan and Peres deliberately, knowing their strengths and their weaknesses. He was an introspective man aware of his own shortcomings. Reading the record, one obtains the feeling that knowing his own inborn skepticism, he needed younger, more confident men around him who would help him overcome it. He did not need doubters to strengthen his doubts; he required men with ingenuity and drive, who would find ways to overcome difficulties which he clearly foresaw, albeit sometimes on an exaggerated scale. And he was willing to assume personal responsibility for decisions taken, whatever their origin or outcome.

In the course of a discussion held in the Knesset Foreign Affairs and Defense Committee immediately following the Sinai Campaign, a member of the Committee observed that what he "had feared had come to pass," to which Ben-Gurion replied: "What I have hoped has come to pass and what I have feared has also come to pass; the hope will prevail and the fear will dissipate."[61]

Several years before—in 1949, then in the context of another critical decision—Ben-Gurion had described himself in the intimacy of his diary as "the greatest coward of all."[62] In the course of one of several acrimonious debates about the withdrawal from Sinai, he approvingly quoted Plato's definition of courage, i.e. being able to differentiate between what should and what should not be feared.[63] He referred to this subject several times in his diary during the following turbulent days, attempting to prove to himself that Spinoza's definition of courage concurred with that of Plato.[64] Quite evidently, he wanted to be remembered as someone who possessed that trait of courage.

The Sinai Campaign was Ben-Gurion's last major undertaking. It gained enormous prestige for the I.D.F., resulted in free navigation in the Straits, and, above all, gave Israel almost eleven years of peace, more than it ever enjoyed before or after.

Notes

1 Moshe Dayan, *Story of My Life*, New York, 1976, pp. 179-180.
2 Knesset Minutes, November 3, 1955.
3 Nadav Safran, *From War to War*, New York, 1969, p. 50.
4 Moshe Dayan, *Milestones* (Hebrew), Jerusalem and Tel Aviv, 1976, p. 175.
5 Ibid., p. 209.
6 Ibid.
7 Knesset Minutes, June 19, 1956.
8 Mohammed Heikal, *Cairo Documents*, New York, 1973, p. 88.
9 Hugh Thomas, *The Suez Affair*, Harmondsworth, 1970, p. 206-210.
10 Michael Bar-Zohar, *Ben-Gurion* (Hebrew edition), Tel Aviv, 1977, p. 1210.
11 Ibid., pp. 1211.
12 Ibid.
13 Michael Bar-Zohar, *Ben-Gurion* (English edition), London, 1978, p. 230.
14 Bar-Zohar (Hebrew edition), p. 1212.
15 Ibid., p. 1214.
16 Ibid.
17 Bar-Zohar (English edition), p. 231.
18 Dayan, *Milestones*, p. 232.
19 Dayan, *Story of My Life*, pp. 192.
20 Ibid.
21 Bar-Zohar, *Ben-Gurion* (English edition), p. 232.

22 Ibid., p. 233.
23 Knesset Minutes, October 15, 1956.
24 Dayan, *Story of My Life*, p. 212.
25 Ibid.
26 Diaries of David Ben-Gurion (manuscript), Ben-Gurion Archives, Sedeh Boqer [hereafter "Diaries"], October 17, 1956.
27 Joseph Evron, *On A Winter's Day* (Hebrew), Tel Aviv, p. 101.
28 Bar-Zohar, *Ben-Gurion* (Hebrew edition), p. 1229.
29 Bar-Zohar, *Ben-Gurion* (English edition), p. 235.
30 Ibid., p. 236.
31 Bar-Zohar, *Ben-Gurion* (Hebrew edition), pp. 1235-1236.
32 Bar-Zohar, *Ben-Gurion* (English edition), p. 237.
33 Diaries, October 22, 1956, p. 160.
34 Michael Brecher, *Decisions in Israel's Foreign Policy*, New Haven, 1975, p. 272.
35 Shimon Peres, *David's Sling*, London, 1970, p. 204.
36 Dayan, *Story of My Life*, p. 225.
37 Bar-Zohar, *Ben-Gurion* (Hebrew edition), p. 1251.
38 Diaries, October 26, 1956.
39 Bar-Zohar, *Ben-Gurion* (English edition), p. 244.
40 Ibid., pp. 245-246.
41 Ibid., p. 246.
42 Dayan, *Story of My Life*, p. 239.
43 Dayan, *Milestones*, p. 302. Many years later, on October 9, 1973, during the course of the Yom Kippur War, Dayan paraphrased Ben-Gurion's 1956 position in a controversial observation. He said that Sinai was not Degania (the venerable kibbutz in the Galilee), by which he implied that there was no justification to defend it at any cost.
44 Brecher, *Decisions in Israel's Foreign Policy*, p. 285.
45 Dayan, *Story of My Life*, p. 252.
46 Bar-Zohar, *Ben-Gurion* (Hebrew edition), p. 1274.
47 Knesset Minutes, November 7, 1956.
48 Brecher, *Decisions in Israel's Foreign Policy*, p. 283.
49 Diaries, November 8, 1956.
50 Based on notes of one of those present. From a private archive.
51 Ibid.
52 Bar-Zohar, *Ben-Gurion* (English edition), p. 251.
53 Dayan, *Milestones*, p. 317.
54 Based on notes of one of those present. From a private archive.
55 Ibid.
56 Dayan, *Milestones*, p. 319.
57 Ibid., p. 208.
58 Bar-Zohar, *Ben-Gurion* (Hebrew edition), p. 1251-1252.
59 Dayan, *Milestones*, p. 260.
60 Based on notes of one of those present. From a private archive.
61 Diaries, November 9, 1956.
62 Ibid., December 14, 1949.
63 Knesset Minutes, November 14, 1956.
64 Diaries, November 14, 1956; November 16, 1956.

CONTRIBUTORS

DR. YEHUDIT AUERBACH: Lecturer in Political Science, Bar-Ilan University.

DR. YITZHAK AVNERY: Emissary Supervisor, World Zionist Organization.
Author: *The Zionist Organization and Illegal Immigration to Eretz Israel from the Beginning of the British Mandate to the Outbreak of World War II* (Hebrew, doctoral thesis, Tel Aviv University).

PROF. URI BIALER: Chairman, Department of International Relations, Hebrew University.
Author: *The Shadow of the Bomber; Between East and West: Israel's Foreign Policy Orientations, 1948-1956.*

PROF. ALLON GAL: Senior Research Fellow, Ben-Gurion Research Center; Associate Professor of History, Ben-Gurion University of the Negev.
Author: *Socialist-Zionism: Theory and Issues in Contemporary Jewish Nationalism; Brandeis of Boston; David Ben-Gurion: Preparing for a Jewish State* (Hebrew, forthcoming in English).

PROF. YOAV GELBER: Head of Strochlitz Institute for Research and Study of the Holocaust; Head of Herzl Institute for Research and Study of Zionism, University of Haifa.
Author: *Jewish Palestinian Volunteering in the British Army During World War II* (four volumes, Hebrew); *The Emergence of a Jewish Army* (Hebrew); *Why the Palmach Was Disbanded* (Hebrew); *New Homeland: Immigration and Absorption of Central European Jews, 1933-1948* (Hebrew).

PROF. YOSEF GORNY: Teaches in the Department of Jewish History, Tel Aviv University.
Author: *Ahdut Ha-Avodah, 1919-1930: Ideological Principles and the Political System* (Hebrew); *Partnership and Conflict: Chaim Weizmann and the Jewish Labor Movement in Palestine* (Hebrew); *The British Labor Movement and Zionism, 1917-1948; Zionism and the Arabs, 1882-1948: A Study of Ideology; The Quest for Collective Identity: Jewish Public Thought in the U.S.A. and in Israel, 1945-1985.*

DR. MENAHEM KAUFMAN: Research Fellow, Institute of Contemporary Jewry, Hebrew University.
Author: *The Non-Zionists and the Establishment of the State of Israel* (Hebrew); *An Ambiguous Partnership: Non-Zionists in America, 1939-1948; The Jerusalem Policy of the United States, 1947-1948; Guide to American Holy Land Studies, v. 4.*
Editor: *Contemporary Jewry Annual* (Hebrew), v. 3, 5-6.

MICHAEL KEREN: Senior Lecturer in Political Science, Tel Aviv University.
Author: *Ben-Gurion and the Intellectuals: Power, Knowledge and Charisma; The Pen and the Sword: Israeli Intellectuals and the Making of the Nation-State.*
Editor: *Visionary Realism and Political Leadership (International Political Science Review).*

PROF. ISRAEL KOLATT: Israel Goldstein Professor of the History of Zionism and the Yishuv, Hebrew University.
Author: *Fathers and Founders* (Hebrew).

PROF. MOSHE LISSAK: Professor of Sociology, Hebrew University.
Author: *Military Roles in Modernization; Elites of the Jewish Community in Palestine* (Hebrew).
Co-author: *The Origins of the Israeli Polity; Moshava, Kibbutz and Moshav: Patterns of Jewish Rural Settlement and Development in Palestine; Trouble in Utopia: The Overburdened Polity of Israel.*
Editor-in-Chief: *The History of Jewish Settlement in Eretz Israel, 1880-1960.*

NETANEL LORCH: Secretary-General of the Knesset, 1972-1983; Former Director, Latin American, African and Information Divisions of Israeli Foreign Ministry; former Head of Military History Dept., IDF; Senior Research Fellow, Truman Center, Hebrew University; Visiting Lecturer, Bar-Ilan University.
Author: *One Long War: Arab vs. Jew Since 1920; The Edge of the Sword: Israel's War of Independence; The Whispering River* (Hebrew); *Israel Amongst the Nations* (Hebrew); *The Knesset from a Different Angle* (Hebrew); *Israel in the Grip of Superpowers: The Threat of Big Power Military Intervention in the Arab-Israeli Conflict* (Hebrew); *Major Knesset Debates, 1948-1981* (forthcoming).

PROF. MATITYAHU MINTZ: Professor of Jewish History, Tel Aviv University.
Author: *Ber Borochov: Circle One, 1900-1906* (Hebrew); *New Times—New Tunes: Ber Borochov, 1914-1917* (Hebrew); *The Lame and the Nimble: The Story of the "Dror" Group in Russia* (Hebrew); *Yitzchak Tabenkin: In the Poaley-Zion Party, 1905-1912* (Hebrew).
Editor: *The Cracow Convention of the Jewish Social Democratic Workers Party (Poalei Zion) in Russia, August 1907* (Hebrew); *The Third Convention of the Jewish Social Democratic Workers Party, 1917; Ber Borochov's Letters (1897-1917)* (Hebrew).

DR. ELHANNAN ORREN: Department of Military History, Israel Defence Forces GHQ.
Author: *Operation "Danny"—July 1948* (Hebrew).
Co-editor: *Ben-Gurion's Diary of the War of Independence, 1947-49* (Hebrew).

MR. SHIMON PERES: Former Prime Minister, Defense and Foreign Minister of Israel; chairman of Israeli Labor Party; former vice-president of Socialist International.
Author: *David's Sling; The Next Phase; Tomorrow Is Now* (Hebrew).

DR. DINA PORAT: Senior Lecturer in Jewish History, Tel Aviv University.
Author: *The Blue and the Yellow Stars of David: Zionist Leadership in Palestine and the Holocaust, 1939-1945.*
Editor: *The Ghetto Everyday: Diary and Documents from the Kovno Ghetto.*

PROF. SHIMON RESHEF (deceased): was Professor of Education and Chairman of the Unit for Jewish Education in the Diaspora, Tel Aviv University.
Author: *The Labor Movement School System in Pre-State Israel, 1921-1939* (Hebrew); *The Sources and History of an Educational Movement* (Hebrew).

DR. SHABTAI TEVETH: Senior Research Fellow, Dayan Center for Middle East Studies, Tel Aviv University.
Author: *The Tanks of Tammuz; The Cursed Blessing; Moshe Dayan: A Biography; Ben-Gurion and the Palestinian Arabs; Ben-Gurion: The Burning Ground, 1886-1948.*

DR. RONALD ZWEIG (Editor): Senior Lecturer in Jewish History, Tel Aviv University; Head of the Institute for Research in the History of Zionism.
Author: *Britain and Palestine During the Second World War; German Reparations and the Jewish World.*
Editor (since 1983): *Studies in Zionism.*

DS 125.3 .B37 D39 1991

David Ben-Gurion